THE RESTRUC
OF THE UK EC

Edited by
Francis Green
University of Leicester

HARVESTER WHEATSHEAF
New York   London   Toronto   Sydney   Tokyo

First published 1989 by
Harvester Wheatsheaf,
66 Wood Lane End, Hemel Hempstead,
Hertfordshire, HP2 4RG
A division of
Simon & Schuster International Group

© Francis Green 1989

Typeset in 10/12 Times
by Witwell Ltd, Southport
Printed and bound in Great Britain by
BPCC Wheattons Ltd, Exeter

British Library Cataloguing in Publication Data

Green, Francis
    The restructuring of the UK economy.
    1. Great Britain.   Economic development
    I. Title
    330.941

    ISBN 0–7450–0657–4
    ISBN 0–7450–0658–2 (pbk)

1 2 3 4 5   93 92 91 90 89

CONTENTS

Part I Introduction

√ Part II The anatomy of structural change

Part IV Policies and agencies for modernisation

Part V Thatcherism in historical perspective

14 The Thatcher revolution

281

Bob Rowthorn
Faculty of Economics and Politics, University of Cambridge

15 Is Thatcherism the cure for the British disease?

299

Meghnad Desai
Department of Economics, London School of Economics and Political Science

FIGURES

TABLES

ACKNOWLEDGEMENTS

The theme running through the contributions in this book is one of the burning questions of the 1980s: has Thatcherism succeeded in arresting the previous seemingly inexorable British economic decline? Or, to put this in a forward-looking manner, has it re-established the UK as a stable base for successful capital accumulation in the foreseeable future? Such questions inevitably pose the issue of structural change in the economy. The theme was introduced in a preliminary manner at a one-day conference on 23 September 1988, hosted jointly by South Bank Polytechnic's Local Economy Unit and the Economic and Social Research Council's Political Economy Group. This conference provided the inspiration for organising the much more comprehensive analyses now presented in this book, and I thank the speakers, participants and organisers on that day for their contributions. In particular I would like to acknowledge Sam Aaronovitch's initiative in setting up the conference on this theme and his enthusiastic support for this subsequent project. Needless to add, while the analyses in each chapter are wholly those of their authors, responsibility for the final project remains with me.

PART I

INTRODUCTION

1 EVALUATING STRUCTURAL ECONOMIC CHANGE: BRITAIN IN THE 1980s

Francis Green

1.1 INTRODUCTION

The British economy in the 1980s is but a small unsheltered inlet on the edge of a turbulent sea. As in the 1970s, as also a century ago, it is organised on capitalist lines. Yet it would be hard to deny that the 1980s have seen both a wider degree of exposure to the rest of the capitalist world and a substantial alteration in its make-up and in the rules which predominantly control economic behaviour. Margaret Thatcher's Conservative government has re-emphasised the philosophy of accepting the 'market's verdict'. In order to support the free market, it has accumulated and centralised its power and set itself against the elements of the previous social democratic regimes that sought to soften capitalism in the cause of workers or specific pressure groups. It has drawn back the boundaries of its own participation in the market. Correspondingly, the private economy has undergone an immense upheaval: manufacturing industries have been decimated, some wiped from the map, while service industries have grown as usual; millions of people have had to grow used to long-term or indefinite unemployment; those in work have received increasingly unequal rewards, and the trade unions that defend them have been on the retreat.

It would be equally hard to contest that *some* form of change was inevitable given the crises which engulfed both the world economy and the economy in Britain during the 1970s. Across the developed countries there was a notable slowing down of productivity growth and a dive in profit rates. While the origins of this decline lay in the previously hidden tensions of the 1950s and 1960s boom years, the traditional Phillips curve relationship collapsed openly in the 1970s. While inflation soared, unemployment was creeping up. The oil price underwent massive shocks in 1974 and 1979. Certain Western cities

I should like to thank Paul Auerbach and Bennett Harrison for helpful comments on an earlier draft.

began running into fiscal crises. Meanwhile, the groundwork was being laid for a major fiscal crisis of Third World states: their massive debts incurred in the 1970s could not be repaid once the world went into recession in the early 1980s, thereby adding to the danger of instability in the banking system. Superimposed on these linked crises was a long-term relative decline in the competitiveness of the British economy. Britain had for a long time experienced slower productivity growth than most other countries – the exception was the US economy, which was in any case far more productive than elsewhere after World War II and which was understandably growing less fast as other economies began to catch up. In the process British manufacturing industries began early on to decline, failing to modernise and expand fast enough into new areas with new technologies. The post-war Keynesian consensus arrived at a critical point when the state could no longer deliver a stable environment of growing private and social wages. Inflation broke out, incomes policies broke down: the economy was increasingly less responsive to the Keynesian medicine.

1.2 FROM DECLINE TO RESTRUCTURING

Our understanding of the changes undergone in the 1980s begins with our perspective on why the economic crises of the 1970s and before had come about. In conventional terms the main culprit is the oil price shock (OECD, 1980) coupled with various degrees of macroeconomic mismanagement. Government spending is thought to crowd out private spending, thereby limiting the effectiveness of Keynesian policies. With the trend towards monetarist thought dominating debates in the UK, the state was increasingly charged with having over-expanded (Bacon and Eltis, 1976), while the unions were said to be overly protected and powerful enough to impose higher wages and restrict the introduction of new technology (Maynard, 1988). Discretionary control of the money supply in order to fine-tune the economy was said to be worse for stability than a steady money growth rule. Those in the Marxist tradition, by contrast, tend to see the periodic appearance of economic crises as unavoidable, even if they can be delayed by state policies (Mandel, 1978; Itoh, 1988).[1] The particular problems in the British economy are seen as rooted deep in its institutions and class structure: the overseas orientation of a significant fraction of capitalists, coupled with the absence of strong centralised institutions representing business and workers and a relatively weak state, had led to there being only weak modernising forces, compared to other advanced countries (Fine and Harris, 1985). Those in an 'institutionalist' framework add their emphasis on the institutional rigidities – both of management and of labour – that have prevented British-based capital from being at the forefront of corporate organisation in the twentieth century (Elmbaum and Lazonick, 1986). These rigidities are the legacy of the success achieved by the atomistic economic organisation that grew up in the industrial revolution. The slothfulness of British industry which was rudely exposed in the 1970s could not therefore be put down to macroeconomic mistakes and instability: it had distant origins.

1.3 THATCHERISM

That there must be change, for good or bad, after crisis is true more or less by definition.[2] The economy changes autonomously as private capitalists sort themselves into winners and losers, and as the winners rearrange their enterprises. It also responds to political change including new government policies. Whatever the diagnosis of the British economy's ills, new policies were going to be needed to make capitalism work successfully in Britain after the 1970s. These radical changes in both economy and policy amount to what is aptly termed a 'restructuring' of the UK economy. 'Restructuring' thus involves not merely the changing composition of industries or of the labour force (though these are relevant) but more generally an alteration in the terms and relations under which the process of capital accumulation for profit takes place. While economic, political and ideological relations may all be restructured, the theme of this book concerns primarily, though not exclusively, the economic aspects.

Two issues that concern any restructuring may be noted. First, the changes can take place either gradually (incrementally) or suddenly. Just as they are believers in incremental adjustments to general equilibrium in markets, many economists have been advocates of gradual change in the policy framework. By contrast, economists from the Austrian school, who tend to see market adjustments as periodic radical re-alignments of values (similar to the Marxian school), have also been advocates of radical and sharp policy changes. An argument for policy radicalism rests on the view that a sharp psychological switch in people's perceptions would be effective in demonstrating the advantages of a return to *laissez-faire* principles.

Secondly, there is more than one way of restructuring an economy. A period of restructuring in a crisis is one of conflict where different groups are vying for power, and the outcome is by no means determinate. The new conservatism – 'Thatcherism' – was the way out of crisis that came to be attempted in Britain. Elements of this philosophy are to be found widely across the global economy in the 1980s, and this can give the impression that there was something inevitable about it. In fact, all countries' economies have been restructuring in the 1980s and many have endured increases in unemployment, but none has experienced mass unemployment and attacks on unions and on the living standards of the poor on quite the same scale. There are some countries which have avoided both inflation and unemployment.[3] Thus, restructuring is an open process, open to political determination. While it may be tempting to see Thatcherism as an 'experiment' with the British economy – there is a sense in which one can stand back to watch whether the medicine works – this may be misleading. Thatcherism was 'won' for Britain not through scientific curiosity but through a political and ideological struggle, first to gain ascendancy in the Conservative Party then to win and maintain control of the government (Keegan, 1984). And whether and how long the experiment continues does not merely depend on a dispassionate analysis of its results.

While the theme here is restructuring as a way out of economic decline and crisis, it is important to note that 'Thatcherism' is not *just* that, nor merely an exclusively economic philosophy. Andrew Gamble (1988) appropriately denotes the core of the 'New Right' thinking, which inspired the development of Thatcherism in the Conservative Party in the 1970s, as a philosophy of both 'the free economy and the strong state'. The strong state is seen as necessary to confront trade unions, pressure groups and other bastions of the social–democratic consensus, to uphold market principles of private property, and even as an end in itself with the free economy of private capital supporting the strength of the state. Policies with major economic effects, such as the early 1980s expansion of defence spending even while committed to cutting state expenditure in general, are understandable in the light of this political objective, but not in terms of an isolated economic approach. The analysis of some political scientists has suggested that Thatcherism can be thought of in Gramscian terms as a 'hegemonic project' – an evolving struggle to establish a successful mode of economic regulation to support capital accumulation, combined with ideological and political dominance in all areas of civil society. Stuart Hall (1988) has dubbed the ideological parts of this (incomplete) project 'authoritarian populism'. It is populist since it draws on popular discontent with traditional state bureaucracy (for example, over council housing); it is authoritarian because it requires an immense centralisation of state power.[4] In fact, the strengthening of traditional ties of authority runs through a range of social policies and attitudes, emphasising parental duties within the family, for example, and reinforcing the police. Authority at work is to be reinforced both by a weakening of union protection and the release of market disciplines.

Thatcherism involves an attack on prevailing social democratic principles such as collectivism in the provision of a substantial proportion of economic necessities, full employment and redistribution of income. One prominent strand of New Right thinking follows the line proposed by F. A. Hayek (1944): that social democracy with rising state provision was bound to lead to authoritarianism. Notwithstanding the refutation of this prediction by the experience of European countries in subsequent decades, the principle that nationalised industries, for example, are at least a potential base for the launch of state control has informed the urge to privatise them. This political motivation exists, whatever may be the objective role being played by particular public-sector corporations within the capitalist economy. The lesson is that one could not explain why Thatcherism has evolved in the way it has, nor why particular policies have been introduced, purely in terms of a supposedly coherent strategy to halt the economic decline of capitalism in Britain and re-establish a successful regime of accumulation.

Yet the economic realm cannot be avoided. The deepest contradiction for Thatcherism arises if its economic project fails, for then it loses its material base. The issue for examination here is primarily not the origin of policies, nor, except indirectly, the ways in which policies were carried through sometimes against considerable opposition. Rather, I shall focus on their effects, in the context of Britain's prior economic decline.

1.4 THE ENTREPRENEURIAL WAY

What basis is there for believing that the 'free economy and the strong state' might provide the route for capital based in Britain to reverse its historic decline and compete actively with capital elsewhere? It is sometimes thought that the conventional economics of free market exchange provides the answer: remove restrictions on competition, particularly the monopoly influences of unions, reduce the distorting effects of government taxation and spending, and the economy approaches closer to a Pareto-efficient allocation of resources. There is, however, no real basis for these prescriptions from mainstream neoclassical theory, since they are based on false assumptions. As soon as public goods, externalities and (necessarily) missing markets are considered, the logical case for state intervention to improve the market, economy is made (Hahn, 1988). Therefore any arguments about, for example, state expenditure should be contingent on circumstances, which may speak for less *or* more spending, rather than couched at an abstract philosophical level wherein less spending is automatically better. And of course conventional Keynesian macroeconomics is no guide to Thatcherite policies either.

As has frequently been pointed out, however, the New Right thinkers who have inspired and rationalised a good many of the Conservatives' policies have relied more on the 'Austrian' school of economics. The distinguishing mark of this school is their conception of economic dynamics, in particular the role of the entrepreneur in changing and modernising the economic structure. F. A. Hayek, the most respected philosopher of Thatcherism, distinguishes between the sort of knowledge that an individual entrepreneur has – i.e., specific knowledge about time and place, and possible improvements to meet potential demands – and a general scientific knowledge of economic affairs. Central planners do not have the specific knowledge, and hence a planned economy will stagnate compared to an atomistic market economy. Competition is the struggle to learn how to reduce costs and this is the stuff of progress. Austrian-school economists stress the special virtues of entrepreneurial alertness – the ability to see quickly the opportunities for gain by producing or trading in some new areas. And as for technical progress, Joseph Schumpeter's conception of waves of creative destruction, a dynamic process of innovation of new technologies, is well known.[5]

In all of these approaches the revitalising spirit of unfettered profit-making is lauded. Thus, for example, even if privatisation of an industry does not change market structure it is claimed to raise efficiency. A corollary of this faith is that the supply of entrepreneurship, and hence of progress and modernisation, can only be helped by riding the tide of increased internationalisation.

Before proceeding to look at the ways of evaluating Thatcherism it is, however, worth noting some inherent contradictions underlying the project, which suggest the possibility that it could lead to regression rather than modernisation.

At the structural level, the hope for modernisation centres around the lure of profits and the exercise of authority: by granting British managers sufficient incentives and the 'freedom to manage' (that is, to take decisions without fear of union interference or needing to care for the effect on employees), entrepreneurs with vision will emerge 'from the woodwork', and the managers they appoint will become efficient and dynamic. But this is a particularly bold assumption which neglects the fact that modern competition is a sophisticated process, which increasingly requires highly educated and trained managers of a kind which has been scarce in British firms. Since the City has always had an arms-length relation with industry, unwilling to intervene and co-ordinate long-term production strategies, a fragmented British industry has been less able to compete with more directed industries in Europe and Japan. Whether entrepreneurs can emerge to produce a long-term growth, in the absence of either a strong educational base or a *dirigiste* strategy of some kind, would seem unlikely. Further doubt arises from the irreversibility of certain kinds of industrial destruction: if a whole industry disappears, so also goes Hayek's specific knowledge in that sphere and it becomes hard or even impossible to resurrect. The destructive aspect of competition easily goes too far.

The achievement of harsher authority and discipline is also a mixed blessing for capital, for it is far from clear whether this is the most effective means of modernising production processes to compete in the world economy. There is little doubt that by imposing greater discipline at the workplace many workers will be induced to toil harder, particularly those in secondary sectors of the labour market where job security is weak (Shapiro and Stiglitz, 1984; Green and Weisskopf, 1988). They are likely to strive harder individually in order to avoid dismissal for poor work, and perhaps collectively to join with management to help ensure their firms' survival. Yet these are one-off achievements which after a few years pale into insignificance behind any changes that can and need to be wrought in the pace of innovation and modernisation.

There is little evidence either way as to whether a regime of greater discipline is generally more or less conducive to dynamic change. Weisskopf (1987) finds evidence that high unemployment can cow workers in the US into accepting innovations more readily, but that in other countries it has no impact or even the reverse is true. It is possible that innovation is more effective when workers sense that it is unlikely to abolish their jobs, since this may induce creative co-operation. This is especially true in many of the newer knowledge-based industries where the skills and inventiveness of employees have to be encouraged and positively motivated. And it has become a central tenet of the labour process restructuring to be found in multinationals such as Toyota, Nissan and the US car companies to provide greater security for core employees in order to elicit their co-operation.

A third issue raised by some writers is the assumed relation between the 'free economy' and the macroeconomic flexibility of the labour market (i.e., the ability of the institutional system in the labour market to come up with wage reductions in times of recession). The Thatcherite presumption is that forcing decentralised individualist bargaining is the best way of achieving such flexibility. Yet the experience of highly centralised bargaining systems in Sweden and elsewhere, with strong union influence and hence a very attenuated authority and freedom for individual managers, suggests that these corporatist mechanisms are as good at producing flexibility as the atomistic system in the US (Calmfors and Drifill, 1988; Freeman, 1988), and far better than the in-between weakly centralised arrangements in Britain.[6]

In brief, even if one accepts that individual entrepreneurs can have an innovative role, there are sufficient reasons to question whether the entrepreneurial strategy could provide a recovery route for capital located in Britain. This issue needs to be posed not at the abstract level of whether capitalist markets in general work harmoniously and stably – as history demonstrates, there are deep contradictions which underlie the periodic crisis to which economies are often subject – but at the historically specific conjuncture of the declining UK economy located in a rapidly changing, increasingly competitive, world market. The Thatcher government's policies *have* opened the way for the entrepreneur, much more so than in previous decades. Whether this will allow this small segment of global capitalism, located in the UK, to adapt more quickly than elsewhere can ultimately be judged only by a detailed analysis of the structural changes which the profit-motivated firms are pursuing.

1.5 LANDMARK POLICIES OF THE THATCHER GOVERNMENT

While the objectives of the Thatcherite strategy are medium- or long-term, and concern a structural alteration in the economy, the policies themselves are both of a macroeconomic and microeconomic nature. To set the scene, the five basic sets of enacted policy programmes will first be outlined. Rather than a detailed tale of their evolution, the landmarks of the decade are noted, as a background for evaluating their overall effects in the next section.

1.5.1 Public Sector Borrowing Requirement (PSBR)

The centre-piece of the new macroeconomic policy, and one which has persisted for a decade, was fiscal rectitude, as embodied in the Medium Term Financial Strategy (MTFS). Launched in March 1980, its stated aim was to reduce the excess of government spending over taxation gradually over a number of years, thereby inducing fiscal confidence in the government and reducing the need for monetary growth. There are many logical holes in the argument that borrowing *per se* is a sign of fiscal irresponsibility, the parallel between corporate and government borrowing being all too obvious. The Public Sector Borrowing Requirement (PSBR) does not distinguish between borrowing for investment and borrowing for consumption purposes, and it arbitrarily counts the income from asset sales as a negative item (presumably indicating an item of prudence). Moreover, it has been forcefully argued that only a comprehensive balance sheet that would account for the government's assets and liabilities can show how stable its finances are (Hills, 1984). The connection of the PSBR with monetary growth is, moreover, contingent on many assumptions and at best indirect (Jackson, 1989). It may be suggested, therefore, that the basic objective of the MTFS may have differed from its stated aim: its underlying intention was to set the political framework for reductions in government spending. Whatever its objective, the policy has by and large been successfully carried out: at 5.89% of Gross Domestic Product (GDP) (at factor cost) in 1980 the PSBR was still larger than in 1978, the last full year of Labour's administration; by 1988 (2nd quarter) the PSBR had been whittled away entirely and there was a 1.98% surplus.

1.5.2 Government expenditure and taxation

The second element of the government's policy has been to lower the level of its own spending, considered an important indicator of how much the state 'interferes' with the free economy. (A favourite game of the 1970s was to choose arbitrarily and publicise a suitable ratio that seemed to suggest that public spending was too high, approaching 'the limits of social democracy'; there being so many definitions to choose from, affecting both numerator and denominator, the conclusions drawn were frequently deeply misleading.) To carry this policy through, sophisticated techniques of financial control were pioneered that allowed the line to be drawn against public demands for spending by reference to what could be 'afforded' – the latter having previously been determined through a political decision, rather than any objective judgment. Nonetheless, the techniques had only a limited overall effect when faced with objective realities. The rise in unemployment and other welfare benefits could not be resisted, despite cuts in the benefit rates; in addition the 'strong state', including Thatcher's commitment to the cold war, meant expanding defence expenditure in real terms. General government spending was 48.4% of GDP (at factor cost) in 1978, Labour's last full year in office; this ratio peaked at 54.3% in 1982, after which the economy improved and the control techniques started to bite, and the ratio fell back to 48.2% in 1987.

The objective of keeping taxes down took second place to the MTFS, with the result that total receipts (from taxes and other income) rose from 42.3% of GDP (at factor cost) in 1978 to 48.3% in 1987. Within this overall constraint, however, some structural changes were effected. The standard income tax rate, which began the Thatcher years at 33%, was down to 25% in 1989, with only one higher-level band at 40%. A number of reforms were effected in 1988, enabled by the buoyant economy. Before then, tax allowances on investment were rationalised; and there was an increase in the importance of indirect taxes.

1.5.3 Monetary policy

In March 1980 the government set a target of 7–11% for £M3 growth for the following 14 months. The underlying strategy was for a gradual reduction in monetary growth as recommended by the monetarist tenets of Milton Friedman. This appeared to represent a defeat for the Hayekian strategy for a very sharp cut in money growth so as to endure high unemployment, but for only a brief period of six months or so while the system was 'cleansed' and 'sound money' restored (rather in the manner of the ending of the 1922–3 German hyperinflation). In the event £M3 grew 22.2%. This was merely a particularly spectacular example of monetary growth widely missing its target, a feature of most years of Conservative-government monetarism. Monetary control, however, is notoriously difficult even at stable times – targets were as often as not missed in earlier days under previous governments (the very first attempt at monetary targeting, the Letter of Intent to the IMF in November 1967, was successful; but only 5 out of 14 attempts to control M3 or £M3 have hit the targeted range).[7] A corollary is that the government has experimented with alternative monetary targets, M0 (mainly notes and coin) alone being favoured in 1987 and 1988. One problem, of which the Bank of England is conscious, is known as 'Goodhart's Law' – the tendency for observed relations between a money definition and economic variables to break down, as soon as that definition is openly targeted (mainly because wealth-holders can switch between assets to avoid the monetary authority's constraints).

Ironically, it is now widely accepted that the money growth figures over 1979 to 1981 presented an especially distorted picture of monetary restraint. De-regulation of financial markets led to increased demand for monetary assets, with the result that despite high growth, interest rates were sky high (see Fig. 1.1, below). Short-term capital inflows responding to these rates and perhaps also to the prospects for North Sea oil revenues (Maynard, 1988, pp. 63–5) brought a further appreciation of sterling (Fig. 1.2, below). The combination of high interest rates, high exchange rates and, later, world recession, combined to create the greatest depression in Britain since the 1930s. Those in the Hayekian mould approving a sharp, as opposed to gradual, tightening of money markets are apt to regard this as a fortunate mistake (Matthews and Minford, 1987), even though the high unemployment became semi-permanent.

1.5.4 Employment policy

While trade unions have been weakened by the economic circumstances of the 1980s (which have tended to hit unionists hard in the manufacturing sector) there have been several landmark policies to hasten this process. The Employment Act 1980 began the attack by restricting unfair dismissal and maternity leave rights, and outlawing 'secondary picketing'. The Employment Act 1982 raised the fines and set unions open to the sequestration of their assets, while further restricting employees' rights. The Trade Union Act 1984 worked to impose a measure of internal democracy within unions, and secret ballots before strikes. The Employment Act 1988 curtailed unions' disciplinary powers and the use of their funds and, without formally abolishing it, made the post-entry closed shop virtually impossible to enforce. Plans, finally, to dispose of the pre-entry closed shop were announced in 1989.

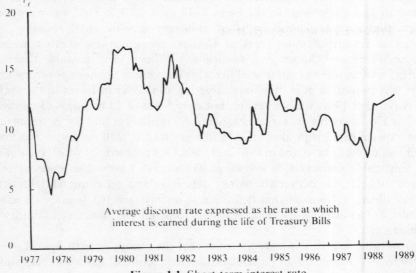

Figure 1.1 Short-term interest rate.

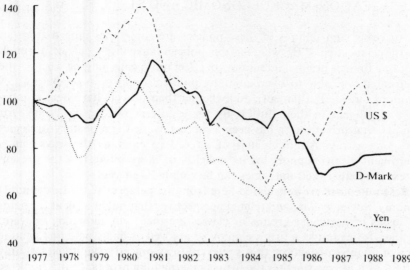

Figure 1.2 Sterling exchange rates (1977.100).

In between these Acts, the government itself as employer conducted a major strategic offensive against organised labour, rarely going so far as to ban trade unions (as at GCHQ), but culminating with its defeat and splitting of the NUM in 1985 after the miners' strike (a success that had parallels both with President Reagan's swifter historic defeat of the air-traffic controllers in the US in 1981, and in Britain with the General Strike in 1926).

1.5.5 Privatisation and de-regulation

While the sale of Local Authority housing began early on in the Conservative programme, privatisation of national assets – perhaps the policy for which Thatcherism will longest be remembered – began in earnest only in the second term. Only about £0.5 billion worth was sold off in 1982–3 but by 1987–8 around £5 billion (about 3% of annual taxes) was being raised from the sale of British Airways and British Gas. The electricity industry which, along with water, is being privatised in 1989–90 in capitalism's biggest-ever auction, is set to realise even more funds.

Alongside such major disposals there has been a general reduction in regulatory functions in many areas. Most prominent are the financial deregulations: the removal of exchange controls, of capital market restraints and of restrictions on bank lending (the 'corset'). There was also a dismantling of controls in other areas, often running alongside privatisation as with bus services, and a general reduction in the policing of businesses in respect of Wages Council orders and safety regulations.

1.6 EVALUATION: MACROECONOMIC AND STRUCTURAL

The successes and failures of these policies are sometimes judged from an inward perspective – by whether the policies have been carried through according to their original intentions. In effect this means judging whether the government was able to overcome any political opposition to the policies (within or outside Parliament), and whether their officers have been competent and diligent in their duties. By these criteria we can easily say, for example, that privatisation has been a success, while the monetary strategies have gone astray. Although it is of interest to examine the ways that a government gleans support for its policies, of more interest in the present context is whether their outcomes can be counted a success.

These outcomes are considered here from the perspective of the capitalist economy. Social welfare and related perspectives that might look at the gains and losses of particular groups or classes are then only indirectly relevant. Whether, for example, a firm's employees are well or badly paid and gaining much or no job satisfaction, this is relevant to an objective capitalist test only in so far as it affects whether the firm is making high profits. In this book we largely leave aside the issue of whether the policies of Thatcherism are at all just or humane in their impact.

Whether the progressive and modernising forces to be unleashed in a Hayekian free economy can overcome such contradictions as we have discussed is ultimately an empirical and historical issue. It is important to

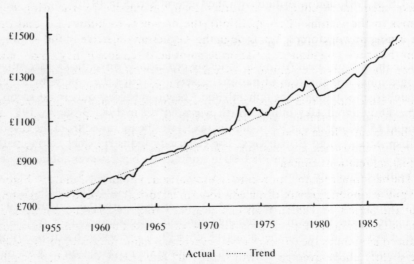

Actual ······· Trend

Figure 1.3 Per capita GDP at factor cost (at 1985 prices, 1955–88 (Q2)).

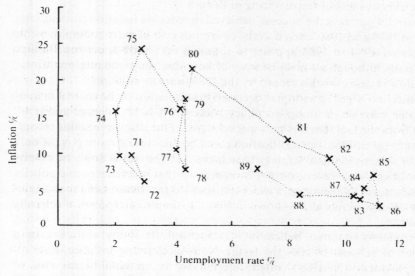

Seas. adj.; 2nd Q, except Feb 89.

Figure 1.4 Unemployment and inflation (1971–88).

assess the changes that have occurred at the appropriate structural level – in terms, for example, of the easing of markets, the restructuring of industries to make them more competitive (rather than the passive restructuring that comes to the victims of competition), the openness to innovation and the retraining of workforces. Yet, though the Keynesian objective of full employment has been abandoned, inflation remains an ostensible policy target, and other macroeconomic data such as real GDP growth are useful as measures of success or failure even though they are no longer targeted. There is, moreover, a close link in that macroeconomic variables can be a direct influence on the structural variables that Thatcherism has tried to alter: thus, high exchange rates have been used to impose strong (often deadly) competition on export industries, and high unemployment has been a factor in altering the industrial relations climate.

The basic macroeconomic record is summarised in Figures 1.3 and 1.4. Figure 1.3 puts economic growth in a medium-term historical perspective, suggesting that the period of Thatcherism has produced roughly speaking an average rate of growth of GDP per capita. This was punctuated by the major recession induced as soon as the Conservative government came to power, followed by the slightly above-average growth from 1982 onwards. Overall there is substantial deviation from trend growth, but the post-1982 recovery was both steady and long-lived, and it is this period that is normally taken as evidence for the effectiveness of restructuring in Britain.

Figure 1.4 portrays the 'success' achieved in reducing inflation from its high levels in 1975 and 1980, even if at the enormous cost of mass unemployment. The period 1980 to 1987 appears to follow a text-book short-run Phillips curve path, although we must be wary of imposing simplistic interpretations. A shadow is cast over this record by the 1989 jump in inflation.

Chancellor Nigel Lawson has declared that inflation is the central macroeconomic variable denoting his policy success – it is both 'judge and jury'. Apart from the fact that this puts a good slant on the macroeconomic record, at least as far as 1988, the justification could be that 'sound money' is the only task for macroeconomic strategy to achieve – all the rest is down to supply-side policies. Nonetheless, once it is recognised that macroeconomic policies have structural implications, a wider test is called for. In assessing the sustainability of such trends as are shown in Fig. 1.1, simple extrapolation is hardly satisfactory.

One macroeconomic indicator of structural flexibility common to a number of schools of thought is the Non-Accelerating-Inflation-Rate-of-Unemployment (NAIRU), often referred to as an equilibrium rate of unemployment.[8] Independent of the actual unemployment rate, the NAIRU captures the effect of structural adjustments in both product and labour markets. If the structural changes are beneficial, leaner and more efficient firms should be able to meet higher demand without inflationary tendencies, while workers in a more 'flexible' labour market can settle for lower wage rises for any given level of aggregate unemployment – in other words, the NAIRU should fall. Unfortunately this is not the whole story, as the radical reshaping of industry brought about during the restructuring process can cause massive structural unemployment of a conventional kind: a mismatch between job vacancies and the unemployed, along both regional and occupational dimensions. A period of time is required before sufficient mobility occurs to eliminate these mismatches, during which the NAIRU can be above the level prevailing before the restructuring programme takes effect. Our expectation, then, is that in the long term the NAIRU should be reduced by successful restructuring – a somewhat weaker prediction.

Unfortunately, too, the NAIRU is not a regularly published hard-and-fast statistic, and can only be obtained by estimation from macroeconometric models whose specifications may be subject to controversy. The small model developed by Layard and Nickell (1986, 1987) has the advantage of allowing a range of theoretical interpretations, while letting the data determine the NAIRU estimates: these are gleaned by setting the expected price equal to the actual price level in the estimated wage-setting and price-setting equations. The results show both that the NAIRU has risen as high as 13% during the 1980s and that its rise tends to follow on a short period after the rise in the actual unemployment rate.[9] This rise of the NAIRU provides a partial proximate explanation for the continued rise in real wages throughout the 1980s

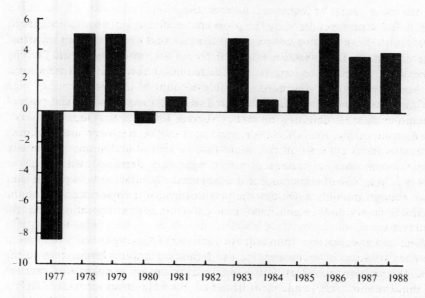

Figure 1.5   Real wages; annual percentage change in average weekly earnings minus inflation.

(Fig. 1.5): after an initial dampening, the weight of mass unemployment became increasingly irrelevant in wage bargains.

Conventional analysis suggests that employer taxes, import prices and the benefit-replacement ratio are important determinants of the NAIRU – indeed, they may have played a role in its two-decade rise through to about 5% by the end of the 1970s. In particular, the oil price shocks had predictable effects on workers' bargaining and firms' pricing strategies. In the 1980s, however, all of these have if anything turned down: tax rates have been cut, the oil price has fallen, the Earnings-Related Supplement to unemployment benefits was abolished in 1982 and benefit payouts are now taxable. The monopoly power of unions, coupled with the assumption that unions tend to impose restrictive work practices, is also used to explain the pre-1979 rise in the NAIRU. The theoretical effect of unions on productive efficiency is ambiguous since by giving workers a 'voice' they can reduce turnover and promote co-operation (Freeman and Medoff, 1984). The Layard–Nickell model suggests, along with commentators on the right, that on balance greater union power tends to raise the NAIRU. But union density and union strength were undoubtedly diminished through the 1980s: if anything this should have lowered the NAIRU. Finally, if the entrepreneurial motive was being successful in restructuring the economy according to the profit motive the NAIRU should be expected to fall.

All these must be balanced against the short-term rise of structural unemployment engendered by the programme of change. Nonetheless, many economists have become concerned at the fact that the high levels of actual unemployment (and NAIRU) seemed to *persist* for many years, thereby questioning whether the long-term predicted fall in the NAIRU is achievable without intervention. The most plausible account of the persistence of high unemployment together with a high NAIRU is to suppose that the path of unemployment is subject to 'hysteresis' (Cross, 1988) – a new term for an old relationship. Thus the NAIRU depends not only on the structural variables just considered but also on the recent past history of actual unemployment. The macroeconomic policies affecting aggregate demand also affect the NAIRU. The rise of unemployment drags up the NAIRU a short period later and, though possibly asymmetrically, a fall in unemployment can drag the NAIRU slowly down again. One reason for this is that in losing their jobs, and remaining unemployed for a while, millions of workers begin to lose their work skills and, just as important, are deprived of the opportunity to develop new skills as industry changes and modernises. Applying these ideas to the UK, the massive recession of 1979–81 itself disrupted the normal procedures of the labour market to an extent from which it has not yet recovered. Only a massive investment in retraining workers, and a regional programme to overcome geographical immobility, could have prevented the semi-permanent rise in the NAIRU, and neither was forthcoming.

It has further been argued that many if not all those excluded from jobs can cease to be effective competitors with the regularly employed (Lindbeck and Snower, 1985). A firm cannot easily substitute unemployed workers ('outsiders') for their existing workforce ('insiders'), even if the reservation wage of the unemployed is lower than the wage they have to pay. This is because the newly employed would then have to undergo training. The turnover costs, including hiring, firing and training, would outweigh the benefits of the wage cuts. (These ideas, too, are implicit in the older and now-voluminous literature on segmented labour markets.) So British firms, after the recession, had to continue to bargain with the existing workforce which, although diminished, increasingly felt less threatened by the dole. And the firms found they had to continue raising real wages in order to attract and retain a quality workforce.

Whichever explanation of hysteresis is accepted, the persistence of high unemployment for many years expressed a contradiction in the Thatcherite programme referred to above: stronger authority is seen as necessary for restoring the 'freedom to manage', yet the means available have adversely affected many other elements of the restructuring which the programme was aimed at. There seems little doubt that the fear of unemployment induced workers to toil substantially harder at their tasks after one term of the Conservative government. The Percentage Utilisation of Labour, an index of work intensity in British manufacturing industries, after an initial drop brought on by the hoarding of relatively idle labour, registered a net rise of about 5% from May 1979 to November 1983; it was still high by the start of 1988 (Smith-Gavine and Bennett, 1988). There was, in effect, a reduction to some degree in 'over-manning', from which British-based capital benefited and which can account for some productivity rises early on. In addition there is plenty of anecdotal evidence of a change in the climate of industrial relations. But the deep recession which engendered these changes may at the same time have ruined the prospects for economic recovery. When substantial sectors of industry are eliminated, the workforce's skills deteriorating in unemployment, there can be an irreversible loss. While neo-Austrians would no doubt argue that no cut was too deep to ensure a change in the climate of industrial relations, the wasting of large numbers of both companies and their workforces is hardly evidence of successful restructuring.

Setting aside the macroeconomic assessments and the somewhat problematic trajectory of the NAIRU, the best judgement as to whether the entrepreneurial forces set free in Margaret Thatcher's strong state are resolving their contradictions lies in a detailed examination of the elements behind the aggregates. The chapters in this book pursue this theme in a number of areas. To begin with, the chapters in Part II are concerned with the composition and balance of industry and of the national economy. Wells dissects the deep problems in store arising from the collapse of manufacturing output in the recession and the creation of a structural trade deficit; Glyn examines the pattern of macroeconomic change, including the financing of the consumption boom through credit and the relative stagnation of industrial investment. Martin examines the tensions that arise from the enormously unbalanced regional development.

In Part III changes in the labour process and labour market are examined. Nolan assesses the debate concerning the factors underlying the growth of labour productivity; Blackaby and Hunt examine whether productivity growth is associated with compositional changes in industries. Ashton, Green and Hoskins review the reorganisation of training systems and the failure to resolve the UK skills problem; Rubery develops and utilises a framework for analysing 'labour flexibility'; and Stark charts the increasing inequality in the distribution of income. In Part IV authors examine various putative sources for modernisation in British industry. Freeman reviews the vital role of technological change through Research and Development (R&D) and investigates whether Thatcherism has done anything to rescue the disastrous record of British firms; Fine examines the possible impact of privatisation, and criticises conventional analyses couched in terms of static competition theory; Toporowski considers the role of financial de-regulation; and Auerbach focuses on the effects of rising competition and increased multi-national involvement in Britain. In Part V, Rowthorn concludes with a political–economic summary of the effects of all these changes, and compares the 1980s with past recessions and recoveries. Finally, Desai examines Thatcherism as a modernising strategy in a century-long historical perspective of British economic decline.

1.7 CONCLUSION

No simple conclusion emerges from this array of studies, even if the balance is strongly weighted in criticism of what Thatcherism has done to the UK economy. That the economy was in need of some form of structural change is nonetheless the implicit starting point of all areas looked at. Thatcherism has come along with and accelerated that process of change in a particular direction.

These changes can only properly be assessed through a structural analysis but they may also be expressed indirectly in the trend path of macroeconomic variables. It has become a conventional wisdom in some circles (*The Economist*, 3.12.88, p. 13; OECD, 1988) that while mistakes may have been made in the macroeconomic management of the economy (such as missing money supply targets, or relying exclusively on high interest rates instead of using fiscal policy), the supply-side policies of the government have worked. This conclusion is typically based on a simplistic analysis of the data, and combined with a belief that market forces should work. On balance the detailed analyses presented in this book present a much less rosy picture of supply-side changes. The rumbles of macroeconomic instability witnessed in 1989 may be expressions of this fact. An unusual conjuncture confronted the Chancellor in his March budget: a large and increasing budget surplus, accompanied by a trade deficit and rising inflation. Old-fashioned Keynesian fine-tuning had to be imposed to curb inflation (despite still-high unemployment). There was therefore no space to cut taxes, as the MTFS allows in order to balance the budget. Instead the policy was justified anew in terms of the advantages of repaying national debt. Unable to raise taxes, owing to the 'supply-side' theory on which the strategy is based, the Chancellor was compelled to conduct the fine-tuning with one arm tied behind his back: that is, by using interest rate policy alone. Thus the macroeconomic 'errors', which some critics of the government have focused on, may be reflecting rather deeper problems in the economy than the technical miscalculations of GDP growth that are said to have informed the expansionary stance taken in 1988.

It is the contention here that such macroeconomic issues are only of a second order of importance. If Lawson is right that the Conservatives' policies are renewing the structure of the economy so that capital accumulation in Britain can proceed smoothly for the medium term, then whatever macroeconomic policy is pursued, even if its fine-tuning is imperfect, as long as it maintains stability in the financial system, there will be continued success for the economy. If he is wrong, and the new philosophy fails to deliver the economic success claimed for it, future Chancellors will continually find themselves caught on the horns of a dilemma. Inflation, unemployment, trade deficits, devaluations – the problems will outnumber the instruments of control any Chancellor can have, and no amount of macroeconomic engine-tuning of either the Keynesian or the modern kind will point the way out of renewed crisis.

NOTES

1. For an introductory survey of theories, see Green and Sutcliffe (1987, Part Five).
2. In its original meaning, a crisis is that point in the course of an illness following which there is either death or recovery.
3. Japan, Sweden, Norway, Switzerland and Austria; see Glyn and Rowthorn, (1988), and Therborn (1986) for analysis.
4. Hall has tended to emphasise the moral and political dimensions above the economic (Hall, 1988, p. 85). Other approaches have identified Thatcherism more closely with the economic interests of dominant fractions of the capitalist class; for a critical survey, see Gamble (1988, Ch. 6).
5. For a sympathetic survey of the Austrian school, see Shand (1984).
6. It is highly questionable, moreover, whether the 'flexibility' available to US-based capital is desirable (even setting aside the blatantly oppressive impact on US workers who have on average suffered real wage reductions since 1973, and endured rising inequality and poverty). The US economy suffers, too, from de-industrialisation and chronic trade deficits and mirrors other features of Britain's economic decline; see Harrison and Bluestone (1988).
7. I thank Paul Herrington for this piece of information.
8. Walrasian neoclassical economists tend to use the term 'Natural Rate of Unemployment'.
9. For estimates up to 1987, and for a critique of the NAIRU concept, see Jenkinson (1987).

REFERENCES

Bacon, R. and Eltis, W., *Britain's Economic Problem: Too Few Producers* (Macmillan: London, 1976).

Calmfors, Lars and Drifill, John, 'Bargaining structure, corporatism and macro-economic performance', *Economic Policy*, **6**: 14–61 (1988).

Cross, Rod (ed.) *Unemployment, Hysteresis and the Natural Rate Hypothesis* (Blackwell: Oxford, 1988).

Elbaum, Bernard and Lazonick, William, *The Decline of the British Economy* (Clarendon Press: Oxford, 1986).

Fine, Ben and Harris, Laurence, *The Peculiarities of the British Economy* (Lawrence & Wishart: London, 1985).

Freeman, Richard, 'Labour markets', *Economic Policy*, **6**: 63–80 (1988).

Freeman, Richard and Medoff, James, *What Do Unions Do?* (Basic Books: New York, 1984).

Gamble, Andrew, *The Free Economy and the Strong State* (Macmillan: London, 1988).

Glyn, Andrew and Rowthorn, Bob, *The Diversity of Unemployment Experience Since 1973*, World Institute for Development Economics Research Working Papers, No. 40, April (1988).

Green, Francis and Sutcliffe, Bob, *The Profit System* (Penguin: Harmondsworth, 1987).

Green, Francis and Weisskopf, Thomas, E., *The Worker Discipline Effect: A Disaggregative Analysis*, Discussion Paper No. 90, University of Leicester, Department of Economics (1988).

Hahn, Frank, 'On Market Economies', in *Thatcherism* (ed. Robert Skidelsky) (Chatto & Windus: London, 1988).

Hall, Stuart, 'No light at the end of the tunnel', in *The Hard Road to Renewal* (ed. Hall, S.) (Verso: London, 1988).

Harrison, Bennett and Bluestone, Barry, *The Great U-Turn* (Basic Books: New York, 1988).

Hayek, F. A., *The Road to Serfdom* (Routledge & Kegan Paul: London 1944, reprinted edn 1979).

Hills, John, What is the Public Sector Worth? *Fiscal Studies,* 5, 1 (1984).

Itoh, Makoto, *The Basic Theory of Capitalism* (Macmillan: London, 1988).

Jackson, Peter, 'Public sector deficit and money supply', in *Current Issues in Monetary Economics,* eds Ghatak, S. and Bandyopadhyay, T. (Harvester Wheatsheaf: Hemel Hempstead, 1989).

Jenkinson, Tim, 'The natural rate of unemployment: does it exist?' *Oxford Review of Economic Policy,* 3 (1987).

Keegan, William, *Mrs Thatcher's Economic Experiment* (Penguin: Harmondsworth, 1984).

Layard, Richard and Nickell, Stephen, 'Unemployment in Britain', *Economica*, special issue on unemployment (1986).

Layard, Richard and Nickell, Stephen, 'The Labour Market', in *The Performance of the British Economy* (eds) (Dornbusch, Rudiger and Layard, Richard) (Clarendon Press: Oxford, 1987).

Lindbeck, Assar and Snower, Dennis J. 'Explanations of unemployment', *Oxford Review of Economic Policy,* 1 (1985).

Mandel, Ernest, *Late Capitalism* (Verso: London, 1978).

Matthews, K. and Minford, P., 'Mrs Thatcher's economic policies 1979–1987' *Economic Policy,* 5, 59–101 (1987).

Maynard, Geoffrey, *The Economy under Mrs Thatcher* (Blackwell: Oxford, 1988).

OECD 'The impact of oil on the world economy', *OECD Economic Studies,* 27, 114–30 (1980).

OECD 'United Kingdom', *OECD Economic Surveys, 1987/1988* (1988).

Shand, Alexander H., *The Capitalist Alternative* (Harvester Wheatsheaf: Hemel Hempstead, 1984).

Shapiro, Carl and Stiglitz, Joseph, 'Equilibrium unemployment as a worker discipline device', *American Economic Review,* 74, June (1984).

Smith-Gavine, Sydney A. N. and Bennett, Alan J., *Index of Percentage Utilisation of Labour: Bulletin to Cooperating Firms,* 53, Leicester Polytechnic, School of Economics and Accounting (1988).

The Economist, 3.12.88.

Therborn, Goron, *Why Some People Are More Unemployed Than Others* (Verso: London, 1986).

Weisskopf, Thomas E., 'The effects of unemployment on labour productivity: an international comparative analysis', *International Review of Applied Economics,* 1, July (1987).

PART II

THE ANATOMY OF STRUCTURAL CHANGE

2 UNEVEN DEVELOPMENT AND DE-INDUSTRIALISATION IN THE UK SINCE 1979

John Wells

2.1 INTRODUCTION

In assessing the economic record of the Thatcher decade (1979–89) one of the most striking features of the past 10 years, taken as a whole, has undoubtedly been the extraordinary divergence in experience comparing manufacturing and services – a divergence which expresses itself in the form of huge differences in the evolution of output, employment and investment.

Let us consider, first of all, the differential experience regarding output growth: following the dramatic slump in manufacturing production during 1979–81, when manufacturing output fell by –19.6% from peak (June 1979) to trough (January 1981) the subsequent recovery in manufacturing activity – halting at first, but then gradually gaining in momentum – has taken manufacturing output to a point where it is now at an all-time high. However, even so, by 4Q 1988, manufacturing output was only +6.8% higher than the level it was at when Mrs Thatcher first came into office (in May 1979).[1]

The rate of growth of output of services,[2] on the other hand, has been vastly in excess of this: after registering a rather modest decline during the 1979–81 slump (–2.4% between 2Q 1979 and 4Q 1980), the output of services is now (4Q 1988) some +28.8% higher than in 1979 (see Fig. 2.1 and Table 2.1).

This extreme divergence in experience between manufacturing and services so far as output growth rates are concerned extends also, of course, to employment (see Fig. 2.2). Between 1979 and 1987,[3] manufacturing employment[4] fell from 7.4 million to 5.4 million – a reduction of 2.0 million or 27.0% of the 1979 manufacturing labour force. Meanwhile, employment[5] in the

Final version of manuscript completed during March 1989. I would like to thank Francis Green for his encouragement and detailed comments on an earlier draft, as well as participants in the ESRC Political Economy Study Group on Evaluating Economic and Distributional Changes in the UK, 1979–88, held on 23 September 1988. Thanks also for useful comments to participants in two Cambridge seminars.

26 *The Anatomy of Structural Change*

Table 2.1 UK: Index numbers of output and expenditure at constant 1985 £million (reference base 1979=100).

	Manufacturing output	Services output	GDP	Total domestic expenditure
1979	100.0	100.0	100.0	100.0
1988	107.6	127.6	121.3	118.5
4Q 1988	110.0	128.8	122.4	n.a.

Sources: CSO, *Economic Trends Annual Supplement 1989*; CSO, *Economic Trends*, January 1989 and *Guardian*, 2.22.89.

services rose between 1979 and 1987 from 14.7 million to 16.7 million – an increase of 2.0 million (or about the same as the decline in manufacturing employment), representing a rise of 13.6% relative to the 1979 services labour force.[6]

These huge manufacturing–services differentials, with respect to output and employment growth rates, comparing 1979 with 1988, have obviously given rise to substantial changes in relative shares (see Table 2.2). Thus, between 1979 and 4Q 1988, the share of manufacturing output in total GDP,

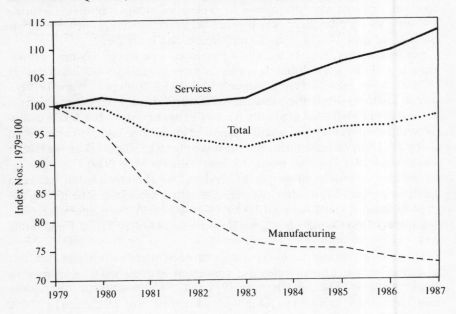

Figure 2.2 UK employment by sector, 1979–87 (Index, 1979=100). (*Sources:* OECD, *Labour Force Statistics*, 1966–86, updated for 1987 with: for (i) employees in employment: *Monthly Digest of Statistics*, May 1988, Table 3.2; (ii) self-employed (Great Britain), Department of Employment, *Employment Gazette*, 'Employment Statistics: Historical Supplement', October 1987, Vol. 95, No. 10, p. 22; self-employed (Northern Ireland): *Northern Ireland Abstract of Statistics*, No. 6, Table 10.4, p. 96.)

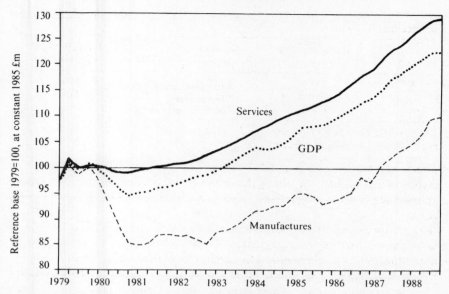

Figure 2.1 UK output, by sector, 1Q1979–4Q1988, at constant 1985 £million, reference base 1979=100. (*Sources: CSO, Economic Trends Annual Supplement 1989*; CSO, *Economic Trends,* January 1989; *Guardian,* 2.22.89.)

measured at constant 1985 £million, fell from 27.1% to 24.4% – a decline of 2.7% of GDP.[7] The share of services' output in total GDP, meanwhile, increased over the same period from 55.8% in 1979 to 58.7% in 4Q 1988 – an increase of +2.9% of GDP. Meanwhile, when it comes to employment, manufacturing's share declined from 29.5% in 1979 to 21.9% in 1987 – a huge reduction in share of –7.6%, whilst the share of the services rose from 58.7% in 1979 to 67.4% in 1987 (an increase of +8.7%).[8]

The differential in experience between manufacturing and services regarding output growth and employment also extends, of course, to the allocation of investment resources (see Fig. 2.3). Even taking into account the manufacturing investment boom which was undoubtedly under way during the course

Table 2.2 UK manufacturing and services: change in percentage shares in total output and employment, 1979–88.

	% GDP at 1985 £million		% total employment	
	Manufacturing	Services	Manufacturing	Services
1979	27.1	55.8	29.5	58.7
1987	–	–	21.9	67.4
4Q 1988	24.4	58.7		
change	–2.7	+2.9	–7.6	+8.7

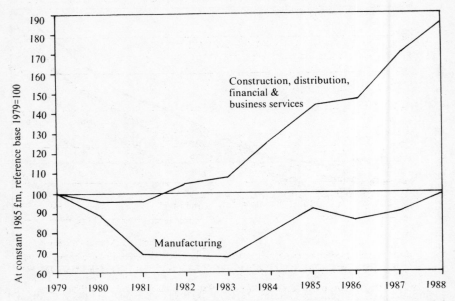

Figure 2.3 UK gross domestic fixed capital formation, by sector, 1979–88, at constant 1985 £million, reference base 1979=100. (*Sources:* CSO, *National Accounts (Blue Book) 1988*, together with DTI, *Press Notice*, 23 May 1989.)

of 1988, gross fixed investment in manufacturing industry (at constant 1985 £million has, according to official figures; only just surpassed the level of 1979.[9] Meanwhile, investment in the services[10] was, by 1988, some 85.3% higher than in 1979 (see Fig. 2.3).

It is these extreme divergences in experience between manufacturing and services, comparing 1979 with the present – expressing themselves in exceptional differences with respect to changes in output, employment and investment – which is our principal focus of enquiry, and the aim of this paper is to provide an explanation for this unusually uneven pattern of economic development. However, before turning to our explanation of such differences, it is important to introduce two caveats.

The first of these is that it would, of course, be quite wrong to believe that such sharp differences in experience between manufacturing and services originated in 1979. Considering the behaviour of output, first of all, the large differential favouring the services relative to manufacturing can, in fact, be said to date from 1973–4 (see Fig. 2.4). Prior to that point in time (and stretching back, at least, to 1948 (see Fig. 2.5)), UK manufacturing output generally grew at a somewhat faster rate than GDP – while the growth of services tended to lag behind GDP growth (see Fig. 2.5). As a consequence, the share of manufacturing output in total GDP, when measured at constant

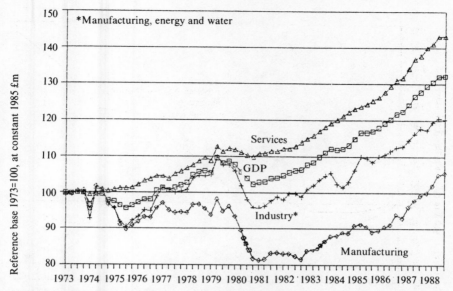

Figure 2.4 UK output, by sector 1Q1973–4Q1988, at constant 1985 £million, reference base 1973=100.

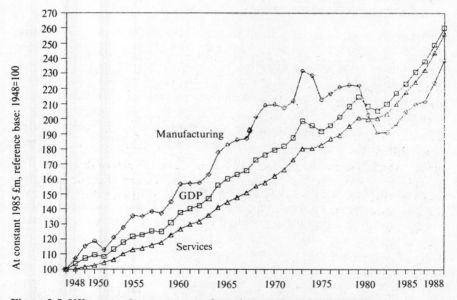

Figure 2.5 UK output, by sector: manufacturing, services, GDP: 1948–88, at constant 1985 £million, reference base 1948=100. (*Sources:* CSO, *Economic Trends Annual Supplement 1989* updated to 1988 with CSO, *Economic Trends*, January 1989, on the basis of figures for the first three quarters.)

Figure 2.6 UK manufacturing output as percentage GDP, 1948–87, at current £million and constant 1985 £million (*Sources:* CSO, *UK National Accounts (Blue Book) 1988* for current price data and CSO, *Economic Trends Annual Supplement 1989* for constant price output series.)

1985 £million, experienced a trend increase between 1948 and 1974, rising from 26.2% to 30.6% – an increase of +4.4% of GDP (see Fig. 2.6).[11,12] That UK manufacturing output growth was so rapid, relative to GDP growth, between 1948 and 1973–4 is all the more surprising, given that UK net manufactured exports underwent a trend decline as a percentage of GDP during most of the pre-1973 period (whether measured at current [13] or constant prices). In practice, two factors appear to account for the fact that UK manufacturing output growth led GDP growth in the period prior to 1973, despite adverse trends in manufacturing trade. The first of these is that, during the 1950s and 1960s, private consumers' expenditure on manufactures was exceptionally income-elastic (as we shall demonstrate below) – experiencing a very large increase as a share of total consumers' expenditure. The second factor tending to boost manufacturing output growth pre-1973 was that investment expenditure represented a gradually increasing percentage of total domestic expenditure: the reason buoyant investment spending tends to boost manufacturing output growth is that, compared with the other components of domestic expenditure (consumption, private and public), investment has a much higher manufacturing component – and a correspondingly smaller service element.[14]

However, despite what went before, 1973–4 appears to mark an important turning-point in the fortunes of the UK manufacturing industry because, since then, the trend in UK manufacturing output has been more or less flat:

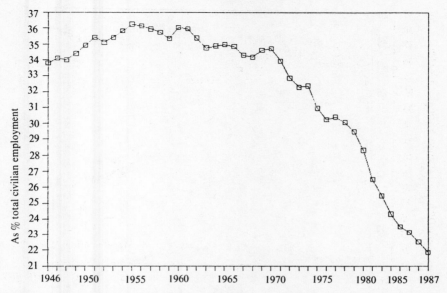

Figure 2.7 UK manufacturing employment as percentage of total civilian employment, 1946–87. (*Source:* see Fig. 2.2; otherwise sources cited in Rowthorn and Wells (1987), chapter 10.)

Figure 2.8 UK manufacturing employment, 1946–87 (millions). Total civilian employment (i.e., employees in employment plus self-employed, including employers). (*Source:* see Fig. 2.7.)

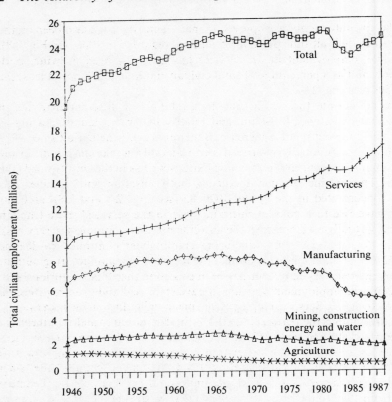

Figure 2.9 UK employment, by sector, 1946–87 (millions). Total civilian employment (i.e., employees in employment plus self-employed, including employers). (*Source:* see Fig. 2.2.).

when all the twists and turns affecting UK manufacturing output are taken into account – the post-OPEC recession of the mid-1970s, the slight recovery in the late 1970s, the deep slump of 1979–81 and the post-1982 recovery – manufacturing output is now only slightly ahead of its previous peak annual and quarterly levels (recorded in 1973 and 2Q 1974, respectively).[15]

On the other hand – and this is quite an amazing result – the output of services is currently (4Q 1988) some 43.5% higher than in 1973 (see Fig. 2.4).

Thus, the marked differential in manufacturing–services output growth rates – with services surging ahead of manufacturing – is a phenomenon which really dates from 1973–74, since when the output structure of the UK economy has undergone a shift of truly enormous proportions.

Nor is the differential manufacturing–service experience with respect to employment changes confined to the post-1979 period. Manufacturing's share in total employment[16] has been undergoing a trend decline (albeit with cyclical variations) ever since its peak (of 36.2%), recorded in 1955 (see Fig. 2.7), while the absolute numbers employed in manufacturing have also been on the decline since their all-time peak of 8.5 million, recorded in 1966 (see Fig. 2.8). Meanwhile, employment in the services has generally been growing, both absolutely and as a percentage of total civilian employment, since at least the mid-1950s (see Fig. 2.9).

However, despite these clear and long-established differential trends in employment experience (absolute and relative decline in manufacturing as against absolute and relative increase in the services),[17] the period since 1979 has, even so, undoubtedly witnessed a considerable acceleration both in the pace of manufacturing employment decline, as well as in the shift towards the services. The decline in manufacturing, both absolute and relative, was mainly concentrated in the period 1979–83 (see Figs 2.7 and 2.8), and this process gave rise to a consequential increase in the services' share (though there was virtually no increase in the absolute numbers employed in services). Between 1983 and 1987 manufacturing employment continued to decline both absolutely[18] and relatively despite the recovery in manufacturing output; however, the recovery in output has been so strong that finally, during 1988, manufacturing employment appears to have stabilised and even registered a slight recovery.[19] Service employment meanwhile has grown extremely rapidly throughout the period since 1983 – both absolutely and relatively.[20]

Having put the uneven development between manufacturing and services since 1979 into a somewhat longer-term perspective, it is also important to introduce our second caveat regarding this development. Namely, that such extreme (manufacturing–services) unevenness did not characterise the entire period from 1979 to the present. As we have seen, during the 1979–81 slump, manufacturing output fell much more dramatically than services' output, which registered only a modest reduction. By contrast, during the post-1982 recovery period, output growth has been much more balanced between the two sectors (see Fig. 2.1), with manufacturing and services experiencing precisely the same increase in output: +27.1%, comparing 1982 with 1988. Thus, so far as different output growth rates during the Thatcher decade as a whole are concerned, it is the huge divergence between 1979 and 1981 which is mainly responsible for the extreme unevenness comparing 1979 with the present.

However, so far as the differential in employment experience is concerned, unevenness has been much more of a continuous phenomenon since 1979 – although, during the slump, unevenness was the product of the sharp fall in manufacturing employment while service employment suffered only mildly, whereas, during the recovery, unevenness in employment experience has been due to the strong expansion in service employment while manufacturing employment has continued to decline, albeit at a slower rate than before.

Anyhow, it is the sharp differential in manufacturing services experience, taking the Thatcher decade as a whole, which is the principal focus of this chapter and it is to an examination of the causal factors responsible for this unevenness to which we now wish to turn. We will consider, firstly, the issue of differential output growth rates. Once these have been accounted for, it is a relatively simple matter to explain the differential employment experience.

2.2 THE EVOLUTION OF THE PATTERN OF DOMESTIC EXPENDITURE

One suggestion as to the cause of the marked shift in the composition of UK domestic output away from manufactures and towards services since 1979 is that it has been the consequence of a shift of a similar kind in the pattern of domestic expenditure. Thus, it is widely believed that, analogous to the shift in expenditure from agricultural products to industrial goods which takes place during the early and intermediate stages of economic development, then, in advanced countries, the pattern of expenditure switches once again – from industrial products to services. This point of view continues to be quite widely held, and tenaciously too, despite the substantial body of empirical evidence to the contrary. In particular, the evidence generated by the UN International Comparison Project which suggests that, using either constant price data (when making inter-temporal comparisons) or weighting expenditures in different countries by a uniform set of relative prices (when making international comparisons), then the share of services in total expenditure appears to be virtually invariant with respect to real per capita income.[21] On the other hand, when either current price data are used (when making inter-temporal comparisons) or use is made of data embodying each country's own relative price structure (when making international comparisons), then it appears that the share of services in total expenditure does indeed tend to increase as a function of real per capita income. However, this is entirely a relative price effect – resulting from the fact that the relative price of services tends to increase as per capita income rises, reflecting the lag in productivity growth in the services relative to the rest of the economy.[22] However, when it comes to trying to account for trends in the (constant price) output data, it is the invariance of the share of services in total expenditure – at constant or uniform (across country) relative prices – which counts.

One of the principal implications to be drawn from the invariance of the services' expenditure share with respect to real per capita income is that, given the continuous decline in the share of agricultural products in total expenditure, then the total elasticity of demand for manufactures (taking into account both income and price effects) is, for most developed countries, certainly as great as unity – and, for many of them in all probability, somewhat in excess of unity.

Leaving these general considerations aside, what does the available empirical evidence suggest concerning the composition of UK domestic expenditure as between manufactures and services – in particular, during the period since 1979? Curiously enough, such an interesting piece of information is not readily available in the published UK statistical source-books, where the data on domestic expenditure are, as is well known, disaggregated according to the conventional national accounts categories of private consumers' expenditure; government current expenditure; gross fixed investment and stock changes. The only readily available data on the composition of UK domestic spending are those on private consumers' expenditure.[23] However, information on the composition of UK domestic expenditure, as a whole, in particular, as between manufactures and services, is available in the form of the unpublished Commodity Flow Accounts (or CFAs).[24]

The CFAs[25] contain estimates of the supply and demand balances for 43 separate sectors of production (including both goods and services), where *supply* is equal to gross output + imports and *demand* is equal to domestic expenditure (C+G+I+S) + exports + intermediate demand (i.e., that arising from other sectors of production). The data are quarterly (currently available from IQ 1978 to 2Q 1987) and at constant 1980 £million. The reason the CFAs are so useful from the point of view of the analysis being undertaken in this chapter is that they enable us to examine the commodity composition (as between the output of agriculture, mining, fuel, construction, manufactures and services) of each component of domestic expenditure (C+G+I+S), as well as the composition of domestic expenditure as a whole.[26]

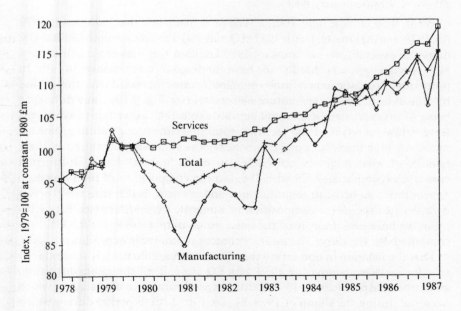

Figure 2.10 UK domestic expenditure (direct content of expenditure): manufactures, services, total; 1978–1987(2Q), at constant £million (Index, 1979=100). (*Source:* Commodity Flow Accounts, see text).

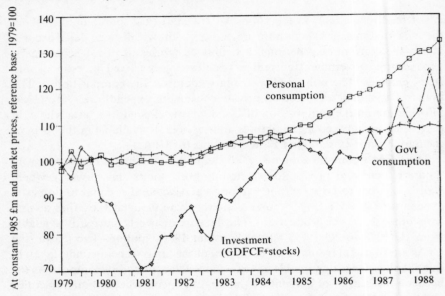

Figure 2.11 UK domestic expenditure: personal consumption, general government consumption and investment, 1Q1979–3Q1988, at constant 1985 £million, reference base: 1979=100. (*Sources:* CSO, *Economic Trends Annual Supplement 1989* and CSO, *Economic Trends*, January 1989.)

What, then, are the main results? The principal one is that, comparing 1979 (or 1978, for that matter) with 1987 (1Q and 2Q), the composition of total UK domestic expenditure – at constant 1980 £million – as between manufactures and services appears hardly to have undergone any change at all. In particular, domestic expenditure on manufactures increased over this period by almost as much as expenditure on services (see Fig. 2.10) – any difference being of no great significance and entirely explicable, as we hope to demonstrate below, in terms of the fact that total investment expenditure (with its unusually high manufacturing component) was somewhat depressed in 1987, relative to what might be considered to be its 'normal' level. This virtual constancy (comparing 1979 with 1987) in the composition of total domestic expenditure, as between manufactures and services, holds true whether we consider just the *direct* composition of domestic expenditure (see Fig. 2.10) or, as we have also done, used the latest input–output tables for the UK,[27] to compute both the *direct* and *indirect* content of domestic expenditure.[28]

That the increase in domestic expenditure on manufactures is so similar to that for services, comparing 1979 with 2Q 1987, is all the more surprising, given the sharp reduction in domestic expenditure on manufactures which occurred during the slump of 1979–81 (see Fig. 2.10), a period during which expenditure on services remained pretty much impervious to the fall in total domestic expenditure. That expenditure on manufactures grew, nevertheless, by almost as much as that on services, comparing 1979 with 1987, attests to

Figure 2.12a UK: percentage of share of total domestic expenditure devoted to manufactures and services, 1978–87(2Q), at constant 1980 £million (*Source: Commodity Flow Accounts, see text.*)

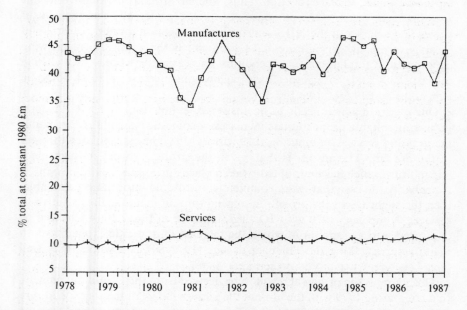

Figure 2.12b UK: percentage share of total investment expenditure (fixed capital formation plus stocks) devoted to manufactures and services, 1978–87(2Q), at constant 1980 £million (*Source:* Commodity Flow Accounts.)

the exceptionally strong recovery in domestic demand for manufactures which has taken place since 1982.

The sharp fall in total expenditure on manufactures during the 1979–81 slump can be ascribed mainly to the sharp contraction in investment spending (fixed capital formation plus stocks) which took place at that time (see Fig. 2.11) – the reason being that, in the case of investment spending, the ratio of spending on manufactures to that on services is much higher compared to the two other components of domestic expenditure (consumption, both private and government) and higher, also, than in the case of total domestic expenditure as a whole (see Fig. 2.12a–b).[29]

In fact, since the composition of each category of domestic expenditure (private consumption, government consumption and fixed investment), as between manufactures and services, though differing enormously one from another, was pretty much unchanged between 1979 and 1987 – then one of the principal determinants of any change in the overall pattern of domestic expenditure, as between manufactures and services, was the changing composition of total spending as between the main categories of final expenditure.

In this respect, it is interesting to note that, since 1979, the growth of domestic expenditure on services (and, hence, the shift to the so-called 'service' economy) has undoubtedly been adversely affected by the Thatcher government's success in curbing the growth of government expenditure, especially on health and education. Thus, whereas around 75% of government spending is devoted to the purchase of services (principally the payment of wages and salaries in the NHS and the state education service), central and local government expenditure have been much the most slowly growing component of total domestic expenditure, increasing between 1979 and 1988 by just 9.3% and 9.5% respectively, against an increase in total domestic expenditure of 19.6%[30] (see Fig. 2.13).

One question which needs to be answered is: how far can the CFA data, indicating roughly proportionate increases in domestic expenditure on manufactures and services, comparing 1979 with 2Q 1987, be extrapolated through to the present? The answer is that, given the strong recovery in investment expenditure which has undoubtedly taken place during the past 12 months, it is probably the case that, were completely up-to-date information available, then the slight lag in the growth of expenditure on manufactures relative to services, comparing 1979 with 2Q 1987, reported in Fig. 2.10, might well be converted into a situation in which the increase in domestic expenditure on manufactures, taking the Thatcher decade (1979–89) as a whole, may well have been greater than that on services.

This, then, is the principal result to be derived from the CFA data: namely, that comparing 1979 with the present the pattern of UK domestic expenditure (measured at constant 1980 £million) as between manufactures and services has remained pretty much unchanged. As a result, domestic expenditure on manufactures has increased at roughly the same rate as expenditure on

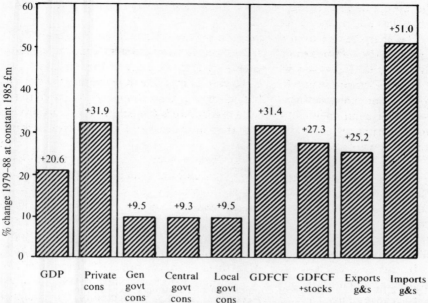

Figure 2.13 UK: percentage change in main macroeconomic aggregates 1979–88, at constant 1985 £million. (*Sources:* CSO, *Economic Trends Annual Supplement: 1989*; CSO, *Economic Trends*, January and February 1989 and HM Treasury, *Financial Statement & Report* (March 1989.)

services – and also at about the same rate as total domestic expenditure as a whole (+19.6%).

Moreover, if this constancy in expenditure patterns extends back to 1973 (and there is every reason to suppose that it does) then domestic expenditure on manufactures will also have increased at about the same rate as expenditure on services over the period 1973 to the present – and also at the same rate as total domestic expenditure: +31.6%. All the more striking, therefore – and a cause for considerable concern – is that manufacturing output in these three years (1973, 1979, 1988) has exhibited a virtually flat trend, whilst the output of services has surged ahead.

One thing is certainly clear: the huge unevenness in output growth rates as between manufacturing and services since 1979 (as well as 1973) cannot be ascribed to any change in the pattern of domestic expenditure between manufactures and services, which, in all probability, has remained more or less constant (comparing the beginning and end of the period).

2.3 CHANGES IN THE PATTERN OF CONSUMERS' EXPENDITURE

The other main source of data on the way the pattern of domestic expenditure has evolved since 1979 is the detailed breakdown of UK consumers' expend-

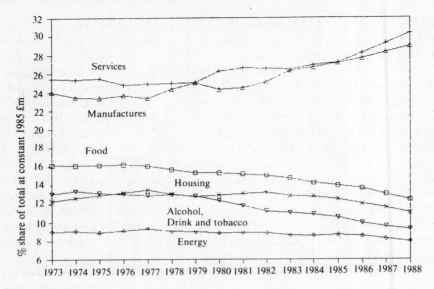

Figure 2.14 UK percentage of composition of consumers' expenditure, 1973–88, at constant 1985 £million. (*Sources:* CSO, *Economic Trends Annual Supplement 1989*, updated with CSO, *Monthly Digest of Statistics*, January 1989.)

iture at both current and constant 1985 £million, which is readily available in the principal UK statistical source-books.[31] The picture presented by these consumers' expenditure data is broadly consistent with that derived from the CFAs. Namely, that comparing 1979 with 1988[32] spending on manufactures and services were much the most dynamic areas of consumers' expenditure (see Fig. 2.14). When measured at constant 1985 £million, expenditure on services increased by +57.8%, while that on manufactures rose by +50.9% – compared with an increase in total consumers' expenditure, as a whole, of just +31.0%.

In fact, comparing 1979 with 1988, these two exceptionally income-elastic items attracted as much as 88.3% of the total increase in consumers' expenditure (services 47.0%; manufactures 41.3%), with many of the other items of consumers' expenditure registering extremely small increases in absolute terms (in the case of tobacco, actually a decline) and quite substantial reductions in relative shares. Moreover, while the percentage increase in expenditure on services was somewhat greater than for manufactures, the difference was hardly that great.

Within these two rapidly growing areas of consumers' expenditure, which were the really dynamic items? In the case of manufactures, the answer is simple enough (ranked in terms of their share of the total increase in expenditure on manufactures, 1979–87,[33] at constant 1985 £million): cars, motorcycles (20.5%); women's clothing (15.8%); sports and recreational goods (12.1%); electronic goods (TV, video, hi-fi, radio) (10.7%); men's clothing (7.7%); domestic electrical appliances (7.4%); DIY goods (+2%). The undynamic areas of manufacturing expenditure were: household furniture and pictures; carpets and floor coverings; books, newspapers and magazines.

When it comes to services, the most dynamic items of consumers' expenditure (ranked, again, in terms of their percentage share of the total increase in expenditure on services) were: catering (meals and accommodation) (16.7%); tourist expenditure abroad (14.4%); other services (14.0%); administrative cost of life assurance (12.6%); housing: contractors and insurance (9.7%); air travel (8.6%); telecommunications (7.6%); vehicle maintenance (4.8%); NHS payments, other medical (4.4%); TV, video: hire charges, repairs, licence fees (3.4%). The least dynamic areas of consumers' expenditure on services were: bus and coach travel: betting and gaming: education; other recreational and entertainment services; hairdressing and beauty care; rail travel and postal services.

There are a number of points to note about these disaggregated data on consumers' expenditure on services. First, by far and away the most important item is expenditure on foreign holidays (tourist expenditure abroad plus foreign travel). On the other hand, a number of the sorts of items which typically come to mind when reference is made to service expenditure – items such as hairdressing, recreational and entertainment services – these have proved to be rather undynamic.[34] Secondly, a certain amount of care is required in interpreting the data on service expenditure: a number of the more rapidly growing items (TV licence fees, NHS payments, vehicle excise duty) are simply taxes, while other forms of taxation (such as VAT and income tax) are not treated as items of consumers' expenditure at all. Finally, the enjoyment of a number of the more dynamic service items, such as air travel, telecommunications, vehicle maintenance and TV and video rental, undoubtedly presupposes the availability of a crucial manufactured item – which, in each case, is absolutely intrinsic to the provision of the service.

Finally, it is worth putting the recent rapid growth in the share of consumers' expenditure on services into perspective. Data on UK consumers' expenditure (at constant 1985 £million) for the period since 1952 (see Fig. 2.15) indicate that the recent growth in the services' share puts it back to just about where it was in 1952: the intermediate period, when the services' share was somewhat lower, being readily explicable in terms of developments such as the consumer durable revolution in the kitchen (e.g., washing-machines replacing laundries) and the substitution of theatre- and cinema-going by TV. The relative price of services has also increased quite substantially since 1952 (see Fig. 2.16).[35] Thus, as the share of food in total consumers' expenditure declined (almost halving since 1952), the major beneficiary was expenditure on manufactures, whose share of total consumers' expenditure has almost doubled since 1952.

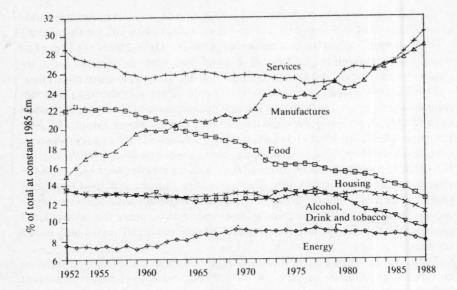

Figure 2.15 UK consumers' expenditure, percentage composition, 1952–88, at constant 1985 £million. (*Sources:* CSO, *Economic Trends Annual Supplement 1989*, updated with CSO, *Monthly Digest of Statistics*, January 1989.)

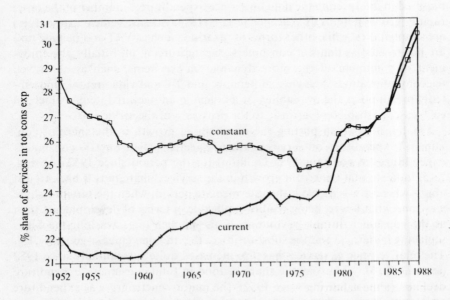

Figure 2.16 UK consumers' expenditure on services, percentage of total, 1952–88 at current prices and constant 1985 £million. (*Source:* see Fig. 2.15.)

Whether the recent rise in the services' share will be maintained into the future is impossible to say: what is clear, however, is that the recent increase is largely due to the rapid growth of expenditure on foreign holidays – not to any revival in demand for traditional personal and entertainment services.

To conclude our discussion of the consumers' expenditure data: they confirm the results derived from the CFAs, namely that domestic expenditure on manufactures and on services have both been quite income-elastic and, during the past decade, have been growing at roughly the same rate – though consumers' demand for services has certainly grown somewhat faster than for manufactures. Meanwhile, the growth of consumers' expenditure in recent years has been dominated by a cluster of five main items: cars, foreign holidays, electronic goods, domestic electrical appliances and clothes. However, these are, it is worth noting, areas of production in which the UK lacks an adequate volume of internationally competitive capacity: for intrinsic reasons, in the case of foreign holidays but also, as numerous studies have established, in the principal areas of consumer durable production (cars, electronic goods, domestic electrical appliances, etc).

2.4 INCREASED NET EXPORTS OF SERVICES?

Since the huge disparities in manufacturing–services output growth rates since 1979 cannot be ascribed to any change in the pattern of domestic expenditure, which, as we have seen, has remained more or less unchanged, an alternative possibility is that the UK may have experienced a change in its pattern of trade specialisation in recent years: in particular, it is widely thought that the UK has experienced an improvement in its trade balance in services and has become increasingly specialised as a net exporter of services.

Now, there is little doubt that a change in the pattern of a country's trade specialisation in the direction of becoming an increased net exporter of services would certainly tend to raise the rate of growth of the output of services relative to manufactures – compared with what would otherwise have happened.[36] This arises on account of both the *direct* effect of an improvement in the services trade balance (as a percentage of GDP) in augmenting the output of services relative to manufactures (compared with what would otherwise have happened), as well as the *induced* effect on the domestic composition of output (favouring services relative to manufactures) arising from the tendency, following the increase in net service exports, for the trade balance as a whole to balance.[37] Similar considerations also apply in the case of an improvement in the balance in factor service payments (interest, profits and dividends).

Whatever the validity of these analytical considerations may be is there, in fact, any evidence to suggest that the UK balance on 'invisibles' has been improving and that the UK has become increasingly specialised as a net

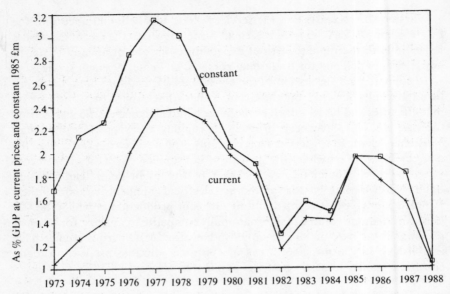

Figure 2.17 UK balance of trade in non-factor services as percentage of GDP, 1973–88, at current prices and constant 1985 factor cost. (*Sources:* CSO, *Balance of Payments (Pink Book)* and CSO, *National Accounts (Blue Book) 1988.*)

exporter of services in the period since 1979? The answer, to take trade in non-factor or commercial services first of all, is: none, whatsoever. On the contrary, comparing 1979 with 1988, UK net exports of non-factor services declined somewhat as a percentage of GDP, whether measured at current or constant 1985 £million (see Fig. 2.17) and, indeed, throughout the 1980s, UK net exports of non-factor services (as a percentage of GDP) have actually been considerably below the levels attained in the mid-1970s.

The reasons for this surprisingly (in view of all the hype) dismal performance are as follows. First, the sharp appreciation in the real exchange rate for the £ sterling which took place in the early 1980s and which, as we shall argue below, wreaked such havoc on manufacturing output, also had an adverse effect on the domestic output of internationally traded services, depressing exports and import-competing activities. Secondly, while in more recent years UK service exports, in particular earnings from financial services (the City) and other services (e.g., consultancy, engineering, royalties, etc.), as well as from overseas tourist expenditure in the UK, have undoubtedly experienced exceptionally rapid growth, there has been an equally rapid growth of service imports: particularly, in respect of shipping, civil aviation and – much the most important factor – the growth of spending by UK tourists abroad.[38] Thus, just as fast as new service export earnings have been generated, so, just as rapidly, they have been spent on increased service imports, leaving net exports of non-factor services virtually constant (at constant 1985 £million) during the period 1985–8.

Thus, so far as trade in non-factor services is concerned, there is no sign of any increase in UK specialisation since 1979 such as would even partly account for the huge divergence in manufacturing service output growth rates since then.

It is only in the case of the balance in respect of interest, profits and dividends plus transfers[39] that we have seen any sign of an improvement comparing 1979 with 1988. The 'IPD plus transfers' balance has gone from a deficit of –0.6% of GDP in 1979 to a surplus of +0.7% of GDP in 1988 – an improvement of +1.3% of GDP (see Fig. 2.18). This improvement is, of course, the consequence of the rapid growth of income accruing from the substantial increase in UK overseas assets, following the relaxation in 1979 of controls on portfolio investment overseas. That the balance on 'IPD plus transfers' is not stronger at the present time – indeed, it is slightly weaker than during the early 1970s – can be accounted for by: (a) the substantial level of IPD remittances from the UK itself, in particular, by operators in the North Sea and (b) the high level of official transfers to the EEC.

Thus, to conclude this part of the discussion: although the 'IPD plus transfers' balance has registered a modest improvement since 1979, when we also take into account the offsetting (and virtually equal) deterioration in the non-factor or commercial service balance there is no evidence to suggest there

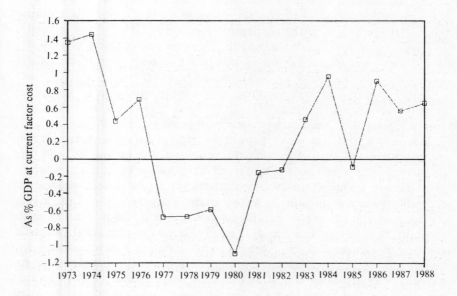

Figure 2.18 UK interest, profits and dividends plus transfers (net) as percentage of GDP, 1973–88, at current £million and factor cost. (*Sources:* CSO, *UK Balance of Payments (Pink Book)* and CSO, *UK National Accounts (Blue Book)*.)

has been a shift in the pattern of UK trade specialisation in favour of 'invisibles' on anything like the scale necessary to even begin to account for the large divergence in manufacturing–services output growth rates since 1979.

2.5 MANUFACTURES: DOMESTIC OUTPUT AND DOMESTIC EXPENDITURE COMPARED

At this point in the development of the argument it is useful to have some idea of the changing relationship between domestic expenditure on manufactures (C+G+I+S) and the domestic output of manufactures available to satisfy final demand, whether domestic or foreign. The CFA data enable us to examine this relationship directly, using quarterly data, at constant 1980 £million, for the period 1Q 1978 to 2Q 1987.[40] In addition, we have attempted to extrapolate both expenditure and output data, forwards and backwards,[41] in order to obtain a picture of the manufacturing output–expenditure relationship for the whole of the period 1Q 1973 to 3Q 1988 (the latter being the latest quarter for which it has been possible to do the exercise).

The resulting graph is quite informative (see Fig. 2.19). Between 1Q 1973 and 3Q 1988 domestic expenditure on manufactures increased by about 30% in real terms – or at about the same rate as total domestic expenditure. Of course, domestic spending on manufactures did not increase continuously throughout this period – suffering somewhat of a setback, first of all, during the mid-1970s, as part of the adjustment/reaction to OPEC 1 and secondly, and much more significantly, during the Thatcher–Howe slump of 1979–81. Nevertheless, despite these setbacks, domestic expenditure on manufactures was roughly 30% higher in 3Q 1988 commmpared to 1Q 1973.

Domestic output of manufactures, on the other hand, can be said to be broadly stationary comparing 1973 with 1979 and 1988 – with large troughs in output registered between each of these local peaks (see Fig. 2.19).

As a result of this divergence between the trend in domestic expenditure on manufactures and that of manufacturing output, the period 1973–88 was characterised, as is well known, by a trend deterioration in the manufacturing trade balance.[42] During the 1970s manufacturing output exceeded domestic expenditure on manufactures by a comfortable margin (see Fig. 2.19), giving rise to a substantial export surplus in manufacturing trade amounting to around 11% of output. In the mid- to late 1980s, on the other hand, domestic expenditure on manufactures exceeded domestic output, also by a substantial margin, giving rise to a large and growing deficit in trade in manufactures. As a result, by 1988 around 11% of total domestic expenditure on manufactures was being satisfied by net imports. The deterioration in manufacturing trade balance, taking the period 1973–88 as a whole, amounts roughly to about 6% of GDP; the deterioration since 1979 being equivalent to about 15% of manufacturing output or roughly 3.6% of GDP.

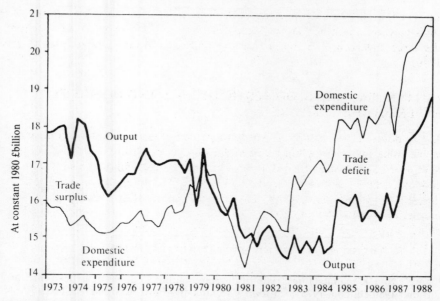

Figure 2.19 UK manufactures: domestic expenditure and output, at constant 1980 £billion, 1973–88. (*Source:* Commodity Flow Accounts, see text.)

This deterioration in the manufacturing trade balance has not, of course, been a continuous process throughout the period since 1973 (or since 1979, for that matter). From the mid- to the late 1970s, the manufacturing trade balance registered a slight improvement, reflecting a certain degree of success in adjusting to the increased cost of net oil imports. Moreover, the manufacturing trade balance also improved during the savage slump of 1979–81 – despite the substantial strengthening in the real exchange rate of the £ sterling which occurred during this period: the reason for this being that, despite the extremely adverse effect of the high exchange rate on UK manufacturing's international competitiveness and, hence, output[43] – the decline in domestic spending on manufactures, especially on capital equipment and stocks, was so great that the fall in domestic expenditure actually exceeded the fall in output (see Fig. 2.19).[44] As a result, the manufacturing trade balance actually improved during the 1979–81 slump – despite the exchange rate-induced loss of international competitiveness.[45] Of course, during the subsequent recovery, domestic expenditure on manufactures recovered much faster than output, with the well-known consequence that the manufacturing trade balance deteriorated sharply, with growth in the volume of manufactured exports lagging sharply behind the growth in the volume of manufactured imports.

Another way of looking at the adverse trends in the growth of domestic output of manufactures relative to the growth of domestic expenditure on manufactures is to examine the ratio of domestic output to domestic expend-

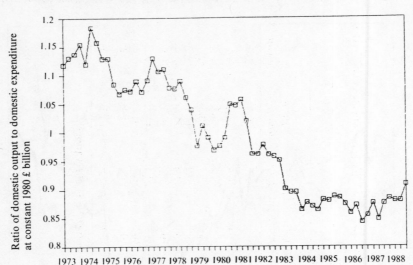

Figure 2.20 UK manufactures: ratio of domestic output to domestic expenditure, at constant 1980 £billion, 1973–88. (*Source:* Commodity Flow Accounts, see text.)

iture for the period 1973 to 1988 (see Fig. 2.20).[46] The downward trend is clear enough. In the early to mid-1970s, domestic manufacturing output was some 10–15% higher than domestic expenditure; however, by 1987–8, domestic manufacturing output amounted to just 88–90% of domestic expenditure. The deterioration in this ratio was virtually continuous – apart from the two periods noted earlier (adjustment to the increased cost of net oil imports in the mid- to late 1970s and the slump of 1979–81).

2.6 HOW WAS THE DETERIORATING MANUFACTURING TRADE BALANCE FINANCED?

How was the deteriorating manufacturing trade balance (resulting from the imbalance between the growth of domestic expenditure on manufactures and the growth of domestic output) actually financed – given, as we demonstrated earlier, that there were no offsetting improvements in the balance of trade in services, comparing 1979 with 1988 (with improvements in IPD plus transfers (net) being offset by a deterioration in commercial services).

The answer lies in three developments. First, in slight improvements in the balances in food, drink and tobacco (FDT) and raw materials: each of these balances improved, comparing 1979 with 1988, by +0.6% of GDP (at current £million) (see Table 2.3). Such improving trends in UK non-fuel commodity trade have been a long-established feature of post-war British economic

Table 2.3 UKs deteriorating manufacturing trade balance and sources of compensatory adjustment, 1979–88, as percentage of GDP(A) at current factor cost.

	Manufacturing	Non-manufacturing current account	Of which			Total services	Of which		Total current account
			Food, beverages and tobacco	Raw materials	Fuel		Non-factor services	IPD + transfers	
Actual 1979	+1.6	-1.9	-1.7	-1.4	-0.6	+1.7	+2.3	-0.6	-0.3
1980	+1.1	+0.7	+0.5	+0.4	+0.5	-0.9	-0.3	-0.6	+1.9
1981	+0.5	+3.0	+0.4	+0.4	+1.9	-0.1	-0.5	+0.4	+3.5
1982	-0.6	+2.9	+0.4	+0.5	+2.3	-0.6	-1.1	+0.5	+2.3
1983 Change	-2.5	+4.3	+0.4	+0.4	+3.0	+0.2	-0.9	+1.1	+1.8
1984 relative	-3.1	+4.1	+0.5	+0.4	+2.5	+0.7	-0.9	+1.6	+0.4
1985 to 1979	-2.6	+4.0	+0.5	+0.5	+2.8	+0.2	-0.3	+0.5	+0.8
1986	-3.4	+3.8	+0.5	+0.7	+1.4	+1.0	-0.5	+1.5	+0.2
1987	-3.7	+3.3	+0.6	+0.6	+1.4	+0.5	-0.7	+1.2	-1.4
1988	-5.3	+1.9	+0.6	+0.6	+0.9	-0.1	-1.4	+1.3	-3.4
Actual 1988	-3.7	-0.0	-1.1	-0.8	+0.3	+1.6	+0.9	+0.7	-3.7

Source: CSO, *UK Balance of Payments (Pink Book)* (various) and CSO, *UK National Accounts (Blue Book)* (various).

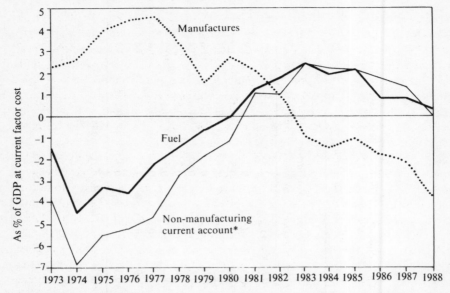

Figure 2.21 UK balance of trade in manufactures, fuel and the non-manufacturing current account as a whole, as percentage GDP, at current £million, 1973–88. (*Sources:* CSO, *UK Balance of Payments (Pink Book)*; DTI, Press Notice, 16.2.89; CSO, *UK National Accounts (Blue Book)*.)
*i.e., current account balance excluding manufactures

development. However, improvements in both areas (but especially in trade in raw materials) were undoubtedly greater than they would have been had the economy as a whole, and, in particular, its manufacturing sector, experienced more vigorous growth during the 1980s. Even so, there were underlying improvements in each of these areas of non-fuel commodity trade, such as to permit some deterioration in the manufacturing balance.

The second main development permitting some deterioration in the manufacturing trade balance to be sustained were improvements in the fuel balance of trade, arising, principally, from the successful exploitation of North Sea energy resources. Thus, between 1979 and 1983–5, the fuel balance of trade improved by some +3.0% of GDP (at current £million) (see Table 2.3). This development also undoubtedly permitted some deterioration in the manufacturing trade balance to be sustained. However, from 1985 onwards the UK's fuel balance of trade deteriorated sharply and by 1988 was only slightly stronger (by +0.9% of GDP) than it had been in 1979.

Thus, we can say that for much of the 1980s favourable developments in primary product trade – FDT, raw materials and, above all, fuel – permitted some deterioration to take place in the UK's manufacturing trade balance.

However – and here we come to the third and final factor sustaining the deterioration in UK manufacturing trade – in recent years, the deteriorating manufacturing trade balance could only be sustained on the basis of a deterioration in the current account balance as a whole and growing current account deficits: that is to say, on the basis of a marked change in resource flows with respect to the rest of the world and a resort to growing dependence on 'foreign savings' (net) (see Table 2.3, page 49). Thus, whereas the severity of the contraction in domestic expenditure during the Thatcher–Howe slump resulted in *surplus* on the current account of +3.8% and +2.6% of GDP in 1981, and 1982, respectively – from then onwards, the current account balance deteriorated to the point where, by 1988, it was in deficit to the tune of –3.7% of GDP.

Thus, to summarise our answer to the question: what sustained the trend deterioration in the manufacturing trade balance between 1979 and 1988? The answer, prior to the mid-1980s, lies in substantial improvements in primary product trade (FDT, raw materials and fuel), which masked the underlying deterioration in the manufacturing trade balance. However, from the mid-1980s onwards, the surplus on the UK's non-manufacturing current account – which had been a wholly exceptional and unusual feature of the UK economy during the 1980s – began to diminish and, by 1988, had for all intents and purposes completely disappeared (see Fig. 2.21). This meant that there was no longer any offset by way of a surplus in non-manufacturing trade, to set against the deficits in manufacturing trade. Thus, by 1988, the manufacturing trade deficit was completely exposed, requiring inflows of 'foreign savings' to finance it in its entirety.

2.7 THE CAUSE OF INADEQUATE MANUFACTURING PERFORMANCE DURING THE 1980s

As we have seen, improvements in UK non-manufacturing trade, at least up until the mid-1980s, followed by a growing dependence on net capital inflow, permitted the UK to experience a deterioration in its manufacturing trade balance during the Thatcher decade.[47] However, while such developments explain why domestic expenditure on manufactures could grow at a faster rate than domestic manufacturing output, they do not explain why output should have performed so badly, remaining broadly flat comparing 1979 and 1988 (the product of a precipitate decline, 1979–81, followed by a gradual recovery). That manufacturing output performance was so poor was by no means inevitable: the growth of domestic spending on manufactures could have exceeded that of manufacturing output – but around a rising, rather than a flat, trend for manufacturing output.

To see why this is so – and what was responsible for the virtual stagnation of manufacturing output comparing 1979 with 1988, we need to divide the Thatcher decade into (a) the years of the sharp slump of 1979–81 and (b) those of the post-1982 recovery. The flat trend in output, comparing 1979 with 1988, is, of course, the product of these two sharply divergent periods –

(i) *Slump, 1979 81*

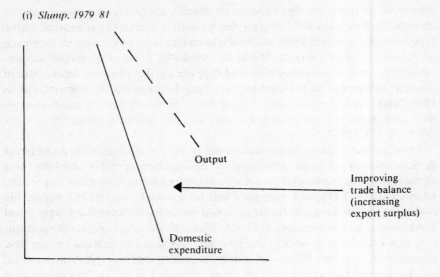

(ii) *Recovery, post-1983*

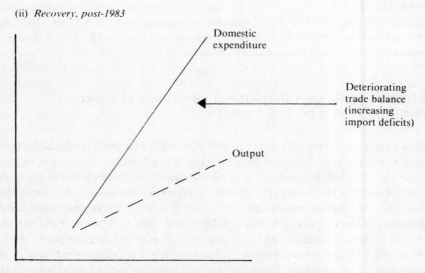

Figure 2.22 Stylised figure: UK manufacturing: output, domestic expenditure and trade balance during slump and recovery. (See Fig. 2.19 for actual data on output and expenditure.)

and accounting for the unsatisfactory manufacturing output performance for the period as a whole largely comes down to a proper analysis of the 1979–81 slump.

The stylised facts of this period (see Fig. 2.22) are that it was characterised by a dramatic reduction in both domestic expenditure on manufactures and output. However, the reduction in domestic expenditure on manufactures (especially in the demand for investment goods) which was the product of the government's strongly contractionary monetary and fiscal policies was even greater than the fall in output. The latter was the product of several factors. First, the contraction in domestic expenditure itself, since, even in the case of a sector as 'open' and exposed to the forces of international competition as manufacturing industry, there exist certain more 'sheltered' or comparatively non-traded segments of production (e.g., the building materials supply industry) where output is mainly sensitive to fluctuations in domestic expenditure. The sharp decline in manufacturing output during 1979–81 was the product, secondly, of the adverse effect on the international competitiveness of both exports, potential exports and import-competing items of the strong appreciation of the real £ sterling exchange rate which occurred during the early 1980s (resulting from the *interaction* between monetary and fiscal tightening and the coming on stream of North Sea oil).[48] Finally, the deceleration in growth in the international economy (itself the product of the growing adoption of monetarist policies throughout the advanced capitalist countries, partly in response to OPEC 2) also exerted its toll of UK manufacturing output.

However, the fact that domestic expenditure on manufactures fell by more than domestic output during the Thatcher–Howe slump meant that the manufacturing trade balance actually improved during this period. And this occurred at the same time that dramatic improvements were also being registered on the non-manufacturing balance, principally on account of increased North Sea production and higher fuel prices. Thus, as a result of drastic cutbacks in domestic expenditure on manufactures and an improving fuel trade balance, the UK generated huge surpluses on its current account overall – which, following the relaxation of exchange controls in 1979, were used to acquire a substantial portfolio of overseas assets.

However, what is clear is that the sharp reduction in manufacturing output which occurred during this period was by no means inevitable. The economy was far from being fully employed in 1979, with considerable margins of unemployed (and underemployed) labour and capital. Thus, it was far from inevitable that adjustment to the strong (oil-induced) improvement in the non-manufacturing balance had to take the form of the 'crowding-out' or substitution of domestic manufacturing output. To see why, we need only examine the second, expansionary phase of Thatcherism.

The 'stylised facts' in this case (see Fig. 2.22) are that domestic expenditure on manufactures and output both increased, with expenditure growing at a faster rate than output. However, the resulting deterioration in the manufacturing trade balance occurred around a rising trend in domestic manufacturing output. The recovery in domestic expenditure on manufactures was the product of the interaction between: (a) liberalisation of the financial sector; (b) strong growth in real earnings and (c) some slight relaxation in the fiscal stance. The recovery in output, on the other hand, can be attributed to: (a) the recovery in domestic expenditure – especially for those sectors of manufacturing production of a more 'sheltered' character, which are less exposed to the forces of international competition and (b) output recovery can also be attributed to improvements in international competitiveness, resulting from the unwinding of the earlier substantial real appreciation of the £ sterling, as well as considerable improvements in labour productivity, both developments enabling UK manufactures better to satisfy the expansion of demand, both at home and abroad.

Be that as it may, the point is: during the recovery, the deterioration in the manufacturing trade balance was not responsible for any 'crowding out' or substitution of domestic manufacturing production by increased net imports, but, on the contrary, coincided with a rising trend in manufacturing output. What made all of this possible was, of course, both that domestic expenditure on manufactures was growing so strongly and that the real exchange rate was much more competitive than during the Thatcher–Howe slump.

That such policies could have been pursued during 1979–81 – rather than the actual policies of monetary and fiscal deflation which provoked such deep cuts in domestic expenditure and such a substantial appreciation of the real exchange rate – and that they could have had positive effects on output rather than triggering the catastrophic slump which actually occurred is obvious enough. Moreover, such expansionary policies were urged on the government[49] as a means of enabling the UK to capitalise on its North Sea windfall and use the opportunity to revitalise and modernise UK manufacturing – rather than, as actually happened, allowing North Sea revenues to 'crowd-out' or substitute domestic manufacturing output and dramatically accelerate the de-industrialisation process. Of course, pursuing expansionary policies of this kind and at that time would undoubtedly have involved taking very considerable risks with inflation (and would have necessitated, in my view, some form of wage-price controls). However, far better this than the actual outcome, in which the UK effectively used a large proportion[50] of its oil revenues to dismantle a considerable chunk of its manufacturing capacity, rather than using such revenues to re-invigorate and modernise manufacturing industry. As a result, the UK made poorer use of its oil resources than any other major oil producer (including virtually all of those in the Third World).

2.8 UNEVEN OUTPUT GROWTH: CONCLUSIONS

We are now in a position to account for the substantial unevenness between manufacturing and service output growth rates, comparing 1979 with 1988 – the central concern of this chapter.

In the main, such unevenness was the product of the huge reductions in manufacturing output and capacity which took place during 1979–81, when, as a result of the tight monetary and fiscal policies being pursued by the government, increased North Sea oil revenues were permitted to 'crowd-out' or substitute for domestic manufacturing production.

That a deterioration in the manufacturing trade balance, consequent upon improvements in oil trade, could have been accommodated with a rising level of manufacturing output is confirmed by what happened during the subsequent recovery period (see Fig. 2.22). Such monumental economic mismanagement – not only failing to use the North Sea windfall productively (to modernise the economy) but using it to destroy a large segment of the industrial base – must be virtually unparalleled in modern economic history, at least so far as the developed world is concerned.

A further issue concerns why it was that, despite the evidently pro-business policies being pursued by the Thatcher government, manufacturing investment did not stage a more substantial (and earlier) recovery[51] – such as might have alleviated the evident supply bottlenecks which arose, following the extraordinary boom in domestic expenditure on manufactures which took place in 1987–8. This is an intriguing question and one which is by no means easy to answer. However, elements of an answer might lie in the following points. First, until as late as 1985 (if not later), the government continued to display an extreme lack of concern regarding the performance of UK manufacturing industry (as exhibited by Chancellor Lawson's replies under questioning by the House of Lords Select Committee on Trade and Industry),[52] particularly given manufacturing industry's central role in securing the UK's future economic well-being. Second, so far as the factors inhibiting manufacturing investment are concerned: it was far from clear, at any time prior to 1987, that the period of extreme contraction in domestic expenditure during 1979–81 would give way to one of such unbridled expansion post-1986. Nor, once expansion was under way, was it clear that it was sustainable (which it has not been) and this element of uncertainty undoubtedly resulted in certain multinational producers sourcing the UK domestic market from, e.g., continental production units, which had ample spare capacity. A further factor tending to inhibit manufacturing investment could have been uncertainty regarding movements in the real exchange rate – again, a factor where in retrospect doubts were certainly amply justified. The only area of manufacturing investment where the government can really claim credit for success is in the attraction of inward, direct (especially Japanese) investment – where government policies of what could be called 'fishing for multinationals' *via* the creation of a sort of 'capitalist paradise' (anti-trade union legislation, de-regulation of all sorts, etc.) can be said to have been quite successful.

A final issue is the following: we have accounted for the lag in manufacturing output growth relative to GDP growth in terms of the 'crowding-out' or substitution effects of increased fuel production on domestic manufacturing output, and, indeed, the rate of growth of output of manufactures *plus* energy and water (which together account for much the greater part of total traded sector output) is much greater than the growth of manufacturing output alone and, indeed, considerably closer to the growth of GDP (see Fig. 2.4). What we had, then, was a situation in which increased fuel output provided the means to sustain increased levels of domestic expenditure on traded commodities (e.g., manufactures) *via* increased resort to net imports, whilst higher levels of domestic expenditure on non-traded commodities (e.g., services) resulted in vastly expanded levels of domestic output and employment.

Nevertheless, how can we account for the very substantial differential which still exists in favour of the growth of service output relative to GDP growth (1979–88: +27.6% versus +21.3%, respectively; a differential of almost 30%)? Surely, if, as we have demonstrated, there really has been no significant change in the pattern of domestic expenditure, as between manufacturing and services, and nor has there been any increase in the country's dependence on net exports of 'invisibles' then we should expect services' output to have grown at roughly the same rate as total GDP (i.e., the aggregate of all the sectors – including energy and manufactures).

Two answers suggest themselves. One is the much discussed possibility of growing specialisation and the hiving-off of certain service functions by manufacturing firms. G. F. Ray[53] estimates that this development may, at the outside, account for 3.2% of the fall in manufacturing output between 1973 and 1983 – and contribute a corresponding amount to the increase in service output.

A second possible explanation of the differential in service output growth relative to GDP growth is that service output growth may be overestimated – despite the downward revisions recently made in the *UK National Accounts (Blue Book) 1988*. For example, although output in 'distribution, hotels, catering and repairs' (see Table 2.4) is estimated to have grown broadly in line with GDP (which is what would be expected, given that 'distribution and

Table 2.4 Disaggregated service output growth rates.

	1979–87
Distribution, hotels, catering, repairs	+18.0
Transport	+10.1
Communication	+39.6
Banking, finance, insurance, business services and leasing	+72.9
Ownership of dwellings	+7.5
Public administration, national defence and compulsory social security	0.0
Education and health services	+8.4
Other services	+34.2
Total services	+21.4
GDP	+15.9

Source: CSO, *UK National Accounts (Blue Book) 1988*, Table 2.4.

repairs' ought, at least, to increase at roughly the same rate as the total supply of material products), while 'communications' is known to have been a very dynamic sector, the size of output increases in 'banking, finance, insurance, business services and leasing' (+72.9%) and 'other services' (+34.2%) are, to my mind, a bit suspect. Although part of the growth of output of banking, etc., can be attributed to growing exports of financial services it nevertheless still seems somewhat excessive.

Moreover, what are we to make of a society whose increased welfare is taking the form of the increased consumption of estate agents services, insurance services, etc?

2.9 MANUFACTURING–SERVICES: DIFFERENTIAL EMPLOYMENT EXPERIENCE, 1979–87

Having done our best to account for the substantial differences in manufacturing–services output growth rates comparing 1979 with 1988, we can now turn to the sharp differential in employment experience between the two sectors: namely, the substantial and continuing decline in manufacturing employment, both absolute and relative, as against the very considerable and continuing increase in service employment, both absolute and relative.

Given the substantial differentials in output growth rates, the even larger differentials in employment experience were the product of the considerably higher rate of growth of labour productivity in manufacturing compared with services – a difference which, though partly the product of measurement problems,[54] is nevertheless real enough.[55] Indeed, during the Thatcher decade, the gap in labour productivity growth rates between manufacturing and services probably widened as a result of the acceleration in manufacturing productivity growth which has undoubtedly taken place. Be that as it may, measured output per person employed in manufacturing increased by 4.5% p.a. (1979–88) whereas, in the economy as a whole, productivity increased by just 2.2% p.a. – yielding a productivity growth rate in the non-manufacturing sector of the economy of 1.4% p.a. (see Table 2.5).

2.10 CONCLUSIONS

The UK's present huge current account deficit – which amounted in 1988 to £14.4 billion or 3.7% of GDP (coinciding with a manufacturing deficit of £14.4 billion) – poses an enormous challenge to the country, especially when taken in conjunction with a net outflow on long-term capital account, which is even slightly larger, at £15.8 billion.[56] Thus, in 1988 the UK had a total overseas financing requirement amounting to around £30.2 billion (or 7.7% of GDP): a figure of quite unprecedented proportions.

Table 2.5   Output per person employed[a] (1985=100).

	Manufacturing	*Non-manufacturing*[b]	*Whole economy*
1979	80.0	92.9	89.4
1988[c]	118.7	105.0	108.7
% per annum 1979–88[c]	4.5	1.4	2.2

[a]The data do not take into account changes in hours of work or in the incidence of part-time working.
[b]Computed as the weighted difference between the other two series, where the weights for manufacturing are a compromise (0.27) between its share in total GDP and its share in total civilian employment.
[c]Estimated by extrapolation on the basis of data for the first three quarters.
Source: ETAS, 1989, Table 23, updated with *Economic Trends*, January 1989, Table 20.

As we hope to have shown in this chapter, the manufacturing component of this sizeable external gap is not simply the product of the exceptionally rapid growth of domestic expenditure which has taken place in recent years, exacerbated by the 'give-away' tax-reducing budget of 1988. It is also the result of acute shortcomings on the supply-side – whose most important feature is the absence of a *sufficient* volume of manufacturing capacity capable of producing the sorts of products which people require in both domestic and overseas markets. These shortcomings on the supply-side are the consequences of many decades of under investment in UK manufacturing capacity, exacerbated by the industrial vandalism of the early 1980s and the subsequent exceptionally weak and precarious character of the recovery in industrial investment in the more recent years of the Thatcher decade.

What the present substantial manufacturing and current account deficits signal is that the rump of UK manufacturing production which remains at the end of the Thatcher decade may well be leaner, fitter, have a higher level of labour productivity and be more profitable than before – but it is totally inadequate in terms of the volume of its internationally competitive capacity and, hence, the scale of its output to meet the requirements which UK society places upon it. The domestic demand for manufactures must be satisfied (either *directly* and/or *indirectly* via exports of manufactures to pay for the imported manufactures which people require) at the same time as attempting to achieve full employment at current UK standards of living.[57]

As a result of these shortcomings on the side of manufacturing supply, the UK today is almost certainly worse off, compared with 1979, in terms of its ability to reconcile the achievement of internal balance (full employment and price stability) with external balance. Comparing 1988 with 1979, unemployment is worse and the current account balance is weaker; only when it comes to inflation is the position slightly stronger today compared with 1979.[58]

Nor is the substantial current account deficit an easy problem to resolve –

even if, which will not necessarily be the case, the UK is able to gain access to a substantial, if diminishing, volume of 'foreign savings' and is able to avoid sudden losses of confidence and runs on the currency. The reason that Britain's imminent external adjustment challenge – of gradually closing its external gap of 3.7% of GDP – is a much more formidable problem than might at first sight appear, is that this increase in output has to come from the traded sector of the economy (via *either* increased exports *and/or* additional import-substitutes). But the traded sector accounts for only a fraction (35%–40%) of total GDP. Thus, the size of adjustment effort required of the traded sector is a multiple of the gap needing to be closed. Moreover, as part and parcel of the external adjustment process, domestic expenditure (and living standards), will have to grow at a substantially slower rate than total UK output and total UK traded sector output.[59]

In all of this, one thing is certain: in the forthcoming process of UK external adjustment, the manufacturing sector has an absolutely crucial role to play. And the supply-side miracle – so often heralded, but so infrequently sighted during the Thatcher decade – will surely have to put in an appearance if the UK is to avoid an exceptionally dismal decade in terms of economic well-being.

NOTES

1. The salient points in the manufacturing output series are as follows (1985 = 100):

1973: 110.5	(previous peak annual output)
2Q 1974: 112.4	(previous peak quarterly output)
1979: 105.9	
1979 May: 109.1	(Mrs Thatcher's election as Prime Minister)
4Q 1987: 109.7	(quarter in which May 1979 output exceeded)
1987: 106.8	(year in which 1979 output exceeded)
2Q 1988: 112.7	(quarter in which previous (1974) quarterly peak exceeded)
1988: 113.9	(year in which previous (1973) annual peak exceeded)
4Q 1988: 116.5	(highest quarterly output ever recorded)

    Thus, by now all of the previous milestones in manufacturing output of what-ever form have been surpassed (data from *ETAS*, 1989, *Economic Trends*, January 1989 and *Guardian*, 22.2.89).

2. The term 'services' is used throughout this paper to refer to all services, the principal components of which are: distribution, hotels, catering and repairs; transport and communication; banking, finance, insurance, business services and leasing; ownership of dwellings; public administration and national defence; education and health services; other services.

3. 1987 is, unfortunately, the latest year for which data providing a complete break-down of the sectoral composition of *total* UK civilian employment (employees in employment plus the self-employed including employer) was available at the time of going to press.

4. Data for 1987 on employees in employment from CSO, *Monthly Digest of*

Statistics, May 1988, Table 3.2; on GB self-employed from Department of Employment, *Employment Gazette*, October 1987, Vol. 95, no. 10, *Employment Statistics Historical Supplement* No. 2, p. 22, and on Northern Ireland self-employed from *Northern Ireland Annual Abstract of Statistics* No. 6, 1987, Table 10.4, p. 96. For 1979–86, see; OECD, *Labour Force Statistics, 1966–86.*

5. Ibid.
6. These statistics assign the same weight to part-time as to full-time employment, which is clearly quite unsatisfactory – especially during the period with which we are concerned, when most of the jobs lost (in manufacturing) were full-time, whereas many of those gained (in the services) were part-time. As a result of this procedure, the estimates quoted in the text undoubtedly *overstate* (relative to a calculation in terms of full-time equivalents), the growth of employment in the services in the 1980s relative to the decline in manufacturing. Estimates which have recently appeared in the *Department of Employment Gazette*, November 1988, p. 614 on the 'number of person hours per week usually worked in Great Britain' undoubtedly remedy this defect. However, these estimates refer only to 1983–7 (and do not extend back to 1979); they also only refer to Great Britain and not to the United Kingdom as a whole.
7. I.e., using the 1985 value added shares in total GDP and extrapolating them backwards and forwards using the constant price output series from CSO, *Economic Trends Annual Supplement: 1989*, CSO, *Economic Trends*, January 1989 and *Guardian*, 22.2.89.
8. These estimated shares in total civilian employment are open to the same objections as those detailed in note 6. In particular, since a higher proportion of service jobs are part-time compared with manufacturing, these data overstate the share of services in total employment. In addition since, as explained in note 6, the manufacturing jobs which have been shed have generally been full-time, whereas a high proportion of the service jobs which have been gained have been part-time, then the *change* in the services' share, comparing 1979 with 1987, is biased upwards using these data.
9. The data are from DTI, Press Notice, 23 May 1989 (capital expenditure in the fourth quarter of 1989: provisional estimates). The estimates for manufacturing include assets leased from the financial sector.
10. The estimate for the services refers to the sum of: construction; distribution, hotels, catering and repairs; banking, finance, insurance, business services and leasing. It did not prove possible to include transport and communication and 'other services' on account of lack of data for 1988. Assets leased to manufacturing are excluded.
11. When measured at *current* prices, on the other hand, manufacturing output experienced a trend decline as a percentage of GDP, between 1948–73 (see Fig. 2.6). However, comparison with the constant price data (see Fig. 2.6) shows that this was entirely a relative price effect – the consequence of a fall in the relative price of manufactures, as a result of an above-average rate of productivity growth in manufacturing compared to the rest of the economy. For a discussion of this point, see R. E. Rowthorn and J. R. Wells, *De-industrialisation and Foreign Trade* (Cambridge University Press: Cambridge, 1987), Chapter 1.
12. There is incidentally, therefore, no evidence whatsoever of any UK 'de-industrialisation', at least in output terms, during the period prior to 1973–4 (though UK manufacturing was undoubtedly performing badly relative to most of its international competitors – in terms of productivity growth, innovation, new product development, etc., trends which were reflected in a comparatively low rate of output growth, by international standards, and an excessively rapid loss of world

market share).

13. See Rowthorn and Wells, op cit., Table 3.2 p. 66, Fig. 5.2, p. 100.
14. The empirical evidence on this point will be presented later in this chapter.
15. See note 1 for the relevant data.
16. As before, this is as a percentage of total civilian employment and includes employees in employment plus the self-employed (including employers).
17. See Rowthorn and Wells, op. cit., pp. 208–9.
18. Albeit at a much slower pace than between 1979 and 1983.
19. See *Financial Times*, 13.3.89.
20. Even so, the growth of service employment in absolute terms, 1983–7, was not particularly rapid compared with the previous decade: 1.4% p.a. compared with 1.7% p.a. (1970–9).
21. See Kravis, I. B. *et al., World Product and Income*, UN International Comparison Project (1982, London) and for a review of the results in Kravis *et al.*, see Rowthorn and Wells, op. cit., Appendix 3.
22. These ideas are set out in diagrammatic form in Rowthorn and Wells, op cit., Fig. 1.2 a–e, pp. 18–19.
23. These are analysed in some detail later in this chapter.
24. These data are available (at a price!) from the Department of Trade and Industry as well as from members of the CFA User Group. I am extremely grateful to Neil Dourmashkin and Terry Barker of Cambridge Econometrics for providing me with a copy of these data.
25. The CFAs provide a link between the quinquennial input–output tables and the quarterly national accounts. Using national accounts estimates of the separate estimates of final demand, together with input–output (I–O) derived estimates of intermediate demand, the CFAs provide estimates of supply and demand for 43 separate commodity groups. The CFAs are, thus both a form of condensed I–O table, where intermediate demand for each commodity is shown in total (not by purchasing industry), as well as an expanded version of the national accounts, in that they are presented in the form of quarterly constant-price series linked to published national accounts of aggregates. For a comprehensive discussion of the CFAs, see *Economic Trends*, May 1985, pp. 82–6.
26. The CFAs are not yet available, as are the national accounts, at constant 1985 £million. There are also a number of other drawbacks with this data, as follows:
    (a) discrepancies exist (quite substantial ones, in the case of certain sectors of activity) between the independently generated estimates of supply and demand;
    (b) the data will almost certainly be revised when they next are made available for limited distribution (during the course of 1989). However, the results presented in this chapter are, we believe, fairly robust with respect to revisions of the sort of order of magnitude which are likely to be made;
    (c) the definitions of sectors of activity (e.g., manufacturing) do not, unfortunately, coincide with those used in, e.g., UK overseas trade statistics, and as a result CFA estimates of exports, imports and trade balance, by sector, do not coincide with those in, e.g., UK overseas trade statistics.
27. CSO, *Input–Output Tables of the United Kingdom, 1984*.
28. The differences between the two calculations are quite minor and mainly affect agriculture's share – which, when taking just the direct effects into account, is exceptionally small (expenditure on unprocessed foodstuffs) but which increases somewhat when the indirect effects (of expenditure on manufactured or processed foodstuffs) are included – largely at the expense of manufacturing's share. The data plot is available from the author on request.
29. Data on expenditure on fixed capital formation have been added to those on

stocks – with the latter being a relatively insignificant item.

30. Another indicator of the slow growth of government expenditure since 1979 is afforded by the disaggregated GDP statistics (1985 = 100).

	1979	1987	% change
GDP	92.9	107.8	+16.0
Total Services	89.6	108.8	+21.4
Public Admin., Defence	100.0	100.0	+ 0.0
Education and Health Services	95.0	103.0	+ 8.4

Source: CSO, *UK National Accounts (Blue Book)* (1988 Edition), Table 2.4, p. 24.

31. *Economic Trends Annual Supplement 1989* for long time series, at both current and constant 1985 prices, on the basis of consistent categories; *Monthly Digest of Statistics* and *Economic Trends* for the latest data; and *UK National Income Accounts (Blue Book)* for the most detailed disaggregation. See also *Economic Trends*, September 1983 for a comprehensive account of the methodology used for classifying the data.

32. Data for 1988 as a whole estimated by extrapolation from 1987 on the basis of data for the first three quarters of 1987 and 1988.

33. Note that 1987 was the latest year for which detailed, disaggregated data was available at time of going to press. For more detailed information on both manufactures and services expenditure see original draft of chapter, available from the author on request.

34. Note that expenditure on catering (which has been revised upwards by several orders of magnitude in the latest *Blue Book* (1988)), though registering the largest single increase in absolute terms for any single item of services expenditure, registered a comparatively modest increase in percentage terms: +23.8% against an increase in total consumers' expenditure as a whole of +22.2%.

35. Note the divergence between the behaviour of the services' share, comparing current and constant prices (see Fig. 2.16), referred to earlier in the chapter. Thus, whereas the services' share, when measured at current prices, has risen almost continuously since 1952, when measured at constant prices, it takes the form of a flattened U and exhibits no trend increase. This divergence is due, of course, to the long-term rise in the relative price of services, resulting from the fact that labour productivity growth in the services lags behind that in the rest of the economy.

36. Considering the effect, initially, of an improvement in the balance of trade in non-factor or commercial services. We consider below the effect of an improvement in the balance in factor service payments (interest, profits and dividends).

37. See original chapter available on request from the author, for a proper discussion of these *induced* effects (p. 31).

38. For the details of all this, see CSO, *United Kingdom Balance of Payments (The Pink Book): 1988*, pp. 19–27.

39. Such transfers are of two types: (a) remittances between private individuals, the balance of which is currently negative, and (b) government remittances, the balance of which is also negative, principally on account of the UK's substantial net contributions to the EEC.

40. Because of errors of measurement, the independently estimated measures of total *supply* (Home Output plus Imports) and total *demand* (C+G+I+S+X+ intermediate demand) do not, in general, coincide. In our work we have, in effect, assigned all of the demand–supply error to intermediate demand (i.e., where total demand exceeds total supply, we have reduced intermediate demand by a corresponding amount, but have not made any correction to the final demand components:

C+G+I+S+X). We have done this in order to ensure that domestic expenditure *less* (output–intermediate demand) = M-X.

41. The methodology used to do this was as follows. The series on output of manufactures (available for final demand) has been extrapolated, using the official index numbers on manufacturing output at 1985 £million, from CSO, *Economic Trends Annual Supplement 1989* and CSO, *Economic Trends* (January 1989) (this must surely be a relatively uncontroversial procedure). The series on domestic expenditure on manufactures has been extrapolated using the official series on *total* domestic expenditure, at constant 1985 £million, from *Economic Trends* and applying it (in index number form) to the 1979 (average) level of domestic expenditure on manufactures. The assumption here is that 1979 was a representative year in terms of the share of manufactures in total domestic expenditure, spanning, as it did, both a pre-election boom and the beginning of the 1979–81 slump. The share of manufactures in total domestic expenditure in 1979 (32%) was certainly higher than in the depths of the ensuing slump, when expenditure on manufactures was particularly depressed. However, as demonstrated earlier, the share of manufactures in total domestic expenditure was remarkably stable, outside of the period 1979–81 – and, thus, the assumption that 1979 was a representative year in terms of the share of manufactures in total domestic expenditure is not unduly sensitive – given the use to which we want to put this data.

42. The definition of 'manufacturing' adopted in the CFAs does not quite coincide with that used in the UK overseas trade statistics. Hence, there are divergences between the two sources, both as to the estimated size of the manufacturing balance as well as the timing of important turning-points (e.g., according to the overseas trade statistics, the manufacturing balance moves from surplus into deficit for the first time in 1983 – whereas, according to the CFAs, this occurs in 1982).

43. Output of exports and import substitutes.

44. This point is further elaborated (with the addition of stylised diagrams) in a subsequent section of this chapter. Note that from the absorption approach, $B \equiv O - E_d$, where B is the trade balance, O is domestic output and E_d is domestic expenditure, one of the principal determinants of O (at least so far as the part of manufacturing – the majority – which is exposed to international competition is concerned) is the real exchange rate, whereas the principal determinants of E_d will be domestic monetary and fiscal policy.

45. That such a mechanism was at work hardly seems to have been appreciated – even at the highest level of the Thatcher government – either at the time or, it would appear, subsequently. See Alan Walters, *Britain's Economic Renaissance: Margaret Thatcher's Reforms 1979–84*, (Oxford University Press: New York, 1986), chapter 9.

46. The data plotted in Fig. 2.20 are a simple transformation of those in Fig. 2.19. Note that the rise in the output: expenditure ratio recorded in 1988 may simply reflect the fact that expenditure is currently being under-recorded in the national accounts (relative to output and income estimates) – though it may also (less likely) reflect an improvement in the capacity of domestic producers to satisfy home demand.

47. Unless the UK had been willing to devote the product of all the improvements on the non-manufacturing side to an increase in net capital outflow.

48. What the late Lord Kaldor referred to as: 'the fact that Mrs Thatcher and North Sea oil came on stream together' (House of Lords Speech, 29 June 1983).

49. Either in the form of a state-led investment and modernisation strategy, as advocated by the Left and a number of Cambridge economists, or a more free market but, similarly, expansionary strategy, such as that set out by William

Keegan, *Britain Without Oil* (Penguin: Harmondsworth, 1985). Note that: since real exchange appreciation of 1979–81 was the product of the *interaction* between restrictive monetary and fiscal policies and the build-up of North Sea fuel production, then, under the counter-factual that more expansionary monetary and fiscal policies had been adopted (1979–81), any appreciation of the real exchange rate would have been much less pronounced – and may, indeed, not actually even have occurred.

50. Note that oil revenues were also used to acquire substantial net overseas assets – which today exist as a sort of congealed North Sea oil wealth.
51. Note that (see Fig. 2.3) the recovery in manufacturing investment which did eventually take place in 1988 only just took it back to a level slightly higher than in 1979 (see DTI, *Press Notice*, 23 May 1989).
52. See House of Lords, *Report from the Select Committee on Overseas Trade*, Session 1984–5: volume II, Oral Evidence: House of Lords, 238–*I*, pp. 553–73.
53. G. F. Ray, 'Services for Manufacturing', *National Institute Economic Review*, August 1986, pp. 30–2.
54. In particular, the problems involved in measuring service output correctly.
55. Reflecting intrinsic differences in the scope for labour productivity growth comparing manufactures with services.
56. Estimated on the basis of the first three quarters from *Economic Trends*, December 1988.
57. And given the position, at full employment, of the non-manufacturing trade balance. Note that manufacturing industry's central role in successful development resides in: (a) the fact that, as demonstrated earlier in the chapter, the domestic demand for manufactures is exceptionally income-elastic and (b) the fact that an exceptionally high proportion of the sector's output can be said to be 'traded' – that is to say, exposed to the forces of international competition. As a result of (a) and (b), if domestic manufacturing output is not sufficiently competitive internationally, the growth of total output and domestic expenditure will inevitably be constrained – unless the country can resort to 'foreign savings' on a growing scale and/or is internationally competitive in some other areas of 'traded' production. However, note that in the case of services, the share of traded output in total output (and, hence, the scope for successful export-expansion and import-substitution) is considerably less than in the case of manufactures. See, for a discussion of the importance of manufacturing to the development process, Rowthorn and Wells, *op. cit.*, chapter 3 and for a discussion of the comparative importance of traded output in total output, comparing manufacturing and services: Wells, letter to *Financial Times*, 16.11.89.
58. The only caveat to the view that the position with respect to the internal–external balance trade-off is worse today relative to 1979 is that the international economic situation is possibly somewhat weaker today (on account of the Third World debt crisis and slow growth in Western and Eastern Europe – and despite the rapid expansion of output and expenditure in North America and Japan). Such weakness in the international economy makes it more difficult for all participants in the international system to reconcile internal and external balance.
59. Whose rate of growth will be determined by (a) the growth of world trade in goods and services and (b) the competitiveness of the UK's internationally traded sector.

3 THE MACRO-ANATOMY OF THE THATCHER YEARS

Andrew Glyn

Over the period of Conservative government since 1979 the growth rate of the UK economy has averaged 2.0% per year[1]: whilst an improvement over the 1.4% per year growth recorded between 1973 and 1979, the rate has fallen well short of that achieved previously. It is only by starting the calculation from the deep recession years of 1981 or 1982 that government apologists can point to growth rates equal to or exceeding the 3% per year achieved in the 1960s or early 1970s.

Although macroeconomic performance as a whole has been unremarkable, the same cannot be said of the macroeconomic *pattern* shown in Table 3.1. First, total spending has been growing nearly one-third faster than production,

Table 3.1 Components of expenditure.

Average annual growth rates (% p.a.)

	1970–9	1979–88	1981–8
GDP	2.4	2.0	2.3
Consumption	2.4	2.6	2.5
Private	2.4	3.1	3.1
Government	2.5	1.0	0.8
Fixed investment	1.0	3.1	4.9
Private housing	3.0	2.7	4.7
Business	2.3	3.8	5.0
Government	−5.4	−1.3	3.9
Exports	5.0	2.6	2.7
Imports	4.4	4.7	5.4
Net exports change in level (% GDP)	0.2	−0.6	−0.7

Sources: CSO, *UK National Accounts 1988*, Tables 1.6, 12.2; CSO, *Economic Trends, Annual Edition*, February 1989; 1989 Budget Statement.

additional resources obtained from a growing balance of trade deficit. Secondly, this has allowed both consumption and investment to grow rather faster than GDP, with investment growing a little faster than consumption. This reverses the pattern of the previous nine years (covering both Conservative and Labour Governments) when investment grew more slowly than consumption. Thirdly, there has been a major growth of private expenditures at the expense of the public sector. Government consumption has grown at about one-third of the pace of private consumption, while over the previous decade the two had grown at similar rates. Government investment in infrastructure has fallen (though less rapidly than previously), while business investment grew at nearly double the rate of GDP (and *private* business investment even faster as previously nationalised industries were transferred to the private sector and those which remained suffered cuts in investment budgets – see Table 3.6). The pattern over the 'recovery' period since 1981 is very similar to that for the whole period 1979–88, except that government investment has recovered much of its decline during 1979–81.

The first task of this chapter is to explore what pattern of incomes (from work, property, transfer payments) has contributed to the remarkably rapid growth of private consumption. This contributes to the picture of the distributional changes of the Thatcher years analysed further by Stark (this volume). Next, there is a brief analysis of the pattern of decline in public expenditure (welfare, military spending and so forth). Finally the pattern of business investment (manufacturing, finance, North Sea oil, for example) is examined for clues as to whether the economy is launched on a sustainable growth path.

3.1 PRIVATE CONSUMPTION AND THE PATTERN OF DISPOSABLE INCOMES

The personal savings ratio – personal disposable income (PDI) less consumption as a percentage of PDI – declined from an average of 13% over the period 1979–81 to only 2% during 1988. As a matter of arithmetic, then, one-third of the rise in private consumption between 1979 and 1988 represented the impact of the declining savings ratio, rather than the rise in PDI (and the same is true for the recovery period 1981–8). This dramatic collapse of personal savings has received much attention (see, for example, Davis, 1988), with analysis of the role of asset price increases and of the expansion of consumer credit encouraged by financial de-regulation (*National Institute Economic Review*, November 1988, pp. 8–9, 36).

All this has naturally diverted attention from the rise in disposable incomes, which accounts for the other two-thirds of the rise in personal consumption. It is possible from the national accounts, however, to make estimates of how various categories of disposable incomes (from employment, from self-employment, from property and from state benefits) have developed (see Table 3.2).[2]

Table 3.2 Components of personal disposable income.

| | billion, 1985 Prices | | | % change | % contri-bution to growth |
	1979	1981	1987	1979–87	1979–87
Income from employment	137.2	132.4	139.6	1.7	7.6
Income from self-employment	17.7	17.3	21.3	20.7	11.7
Rent, dividends, interest	33.4	35.1	46.7	39.7	42.5
Social security benefits	33.5	38.6	47.2	41.0	44.0
Personal disposable income	220.5	221.5	251.7	14.1	100.0

Note: All incomes are after deduction of taxes and interest. See Note 2. Total PDI excludes small items for net transfers, etc.
Source: CSO, *UK National Accounts 1988*, Tables 3.7, 4.1, 4.4, 4.7, 7.5, 9.6.

The most striking finding reported in Table 3.2 is that disposable income from employment (after deducting tax, social security and interest payments) barely increased at all (0.2% per year) between 1979 and 1987, so virtually none of the growth of consumption up to 1987 was derived from the additional purchasing power of wage and salary earners (though of course reduced savings out of this category of income did play an important part). In the next section the question of reconciling this with the rise in real wages is discussed. Disposable income from self-employment seems to have fared rather better, rising by one-fifth; but such a rise is still very small in comparison to the estimated rise of one-half in the numbers of self-employed.

The considerable rise in real personal disposable income which did occur (14% over the eight years) was thus almost entirely due to the rise in real receipts of rent, dividends and interest (RDI) and of social security benefits (SSB). Each of these categories rose by around 40% in real terms and contributed about four-tenths of the total increase in PDI. Some rough estimates which can be computed for the first half of 1988 slightly modify the picture, since real disposable earnings rose by around 5% as compared to 1987 while RDI and SSB both stagnated; but even in absolute terms the rise in disposable wages and salaries was still much less important than RDI and SSB in accounting for the rise in personal disposable income between 1979 and 1988; so the general conclusion is that the main factors behind rising consumption were growing receipts of RDI and SSB, together with the fall of the savings ratio.

3.1.1. Income from employment

How can the stagnation of aggregate disposable wage and salary income be reconciled with increases in conventional measures of real wages? The explanation lies both in the decline in employment and in the increase in deductions from gross income from employment (with the calculations in Table 3.3

Table 3.3 Income from employment.

	1979	1987	% change 1979–87
(1) Employees (1,000)	23,487	22,129	–5.8
(2) % part-time	16.4	22.5	
(3) Employees (full-time equivalent) = (1) × (100 – 0.5 × (2))	21,561	19,639	–8.9
Disposable income from employment			
(4) Per head (£. 1985)	6,365	7,109	11.7
(5) Total (£billion, 1985) = (4) × (3)	137.2	139.6	1.7
Income from employment per head and deductions			
(6) Gross (£ 1985 prices)	8,781	10,632	21.1
(7) Net of taxes and social security	6,734	7,953	18.1
(8) Net of taxes, social security and interest	6,365	7,109	11.7
(9) Net of tax, social security, interest and pension contributions	5,535	6,212	12.2
Memo: Shares of gross income from employment (%)			
(10) Taxes and social security	23.3	25.2	
(11) Interest payments	4.2	7.9	
(12) Pension contributions	9.5	8.4	

Source: as Table 3.2 plus CSO, *UK National Accounts*, Table 16.1.

showing that both factors were of a similar order of magnitude). The combination of falling numbers employed (line 1) and increased numbers of part-time workers (line 2) led to a fall in the number of 'full-time-equivalent' workers of 8.9% between 1979 and 1987. This nearly offsets the rise of 11.7% in disposable income from employment per head (line 4) so that total disposable income from employment barely increases (line 5). The remainder of the table shows how the 21.1% rise in gross income from employment per head is successfully whittled down to 11.7% (line 8) by the deduction first of taxes and social security (line 7) and then debt interest on mortgages and consumer credit (line 8). Of these two deductions, interest payments are more important than taxation; a comparison of lines (10) and (11) shows that the former increased their share of gross incomes by more than the latter. Over this period the share of pension contributions actually fell (line 12).

Thus, although the average weight of direct tax (and social security) rose somewhat, this factor was less important in holding down disposable income from employment than were increasing interest payments on debt obligations. The personal balance sheet data now published in the *National Accounts* (Table 11.2) shows that the increasing burden of interest payments on disposable incomes mostly reflected the greater level of debts incurred in relation to average incomes, since the average interest rate paid rose only slightly between 1979 and 1987.[3] The remarkable fall in the importance of disposable wages and salaries is underlined by their decline from 42.3% to only 36.0% of GNP between 1979 and 1987. Only one-sixth of this decline took place in the

Table 3.4 Income from self-employment.

	1979	1987	% change 1979–87
Number of self-employed (1,000)	1,906	2,861	50.1
Disposable income of self-employed per head (£ 1985 prices per year)	9,279	7,462	–19.6
Total disposable income from self-employed (£billion, 1985 prices)	17.7	21.3	20.7
Ratio of income per head of self-employed to employees			
Gross	1.47	0.99	
Disposable	1.25	0.93	

Note: Disposable income is net of tax, social security and interest payments and (for comparison with employees) of capital consumption.
Source: as Table 3.3.

recession years 1980–1, despite the concentration of employment decline in those years.

The modest increase in disposable earnings per head which has occurred since 1979 has been disproportionately concentrated among the better paid as a result of two trends. There has been increasing dispersion of pre-tax earnings (see Adams (1988) and Stark, this volume). On the other hand, reductions in tax rates have also disproportionately benefited higher earners.

3.1.2 Income from self-employment

Real income from self-employment per head fell drastically between 1979 and 1981 (13% in gross terms, 15% net of taxes, interest and capital consumption) and fell a little thereafter. Average gross self-employment incomes were nearly 50% higher than average income from employment per head in 1979; by 1987 the difference was negligible (Table 3.4). This drastic decline in *relative* self-employment incomes suggests that the huge increase in numbers of self-employed has taken place predominantly in poorly paid occupations.[4]

3.1.3 Rent, Dividends and Interest (RDI)

Table 3.5 shows that the fastest growing component of the personal sector's receipts of RDI was receipts by Pension Funds and Life Assurance Companies. Rent from owner-occupied dwellings (an imputed figure based on rateable values) increased rather slowly. Household receipts, the only part directly available to finance consumption, grew in real terms by over 40% between 1979 and 1987. The tax burden on cash receipts of RDI actually appears to have fallen slighly over this period.

The memorandum items in Table 3.5 also show the origin of the sharp rise

Table 3.5 Personal sector receipts of rent, dividends and interest.

	1979	1987	% change 1979–87
Gross RDI receipts (£billion, 1985 prices)	37.5	54.6	45.8
Households RDI receipts	16.4	23.3	42.2
Pension and life assurance receipts	10.5	17.9	70.7
Rent of owner-occupied dwellings	10.7	13.5	26.7
Disposable RDI	33.4	46.7	39.7
Memorandum items			
Payments of dividends and interest			
Industrial and commercial companies	15.1	20.8	38.2
Government	14.2	16.3	15.0
Personal sector	11.0	23.4	112.8
Overseas (net)	2.0	5.1	159.2
Corporate income % GNP net of tax, depreciation	15.0	16.3	
Corp dividends and interest as % corporate income	49.4	54.8	

Notes: Levels of RDI are deflated by Consumer Price Index. Corporate sector refers to companies plus public corporations.
Sources: CSO, *UK National Accounts*, Tables 3.1, 3.2, 3.7, 4.1, 5.4, 13.3.

in RDI payments; well over half the rise came from the personal sector with government payments rising much less rapidly. Net receipts from overseas rose very fast, but from a low base. Payments from industrial and commercial companies rose quite rapidly in real terms reflecting increases (of about one-tenth in both cases) in the share of corporate post-tax income in GDP and in the share of corporate income paid out as dividends and interest.

Two further matters concerning RDI receipts are worth consideration. First, receipts of RDI by pension and life assurance funds are included as part of personal income in the national accounts even though they do not accrue directly to households. The pensions they pay out certainly do, however. Between 1979 and 1987 such private pensions (and life assurance payouts) actually rose by £12 billion (1985 prices), or over 90%, faster even than the 71% rise in the funds' receipts of RDI (while the funds' 'surplus' was maintained in real terms by the rapid increase in contributions).[5]

In an important respect the rapid rise in RDI receipts documented in this section underestimates the returns to owning property since it leaves out of account all real capital gains (or losses). The balance sheet data for the personal sector allows calculations to be made of the real rate of capital gain on personal net assets. The category of net assets can be drawn more or less widely but over the whole period 1979–87 (end year 1978 to end year 1987) there were real rates of capital gain in the range 4–5% per year (around half a percentage point higher over the period 1981–7).[6] The real rate capital gain fluctuates a good deal from year to year (see Davis, 1988; Table 2), but applying the average return of 5% to net worth (the broad concept including housing and including equity in pension funds, etc.: see note 6) gives a real capital gain in 1987 of some £60 billion (1985 prices), of a similar order of magnitude to gross RDI receipts. This indicates the severe understatement of real returns to property involved in looking just at RDI receipts over the 1980s, and in particular the transformation as compared to the mid- and late 1970s when real capital losses were sustained (see Bryant, 1987).

3.1.4 Social security benefits

The rise in the total real receipts of social security benefits and other government current grants does underline the fact that the various income categories of PDI are not independent. The fall in employment and thus the stagnation in employment incomes has been partly compensated for by rising numbers receiving social security payments. Conversely, the rise in such payments has tended to increase taxation (and thus reduce the disposable income of recipients of earned income and RDI).

It is worth emphasising, however, that the rising share of benefit payments is entirely the result of increased numbers of recipients rather than the relative generosity of benefits. As compared to average earnings, rates of benefit typically fell by some 10–15% between November 1978 and April 1987 (*Social Security Statistics* 1987; Tables 46.05, 46.06, etc.).

3.2 GOVERNMENT EXPENDITURE

The slow growth of total government expenditure on goods and services noted has been felt in all the major categories of spending. Table 3.6 shows that in public services, defence and law and order growth was of a similar magnitude to that of the 'welfare' category (education, health, housing, etc.). There was no growth at all, however, in expenditures on industry and other non-welfare infrastructure.[7] This category excludes real investment by public corporations, which fell by nearly one-half over the period. The growth in real social security transfers swamps such increases in other programmes as have occurred – accounting for some two-thirds of the increase in real public spending.

3.3 BUSINESS INVESTMENT

Two important issues concerning the growth of business investment since 1979 are its sectoral composition and its relation to the recovery in profitability.

Table 3.6 General government expenditure on goods and services.

	£billion, 1985 prices		% change
	1979	1987	1979–87
Public services, defence, law and order	26.6	28.9	8.6
Education, health, housing and welfare	44.2	47.4	7.2
Industry	6.4	6.5	1.6
Memo items			
Social security benefits	33.5	47.2	40.9
Pub corporations fixed investment	8.7	4.4	–49.4

Source: CSO, *UK National Accounts 1988*, Tables 1.6, 9.4, 12.2.

3.3.1 The pattern of investment

Table 3.7 presents the sectoral breakdown for the most conventional indicator of investment effort between 1979 and 1987 – the growth of real gross fixed investment. Leaving aside the rather special case of oil and gas extraction (the run-down of North Sea oil development) there are still enormous variations. Real manufacturing investment in 1987 was nearly one-tenth lower than in 1979 (after including leased assets). Investment by banking, finance and insurance, by contrast, more than doubled (excluding leased assets), with investment in business services close behind. All the growth of investment occurred in services, with falling investment in agriculture and industry.

The growth of real investment shows improvement or deterioration, but gives no idea of its absolute level. The best indicator of the investment level is its impact in extending the existing stock of capital equipment, that is the growth rate of the gross capital stock.[8] Table 3.7 shows this measure first for 1979 (the growth of the stock during 1979 which is the best indicator of investment effort when the Tories came to power), then for 1987 (to show the position after years of 'recovery') and finally for the whole period 1979–87 (to show overall performance). The very weak investment performance in all the industrial sectors is underlined – by 1987 the capital stock was growing at around 1% per year or less in all industrial sectors (including North Sea oil) and agriculture, with an average growth rate of only 0.6% per year. With the exception of North Sea oil, where accumulation was very high at the beginning of the period, the average growth rate of the capital stock over the whole period was around 1% per year or less – an *unprecedentedly* poor performance in the whole post-war period. In manufacturing, vital for trading performance, the trend was especially poor, with the growth rate of the capital stock during the whole period only 1% or so (the true figure is probably somewhat lower still, as no account is taken of exceptional scrapping of capital during 1979–81, some of which presumably would not otherwise have happened by 1987; see Wadwani and Wall, 1986). In 1987 the manufacturing capital stock was growing at less than 1% per year, around

Table 3.7 Business investment.

	Gross investment % change	1979–87 Share of total increase (%)	Growth of gross fixed capital stock % pa		
			1978–9	1986–7	1979–87
Business	14.0	100.0	2.8	2.0	1.9
Industry and agriculture	−16.0	−63.9	2.5	0.6	1.2
Services	52.0	163.9	3.5	4.3	3.2
Agriculture	−36.9	−11.1	1.4	−2.1	−0.3
Oil and gas	−36.0	−22.4	14.9	1.1	6.5
Energy	3.0	2.4	0.9	0.5	0.9
Manufacturing	−9.5	−22.0	2.6	0.9	1.0
Construction	−41.8	−7.6	3.4	−0.6	0.0
Distribution	39.3	37.0	5.2	5.1	4.0
Transport	−19.7	−17.2	−0.7	−2.3	−2.3
Communication	49.9	18.1	2.9	2.6	2.5
Banking and finance	122.1	35.4 [B,F,BS(1)	5.9	8.2	7.5]
Business services	85.9	38.6 L B,F,BS(2)	8.6	8.1	8.2]

Notes: The gross investment figures for agriculture, manufacturing and transport and the capital stock figures for manufacturing include assets leased by the industry; for other industries leased assets cannot be allocated to investment or capital stock. Investment by banking and finance excludes assets leased out. The two capital stock figures for Banking, Finance and Business Services exclude (B,F,BS(1)) and include (B,F,BS(2)) rough estimates of the stock of leased assets.

The category 'Other Services' (SIC 91–99) which contains some marketed services (R&D, films, TV, music, sport, laundries, hairdressing, etc.) is omitted as it is largely non-market.

Source: CSO, *UK National Accounts 1988*, Tables 12.6, 12.7, 12.8, 13.8, 13.10 and page 133.

one-third of the 1979 rate. Even if manufacturing investment rose as much as 25% between 1987 and 1989 (as the National Institute currently forecasts) the growth rate of the manufacturing capital stock would only reach about 2% during 1989 and it is expected to slow down thereafter.

The investment boom in parts of the services sector did not commence with the Thatcher government – the growth rate of the capital stock in distribution in 1987 was similar to that in 1979. Only in banking, finance, insurance and business services does the growth rate of the capital stock appear to have accelerated (from an already fast rate in 1979), and then only when the assets bought by that sector for leasing to other sectors are left out.

3.3.2 Investment and profits

One of the most prominent features of the recovery since 1981 has been the sharp increase in the profit rate (Table 3.8). Having fallen in 1981 to a level below even the 1975 trough, the rate of profit had recovered by 1987 to a level close to that of the later 1960s. Once the rather special case of North Sea oil is left to one side, this is true of both manufacturing and the industrial and commercial sector as a whole.[9] Before dissecting this recovery, we should note the extent to which the recovery in profitability has *not* been paralleled by a recovery in capital accumulation. If the growth of the capital stock in manufacturing had maintained in 1987 the same relationship to the profit rate as the early 1970s, then it would have been three or four times faster than was actually achieved.

One factor which may have moderated somewhat the impact of rising pre-tax profitability is the increased corporate tax burden implicit in the change in tax regime after 1983/4. Over the preceding decade 'free depreciation' on plant and machinery had wiped out the impact of a 52% corporation tax rate and left pre-tax and post-tax returns on new investment practically equal. However, the shift to regular depreciation allowances (25% for machinery) and abolition of stock relief more than outweighed the cut in corporation tax to 35% and reduced the post-tax rate of return somewhat (*Bank of England Quarterly Bulletin*, June 1985, p. 232). A detailed analysis of the impact of the system concluded that 'in the long run, and on average, the new system acts as a disincentive to new investment' (Devereux, 1988), but the impact of the change was not very large. In any case the new regime was not unfavourable in terms of effective taxation of profits from new investment as compared to the situation in the late 1960s, when the pre-tax profit rate was similar. So the poor performance of manufacturing investment relative to the pre-tax profit rate cannot be substantially attributed to tax changes. With the stock market, and thus valuation ratios, at high levels even after the 1987 crash, depressed expectations as to continued growth of the home market and competitiveness overseas seems the most important explanation.

We do not have the disaggregated data which would permit a comprehensive comparison of the changing profitability of different sectors of the economy. The poor performance of manufacturing investment, against the backdrop of a comparable recovery in profitability to that of the industrial and commercial sector as a whole, has already been noted. It is interesting that between 1979 and 1987 net equity profits in the financial sector actually grew slower than those in industry and commerce (159% against 194%[10]). These comparisons suggest that the very strong real investment boom in the financial sector, as compared to weak investment in manufacturing, cannot be explained simply by a changing pattern of realised profitability.

3.3.3 The pattern of profitability

The final set of calculations analyses the factors behind the strong improvement in profitability since 1979. We focus on manufacturing for which data is more easily available, and which we have seen displays a rather similar pattern of profits to the corporate sector as a whole. A change in the rate of profit can be split into the change in the profit share and the change in the

Table 3.8 Trends in the profit rate.

%	1965–73 average	1975	1979	1981	1987
All industrial & commercial corporations	9.8	3.9	7.4	6.1	11.3
excluding North Sea oil	9.9	4.2	5.6	2.8	10.2
All manufacturing corporations	9.0	2.8	4.3	2.3	9.2

Note: Profit rates are net corporate profits divided by net capital employed (fixed plus stocks) at current replacement cost.
Source: see Table 3.9.

output capital ratio. Table 3.9 further decomposes the change in the profit share into the change in the balance between productivity and wages, and the change in the output capital ratio into a 'real' and a relative price component.

Labour productivity cannot be directly compared to the real wage (in terms of consumer goods) without adjusting for the fact that domestic manufacturing output comprises only part of the bundle of consumer goods. So in order to assess what growth of real wages is consistent with a constant wage share in manufacturing value added, manufacturing productivity growth per hour worked (line 1) has to be converted into purchasing power over consumer goods (line 3) by subtracting the change in relative price of consumer goods as compared to manufacturing value added (line 2). If the real wage (line 4) rises faster than this category of 'real manufacturing incomes' (line 3), then the wage share rises (line 5) and the profit share declines (line 6).

Table 3.9 presents a striking picture. Both the wage share (line 5) and the output capital ratios reverse their trends after 1979. Much the more important quantitatively in its effect on the rate of profit is wage share (for it translates into a much larger relative effect on the smaller profit share – line 6). The reversal in the trend of the wage share reflects the much faster productivity growth. This was slightly moderated in its effect on the growth of real manufacturing incomes due to faster relative rise of consumer prices (line 2), but still the acceleration of productivity growth dominates. With real wages growing at virtually the same rate, most of the faster productivity growth is translated into a growing profit share. Up to 1979 workers had achieved real wage increases substantially exceeding what was available in terms of the growth of real factor incomes, even allowing for slow relative growth of consumer prices.[11]

The trend in the output capital ratio is also much more favourable after 1979. The decline in the ratio of real output to gross fixed capital stock (the usual measure, given in line 7) slowed down from 3% p.a. to 1%.[12] The faster fall in the relative price of components of the capital stock (line 8) meant that the current price output capital ratio, which is the measure relevant for profitability, actually rises after 1979, reversing a twenty-year downward tendency.

Table 3.9 UK manufacturing profit shares and rates.

% change per annum	1973–79	1979–87
(1) Hourly productivity	0.6	4.5
(2) Consumer prices/man VA prices	–0.6	0.4
(3) Real manufacturing incomes =	1.2	4.1
(1) – (2)		
(4) Real wages per head	2.7	2.6
(5) Wage share = (4) – (3)	1.5	–1.5
(6) Profit share	–8.2	8.4
(Change in % points pa)	[–1.2	1.3]
(7) Real output/fix cap ratio	–3.1	–0.9
(8) Price effects	1.3	2.4
(9) Current price output/capital =	–1.8	1.5
(7) + (8)		
(10) Profit rate = (6) + (9)	–9.9	10.0
(Change in % points pa)	[–0.6	0.6]

Notes: Price effects in line (8) include the relative prices of
stocks and of fixed assets compared to manufacturing value
added, as well as the ratios of net to gross capital stock and net
to gross value added (see Glyn *et al*. 1989. Appendix). In
addition, any changes in the real ratios of stocks to fixed capital
are also included, since this data includes stocks of commodities
as part of the capital stock. The basic data source is for
manufacturing companies (i.e., excluding public corporations
and self-employed enterprises); this had to be complemented
with data on output, employment for the manufacturing sector
as a whole involving some approximations.
Sources: Department of Trade, data on manufacturing
companies: rates of return; supplemented with CSO, *UK
National Accounts,* Tables 2.1, 2.2, 2.4, 13.10, 16.1.

CONCLUSIONS

The most important features of the macroeconomic pattern during the
Thatcher years which have been explored in this paper are as follows:

1. The relatively small contribution of increased disposable wages and
salaries in generating the spending power behind the rise in consumption.
There has been a marked redistribution of income towards returns from
holding assets (both interest receipts and real capital gains) and state benefits
have risen sharply due to increased numbers of recipients. These two sources
of income have sustained the growth in consumption, along with the fall in
the savings ratio.
2. The extreme weakness of industrial investment, especially when this is
assessed in the most appropriate way, by the growth of the capital stock. The
strength of service investment is a continuation of earlier trends. Only within
the finance sector does the accumulation rate appear to have accelerated, but

with the effect of generating excess capacity as first financial markets and then consumer credit lost buoyancy.

3. Increased profitability has reflected the increase in productivity growth (of labour and capital), with real wage growth remaining very steady. While failing to promote an investment boom in industry, increased profits have contributed to the growth of returns from assets held by the personal sector.

The macroeconomic pattern of development under the Thatcher government has been extraordinary: a consumption boom financed from borrowing, from dividend and interest incomes and from state benefits, and a pattern of investment skewed towards sectors which service the consumption boom (distribution, credit) rather than those which produce, or contribute to the production of, tradeable commodities. This has been partially disguised by productivity increases in industrial sectors which undertook substantial reorganisations in the wake of the 1981 shock (see Chapters 5 and 6, this volume). A sustained expansion, however, must be based on the investment in new processes and products which alone can ensure long-term competitiveness in world markets. The attempts to rein in the Thatcher–Lawson boom through high interest rates and exchange rates will further worsen the prospects for this.

NOTES

1. As measured by the average growth rate of GDP from 1979 to 1988 (see Table 3.1). Unless otherwise specified all the data in this chapter are calculated directly from *Economic Trends* or *United Kingdom National Accounts* (UKNA) 1988 edition. The more detailed data in subsequent tables require data from the UKNA which are only available up to 1987.

2. To take the example of income from employment, the first deduction is for taxes. The figure (UK National Accounts (UKNA) 1988, Table 9.6) for taxes on wages and salaries in fact includes taxes on receipts of occupational pensions. This total was prorated between income from employment and pension receipts (UKNA, Table 4.9) assuming the same proportions taken in taxation. The second deduction, to reach post-tax income from employment, is for social security contributions (UKNA, Table 9.6). The next deduction is for interest payments (on mortgage, consumer credit and other debts) in order to show what is potentially available for the purchase of goods and services. The figure for total interest payments by the personal sector (UKNA, Table 3.7) less interest on business loans being paid out of self-employment incomes (UKNA, Tables 3.1 and 3.7) is prorated, between income from employment, self-employment incomes and rent, dividends and interest received directly by the personal sector, in proportion to the level of post-tax income of the particular category. This gives us the basic category of disposable employment income which is a component of personal disposable income. Contributions to pension funds (employer and employee) may also be deducted (UNKA, Table 4.9) to give another measure of disposable income corresponding more closely to Table 4.9 of UKNA which views such contributions (though not life assurance premiums) as not at the discretion of the person concerned. In the case of income from self-employment the deductions are the

same except that capital consumption represents an additional deduction. Only tax and interest payments are deducted from property incomes, and only tax from state benefits.

3. The implicit average interest rate on the personal sector's liabilities rose from 9.4% to 9.7% between 1979 and 1987 (UKNA Tables 3.7 and 11.2). In fact the general level of (nominal) short-term interest rates was considerably lower in 1987 – on average banks' base rates were 14.0% in 1979 and 9.7% in 1987.

4. An obvious explanation for the decline in relative self-employment incomes would be the decline in farm incomes. In fact, they only decline at a slightly faster rate than other self-employment incomes and thus do not explain the overall fall. Summary data for the distribution of self-employment incomes are published in the Inland Revenue's annual *Survey of Personal Incomes*. The latest data for 1984–5 (Table 17) show that slightly over 10% of the self-employed earned incomes in excess of £15,000 per year (whilst the median income was about £5,000).

5. An alternative to PDI is to calculate household disposable income, which deducts contributions to pension funds (and life assurance premiums) and includes pension receipts from them and life assurance companies rather than treating the operations of the LAP sector as part of the personal sector. Rent of owner-occupied dwelling is also left out as an imputed item (as is the capital consumption of the self-employed which does not in principle represent disposable income). This category of HDI rose by 13.4% between 1979 and 1987 (as compared to 14.1% for PDI), whilst the corresponding category of consumption (leaving out both rent on owner-occupied dwellings and the costs of the LAP sector) rose by 22.2% (as compared to 23.1% for conventional private consumption). Thus, the fall in the 'discretionary' savings ratio of the household sector (i.e., leaving out all pension contributions and life assurance premiums) from 3.1% to –4.4% between 1979 and 1987 accounted for all of the fall in the conventional savings ratio of the personal sector.

6. In the UKNA Table 11.2 the net worth of the personal sector is calculated including an item of 'non-marketable tenancy rights'. For our purposes it seems desirable to exclude this. This gives us a 'gross' concept of net worth. A category of 'marketable' net worth may also be calculated excluding both housing and equity in LAP (worth over one-fifth of net worth in 1987). At the end of 1987 'gross' and 'marketable' net worth amounted to £1,414 billion and £247 billion, respectively. The real rates of return for these various categories are computed by a simple DCF exercise from base year real net worth, annual real savings and end year real net worth; they were 4.9% and 4.3% respectively, for 1979–87, and 5.6% and 4.7%, respectively, for the years 1981–7. Data in Bryant (1987), Table 8, shows that (gross) real personal wealth declined (by 0.9% per year) over the period 1973–9, implying substantial real capital losses, given a substantial level of real personal investment.

7. The first category includes expenditure on parliament, tax collection and diplomacy. The second category comprises education, health, social security, housing and community amenities and recreation and cultural affairs. The third category comprises fuel and energy, agriculture, industry, transport and communication and other economic and unclassified expenditures. The current price data in UKNA, Table 9.4 is converted to constant prices by applying the government current and capital expenditure deflators to each of the three categories. Note that these are 'general government' expenditures on goods and services; the most important other items of public sector expenditure, transfer payments and public corporations investment, are shown as memorandum items.

8. The growth rate of the gross capital stock is close to a normalised net investment measure, since retirements (which approximate to capital consumption) are

deducted from gross investment and the remainder is divided by the existing gross stock. Note that retirements are based on conventional assumptions about asset lives, and do not include abnormal scrapping such as is believed to have occurred, especially in manufacturing in the recession of 1979–81.

9. Privatisations since 1979 have affected the trend in (private) corporate profitability, since the relatively low profit rate, even of the privatised public corporations, has slightly restrained the measured recovery. The effect is not very big, however. If we add public corporations to private companies, the net rates of return in 1979, 1981 and 1987 are 3.8%, 2.1% and 7.7%, respectively – a very similar pattern to that for the private sector shown in Table 8.

10. It is difficult to decide on a concept of profits for the financial sector, comparable to operating profits for industrial and commercial companies. It seems best, therefore, to evade the question of the treatment of interest payments by taking a measure of equity profits, net of stock appreciation and depreciation but including profits due abroad, and because of data problems, debenture interest (data from UKNA; Tables 5.1, 5.3, 5.7, 5.9).

11. The data for the business sector as a whole (companies, public corporations and unincorporated enterprises) show a rather similar pattern. The acceleration in productivity growth is less dramatic than in manufacturing, but is again paralleled by a reversal of the upward trend in the wage share – real wage growth continues at roughly the same rate. The output capital ratio also increases after 1979, but only when reckoned (as it should be) at current prices and including stocks of goods as well as fixed capital.

12. To the extent that the growth of the gross fixed stock is exaggerated due to failure to record increased scrapping in the recession after 1979, then the trend in the real output capital ratio may be somewhat better than recorded. To the extent that premature scrapping was mainly of old plant, the inaccuracy in the capital stock data decreases after 1981 or 1982 as some of the excess scrapping is caught in the regular retirements data.

REFERENCES

Adams, M., 'The distribution of earnings 1973 to 1986', *Department of Employment* (1988).

Bank of England Quarterly Bulletin (June 1985).

Bryant, C. 'National and sector balance sheets 1957–85', *Economic Trends* (May, 1987).

Central Statistical Office, *United Kingdom National Accounts 1988 Edition*, HMSO (London 1988).

Central Statistical Office, *Economic Trends*, HMSO (October 1988).

Davis, E. P., 'Revaluations of personal sector assets', *The Royal Bank of Scotland Review*, No. 159 (September 1988).

Devereux, M., 'Corporation tax: the effect of the 1984 reforms on the incentive to invest.' *Fiscal Studies*, Vol. 7, No. 1 (February 1988).

Glyn, A., Hughes, A., Lipietz, A. and Singh, A. 'The rise and fall of the Golden Age' *The End of the Golden Age* (eds Marglin, S. and Schor, J.) (Oxford University Press: Oxford, 1989).

National Institute Economic Review, pp. 8–9, 36 (November 1988).

Social Security Statistics (1987).

Wadwani, S. and Wall, A. 'The UK Capital Stock', *Oxford Review of Economic Policy*, Vol. II, No. 2 (1986).

4 REGIONAL IMBALANCE AS CONSEQUENCE AND CONSTRAINT IN NATIONAL ECONOMIC RENEWAL

Ron Martin

4.1 BRITISH ECONOMIC RENEWAL AND THE THATCHER PROJECT

During the ten years after Mrs Thatcher's Conservative Government first took office the British economy underwent its most intense phase of restructuring and reorganisation since the inter-war decades. Few would probably deny that some such upheaval was sorely needed. By the close of the 1970s Britain had acquired the dubious distinction of having one of the slowest rates of output growth and lowest per capita incomes of the advanced industrial nations. All of the latter experienced a sharp deterioration of economic performance in the 1970s, as the Fordist regime of accumulation on which the long post-war boom or 'golden age' was based became increasingly undermined by structural crisis (Cooke, 1987; Lash and Urry, 1987; Glyn *et al.*, 1988; Allen and Massey, 1988; Martin, 1989a). But in Britain this crisis was superimposed on and compounded by a further process of deep-seated long-term relative economic decline that had begun a century earlier (Gamble, 1981; Matthews *et al.*, 1982; Feinstein, 1988; Mann, 1988). As a result, the slowdown was much more acute than in other countries, and by the late 1970s de-industrialisation, accelerating inflation and the breakdown of state intervention appeared to have become endemic features of British economic life.

There had, of course, been various attempts to modernise and renew the national economy: between 1964 and 1979 three quite different modernisation strategies were tried. Under Harold Wilson's Labour government of 1964–70, the aim had been to use centralised planning to reforge the economy in the 'white heat of new technology', to take British industry 'by the scruff of the neck and drag it kicking and screaming into the twentieth century' (Wilson,

This chapter was written while the author was Visiting Research Professor in the Department of Geography at the University of California, Los Angeles. The research support provided by that Department is gratefully acknowledged.

quoted in Fry, 1975, p. 14). By contrast, the Conservative government of 1970–4 under Edward Heath sought to rebuild the economy and improve industrial efficiency by means of a 'Quiet Revolution' driven less by state planning and more by market forces. This was then followed between 1974–9 by Labour's programme to renew growth and foster structural change through a corporatist 'New Industrial Strategy'. What united these different endeavours to renew the economy, however, was their lack of success (Martin, 1989b): together they chart a depressing catalogue of abortive and thwarted policies, a tale of 'modernisation frustrated' (Newton and Porter, 1988).

When compared with these previous policies, the Thatcher project of the past decade stands out as the most ambitious and radical yet attempted. Certainly by the close of the 1970s the much overdue task of restructuring and reviving the UK economy had reached critical proportions, so that the newly elected Conservative government could justifiably claim that drastic and determined therapies were necessary. And without doubt, since 1979 the Thatcher governments have sought to change almost every facet of the post-war economy and its management. Their underlying and motivating conviction has been quite simple: the only way to secure a thoroughgoing restructuring of the economy and revival of economic growth is by exposing the nation's industries, workers and social institutions to the full rigour of unfettered market forces, that is, by 'freeing the economy' (see Gamble, 1988; Hoover and Plant, 1989) so as to allow capitalism's natural process of 'creative destruction' to operate unhindered. In this way, they argue, obsolete and inefficient industries, firms, products and skills should be driven out, to be replaced by new, innovative and efficient industries, firms, products and skills. In its effort to ensure that this assumed process can function properly, the government has acted to weaken or even dismantle those social, public and political infrastructures whose historical evolution is seen as largely responsible for generating Britain's secular decline and retarding the process of economic adaptation. Thus, the government's policies to privatise public industries and services, to emasculate the power of the unions, to de-regulate markets, to reduce taxes, to curb public expenditure and to promote individualism and self-reliance have all been intended to 'de-rigidify' the economic structures and social attitudes believed to have suffocated competition, incentive and enterprise. The Thatcher restructuring project, then, has extended well beyond the purely economic realm to embrace the recasting of the accepted cultural, ideological and political bases of post-war social democracy (King, 1987).

How far and in what ways this particular route to the renewal of Britain has been successful is, of course, the subject of fierce ongoing debate (for two very recent assessments see Leadbeater, 1989; Wells, 1989). Almost all of this debate has been preoccupied with the performance of the aggregate economy, and the question of the unequal distribution of the costs and benefits of restructuring, though widely acknowledged, has received much less attention, especially from economists. Yet one dimension of this inequality has become the focus of considerable public and political controversy and has proved embarrassing to the government, namely the widening of spatial disparities in economic growth and social welfare across the country, and in particular the opening up of a major 'North–South divide'. The government and its supporters have argued that no such stark division of the country exists, that prosperous areas can be found in parts of the 'north' just as depressed areas can be found in the south. However, this observation, which few would contest, is not the issue, for whether at the level of broad regions or local areas the evidence points unequivocally to the development of a North–South 'two nations' divide during the 1980s (see, for example, Armstrong and Riley, 1987; Massey, 1987; Champion and Green, 1988; Martin, 1988a; Lewis and Townsend, 1989). Furthermore, this regional imbalance in its turn has had adverse effects on the performance of the national economy and on the government's macroeconomic and anti-inflation policies. Economists have tended to ignore the geographical dimension in their assessments of the impact and progress of the Thatcher restructuring project. My purpose in this chapter, therefore, is to focus on this important but neglected issue.

4.2 THE RATIONALISATION OF MANUFACTURING: SPATIAL BIAS IN DE-INDUSTRIALISATION

The significance of geography in the economic restructuring process arises in several ways. In the first place, within a capitalist system uneven regional development is a fundamental mechanism of economic accumulation. A given regime or phase of economic expansion will be associated with the construction and stabilisation of a particular form and pattern of uneven regional development which will reflect both the specific nature of capital accumulation and the differential opportunities provided by the inherited spatial surface of socio-economic differentiation, or spatial division of labour (Massey, 1984). Once established, a given pattern of uneven regional development tends to be cumulative, in that the leading growth areas typically maintain their advantageous edge over the lagging ones. However, if a major alteration in the nature and character of economic growth occurs, this will stimulate a corresponding restructuring of the form and pattern of uneven regional development. During the course of such an upheaval, as capital moves into new forms and sources of profitable accumulation, a new technological and spatial 'fix' (Harvey, 1982), the pressures on and capacities of different social groups and localities to restructure will vary according to their role in the old declining pattern of development and their relative suitability with respect to the needs of the new succeeding phase of growth.

Thus, the uneven spatial landscape of production, employment, labour skills and class interests built up by capital in one phase of development

Table 4.1 Uneven geography of economic restructuring, 1971–9 and 1979–88.

	Change in the number of employees in employment in manufacturing and services							
	Percentage change				Absolute change (000s)			
	1971–79		1979–88		1971–79		1979–88	
	Manufacturing	Services	Manufacturing	Services	Manufacturing	Services	Manufacturing	Services
South-east	-15.2	10.7	-29.4	14.9	-336	489	-550	750
East Anglia	7.2	27.2	5.8	33.3	14	86	12	134
South-west	3.8	34.5	-17.1	10.9	16	256	-75	109
East Midlands	1.0	34.3	-18.6	22.2	7	192	-113	167
'South'	-8.7	16.6	-23.2	16.1	-299	1023	-726	1160
West Midlands	-11.0	17.9	-29.3	15.8	-122	163	-228	169
Yorkshire–Humberside	-9.2	22.2	-37.4	14.4	-72	190	-265	151
North-west	-15.9	11.6	-38.2	-2.2	-184	155	-371	-33
Northern	-7.7	13.7	-36.3	9.2	-14	80	-149	61
Wales	-2.8	21.1	-32.4	2.5	-9	106	-102	-2
Scotland	-11.9	14.4	-36.3	5.6	-72	171	-219	68
'North'	-11.0	16.5	-34.8	7.4	-493	859	-1386	451
Great Britain	-10.0	16.5	-29.7	12.0	-792	1882	-2112	1611

Notes: (1) Changes calculated from mid-year to mid-year; (2) comparable data for Northern Ireland not available.
Source: Department of Employment.

becomes the barrier that must be broken down and reorganised if fresh room is to be opened up for the next phase of accumulation and economic growth. The problem is that this process of 'creative destruction' will not be spatially neutral in its effects. Those areas most dependent on the industries and jobs in decline, and hence the most in need of rationalisation and reorganisation, are by the same token likely to be the most difficult and painful to restructure. Understandably, in such localities workers and unions are likely to resist attempts by declining industries to slim down capital and shake out labour. In addition, the skills of much of the locally redundant workforce are unlikely to be those required by the new industries and new technologies. As a result, in these areas economic adjustment and adaptation could be slow and conflictive. Conversely, those areas less dependent on and less burdened by the declining industries and structures of the 'old' economy will be simultaneously more attractive as locations for, and quicker to adjust to, the emergent growth sectors of the 'new' (Heim, 1984; Norton, 1986).

The process of economic renewal, particularly if left to market forces, is therefore almost certain to be spatially uneven and divisive. Thus, when Lord Young, Secretary of State for Trade and Industry, argued that because 'there was more industrialisation in the North originally, therefore there now has to be more de-industrialisation' (quoted in *Business*, 1987), to some extent his simple appeal to the inevitable imperatives of economic history was correct. As the post-war boom ground to a halt in the 1970s, it was those areas of the country that historically had been most dependent on old-line and large-scale manufacturing that began to experience the most serious problems of industrial stagnation and the onset of de-industrialisation (Table 4.1). Between 1971–9 the 'north' lost some 493,000 jobs in manufacturing (a decline of 11.0%) compared to a loss of 299,000 (8.7%) in the 'south' of the country. In the latter the decline was entirely attributable to London, whereas in East Anglia, the South-west and the East Midlands manufacturing employment actually increased. Although regional policy certainly created valuable industrial jobs in the northern regions during this period (Moore *et al.*, 1986), through the diversion of investment activity from the South-east and West Midlands to assisted areas in the 'north', these were not enough to stem the rising tide of de-industrialisation there. And this diversion of industry from the 'source' regions of the South-east and West Midlands deprived them of investment at a time when they themselves were beginning to experience job losses in manufacturing.

But during the Thatcher era the situation has deteriorated dramatically. Since 1979 the rate of de-industrialisation has accelerated threefold, involving the loss of more than 2.1 million jobs in the manufacturing sector. While this intense wave of labour shakeout has been much more widespread geographically than that of the 1970s, affecting all regions of Britain except East Anglia, nevertheless there has been a clear 'north–south' differential to the decline (Table 4.1). The fall in manufacturing employment in the 'north' amounted to a staggering 1.386 million (34.3%) between 1979–88, as against a reduction of 726,000 (23.2%) in the 'south'. The greater part of this collapse occurred during the deep recession of the early 1980s. Although surprised by the scale of the shakeout, the government viewed it as the necessary elimination of the unproductive labour and capital that had long plagued British industry and which had been encouraged and protected by years of Keynesian policies and state support. In the words of Mrs Thatcher, the size of the fall in manufacturing employment and the consequent rise in unemployment were the price of the overmanning of the 1960s and 1970s. Moreover, the fact that the shakeout has been much higher in the northern regions is seen as confirmation that it was in this part of the country that the post-war rigidities and inefficiencies responsible for industrial decline were most concentrated; while conversely the less severe de-industrialisation of the 'south', with the exception of parts of London, can be partly explained, it is argued, by the lower incidence there of the problems of industrial maturity, low productivity and disruptive unions found in the 'north'.

In some respects it is difficult to disagree with this view, although the uneven geography of de-industrialisation also reflects regional differences in corporate organisation and structure, in that the 'south' has a higher concentration of secure corporate head offices and a smaller share of vulnerable production and assembly plants than does the 'north'. But equally, both the magnitude and the uneven regional impact of de-industrialisation in the 1980s have been partly of the government's own making. For despite the fact that the Thatcher government came to power at a time when the capitalist world was moving into sharp recession, it introduced policies that had highly deflationary effects on the economy and which added considerably to the decline of industrial employment. The fiscal regime imposed by the government was four times as restrictive as elsewhere in the OECD (Riddell, 1983; pp. 90–1), and the sharp increases in interest rates and the exchange rate dramatically raised the costs and reduced the competitiveness of British industry precisely when domestic and international demand were falling (MacInnes, 1987; p. 65).

Not only did this deflationary squeeze intensify the rationalisation of industry in the older manufacturing regions of northern Britain, the government's abolition of exchange controls enabled many firms there to shift production and jobs to less hostile environments overseas (Cowling, 1986). Between 1979–86 the country's 40 largest manufacturing firms cut their home-based employment by 415,000 while increasing employment abroad by 125,000 (Wintour, 1987). The North-west, North-east and West Midlands regions were particularly hard-hit by this internationalisation process (see Gaffikin and Nickson, 1984; Martin, 1986). And on top of these pressures, the government itself has pushed through an ongoing rationalisation of the nationalised industries. Since 1979 more than 500,000 jobs have disappeared as part of the reorganisation and restructuring schemes imposed in steel, shipbuilding, coal, the national airline, vehicles and the railways. Again it has been the older industrial regions of the 'north', where nationalised industries dominate many local communities, that have borne the brunt of the job losses involved (Hudson, 1986).

The nation's manufacturing base and particularly that of northern Britain is obviously now much 'leaner' and more efficient, with considerably improved levels of productivity and profitability. But it is also much smaller, and this has had both local and national implications. At the macroeconomic level it seems that perhaps too much industrial capacity has been slimmed down or internationalised over the past decade. Certainly, manufacturing production has not be able to keep pace with the post-1983 'Thatcher boom' in domestic demand, fed by rising incomes and especially the explosion of consumer credit (which has more than doubled in real terms since 1983), with the result that huge flows of imports have been sucked in and the manufacturing trade balance has moved into a deteriorating structural deficit (£20.6 billion in 1988). Within the 'north' itself the rapid loss of so many jobs in manufacturing has put acute strain on local labour markets in terms of high unemployment rates and the need for alternative job opportunities. Yet in the face of this de-industrialisation the government has progressively abandoned its support for manufacturing (Martin, 1989b) and instead has increasingly pinned its hope on, and directed its support to, the service sector as the source of compensating job growth. But here too, developments have favoured the 'south' as against the 'north'.

4.3 REGIONAL IMBALANCE IN THE GROWTH OF THE SERVICE ECONOMY

The Thatcher government views the rapid de-industrialisation of Britain not so much as problematic, but rather as part of the process of continuous adjustment to a 'post-industrial' economy in which service activities are the major source of wealth creation, exports and employment growth. Although services already account for the bulk of GDP and total employment, the question of whether they can take over from manufacturing as the basis of the growth dynamic is debatable. Also, there can be no guarantee that services will automatically fill the trade gap that now exists in manufacturing because many services cannot be traded internationally. And to compound the problem, over the past two decades Britain's share of world invisible exports has fallen in percentage terms by more than its share of world trade in manufactured exports (Aldington, 1986; British Invisible Exports Council, 1988). However, it has been the employment-generating potential of services that has attracted particular political attention.

During the 1970s service employment expanded by some 1.88 million, which easily offset the decline of 792,000 in manufacturing (Table 4.1). In broad geographical terms this growth in service employment was evenly spread between the 'north' and 'south': between 1971–9 the northern regions as a whole gained 859,000 new jobs in services (an increase of 16.5%), not far short of the rise of 1.02 million (16.6%) in the 'south'. And in every region of the 'north' except the North-west the number of new service sector jobs was sufficient to compensate for the decline in manufacturing employment. However, during the 1980s both the nature and pattern of job creation in the service sector have been rather different. In contrast to the previous decade when public services were an important source of employment growth, job expansion is now concentrated in the private sector services and within these the professional, financial and business services on the one hand, and the retail, leisure and hotel and catering divisions on the other, are the fastest growing groups. In further contrast to the 1970s, the recent growth of the service economy has been highly unequal across the regions. Between 1979–88 service employment in the four southern regions rose by 1.16 million or 16.1%, thus more than making up for the contraction in manufacturing in that part of the country. By comparison, the numbers employed in services in the 'north' increased by only 493,000 or 7.4%, far from sufficient to fill the gap left by the loss of jobs in manufacturing industry there, and in the North-west and in Wales service employment actually fell.

In fact, across the various regions of the country there has been a clear inverse relation between the scale of de-industrialisation and the growth of the service economy (Martin, 1989c). Those areas which have suffered the highest rates of decline in manufacturing employment have benefited least from service sector development. To some extent this has been a consequence of the very depth of industrial contraction and economic recession in these areas, which has not only had a direct impact on those services associated with and dependent on the local manufacturing base, but also a depressive effect on local incomes. In addition, following the argument advanced earlier, these economically debilitated areas do not offer the most conducive market opportunities for new capital investment, so that their regeneration has been a much slower process. The 'south' on the other hand has led the shift to a service-based 'post-industrial' economy, in part because London and the South-east already had the advantage of a well-established producer, business and financial services sector, and has therefore been particularly favourably placed to benefit from the government's de-regulation and expansion of financial markets, its monetary policies and its various measures to assist small firms and new businesses. Added to this, there are the nearby rural environments of East Anglia and the South-west which offer the sort of accessible non-industrial 'greenfield' locations desired by many new high-tech and related service activities, and which are viewed as having good investment potential by London-based firms and financial institutions.

Thus, in employment terms the restructuring of the economy away from manufacturing towards services engineered to a significant degree by the

Table 4.2 Regional divergence in employment growth, 1971–9 and 1979–88.

	Percentage change in number of employees in employment			
	1971–9	*1979–83*	*1983–8*	*1979–88*
South-east	1.6	–5.2	6.9	1.3
East Anglia	15.6	–0.1	21.2	18.8
South-west	20.6	–5.2	5.5	0.1
East Midlands	14.1	–7.6	9.3	0.3
'South'	6.5	–5.4	8.0	2.0
(absolute change)	691,000	–617,000	849,000	232,000
West Midlands	1.1	–11.2	5.7	–6.5
Yorkshire–Humberside	0.2	–11.9	2.6	–9.5
North-west	–1.5	–13.9	–1.6	–15.4
Northern	1.5	–14.3	4.5	–11.5
Wales	7.4	–14.0	–1.6	–15.4
Scotland	4.9	–9.6	–0.5	–10.2
Northern Ireland	1.3	–7.2	0.0	–7.2
'North'	2.8	–12.5	2.0	–10.8
(absolute change)	323,000	–1,476,000	202,000	–1,274,000)
United Kingdom	4.6	–9.0	5.0	–4.5
(absolute change)	1,014,000	–2,093,000	1,051,000	–1,042,000)

Note: (1) Change calculated from mid-year to mid-year.
Source: Employment Gazette (various).

Thatcher government over the past decade has produced a distinct cleavage between the northern and southern halves of the country. The recovery in employment since 1983 is frequently cited by the government as evidence that its policies have wrought a national 'economic miracle'. Leaving aside the fact that much of that employment growth has consisted of part-time and low-wage jobs, the employment 'miracle' has hardly been nation-wide. Of the million or so net new jobs created since 1983, the great bulk, some 849,000 or 80%, have been located in the four southern regions (Table 4.2). The corresponding increase of only 200,000 or so in the 'north' has been marginal, especially when compared to the decline in employment of nearly 1.5 million that took place in that area of the country during the first period of Thatcher government between 1979–83. By mid-1988 the number of employees in employment in the 'south' had climbed back to more than 230,000 above the mid-1979 level, but in the 'north' the number was still 1.27 million below the mid-1979 position. Since its inception Thatcherism has been presented and prosecuted as a new 'one nation politics' of economic regeneration and remodernisation; instead it has created a 'two nation politics' of increased spatial inequality in socio-economic welfare (Gamble, 1987; Martin, 1987; see also Jessop *et al.,* 1984).

4.4 THE 'POST-INDUSTRIAL' SOUTH: THE THATCHERITE EXEMPLAR OF THE 'NEW BRITAIN'

Undeterred, however, the government has pointed to the success of the 'south' as proof of what its free-market economic policies have achieved and of what the market forces and individual enterprise unleashed by those policies will in time also bring to the 'north'. In several respects, in fact, the south of England is used by Mrs Thatcher and her government as the economic and cultural exemplar of their vision of the post-industrial, post-modern Britain they are seeking to create.

From an economic standpoint this use of the buoyant 'south' by the government to justify its approach to restructuring would seem logical enough. It is here, as we have just seen, that the recovery of employment has been significant. In addition, it is from the 'south' that the rapid upturn in the rate of economic growth since 1983 has emanated, and where levels of per capita output are highest (Table 4.3). It is also in this part of Britain that the sort of

Table 4.3 Growing gap in regional wealth generation, 1971–1987.

	GDP Per head relative to UK average					Percent growth in real GDP per head
	1971	1975	1979	1983	1987	1983–7
South-east	113.7	112.9	116.2	116.4	118.5	23.7
Greater London	124.5	123.9	128.4	124.4	129.4	25.3
Rest of South-east	105.5	103.7	107.9	111.1	111.6	22.5
East Anglia	93.6	92.9	94.4	96.6	99.8	30.6
South-west	94.8	90.6	91.3	94.8	94.0	23.5
East Midlands	96.6	96.1	96.6	96.5	95.1	20.4
'South'	106.7	104.9	108.7	108.9	110.4	23.7
West Midlands	102.8	100.1	96.2	90.4	91.6	21.9
Yorkshire–Humberside	93.3	94.1	92.7	92.4	92.7	19.6
North-west	96.2	96.3	96.1	93.9	92.8	16.9
Northern	86.9	93.6	90.7	92.0	88.9	13.7
Wales	88.3	88.7	85.2	86.0	82.0	14.9
Scotland	93.0	97.1	94.6	97.3	94.5	14.4
Northern Ireland	74.3	76.6	78.2	79.0	77.4	19.5
'North'	93.6	94.6	93.1	91.9	90.6	17.3
United Kingdom	100.0	100.0	100.0	100.0	100.0	20.7

Notes: (1) GDP measured at factor cost in current prices; (2) UK base excludes Continental Shelf; (3) real GDP growth measured at factor cost in 1985 constant prices; (4) figures for 'South' and 'North' calculated as population weighted averages of regional estimates.
Source: Economic Trends (various).

activities identified by the government as forming the basis of a renewed economy are concentrated. Thus, the 'south' dominates the national high-technology, producer, financial and research and development services: the South-east region alone accounts for 50% of national employment in these sectors (Martin, 1988b). Yet further, the 'south' leads in the development of the two forms of capitalist enterprise that have become central pillars of Thatcherite economic ideology: large multinational financial institutions that generate considerable overseas invisible earnings, and the small-firm sector that is seen as epitomising individual entrepreneurship and innovation. Socially and politically the 'south' is also Thatcher land. It has the lowest rates of unionisation amongst the workforce, the highest proportion of employment in services, the largest proportion of workers in the professional, managerial, technical and scientific occupational classes and the greatest concentration of shareholders (see Martin, 1988a). Given these features, and fuelled by its leading role in the emergent growth economy, the 'south' of Britain has become the primary stronghold of Mrs Thatcher's politics of 'popular capitalism' and 'enterprise culture'. It is not surprising, therefore, that this area is also the Conservative's main electoral base.

Of course, this is not to suggest that virtually all economic growth, employment and wealth is concentrated in Tory southern England, or even the South-east, or that the remainder of the country is a zone of relentless economic depression and social deprivation. As the government itself has continually stressed, there are successful areas in the 'north' as well as in the 'south'. Indeed, the use of individual localities as exemplars has been a key device in the government's political rhetoric. In particular, jewels in the southern crown such as Cambridge, Milton Keynes, Swindon, Crawley, Newbury, Bracknell and Basingstoke, all low-unemployment, fast-growing, high-tech or service towns, are singled out as model examples of the new flexible capitalism that other localities across the nation should aspire to and emulate. That such growth towns contain their own sharp internal economic and social divides (SEEDS, 1987; Crang and Martin, 1989; Murray, 1988) is rarely acknowledged. And whether the specific experience of these southern towns can or should be replicated elsewhere is surely open to question. The government and its supporters claim that the economic revival of northern towns will be best achieved by relying on the market forces and minimal state support that are alleged to have promoted the rapid recovery of areas in the 'south', and point to specific cities such as Chester, Glasgow, Bradford and even Liverpool, as areas where market forces are starting to take effect as local councils, indigenous entrepreneurs and businesses moving from the 'south' are beginning to rebuild the economic base.

The reality is that the south and east of the country has been much better placed than the 'north' to recover from the effects of de-industrialisation and to lead the growth process, in part because of its more favourable inherited economic structure, but also in part because of the extent to which the economy of this area of Britain is underwritten by the state. What is too little understood is that much of the success of the South-east is not just attributable to market forces. There is of course an economic market place with its own logic and momentum. But added to that market, and a major factor shaping how and where it operates, is the discretion of government in relation to public spending, procurement, the centralisation of power and the location of private investment and prosperity. For decades the 'south' has been the most subsidised part of the country, and many of Mrs Thatcher's policies have actually increased this spatial bias in state support and further encouraged the agglomeration of wealth and jobs in the 'south'. Thus the government's reductions in personal taxes, its various social capital and infra-structural investment programmes, its defence procurement spending, its schemes for new and expanding small businesses, its de-regulation of financial markets and its sale of public industries have all helped to boost economic activity more in the 'south' than in the 'north'.

This is not to ignore the urban and regional aid that has gone to the north of Britain over the past decade but, as Michael Heseltine (1988, pp. 7–8) commented, regional incentives are small when compared with the real sub-sidies, the counter-regional subsidies, amounting to billions of pounds a year which are likely to concentrate wealth in the 'south'. And, in any case, since 1979 regional policy has been considerably weakened. Under the Thatcher government, spending on regional industrial assistance has fallen by more than 25% in real terms, and current policy can only be described as confused. While Peter Walker, Secretary of State for Wales, emphasises the importance of the interventionist regional policy that he practises in that region, Lord Young, the Secretary of State for Trade and Industry, does not speak of regional policy but plays up the role of Thatcherism in creating the overall business climate which he believes has made the British regions successful in recent months in the international bidding game for inward foreign invest-ment (Nissan and Fujitsu in the North-east, Bosch in South Wales, Toyota in Derbyshire). But at the same time that inward investment appears to have become the government's preferred form of 'regional policy' for the 'north', Mrs Thatcher is dismantling the Scottish Development Agency, an instrument generally considered to have been successful in attracting foreign investment into Scotland.

The dual notion, advanced particularly by Lord Young, that the dynamism of the southern economy is solely the product of market forces and is some-thing that can be expected to be reproduced spontaneously in the 'north' simply by making the business climate there more competitive is, then, rather misleading. Not only is the Thatcherite paradigm of a free-market post-industrial society a false characterisation of the 'south', the 'freeing' of the northern economy though necessary is unlikely to be sufficient to regenerate the 'north' unless many of the key institutions of economic and political power that underpin the southern economy are decentralised. Although the dependence of the 'north' on heavy industry and manufacturing has been reduced in recent years as a result of the restructuring process, this part of the economy still differs significantly in structure and operation from the 'south'. The latter, containing as it does the core of the nation's financial system and high-tech sector is linked into different international markets, is subject to different pressures, and responds in a different way to government policies than the northern economy, which has only just begun to develop new industries and services to add to its streamlined manufacturing base. Over the past two years or so the latent contradictions of this regional imbalance have begun to impinge on the performance of the overall economy and the government's economic policies.

4.5 THE UNEVEN THATCHER BOOM: CONSEQUENCES AND CONSTRAINTS

Throughout the post-war period regional imbalance has been a recurring constraint on British economic growth and management, although few governments have accorded the problem the attention it warrants. Given their different economic structures, the different regions of the country contribute in different ways to national output, exports, imports and inflationary pressures, and similarly respond differentially to government policies and international conditions. Both expansionary and deflationary macroeconomic policies are likely, therefore, to have different effects in different regions. This has been the case during both the Keynesian and Thatcher eras (Martin, 1989b). For example, in the 1960s the expansionist position adopted by the governments of that period towards the national economy generated inflation in the tighter, higher-wage labour markets of the South-east and West Midlands well before the full utilisation of labour and industrial capacity was reached in the higher unemployment regions of the industrial periphery of the country. In this way the uneven geography of growth imparted an inherent inflationary bias to the national economy, and this contributed to the need for the periodic deflationary intervention that characterised the 'stop-go' policy syndrome that emerged in the course of that decade.

Twenty years on, the same basic problem has reappeared in relation to Thatcherism. As we have seen, both the recession of the early 1980s and the subsequent recovery have been uneven across the regions. From the mid-1980s that recovery quickened into a boom. The government talks of this boom as a national phenomenon, the result of its liberalisation policies. But a different picture emerges if this 'national' boom is disaggregated geographically. In the first place it has been a boom focused in the 'south'. Between 1983–8 real GDP per head grew by 23.7% in the 'south' compared to 17.0% in the rest of the nation (Table 4.3). Within these two broad divisions the most rapid growth has been in Greater London (25.3%) and East Anglia (30.6%),

Table 4.4 Inflationary over-heating of the 'south' during the Thatcher boom.

| | Percentage increase, 1983–8, in | |
	average house prices	average hourly earnings
South-east	156.7	52.5
Greater London	169.8	55.0
Rest of South East	138.6	48.9
East Anglia	148.3	43.1
South-west	115.5	42.7
East Midlands	92.0	40.7
'South'	145.9	47.3
West Midlands	90.4	40.4
Yorkshire–Humberside	57.6	38.1
North-west	57.7	39.3
Northern	43.1	36.6
Wales	58.1	36.0
Scotland	29.8	38.8
'North'	56.7	37.6
Great Britain	104.8	43.9

Notes: (1) Average hourly earnings refer to full-time adult males, and exclude effects of overtime; (2) house price data based on mortgage approvals.
Sources: Nationwide Building Society (Housing Statistics Division), London; *New Earnings Survey (Part E)*, 1983 and 1988.

and the slowest in the northern region (13.7%), Wales (14.9%) and Scotland (14.4%). By 1986 the boom in the 'south', and especially in the congested South-east, had begun to fuel a process of inflationary over-heating, manifested by fast wage growth and a spiralling of house and property prices. Over the 1983–8 period male average hourly earnings in the South-east rose 50% faster than those in the 'north', and average house prices three times as fast (Table 4.4).

The government sees this inflationary pressure in the 'south' as the product of economic success, and argues that the rising costs and congestion in this part of the country should trigger off automatic market mechanisms to diffuse that success to the rest of Britain because 'the workings of the market mean that industries are forced further and further north to take business opportunities' (Lord Young, quoted in *Business,* 1987). Recent office decentralisation suggests that such cost-induced dispersion is occurring: examples include Barclays' move of head office staff from London to Coventry, National Provident's move from Kent to Cardiff, the relocation of insurance companies and Lloyd's Bank to Bristol, the Bank of England's Registrar's

Department to Gloucester, and the transfer of Shell Chemicals' head office to Chester. Most of the moves, however, have been to areas in regions bordering on the South-east: the farther from London the slower the growth and the less chance a location has of being chosen as a destination for decentralising business. Furthermore, for the most part it is the routine functions that have moved out of the South-east, leaving the strategic functions in London and its environs. Thus, while the growth core in the 'south' may be moving outwards, the rate and extent of that dispersion is limited, and there is still a regional hierarchy within it. The South-east, at the top, remains the main focus of accumulation based on the leading edge of the private economy and the control centres of the public sector.

Even within the 'south' itself the boom has been very uneven, a boom of some places and people rather than others. The problems of inner London's so-called 'crescent of depression' contrast markedly with the affluence and growth of the rest of the city. But there are other 'south–south' divides within the region, for example between the lagging industrial towns of high 'Fordism' (Basildon, Luton, Bedford, Oxford East) and the expanding centres of the new 'post Fordist' era (Newbury, Cambridge, Bracknell); and between the depressed coastal towns and the hinterland (SEEDS, 1987; Murray, 1988). The high unemployment rates in the older industrial towns and coastal areas contrast sharply with the growing problems of acute labour shortage in the high-tech and commuter 'sunrise corridors' along the M4 and M11 motorways. In these areas, full or nearly full employment, skill shortages and high housing costs have created serious labour recruitment problems for employers, both in the sunrise and associated industries themselves and in consumer and public services. Increasingly private sector employers are resorting to new strategies, such as generous fringe benefits, new flexible work shifts, jobsharing, contract arrangements (often involving labour brought down from northern regions), casualisation and even retired workers, in an attempt to attract labour. For the professional, technical and skilled classes this labour and skills crisis in parts of the 'south' has meant higher wages and improved benefits; for many of the unskilled and the additional females drawn into employment, however, it has meant enforced restriction to part-time, low-paid and 'flexible' jobs. The boom, then, has increased the divisions between core or primary and peripheral or secondary labour.

Within the 'south', and especially the South-east, the boom in growth has strained the limits of supply. Labour shortages, inadequate skills, rising wages, lack of housing, excessive house prices and congestion of transport services, these are the contradictions of the boom that threaten to constrain the very economic renewal that is used by the Thatcher government to symbolise the success of its policies. As the national rate of inflation has accelerated the government has sought to dampen the growth in demand by a new round of deflationary interest rate rises. Those inflationary pressures have emanated primarily from the South-east. The irony is that the over-heating of the 'south', itself a product of Thatcherism, now appears to be hindering the government's anti-inflation goals. And to the extent that retaliatory deflationary action by the government succeeds in cutting the boom in demand, it does so as much in the slower-growing 'north' as in the 'south', and thereby does little to reduce the imbalance between these two broad areas of the country or the structural constraints that this imbalance implies for the national economy. The task of regenerating the 'north' without creating bottlenecks and inflation in the 'south' continues to pose a major challenge to the Thatcher project and its market-based philosophy.

REFERENCES

Aldington, Lord, 'Britain's Manufacturing Industry', *Royal Bank of Scotland Review*, **151**, 3–13 (1986).

Allen, J. and Massey, D. (eds), *Restructuring Britain: The Economy in Question*, (Sage: London, 1988).

Armstrong, H. and Riley, C., 'The North–South controversy and Britain's regional problem', *Local Economy*, **2**, 93–105 (1987).

British Invisible Exports Council, *Invisible Trade in the World Economy, 1972–1986*, (BIEC: London, 1988).

Business, 'Across the North–South divide', pp. 45–58 (September 1987).

Champion, T. and Green, A., 'Local prosperity and the North–South Divide: winners and losers in 1980s Britain', *Report*, University of Warwick: Institute of Employment Research: Warwick, 1988).

Cooke, P., 'Britain's new spatial paradigm: technology, locality and society in transition', *Environment and Planning*, **A19**, 1289–301 (1987).

Cowling, K., 'The internationalisation of production and deindustrialisation', in *Technological Change, Industrial Restructuring and Regional Development* (eds Amin, A. and Goddard, J.) (Allen & Unwin: London, 1986).

Crang, P. and Martin, R. L., 'Mrs Thatcher's Vision of the New Britain and the Other Sides of the "Cambridge Phenomenon"', *Society and Space* (1989) (in press).

Feinstein, C., 'Economic growth since 1870: Britain's performance in international perspective', *Oxford Review of Economic Policy*, **4, 1**, 1–13 (1988).

Fry, G. K., 'Economic policy making and planning 1945–70', *Public Administration Bulletin*, **18**, 3–22 (1975).

Gaffikin, F. and Nickson, A. *Jobs Crisis and the Multinationals: The Case of the West Midlands* (Birmingham Trade Union Resource Centre: Birmingham, 1984).

Gamble, A., *Britain in Economic Decline* (Macmillan: Basingstoke, 1981).

Gamble, A., *Thatcherism and the Politics of Inequality*, Paper presented at the Annual Conference of the Institute of British Geographers, Portsmouth Polytechnic, January 1987.

Gamble, A., *The Free Economy and The Strong State* (Macmillan: Basingstoke, 1988).

Glyn, A., Hughes, A., Lipietz, A. and Singh, A., 'The rise and fall of the Golden Age', *Working Paper No. 884*, University of Cambridge: Department of Applied Economics (1988).

Harvey, D., *The Limits to Capital*, (Basil Blackwell: Oxford, 1982).

Heim, C., 'Decline and Renewal in Britain and the United States: The Role of Less Developed Areas Within Mature Economies', unpublished typescript, Department of Economics: Harvard University (1984).

Heseltine, Rt. Hon. M., Speech to the Brick Development Association, London, 18 May, 1988.

Hoover, K. and Plant, R., *Conservative Capitalism in Britain and the United States*, (Routledge: London, 1989).

Hudson, R., 'Producing an industrial wasteland: capital, labour and the State in North-east England', in *The Geography of De-industrialisation* (eds Martin R. L. and Rowthorn, R. E.) (Macmillan: Basingstoke, 1986).

Jessop, B., Bonnett, K., Bromley, S. and Ling, T., 'Authoritarian Populism, Two Nations and Thatcherism', *New Left Review*, **147**, 32–60 (1984).

King, D., *The New Right: Politics, Markets and Citizenship*, (Macmillan: Basingstoke, 1987).

Lash, S. and Urry, J. *The End of Organised Capitalism* (Polity Press: Cambridge, 1987).

Leadbeater, C., 'New Times: back to the future', *Marxism Today*, pp. 13–17 (May 1989).

Lewis, J. and Townsend, A. R., *The North–South Divide: Regional Change in Britain in the 1980s* (Paul Chapman: London, 1989).

MacInnes, J., *Thatcherism at Work* (Open University Press: Milton Keynes, 1987).

Mann, M., The decline of Great Britain, in *States, War and Capitalism*, (Basil Blackwell: Oxford, 1988).

Martin, R. L., 'Thatcherism and Britain's industrial landscape', in *The Geography of De-industrialisation* (eds Martin, R. L. and Rowthorn, R. E.) (Macmillan: Basingstoke, 1986).

Martin, R. L., 'Mrs Thatcher's Britain: a tale of two nations', *Environment and Planning*, **A19**, 571–4 (1987).

Martin, R. L., 'The political economy of Britain's North–South Divide', *Transactions of the Institute of British Geographers, New Series*, **13**, **4**, 389–418 (1988a).

Martin, R. L., 'Industrial Capitalism in transition: the contemporary transformation of the British space economy', in *Uneven Redevelopment: Cities and Regions in Transition* (eds Massey, D. and Allen, J.) (Hodder & Stoughton: London, 1988b).

Martin, R. L., 'The reorganisation of regional theory: alternative perspectives on the changing capitalist space economy', *Geoforum*, **20**, 187–201 (1989a).

Martin, R. L., 'De-industrialisation and State intervention: Keynesianism, Thatcherism and the regions', in *The Political Geography of Contemporary Britain* (ed. Mohan, J.) (Macmillan: Basingstoke, 1989b).

Martin, R. L., 'The New Economics and politics of regional restructuring: the British experience', in *Regional Policy at the Crossroads: European Perspectives* (eds Albrechts, L., Moulaert, F., Roberts, P. and Swyngedouw, E.) (Jessica Kingsley: London, 1989c).

Massey, D., *Spatial Divisions of Labour: Social Structures and the Geography of Production* (Macmillan: Basingstoke 1984).

Massey, D., 'Geography Matters', *Geographical Review*, **1**, **1**, 2–9 (1987).

Matthews, R. C. O., Feinstein, C. H. and Odling-Smee, J. C., *British Economic Growth, 1856–1973*, (Stanford University Press: Stanford, 1982).

Moore, B., Rhodes, J. and Tyler, P., *The Effects of Government Regional Economic Policy*, (HMSO: London, 1986).

Murray, R., *Crowding Out: Boom and Crisis in the South East* (South East Economic Development Strategy: Stevenage, 1988).

Newton, S. and Porter, D., *Modernization Frustrated: The Politics of Industrial Decline Since 1900* (Unwin Hyman: London, 1988).

Norton, R. D., 'Industrial Policy and American Renewal', *Journal of Economic Literature*, **XXIV**, **1**, 1–40 (1986).

Riddell, P., *The Thatcher Government*, (Martin Robertson: Oxford 1983).

SEEDS, *South–South Divide* (South East Economic Development Strategy: Stevenage, 1987).

Wintour, P., 'Manufacturers shift spending to overseas jobs', *The Guardian*, 5 May 1987.

Wells, J., 'Miracles and Myths', *Marxism Today*, 22–25 (May 1989).

PART III

PRODUCTION PROCESS AND LABOUR MARKET

5 THE PRODUCTIVITY MIRACLE?

Peter Nolan

> One of the most striking economic developments of the 1980s has been the large improvement in the productivity of manufacturing. (*Economic Progress Report*, January–February, 1987).

Not for the first time, Britain's industrial productivity has become a subject of intense controversy and debate. Past interest in this topic was fuelled by accumulating evidence of a major productivity shortfall in Britain, as compared with other leading capitalist economies. Now, however, the issue is under the spotlight because, after ten years of Conservative government, industry is supposedly experiencing a renaissance. The performance of manufacturing has attracted most attention. For unlike the service sector, in which productivity has advanced by an average of less than 1% per annum since 1979, British manufacturing boasts one of the highest productivity growth rates in Europe, is some way ahead of the United States, and now stands in sight of Japan's remarkable record.

The government, predictably enough, has linked these performance gains to its policies on taxation, privatisation and industrial relations; as it were, the productivity figures have become 'judge and jury' of its supply-side strategy But the government is by no means alone in arguing that Britain's manufacturing performance has been miraculously transformed under its stewardship. Among economists there is considerable support for the proposition that industry is leaner and more efficient than it has been for many years.

Taking manufacturing as its focus, this chapter challenges this cosy consensus by arguing that the long-standing sources of structural weakness in production have not been tackled. Recent productivity gains do not stem from a fundamental reorganisation of the forces of production in Britain, but instead are the product of a series of step-by-step changes dictated by short- rather than long-term aims and perspectives.

The post-war productivity record is briefly reviewed in the first section. Section two focuses on developments since 1979, and considers the argument that there has been a trend shift in the underlying rate of productivity growth.

The discussion focuses on Muellbauer's influential econometric study (Muellbauer, 1986), for this has formed the starting point for subsequent debate. Section three develops the argument that the basic character of the manufacturing sector in Britain has not been transformed by the Government's supply side measures. It suggests that the policies of the present have entrenched the weaknesses of the past. The main ingredients of the recent productivity surge are discussed, as is the relationship between productivity and production efficiency. The chapter concludes by addressing the question of whether or not the recent gains are likely to endure.

5.1 THE PRODUCTIVITY RECORD

The analysis of productivity is fraught with empirical problems. How should productivity be measured? What procedures should be used to sum heterogeneous capital and labour inputs? And how, in time series analysis, should trend and cyclical movements be disentangled? These difficulties are formidable enough, but they are underpinned by deeper conceptual issues which have scarcely been addressed, let alone resolved in the economics literature.

Particularly salient is the dynamic relationship between social and economic structure and industrial performance. Given that productivity is the *outcome* of a collective social process, how should the interplay of economic, technical and social relations in production be conceptualised? Economists have traditionally eschewed an analysis of relations *in* production, preferring instead to focus on the measurement of outcomes. But the events of the recent past have forced such issues to the forefront of debate. Are recent productivity gains in Britain sustainable, the product of enduring social and economic changes, or do they merely reflect short-term, cyclical factors? An adequate response to this question requires detailed knowledge of the evolution of the key economic and social forces acting in and on production. Yet, as we shall see, most contributions to this subject have lacked the direct evidence and conceptual tools to deal with these issues.

Ironically, while economists have directed most of their effort towards the task of measurement, the two most widely used descriptive statistics – labour productivity and total factor productivity – are in many respects profoundly inadequate. The former is a measure of output per employee (or employee hour) and is often presented as a rough and ready index of labour efficiency. In fact, however, the figures for labour productivity say nothing whatsoever about the conditions of work, variations in physical capital, plant layout, or management performance, all of which might be expected to have a bearing on labour efficiency.

Total factor productivity conveys more information because it allows for inputs in production other than labour, but it is estimated as a *residual*. It is defined as the rate of output growth minus the weighted sum of the growth of the inputs, the weights being determined by each input's share of total income. Presented as a broad measure of technical progress, as a record of the gains in output which are not attributable to inputs, total factor productivity has in practice served as a crude 'catch all' term. As discussed more fully below, the concept has been used to describe the dynamic aspects of capitalist production which are not directly theorised in mainstream economics.

With these important caveats in mind, what does the productivity record show? The evidence on labour productivity is pretty clear-cut. Workers in Britain produce less output per unit of labour time than their counterparts in other advanced capitalist countries. The United States built up a vast productivity lead over Britain, equivalent on average to a threefold differential, long before the Second World War. Yet Britain's relative decline within Europe started much later, during the 1950s and 1960s. In 1945, living standards and the level of productivity in Britain were among the highest in Europe, but after a decade of sluggish productivity growth, Germany and France began to pull ahead. As Table 5.1 reveals, this gap widened during the 1960s and 1970s. Comparing the growth of labour productivity in six countries, it shows that Britain's performance lagged behind all the other countries with the exception of the United States. Thus, while Japan and most of Europe succeeded in eroding the United States' productivity lead during this period, the differential between Britain and the United States remained more or less constant.

Table 5.2 focuses on total factor productivity growth and compares Britain's performance since 1979 with the previous two decades and also with the other countries. The data are grouped into three periods: before and after the oil crisis in 1973, and post-1979. Before 1973, total factor productivity in Britain grew at an average annual rate of 3.3%, somewhat faster than the United States but much slower than in Japan, France, Italy and Belgium. After 1973, Britain experienced no growth at all. Other countries also experienced a productivity slowdown, but (with the exception of the United States) on a far less dramatic scale than in Britain.

Table 5.1 Productivity: real value added in manufacturing per person employed. Average annual percentage rates of change.

	1960–8	*1968–73*	*1973–9*	*1979–86*	*1960–86*
United States	3.2	3.5	0.9	3.3	2.7
Japan	9.0	10.4	5.0	6.3[a]	7.5
France	6.8	5.8	3.9	n.a	5.0
West Germany	4.7	4.5	3.1	2.0	3.5
Italy	7.2	5.6	2.9	3.6	4.9
Belgium	4.9	8.2	5.0	4.9	5.5
United Kingdom	3.4	3.9	0.6	4.1	3.0

Note: (a) 1979–1985.
Source: OECD, *Historical Statistics,* 1960–86.

Table 5.2 Total factor productivity growth in manufacturing (hourly)[a]. Average annual percentage change.

	Pre-1973[b]	1973–9	1979–85
United States	2.6	0.4	2.4
Japan	6.9	2.4	4.4
France	5.4	3.0	1.9
West Germany	3.6	2.8	2.0
Italy	5.6	2.1	1.6
Belgium	6.6	5.0	3.7
United Kingdom	3.3	0.0	2.3

Notes: (a) Output is valued added at constant prices. (b) The starting years are as follows: United States, 1960; Japan, 1966; Germany, 1961; France, 1964; United Kingdom and Italy, 1960; Belgium, 1962.
Source: OECD, *Economic Outlook*, December 1987.

Since 1979, total factor productivity has grown faster in Britain than in France, West Germany and Italy. If the relevant point of comparison is Britain's record before 1973, however, recent figures appear less favourable. Thus, one plausible interpretation of this record is that Britain has begun to recover in the 1980s from the effects of the world-wide economic crisis and recession of the 1970s and, in consequence, has seen a return to the underlying productivity trend which prevailed in the 1960s and early 1970s. Such an interpretation, as we shall see, is at variance with much of the recent literature on this topic.

5.2 THE 1980s 'BREAKTHROUGH'

Many economists have argued that Britain's declining fortunes have been checked and reversed since the Conservatives took power in 1979. Maynard thus recently argued that, as a result of rapid productivity advances and greatly improved production efficiency, manufacturing in Britain 'is now in a better position to take oil's place' (Maynard, 1988: 174). Other writers, Crafts (1988a) and Metcalf (1988) for example, have pointed to the diminishing productivity gap between Britain and the other leading industrial nations, while Muellbauer (1986) has suggested that the conditions for sustainable high productivity growth in Britain may now be in place. Muellbauer's analysis of manufacturing has been especially influential, so it is important to look at it in detail.

5.2.1 Trends and cycles

Muellbauer examined the productivity record since 1956. He estimated a Cobb–Douglas production function relating output to input (physical capital and labour) and a shifting time trend to capture movements in total factor productivity. Because productivity is estimated as a residual it is critically important that input and output are recorded accurately, for any undetected measurement errors will feed directly into (and hence bias) the productivity results. Muellbauer's study has proved significant for two connected reasons: first, it attempted to disentangle underlying productivity trends from short-term, cyclical movements; and secondly, it corrected for the most glaring deficiencies in the official data on output and labour input.

Muellbauer gave most weight to the labour input. Based on paid-for hours, the official statistics provide an *extensive* measure of labour input and yield no information about labour *intensity*. For Muellbauer, however, variations in labour intensity hold the key to an understanding of the cyclical shifts in labour productivity in the 1980s.

Labour utilisation rates may rise or fall either because of changes in the intensity of work – perhaps reflecting power shifts between employer and employee – or because employers deliberately 'hoard' labour as a cost-cutting strategy. This distinction is elaborated in section three. For the moment, note that Muellbauer's account centres on hoarding and the idea, put forward many years ago by Oi (1962), that labour is a quasi-fixed factor of production. The implication is that firms face potentially large hiring and firing costs, and hence will respond to sudden shifts in output by varying labour utilisation rates rather than employment levels. The gap between paid-for hours and actual hours worked will rise as output falls and contract as output rises.

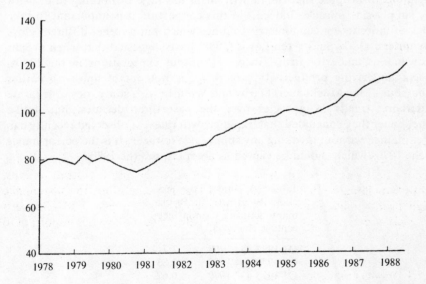

Table 5.1 UK manufacturing productivity 1978–88, output per person employed 1985=100. (*Source*: CSO, *Economic Trends*.)

Figure 5.1 shows that output per employee fell sharply in 1979–80 and again in 1985–6, while the intervening period was characterised by recovery and rapid productivity growth. These amplitudes, on Muellbauer's reckoning, can be almost fully accounted for by changes in the labour utilisation rate. Labour utilisation dropped dramatically in 1979–80 as the level of output collapsed; thereafter it began to rise as firms shed workers (approximately one and a half million were sacked), and after a period of stability it fell again in 1985. Muellbauer's account stops in 1986, but the force of his analysis has relevance for the past couple of years. Since 1986 manufacturing output has surged, but there has not been a corresponding rise in employment. In fact, employment has continued to decline. The result is that utilisation rates have increased as employers have sought to raise output without incurring additional hiring and training costs. We return to these issues in section three.

What about the underlying productivity trend? According to Muellbauer, a trend shift in total factor productivity growth can be detected from about Q3 1980. On his reading, there has been a marked and sustainable shift in supply side performance. His estimates for the first half of the 1980s and the preceding 25 years are given in Table 5.3.

These figures, it should be stressed, are open to different interpretations, notwithstanding the fact that most writers cites them to confirm the force of Mrs Thatcher's economic 'cure' (e.g., Ball, 1988; Maynard, 1988). While there seems little reason to resist the implication that total factor productivity has been growing faster on average in the 1980s than the 1970s, it is by no means ridiculous to propose that the improvement has little or nothing to do with any supply-side miracle. Indeed, in this connection it is important to take stock of more recent econometric findings which put a rather different gloss on matters. Darby and Wren-Lewis (1988) have suggested that when proper allowance is made for firms' 'incorrect' output expectations in the 1970s, 'recent underlying productivity growth ... is not out of line with earlier behaviour'. Like Muellbauer, Darby and Wren-Lewis's study tries to separate underlying trends from cycles over the past three decades, but unlike Muellbauer they concluded that 'rapid growth rates ... observed recently can be explained without invoking any supply side miracle'. It is the performance of the 1970s which should be viewed as aberrant, not the 1980s.

Table 5.3 Total factor productivity growth in British manufacturing (annual percentage changes).

Q1 1956–Q3 1959	1.71
Q4 1959–Q4 1972	2.63
Q1 1973–Q2 1979	0.62
Q3 1979–Q2 1980	−1.93
Q3 1980–1985	2.76

In citing Darby and Wren-Lewis's results it is not intended to imply that they are sufficient to overturn the miracle thesis. This would be quite wrong, for neither this study nor Muellbauer's is able to shed any direct light on supply-side behaviour, particularly the sort of structural changes in production which proponents of the miracle argument allege are at the root of recent performance gains. Indeed, both studies could be interpreted as saying more about changing demand side conditions than the supply side.

5.2.2 Measurement problems

With these qualifications in mind, and in pursuit of a more sober assessment of the productivity evidence, it is important to record some of the measurement problems which Muellbauer encountered and which he was unable to overcome. As Muellbauer himself pointed out, he was forced to rely on the official capital stock series which is limited in two important respects. Like the series on labour input, the capital stock figures make no allowance for variations in utilisation rates and they are constructed on the assumption that retirements from the capital stock occur at a constant rate, irrespective of wider economic conditions. Both assumptions, however, seem highly dubious and all the more so given the dramatic shifts in economic activity which occurred during the 1970s and 1980s.

Muellbauer focused on the consequences of the oil price rise in 1973. Suppose, as seems likely, profit-seeking firms switched away from energy intensive production processes towards more labour-intensive techniques. In all probability, both the rate of capital scrapping and the rate of capital utilisation would have changed: more plant and equipment would have been scrapped where substitution was an option, and where it was not utilisation rates would have fallen. By failing to record these changes, official statistics in effect overstate the magnitude of the capital input in that period. In the 1980s, in contrast, official statistics have probably understated the growth of capital stock. For if large quantities of capital had been scrapped during the 1970s and again in the crisis of 1979-80, thereafter the scrapping rate probably fell below the constant rate assumed in the official series.

Now if Muellbauer is right about scrapping, then his estimates for total factor productivity growth include potentially large capital stock measurement errors. In short, his estimates for 1973-9 and post-1980 *understate* and *overstate*, respectively, the true rate of total factor productivity growth. This raises a further issue.

If the capital stock has been growing faster than official statistics suggest for the 1980s, then it is possible (as Muellbauer proposed) 'that the trend rate of growth of output per head can indeed stay permanently higher than its 1973-80 rate'. Certainly this is the view taken by Metcalf (1988) and Maynard (1988), who cite Muellbauer on this point. Yet this is to give Muellbauer's conjecture far too much weight, for there are good reasons for arguing that a higher rate of capital stock *retention* in the 1980s is alone not sufficient to guarantee 'permanently higher' growth rates.

First, it is necessary to consider what has been happening to the *quality* of the capital stock. Muellbauer, it should be stressed, did not ignore this issue. Among the various hypotheses which he put forward to account for recent advances in productivity was the so-called 'batting average' effect. Basically, the idea is that the average quality of the capital stock may have been given a significant, once-and-for-all boost by the massive shake-out of plant and equipment in the early 1980s. By removing the 'tail enders', the least efficient capitals, scrapping may have boosted, again on a once-and-for-all basis, the average level of productivity. However plausible this argument may seem, it has since been investigated and rejected by Oulton (1987). Oulton found that larger plants were disproportionately represented among the casualties of the early 1980s, and that while these plants tended to be less profitable, they were more, not less productive.

Secondly, and of related significance, is the qualitative impact of new capital formation. Any deterioration in quality due to scrapping may have been offset by the introduction of new capital equipment, embodying the latest technical advances. This seems unlikely, as manufacturing investment more or less collapsed during the first half of the 1980s. In a number of sectors (metals, mechanical engineering, motor vehicles) it had halved by 1982, and though there have been some signs of recovery since then it has yet to reach its previous peak level of 1979. This appalling investment record is to some extent confirmed by the figures for capacity utilisation, which show that despite the modest growth of output over the past decade, the utilisation rate has surpassed its previous peak of 1973 (*Economic Survey of Europe*, 1988). It thus seems reasonable to suppose, in light of Oulton's evidence and the investment record, that the average quality of physical capital has deteriorated.

Thirdly, there is the question of labour force skills. There are two distinct points here. Muellbauer's productivity estimates make no allowance for compositional changes in labour force 'quality', which is surprising given that economic analysis posits human capital (the accumulation of general and specific skills) as a key determinant of productivity. In the same way that compositional changes in the capital stock are relevant to the argument, one might expect compositional changes in the labour force to have some significance. Quite apart from this, any adequate assessment of the sustainability of recent productivity advances ought surely to take account of the changing stock of labour force skills, the provision for training and so forth, yet Muellbauer says nothing whatsoever about such issues. These, and related questions, are taken up in section three, where we set out our own analysis of the main ingredients of the productivity record. Before doing so, however, it is useful to amplify our earlier criticisms of the concept of total factor productivity, and the method of growth accounting used by Muellbauer and others.

5.2.3 Growth accounting: a licence to speculate?

The method of growth accounting (total factor productivity analysis) has attracted numerous critics over the years, for it is based upon a number of strong and highly restrictive assumptions: homogeneous factor inputs, perfect and universal market competition and constant returns to scale. Exponents of this technique usually take the view that, however imperfect, it is able to shed some light on the scale and sources of economic growth. Our aim here is not to restate well-known criticisms, but rather to highlight a further, critically disabling weakness of this approach. Growth accounting entails a forced separation between economic and social relations in production.

As noted, the tendency in economics to treat production as a narrow, technical relationship between inputs and output is deeply entrenched. In growth accounting, as we have seen with Muellbauer, primary emphasis is given to (input) measurement problems, while social relations are subsumed under the residual, total factor productivity term. The significance of social structure for the growth process can scarcely be denied, however, for it is usually the case that total factor productivity is the largest element in the estimated equation. Nevertheless, when it comes to the specification of the connections between social and economic forces growth accounting has encouraged the worst kind of ungrounded speculation. This happens because social structure enters the argument at the end, and not the beginning; it is tacked on as an afterthought. The point is well illustrated with the example of industrial relations, which has been one of the most keenly advocated explanations of past and present productivity trends.

Muellbauer thus suggested, without pursuing the issue, that the changed climate of industrial relations in the 1980s may be an important part of the explanation of the measured improvement in trend productivity. His suggestion has since been taken up and reinforced by other writers, with more or less substantive evidence at hand. Maynard, with no evidence, proposed that 'there would probably be general agreement that the government's legislative assault on trade union power and privilege and its willingness to stand up against crucial strikes ... have played a significant role in reducing trade union opposition to the introduction of new technology and to changes in working practices' (Maynard, 1988; p. 156). Crafts (1988a), similarly, has argued that the erosion of trade union restrictive practices, and the fact that the Government has stopped seeking an accommodation with the unions at national level, has helped release a formidable constraint on productivity.

What is striking about these arguments is that they are not grounded in a developed theory of the nature and role of collective social forces in the economy. In identifying unions as a major cause of economic weakness, their central reference point is the standard textbook model of atomistic competition, according to which any collective institution (whether it be unions, government, or whatever) is a source of economic inefficiency. Plainly this highly abstract analysis, which in any case is elaborated for static allocation issues and not the question of dynamic change, is inappropriate for the task in hand (see Nolan and Marginson, 1988). It assumes what should be demonstrated. It advances as 'common sense' and uncontroversial the entrenched idea that the capitalist economy works best when it is unregulated and when workers do not combine to advance their material interests, either in production or the market place. Such propositions ought to be subject to explicit theorisation and empirical investigation and not inserted into the analysis by recourse to *ad hoc* argument.

A more satisfactory approach is to recognise from the outset that the economy is a social process and that production is structured by power relationships and struggles which cannot be confined to a footnote or residual term. Then the relevant research agenda is to examine the interplay of different social forces in the growth process, to ask how and why particular (national and international) institutional configurations are more or less conducive to rapid productivity growth. Such an approach would caution against the easy scapegoating of one social agency, the trade union for example, and would entail a more precise account of the dynamic relationships involved. These are the primary concerns of the next section.

5.3 THE LIMITS TO PRODUCTIVITY GROWTH

A number of developments over the past decade have allegedly combined to produce a sea change in the performance of British industry. It is said that the government's union legislation, harsher competitive conditions, higher unemployment, privatisation, tax changes and the freeing of markets have given management both the incentive and opportunity to restructure work, introduce more efficient techniques and claw back the 'right to manage'.

There can be little doubt that unions and workers have taken a bashing in the 1980s, and that managers now have the whip-hand in production. But is there any solid evidence to suggest that this new power structure has promoted economic dynamism and greater efficiency? We confront these questions by identifying the salient characteristics of manufacturing industry in Britain and the sources of productivity weakness in the past. Then we look at recent developments with a view to drawing out the changes and the continuities with the past.

5.3.1 The historical legacy

Britain emerged from the post-war boom years as a producer of relatively labour-intensive, low value-added goods. Once renowned for its advanced engineering and electrical products, Britain now has a comparative trade advantage in low research intensive industries, such as food, drink and tobacco. Thus Smith (1986) has shown that Britain's trade performance in high research intensive industries (automobiles, consumer electronics, semiconductors, computers, etc.) has deteriorated steadily since the early 1970s, as reflected in a near doubling of imports in these sectors. (See also Freeman, this volume). In fact, Britain now trades at a surplus in only two high technology industries – chemicals and aerospace equipment – and in both cases there has been a marked erosion of the surplus over the past decade.

While these structural trends have been consolidated and reinforced in the 1980s, they are the product of long-standing weaknesses. Many writers, as we have seen, trace the problem to the effects of particular institutional 'rigidities' – trade unions, inept management, or whatever. But such an approach is far too simplistic, for it fails to place Britain's industrial development in the context of the shifts and transformations of the world economy. Britain's post-war industrial development has been conditioned by the combined effects of international and domestic structural forces.

The policies and practices of the multinational corporations have been crucial. In chameleon-like fashion, they have adapted to the economic conditions of Britain in ways which have militated against the progressive upgrading of plant and equipment, of labour force skills, of work organisation and management techniques. Domestically, there has been a critical absence of strong and decisive modernising forces (Fine and Harris, 1985). The social agencies and pressures which might have led to the establishment of a high-wage, high-productivity industrial system have been weak and ambiguous in their effects. The key social agencies in question are the state, the trade unions and industrial capital.

In stressing the effects of particular social agencies in Britain, the aim is not to reproduce the argument that productivity growth has been obstructed by powerful institutional 'rigidities'. The argument, rather, is that the agencies which might have generated the pressure for change have been too *weak*. Thus, for example, it is not the case that unions have wielded too much influence and have blocked productivity-enhancing changes in production. The problem has been that unions have been ineffective in closing off routes to profitability based on low wages, labour intensification and job segmentation. Fractured by sectional material concerns and by the ever-shifting contours of industrial production in Britain, trade unions have been unable to mount sufficient pressure – at plant, industry and national level – to secure a coherent programme of modernisation conducive to stable, well remunerated employment.

Nor has there been any clear direction from employers and their representative organisations. Divided and fragmented by the irrepressible forces of competition, and by differences in size, market and technology, employers in Britain have failed to push for and unite around a co-ordinated programme of modernisation for industry (for an elaboration see Leys, 1985). The combined weaknesses of the trade unions and employers have been reflected in the policies of the British state (Jessop, 1980; Fine and Harris, 1985).

Potentially, at least, the state can assume a pivotal co-ordinating role, guiding and underwriting new investment, rationalisation and restructuring – as has been the case, in varying degrees, in Japan, France, and West Germany (House of Lords, 1985). In Britain, however, the state has not assumed this role, despite brief flirtations with the principle of indicative planning during the Labour administrations of the 1960s and 1970s. Successive governments have sought to manage the economy at arms' length and mainly from the demand side. The resulting vacuum has given rise to a number of specific effects.

From the standpoint of the advanced capitalist countries, Britain as early as the 1960s was becoming a centre for relatively cheap, disposable labour. This is brought out in Table 5.4 which gives figures on total labour costs, derived by summing average hourly earnings and social charges (eg., national insurance, holiday and sick pay). It shows that in 1970, of the leading capitalist countries only Japan had lower labour costs than Britain. Rising wages in Japan since then has meant that Britain has gained the dubious distinction of being the lowest of the low labour-cost countries. Furthermore, by the standards of most European countries, employers in Britain face few legal and financial constraints in respect of the hiring and firing of workers. Such flexibility has allowed employers to operate with short-term business horizons and to abstain from the long-term investment required to progressively upgrade production facilities and labour force skills (cf. Streeck, 1986).

Britain's position as a low-wage economy is commonly thought to be the consequence of low productivity. Wages are the product, not the cause of the underlying situation (cf. Alford, 1988). Certainly such thinking has informed

Table 5.4 Labour costs in manufacturing, 1960–86[a].

	1960	1970	1980	Total hourly labour costs 1982	1984	1986
			(UK = 100)			
United States	296	250	126	158	194	161
Japan	30	57	80	86	109	129
France	94	105	121	110	114	122
West Germany	98	144	165	147	153	173
Italy	72	113	108	104	117	127
Belgium	94	122	176	142	140	149
Netherlands	n.a.	126	160	142	142	156
Norway	113	150	153	152	163	164
Sweden	138	181	170	142	147	154
United Kingdom (GB)	100	100	100	100	100	100

Note: (a) Labour costs are compared at current market exchange rates.
Source: Ray (1962 and 1987).

the character of government policy over many years, for wage restraint has been seen by successive governments as the key solution to Britain's declining industrial fortunes. Yet there is compelling evidence that low wages and low productivity have become self-reinforcing and indissolubly linked.

The multinational companies, in particular, have come to see Britain not as a base for highly skilled, high value-added production, but as an ideal location in which to carry out labour-intensive, assembly and sub-assembly work. As major transmitters of technology, the multinationals have had and continue to have a significant impact on industry structure and performance. The composition of world trade and the distribution of economic activity within and between countries is increasingly patterned by their global sourcing and investment strategies.

In Britain, their impact is graphically illustrated by the declining fortunes of the motor industry (including component supplies). Accounting for about a third of Britain's visible trade deficit in 1988, and roughly 5 and 4% of GDP and employment, respectively, car production in Britain is dominated by four foreign-owned multinational companies (Ford, General Motors, Peugeot and Nissan) and two British firms, Rover and Jaguar (formerly parts of the state-owned British Leyland).

The growing surplus of car imports over exports, and the associated decline of the British components industry, reflect the progressive marginalisation of British branch plants. Thus, the two leading American-owned firms, Ford and General Motors, now source about 50% of their British sales from overseas and both firms, like Peugeot, the French-owned company, use Britain predominantly as a base for the assembly of imported parts and sub-assemblies. Ford developed this strategy early on in the post-war period. Seeing Britain as a source of low-cost, readily disposable labour, it elected to situate its least capital intensive assembly plants here, while in countries such as West Germany – where the institutional and legal context militated against cheap and disposable labour – it was forced to implement the most advanced productive techniques, making for a high productivity, high-wage virtuous circle (Roots, 1986).

Over the past decade this pattern of international specialisation has been further entrenched as the gap between Britain's labour costs and those of the other major car-producing countries has widened. Spain is the notable exception, for like Britain it also competes on the basis of low labour costs (*Financial Times*, 24.2.1989). In West Germany, the United States, Sweden, Japan and Belgium labour costs in 1988 were between 33 and 50% higher than in Britain. Yet contrary to the government's persistent refrain that lower costs are necessary to secure industrial regeneration the motor industry (in common with other high technology industries) has continued to experience decline.

The United States multinationals in particular have weakened their commitment to British production facilities as part of a world-wide restructuring of their operations. Thus, integrated plant (such as Ford's Dagenham site) has been broken up, technology has been allowed to fall behind the standards of other European countries, and output has been confined mainly to labour-intensive, low value-added assembly work. In 1988, Ford announced its intention to shift the production of the Sierra – one of its more technically sophisticated models – to Belgium, while concentrating production in Britain on the more basic, lower-priced Fiesta. Nissan, then a relatively recent arrival in Britain, has no plans to locate any research and design functions here and currently imports engines and gearboxes, the most capital intensive stages of the car manufacturing process, from Japan, thus leaving workers at its Washington (UK) plant to carry out the relatively unskilled (and poorly remunerated) operations.

5.3.2 Continuity and change

Breaking with the legacy of the past has been the government's self-professed aim since it took power in 1979. To this end it has sought to break down the institutional and class structures which conditioned economic development before 1979, and which constituted what is often termed the Keynesian welfare state. The productivity growth of manufacturing in the 1980s has been held up as evidence of the government's achievements, but the interpretation presented here casts a different light on recent events. The argument in a nutshell is that the social and economic relations which in the past inhibited the movement towards a high wage, high productivity, high research-intensive production system have been consolidated and not dislodged over the past decade.

The productivity gains of the 1980s are the product of three basic ingredients: the recovery of output since 1982, accompanied by continuing large-scale job losses; a power shift in the relationship between employer and employee; and changes in work organisation and production technology. These three elements have *interacted* to produce a series of step-by-step increases in measured productivity. The notion of step-by-step changes is used to gain distance from the idea that there has been a fundamental and sweeping transformation of production relations which has resulted in greater efficiency and economic dynamism.

The output–employment ratio has been transformed since 1979 by successive waves of redundancy. The collapse in output in 1979–80 was followed in 1981 by an even larger collapse in employment. Output began to recover in 1982, but this recovery was not accompanied by employment growth, perhaps because as Muellbauer and others have proposed employers were (and still are) keen to avoid the transactions costs of recruitment. Employment at the end of 1988 was 30% lower than it was in 1979, which in absolute terms amounts to a loss of more than 2 million jobs. Manufacturing output, in contrast, returned to its 1979 level in 1987 and its previous peak of

1973 in late 1988, under the impetus of rising (domestic and international) demand. With many fewer workers producing this expanding level of output labour productivity was bound to rise. This much is uncontroversial, for it is nothing more than a description of the three elements of an identity.

Yet the real issues at the centre of the productivity controversy is how these gains in output per employee have been achieved. Are workers expending more effort in production, in order to make up for the contribution of the labour power which has been expelled, or is labour productivity rising because of the introduction of new and more efficient production techniques? Are the gains sustainable, or do they merely reflect a shift in the power relationship between workers and bosses which may eventually be reversed?

In approaching these problems, two difficulties present themselves. First, there is a scarcity of direct, systematic evidence on the changing pattern of production relationships. Secondly, the concept of power is alien to mainstream economics, which makes the task of interpretation and dialogue so much more difficult. What for one analyst is evidence of a shift in power is for another a welcome move towards technical efficiency. Be that as it may, most economists writing on this topic have been forced to engage with the messy realities of production politics, and in so doing have had to try to adapt the narrow concepts of neoclassical production theory to the problems in hand.

Muellbauer is a good case in point for, as discussed above, he identified variations in labour utilisation as a key element in the explanation of cyclical movements in labour productivity. Unfortunately his treatment is confined to the concept of labour hoarding, to the idea that risk-averse employers do not immediately lay off (hire) workers as demand dictates a downward (upward) revision of planned output. Doubtless this is part of the explanation, but it remains incomplete. For it does not grapple with the implications of the massive labour shake-out for the *politics* of productivity. Is it not the case that workers, faced with the threat of job loss, are more likely to submit to new work routines and productivity targets than those with greater job security in an expanding situation?

In ignoring such questions Muellbauer and others have failed to grasp the possibility that recent labour productivity gains have been secured in rather unusual circumstances, as a result of what Metcalf (1988) has recently termed the 'fear' factor, and as such may prove to be short-lived. To be sure, other writers have registered the salience of power as a factor in recent economic developments, but so often the issue is shrouded in vague, ungrounded references to changes in the 'climate of industrial relations', to a 'new realism', or some equally nebulous notion of naked 'individualism' on the part of workers (e.g., Richardson and Wood, 1989). The problem with such terms is that they encourage writers to speak misleadingly of an enduring 'trend shift' in supply side conditions, when in fact what they are merely describing is a new, and intrinsically fragile, power shift arising from the exceptionally brutal crisis conditions of the early 1980s.

The evidence – what little there is – supports this interpretation. There are two main sources: case studies from particular plants and industries (e.g., Tailby and Whitston, 1989) and survey evidence from a panel of manufacturing establishments (e.g., Batstone and Gourlay, 1986). One of the most widely cited references is Bennett and Smith Gavine's so-called Percentage Utilisation of Labour Index (PUL). The PUL index has monitored changes in work effort – the intensity of the labour input – in a panel of manufacturing firms (covering 135,000 operatives) since 1971, using management's own work study measurements. The PUL index increased sharply after 1981, by approximately 7% over the recorded levels of 1980–1, and then reached a new peak in 1984.

Based on management's work study methods, the PUL index is probably an imperfect measure. But it is consistent with academic and anecdotal reports. Respondents to Batstone and Gourlay's workplace survey reported significantly increased effort levels after 1980, while Metcalf (1988) found a positive correlation between the scale of job losses and productivity gains at the industry level. His interpretation of this result is that the massive labour shake-out from manufacturing rendered workers far more compliant and hard-working than before. From outside manufacturing, Glyn's study of the coal industry adds weight to this argument. He found that, in the wake of recent closures, labour productivity has increased rapidly as a result of 'changing working practices and pace of work rather than new equipment' (Glyn, 1988).

These findings, moreover, mesh with the aggregate picture. For, as noted above, one of the most striking features of the Thatcher years is the extent of the decline in new investment: in physical capital, research and development, and education and training. Fixed capital investment in manufacturing plant and machinery and new building work fell dramatically in real terms after 1979 and continued to fall until 1985. The modest recovery since then has been experienced unevenly across industries, with metals, mechanical engineering and chemicals, for example, remaining heavily under-resourced by the standards of 1979. Moreover, investment shows signs of being choked off in 1989 by higher interest rates. Of the major capitalist countries, Britain devotes the smallest share of its national income to non-defence investment projects (House of Lords, 1986), while the proportion of income devoted to education and training is now lower than in 1979. Industry studies have thus revealed major skill deficiencies (e.g., Steedman and Wagner, 1987; Ashton, Green and Hoskins, this volume) and have highlighted the lack of training as a major impediment to the introduction of new, microelectronic technologies.

Commonly, such weaknesses are discussed in abstraction from the particular structures and social relations which have perpetuated the so-called British 'disease'. Thus Crafts (1988b), for example, recently complained that while the government had succeeded in taming the unions, it had failed to rectify Britain's inferior record in research and development and training.

Why exactly he should expect the government to tackle such problems is by no means clear, but this is not the point. The central issue is that the policies of the present are making it more, not less, likely that these deficiencies will become increasingly pronounced in the future. Why should companies such as Ford or Nissan locate vital research and development functions in Britain, or engage in the upgrading of workforce skills, when they are currently using their British plants to undertake relatively unskilled, labour-intensive assembly work? However paradoxical it may seem to advocates of the miracle thesis, the route to high technology, high research-intensive industry lies in closing-off the open access that firms currently have to a weak, low-paid workforce.

This leads to the third ingredient of recent productivity gains, namely changes in work organisation and production technology. It is common to see new technology (the 'microchip') and labour intensification counterposed in the literature as two distinct routes to higher productivity. But this is a false dichotomy, for the evidence shows that new investment is often geared towards the promotion of changing working practices and more intensive effort. Illuminating case study research is provided in Tailby and Whitston (1989). Documenting the process of social and technological change in, *inter alia*, textiles, the truck lift industry, motor components and foundries, their studies provide a complex picture of piecemeal and uneven adaptation to new design, production and marketing systems. Above all else they show how firms in the 1980s, often hedged in by cash shortages and fierce market pressures, have sought incrementally, and not always successfully, to apply new microelectronic systems and a range of not so much new as different labour management techniques. The process of change has been partial and slow.

Such an account suggests that the much-vaunted 'Japanisation' of British industry has been greatly exaggerated. Take the over-worked notion that management is making a decisive shift towards positive human resource management techniques. All too often, in practice, this has entailed little more than a cynical application of new representation and communication structures, designed first and foremost to displace traditional collective mechanisms. Likewise, the search on the part of employers for greater 'flexibility' – another powerfully seductive term – has tended to stop short of the large investments required to upgrade workers' technical skills to achieve so-called 'functional' flexibility (the super, multi-skilled person). More often, firms have sought 'numerical' flexibility (ACAS, 1988) by eroding job security and by targeting disadvantaged groups.

More fundamentally, the diffusion of so-called Just-in-Time (JIT) production and inventory techniques – the apotheosis of the Japanese production system – has proved difficult on a number of fronts. Based on the application of advanced computerised technology, and chiefly intended to cut the turnover time of capital, JIT production works best on greenfield sites where client companies are able to enforce the toughest quality and delivery requirements on their supplier companies. These structures, however, have been difficult to foster in Britain because of the shortage of suitable industrial locations and also because of entrenched skill shortages (Sayer, 1986).

Where JIT has been introduced the most significant effect has been at the level of workplace relations. The case studies (Tailby and Whitston, 1989) show that by supplanting traditional functional workplace layouts (wherein work passes from one discrete stage to another, often with notable delays), JIT entails a new module system grouping workers and machines together, and linking different stages of production into a closely integrated totality. The consequence has been to erode worker autonomy and job control, and invade further the porosity of the working day.

5.3.3 The miracle exposed

Several points emerge from the foregoing discussion. First, the (survey and case study) evidence seems to point to labour intensification as a key element in recent productivity gains. This has been facilitated by high job loss and output recovery on the one hand and technological and organisational change on the other. As argued, it is erroneous to view technology and intensification as mutually exclusive routes to higher productivity. Both can, and have, played a role.

Secondly, looking at the record for manufacturing as a whole, the evidence shows clearly that there has not been an investment breakthrough (cf. Oulton, 1989). Nor should this be particularly surprising, for it has become increasingly possible for firms to make productivity (and profitability) gains without undertaking large-scale investment. The progressive weakening of labour, both collective and individual, has helped entrench the legacy of the past. Firms have sought short-term gains, through a series of step-by-step adaptations, which have left untouched basic structural weaknesses.

Thirdly, there is the question of the relationship between productivity and production efficiency. Is it the case that gains in productivity necessarily imply an improvement in production efficiency? The short answer to this question is no. For the concept of production efficiency specifies a relationship between input and output. If output is increased without a corresponding rise in input then it is accurate to speak of an efficiency gain. If, in contrast, the gains in output are secured by increasing input then the situation is not clear-cut. Productivity increases may be consistent with no change, or even a loss of efficiency. For Britain in the 1980s the evidence points strongly towards an association between rising productivity and rising labour input; in other words, it suggests that production efficiency has not improved. Indeed, without significant investment in new technological systems, it is plausible to argue that dynamic efficiency may have been impaired. Static gains may have been secured at the expense of the more fundamental production reorganisation needed to sustain future growth.

5.4 CONCLUSIONS

Is it likely that the higher rate of productivity growth of the past six years or so will endure? The analysis presented above has sought to focus attention on four interrelated aspects of the structure of British industry which bear on this question. First, the productivity gains have been secured against a backdrop of long-standing and deepening structural imbalances in British manufacturing, with a progressive movement towards low-skill, low-technology activities. Secondly, there has been a surge in domestic and international demand, particularly pronounced in the past two years or so, which has stimulated a recovery of manufacturing output without any corresponding recovery of employment. Thirdly, the position of trade unions has been weakened by a combination of factors (high unemployment, government legislation and structural shifts in the economy) which has made it easier for firms to intensify existing production processes and maintain a low-wage regime, at least by the standards of other major industrial economies. Fourthly, there has not been a root and branch modernisation of production conditions, but rather a series of incremental, piecemeal changes often geared towards labour intensification.

These considerations suggest that the gains of the recent past are not the product of an enduring social and economic transformation of supply side conditions. Industry in Britain remains badly placed to share in the expanding markets for high technology, high research-intensive products. Moreover, any weakening of domestic demand conditions in the near future would place in jeopardy the output (and hence productivity) advances which have been aided by recent expansionary policies. To the extent that Britain's poor, and rapidly deteriorating, trade performance forces the government to deflate the domestic economy, so it is more likely that productivity growth will begin to tail off. More fundamentally there are definite limits to a productivity boom based on a necessarily fragile shift in the power relationship between employer and employee and the associated intensification of existing production systems.

REFERENCES

Advisory Conciliation and Arbitration Services (ACAS), *Labour Flexibility in Britain: the 1987 ACAS Survey*, ACAS Occasional Paper 41 (1988).
Alford, B. W. E., *British Economic Performance 1945–1975*, (Macmillan: London, 1988).

Ball, J., 'The United Kingdom economy: miracle or mirage?' Cardiff Business School (1988).

Batstone E. and Gourlay, S., *Unions, Unemployment and Innovation*, (Blackwell: Oxford, 1986).

Bennett, A, and Smith Gavine, S., 'The percentage utilisation of Labour Index', *Working Below Capacity* (ed. Bosworth, D.) (Macmillan: London, 1988).

Crafts, N. F. R., 'The assessment: British economic growth over the long run', *Oxford Review of Economic Policy,* **4**(1) (1988a).

Crafts, N. F. R., 'British economic growth before and after 1979: has economic decline been reversed?', Centre for Economic Policy Research Discussion Paper No. 292 (1988b).

Darby, J. and Wren-Lewis, S., 'Trends in manufacturing labour productivity', National Institute of Economic and Social Research Discussion Paper No. 145, October (1988).

Economic Commission for Europe, *Economic Survey of Europe in 1987–1988*, United Nations, New York (1988).

Economic Progress Report, January–February (1987).

Financial Times, 24.2.89.

Fine, B., and Harris, L., *The Peculiarities of The British Economy* (Lawrence & Wishart: London, 1985).

Glyn, A., 'Colliery results and closures after the 1984–85 coal dispute', *Oxford Bulletin of Economics and Statistics,* **50** (2) (1988).

House of Lords, *Report From the Select Committee on Overseas Trade*, Session 1984–5, (238–I), London, HMSO.

House of Lords, *Select Committee on Science and Technology, Report on Civil Research and Development*, London, HMSO (1986).

R. Jessop, 'The Transformation of the State in Post-war Britain', *The State in Western Europe*, (ed. Scase, R.) (Croom Helm: London, 1980).

Leys, C., 'Thatcherism and British manufacturing: a question of hegemony', *New Left Review,* **151**, May/June (1985).

Maynard, G., *The Economy Under Mrs Thatcher*, (Blackwell: Oxford 1988).

Muellbauer, J., 'The assessment: productivity and competitiveness in British manufacturing', *Oxford Review of Economic Policy,* **2**, 3, (1986).

Metcalf, D., 'Water notes dry up', Centre for Labour Economics London School of Economics Discussion Paper 314 (1988).

Nolan, P., 'Walking on Water? Performance and industrial relations under Thatcher', *Industrial Relations Journal,* **20** (2) (1989).

Nolan, P., and Marginson, P., 'Skating on thin ice: David Metcalf on Trade Unions and productivity', Warwick Papers in Industrial Relations, University of Warwick, No. 22 (1988).

OECD, *Economic Outlook: Historical Statistics, 1960–85* (June 1987).

Oi, W., 'Labour as a Quasi-Fixed Factor', *Journal of Political Economy,* **LXX**, 6, (1962).

Oulton, N., 'Plant closures and the productivity "miracle" in manufacturing', *National Institute Economic Review*, No. 121 August (1987).

Oulton, N., 'Productivity growth in manufacturing, 1963–85: the roles of new investment and scrapping', *National Institute Economic Review*, no. 127, February (1989).

Ray, G., 'Labour costs and international competitiveness', *National Institute Economic Review*, No. 61, August (1962).

Ray, G., 'Labour costs in manufacturing', *National Institute Economic Review*, No. 120, May (1987).

Richardson, R. and Wood, S., 'The Coal Industry and the New Industrial Relations', *British Journal of Industrial Relations,* **XXXVII** (1) March (1989).

Roots, P., 'Collective bargaining: opportunities for a new approach', Warwick Papers in Industrial Relations, University of Warwick, No. 5 (1986).

Sayer, A., 'New developments in manufacturing: The Just in Time system', *Capital and Class*, No. 30, Winter (1986).

Smith, M., 'UK manufacturing: output and trade performance', *Midland Bank Review*, Autumn (1986).

Steedman, H., and K. Wagner, 'A second look at productivity, machinery and skills in Britain and Germany', *National Institute Economic Review*, November (1987).

Streeck, W., Industrial Relations and industrial change in the motor industry, Industrial Relations Research Unit, Warwick University (1986).

Tailby, S., and Whitston, C., (eds), *Manufacturing Change*, (Blackwell: Oxford, 1989).

6 THE MANUFACTURING PRODUCTIVITY 'MIRACLE': A SECTORAL ANALYSIS

David Blackaby and Lester Hunt

6.1 INTRODUCTION

The increase in Britain's manufacturing productivity growth in the 1980s compared to the 1970s has by now been well documented.[1] A full account of the reasons for the increase, and an assessment of its significance, has yet to be produced. It has been suggested that one element in the increase may have been a 'batting-average effect', whereby low-productivity plants went out of business and high-productivity establishments survived, thereby raising productivity on average (Muellbauer, 1986; Matthews, 1988). Some doubt has been shed on whether this has been of practical importance (Oulton, 1987).[2] It is possible, however, that a similar effect could be working at a sectoral level, whereby structural shifts in the sectoral balance within manufacturing industries from low- to high-productivity industries could bring about an overall productivity rise.

This chapter seeks to examine the issue of sectoral change and productivity by analysing 12 sub-sectors of manufacturing for which disaggregated data are readily available. The hypothesis that the manufacturing productivity 'miracle' is no more than a re-allocation of resources from low-productivity to high-productivity sectors is tested. If this hypothesis is accepted, it implies that the major contribution to the improved manufacturing productivity performance has essentially been a one-off affair and the relative gain cannot be expected to continue in the future.

6.2 OVERVIEW OF INDIVIDUAL SECTORS PRODUCTIVITY GROWTH

Labour productivity is defined as output per employee. (Details of the data used and sources are given in the appendix.) A summary of the growth in

We would like to thank Francis Green and Ted Nevin for comments on an earlier draft of this paper. Of course, all remaining errors and omissions are entirely our own.

labour productivity over the periods 1973–9 and 1979–87 is given in Table 6.1. The years 1973 and 1979 were chosen as cyclical peaks, as identified by the CSO's Coincident Index (see *Economic Trends*, January 1989, pp. 70–1). The year 1985 could also be interpreted as a peak, but it is stated that:

> The interpretation of the indices since 1981 is that they could show a cyclical peak in economic activity in early 1985. There may have been a mild trough in 1986, although the decline in the indices before their renewed growth is less marked then previous cyclical movements . . . Recent values of the indices are particularly subject to revision as more information becomes available so any interpretation remains provisional. (*Economic Trends*, January 1989)

Therefore, 1987 has been used as the end year since it is the most recent data point. These short-run cyclical peaks are used in an attempt to obtain a more accurate measure of trend productivity growth. Only two periods are analysed (because of data limitations) and the possibility that these are part of a longer cycle is ignored.

Table 6.1 shows that the majority of the sub-sectors experienced a marked improvement in productivity growth in the period 1979–87 compared to 1973–9. The main exception is Clothing, Footwear and Leather, which had well above average productivity growth during the 1973–9 period and only showed an improvement of 0.2 percentage points per annum. Food, Drink and Tobacco, Paper, Printing and Publishing, and Other Manufacturing were also at the lower end of the range with improvements of only 2.2, 1.8 and 1.6 percentage points per annum, respectively.

Although the so-called 'miracle' has taken place in productivity growth, manufacturing industry has experienced a loss of over 2 million jobs and a failure to regain its 1979 level of output until 1987. Since the growth in labour productivity is approximately the difference between the growth in output and employment, these separate components for the 12 sub-sectors are given in Table 6.2. It can be seen that total manufacturing output growth was relatively poor: the average annual growth rate was actually negative over the period 1973–9 (–0.7%) and barely positive over the period 1979–87 (0.2%). At the disaggregated level only four sectors during the period 1973–9 experienced growth, while in the latter period this rises to six. The figures for employment are much more dramatic with Chemicals and Man-made Fibres the only sector experiencing employment growth in the first period. No sectors at all experienced growth in the latter period. All sub-sectors experienced a bigger decline in employment over the period 1979–87 compared to 1973–9. Moreover, the sub-sectors noted above which experienced the smallest improvements in productivity over the two periods also experienced the smallest change in the decline in employment. Thus, the low productivity growth in the first period was associated with declining output and steady but falling employment, while in the latter period the productivity 'miracle' is associated with negligible growth in output and rapidly declining employment.

Table 6.1 Average annual growth in productivity (%).

1980 SIC	Sector Name	1973–9	1979–87	Change 1973–9 to 1979–87
21–4	Metals, Other Minerals and Mineral Products	0.0	5.8	5.8
25–6	Chemicals and Man-made Fibres	1.9	5.2	3.4
31	Metal Goods, (not elsewhere specified)	–0.8	5.1	5.9
32	Mechanical Engineering	–0.7	2.6	3.3
33–4, 37	Office Machinery, Electrical Engineering and Instruments	2.0	7.2	5.2
35	Motor Vehicles and Parts	–1.2	5.6	6.8
36	Other Transport Equipment	–0.5	6.9	7.4
41–2	Food, Drink and Tobacco	1.8	4.0	2.1
43	Textiles	0.8	4.6	3.7
44–5	Clothing, Footwear and Leather	3.2	3.5	0.3
47	Paper, Printing and Publishing	0.3	2.1	1.8
46, 48–9	Other Manufacturing (including Timber, Furniture, Rubber and Plastics)	1.0	2.6	1.7
2–4	Total	0.6	4.6	3.9

Note: Totals may not equal sums of constituent items due to rounding.

6.3 A SHIFT-SHARE ANALYSIS OF MANUFACTURING PRODUCTIVITY

Aggregate labour productivity is affected over time by productivity change within each sector and by shifts of output and employment between sectors with different levels of productivity. Beebe and Haltmaier (1983) show how aggregate labour productivity growth may be decomposed as follows:

$$\Delta P/P = (1/P)\Sigma p^i \Delta s^i + (1/P)\Sigma s^i \Delta p^i + (1/P)\Sigma \Delta p^i \Delta s^i$$

where P = total manufacturing labour productivity
  s^i = the share of employment in sub-sector i i = 1,..,12
and p^i = the labour productivity in sub-sector i i = 1,..,12
The first term represents the contribution brought about by changes in the composition of employment (thereafter referred to as the 'distributional effect'); the second term represents the contribution made by the growth in productivity within the individual sub-sectors (henceforth referred to as the 'sectoral effect'); and the third term represents the contribution made by the interaction of the distributional and the sectoral effects which results from the compounding of the two effects with discrete time data.[3]

The distributional effect, therefore, estimates the contribution made by each sector to the growth in total manufacturing productivity which results

Table 6.2 Average annual growth in output and employees in employment (%).

1980 SIC	Sector Name	Output			Employment		
		1973–9	1979–87	Change 1973–9 to 1979–87	1973–9	1979–87	Change 1973–9 to 1979–87
21–4	Metals, Other Minerals and Mineral Products	-2.2	-0.7	1.5	-2.1	-6.1	-4.0
25–6	Chemicals and Man-made Fibres	2.1	1.9	-0.1	0.2	-3.1	-3.3
31	Metal Goods (not elsewhere specified)	-2.4	-1.8	0.6	-1.6	-6.4	-4.8
32	Mechanical Engineering	-1.0	-2.2	-1.2	-0.3	-4.6	-4.4
33–4, 37	Office Machinery, Electrical Engineering and Instruments	1.1	3.9	2.9	-0.9	-3.1	-2.2
35	Motor Vehicles and Parts	-2.7	-2.6	0.1	-1.5	-7.8	-6.3
36	Other Transport Equipment	-1.5	1.7	3.1	-0.9	-4.8	-3.9
41–2	Food, Drink and Tobacco	0.8	0.5	-0.4	-1.0	-3.3	-2.4
43	Textiles	-3.3	-1.8	1.5	-4.1	-6.1	-2.0
44–5	Clothing, Footwear and Leather	0.6	-0.5	-1.1	-2.5	-3.9	-1.4
47	Paper, Printing and Publishing	-0.1	0.7	0.7	-0.3	-1.4	-1.1
46, 48–9	Other Manufacturing (including Timber, Furniture, Rubber and Plastics)	-0.5	0.6	1.1	-1.4	-2.1	-0.6
2–4	Total	-0.7	0.2	0.9	-1.3	-4.2	-2.9

Note: Totals may not equal sums of constituent items due to rounding.

Table 6.3 Contribution to total manufacturing productivity growth due to the distributional effects (average annual percentage change).

1980 SIC	Sector name	1973–9	1979–87	Change 1973–9 to 1979–87
21–4	Metals, Other Minerals and Mineral Products	–0.08	–0.19	–0.10
25–6	Chemicals and Man-made Fibres	0.13	0.11	–0.01
31	Metal Goods (not elsewhere specified)	–0.02	–0.13	–0.11
32	Mechanical Engineering	0.15	–0.06	–0.22
33–4, 37	Office machinery, Electrical Engineering and Instruments	0.03	0.13	0.10
35	Motor Vehicles and Parts	–0.02	–0.23	–0.21
36	Other Transport Equipment	0.02	–0.03	–0.05
41–2	Food, Drink and Tobacco	0.03	0.12	0.08
43	Textiles	–0.11	–0.07	0.04
44–5	Clothing, Footwear and Leather	–0.04	0.01	0.05
47	Paper, Printing and Publishing	0.10	0.31	0.21
46, 48–9	Other Manufacturing (including Timber, Furniture, Rubber and Plastics)	–0.01	0.17	0.18
2–4	Total	0.18	0.14	–0.04

Note: Totals may not equal sums of constituent items due to rounding.

solely from shifts in labour among sectors. It is the part of growth that would have occurred had productivity levels remained constant within sectors. These estimates are given in Table 6.3.[4] Over the period 1973–9 the contributions of individual sectors due to changes in the composition of employment were typically rather small, the exceptions being Chemicals and Man-Made Fibres and Mechanical Engineering, both of which had relatively large positive distributional effects. Over the period 1979–87 the contributions are again rather small except for Paper, Printing and Publishing which had the largest positive contribution. The final column shows that there were positive and negative changes, for the different sectors, over the two periods analysed; they tended to cancel each other out so that the total contribution made by changes in the composition of employment to the manufacturing productivity 'miracle' of the 1980s is marginally negative. Of course, the distributional effect may be affected by the degree of disaggregation, so that there may have been some reallocation of resources within the 12 sub-sectors identified. Beebe and Haltmaier (1983), however, did find very similar results for the US with both broad and narrow levels of disaggregation.

The sectoral effect shown in Table 6.4 estimates the contribution of each sector to the growth in total manufacturing productivity that comes about as a result of changes in productivity within sectors. It is the part of total manufacturing productivity growth that would have occurred if each sector's share of employment had remained constant.

The contribution of each sector due to the sectoral effect over the earlier period tended to be fairly small on the whole, with both positive and negative contributions. Over the later period, however, the contributions for *all* sectors are positive and are larger than for the previous period (as well as being generally larger than any of the contributions due to the distributional effect over the two periods). Thus, the sectoral growth in productivity is the major contributor to the total growth in manufacturing productivity over the period 1979–87. The sector with the greatest contribution due to the sectoral effect during the period 1979–87 is Office Machinery, etc., which also shows the greatest increase over the earlier period (as shown in the final column of Table 6.4): this is despite it being one of the sectors with the highest contribution attributable to the sectoral effect during the period 1973–9. In fact, this sector, together with Metals, Other Minerals and Mineral Products, accounts for over 30% of the improvement in the total contribution due to the sectoral effect over the two periods analysed. The remaining sectors show fairly significant though smaller improvements, except for Clothing, Footwear and Leather which has not shown any substantial increase in productivity growth in the 1980s.

Table 6.4 Contribution to total manufacturing productivity growth due to the sectoral effects (average annual percentage change).

1980 SIC	Sector name	1973–9	1979–87	Change 1973–9 to 1979–87
21–4	Metals, Other Minerals and Mineral Products	−0.02	0.51	0.53
25–6	Chemicals and Man-made Fibres	0.15	0.52	0.36
31	Metal Goods (not elsewhere specified)	−0.06	0.26	0.32
32	Mechanical engineering	−0.11	0.32	0.43
33–4, 37	Office Machinery, Electrical Engineering and Instruments	0.20	0.91	0.71
35	Motor Vehicles and Parts	−0.10	0.30	0.40
36	Other Transport Equipment	−0.03	0.38	0.41
41–2	Food, Drink and Tobacco	0.22	0.54	0.32
43	Textiles	0.03	0.14	0.11
44–5	Clothing, Footwear and Leather	0.11	0.12	0.01
47	Paper, Printing and Publishing	0.01	0.21	0.20
46, 48–9	Other Manufacturing (including Timber, Furniture, Rubber and Plastics)	0.07	0.21	0.13
2–4	Total	0.48	4.41	3.93

Note: Totals may not equal sums of constituent items due to rounding.

Table 6.5 Summary of the contributions to total manufacturing productivity growth (average annual percentage change).

	1973–9	1979–87	Change 1973–9 to 1979–87
Distributional effect	0.2	0.1	0.0
Sectoral effect	0.5	4.4	3.9
Total	0.6	4.6	3.9

Note: Totals may not equal sums of constituent items due to rounding.

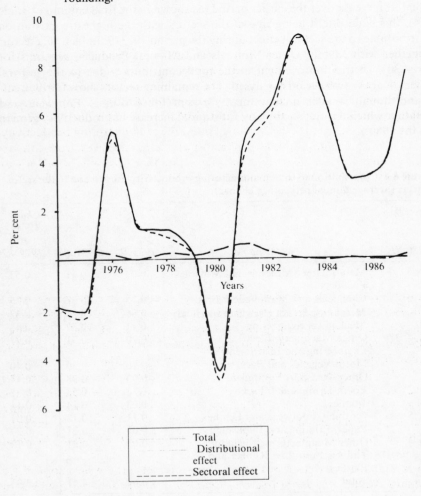

Figure 6.1 Growth in manufacturing productivity.

Looking at Table 6.5, which summarises these results (and Fig. 6.1, which shows the annual results), it is clear that it is the change in productivity *within* individual sub-sectors that dominates the growth in manufacturing productivity as a whole. Over the periods 1973–9 and 1979–87, the sectoral effect contributed 0.5 and 4.4% per annum, respectively, to the total, compared with a contribution of 0.2 and 0.1% per annum, respectively, from the distributional effect. The change in total manufacturing productivity growth over the two periods is thus almost entirely due to the change in the sectoral effect, i.e., the productivity growth of the individual sub-sectors.

6.4 SUMMARY

Although all sectors analysed have shown an improvement in productivity growth in the 1980s, the so-called 'Thatcher productivity miracle' has not been evenly distributed. Yet the increase in total manufacturing productivity growth cannot be attributed to a change in the composition of manufacturing employment. It *is* attributable to productivity growth within each of the sub-sectors analysed. Hence, the hypothesis that the manufacturing productivity 'miracle' was no more than a re-allocation of resources away from low- to high-productivity sectors is rejected, suggesting that this rapid productivity growth need not be a once-and-for-all effect. Yet while productivity growth in the 1980s is an improvement on the 1970s, this productivity 'miracle' does not seem to have been accompanied by a supply side output 'miracle'.

DATA APPENDIX

Labour productivity is defined as output per employee in employment in 12 sub-sectors of manufacturing according to the 1980 SIC. Self-employment is ignored since data are not published at a disaggregated level. (Although self-employment has grown significantly in the 1980s it is still a small proportion of total manufacturing employment, about 4% in 1986.)

The UK indices of output at constant factor cost for each sector (1985=100) were extracted from the CSO Data Bank at the University of Bath (using the December 1988 update). The levels of output, necessary for the shift share analysis, were calculated by multiplying the index of output for each sector by each sector's GDP in 1985 taken from the *United Kingdom National Accounts, 1988 Edition*.

UK employees in employment for June of each year were supplied (in January 1989) by the *Department of Employment*. The data only go back to June 1971 because of the switch from the 1968 to the 1980 SIC.

NOTES

1. For a survey and critique, see Chapter 5 by Peter Nolan.
2. Oulton (1987) noted that it was the largest plants which were closed in the 1980–1 recession, with employment shifted away from the size of plant which had the highest level of productivity in 1979 and the highest growth in subsequent years.
3. This interaction effect is ignored since it is very small: it is easily computed as the difference between the actual productivity growth and the sum of the distributional and sectoral effects.
4. The average annual growth rates for the periods 1973–9 and 1979–87 have been calculated by taking the average of the annual growth rates rather than calculated over the entire period, thus allowing the weights to change each year. (For consistency, therefore, all growth rates calculated in this chapter are derived in a similar way.)

REFERENCES

Beebe, J. H. and Haltmaier, J., 'Disaggregation and the labour productivity index', *Review of Economics and Statistics,* **65**, 487–91 (1983).
Matthews, R. C. O., 'Research on productivity and the productivity gap', *National Institute Economic Review,* **124**, May, 66–72 (1988).
Muellbauer, J., 'Productivity and competitiveness in British manufacturing', *Oxford Review of Economic Policy,* **2**, 3, I–XXV (1986).
Oulton, N., 'Plant closures and the productivity "miracle" in manufacturing', *National Institute Economic Review,* **121**, August, 53–9 (1987).
United Kingdom National Accounts, 1988 Edition (HMSO; London, 1988).

7 THE TRAINING SYSTEM OF BRITISH CAPITALISM: CHANGES AND PROSPECTS

David Ashton, Francis Green and Martin Hoskins

> In 1869 [the so-called 'public schools'] were more or less set free from all government control and set about elaborating that actively anti-intellectual, anti-scientific, games-dominated Tory imperialism which was to remain characteristic of them. ... Unfortunately the public school formed the model of the new system of secondary education. ... Knowledge, especially scientific knowledge ... took second place in the new British educational system, to the maintenance of a rigid division between the classes. In 1897 less than seven per cent of grammar-school pupils came from the working class. The British therefore entered the twentieth century and the age of modern science and technology as a spectacularly ill-educated people. (Hobsbawm 1968, p. 169)

Concern at the declining ability of British capital to compete in world markets goes back at least to the Paris exhibition of 1867 where Britain won an embarrassingly small proportion of the awards available compared to an almost universal success at the Great Exhibition in London in 1851. The decline in economic power since then has been attributed fairly consistently, at least in part, to the relatively poor training and education provided in Britain compared to that provided by major competitors. Adverse comparisons were drawn early by, amongst others, Sir Lyon Playfair (1852) and Matthew Arnold (1868), and have continued to be drawn ever since. Modern historians with as diverse outlooks as Corelli Barnet (1986) and Eric Hobsbawm (1968) have given education and training an important place in their explanations for the failure of British industry to modernise at the forefront of global competition.

Among economists and political scientists, however, the issue has till recently taken a decidedly back seat. Although no single element can carry the weight of explaining deep and long-running historical trends, it is surprising that both orthodox and radical accounts of Britain's economic crises have either ignored training or else allotted it a minor place below other major 'culprits' such as high state spending, entrepreneurial failure, poor R&D, strong unions òr the role of the City of London.[1] In conventional analyses, skills were treated unproblematically, and were not connected to any historical processes. Among Marxian analysts, there was perhaps a feeling, engendered by Harry Braverman's inspiring and influential 'Labor and Monopoly Capital' (1974), that for the large majority of workers, training for technical and intellectual skills did not matter. In the age of Fordist technology and Taylorist work organisations, jobs had been sufficiently de-skilled, and all capital needed was a morally work-conditioned proletariat (Bowles and Gintis, 1976) and sufficient institutions to impart and develop the technical knowledge that was now the monopoly of the managerial class.

Two factors have forced economists and politicians now to focus on this issue: the outrageous and tragic waste of massive youth unemployment in Britain in the 1980s simply commanded that an alternative be sought; meanwhile the increasing competitiveness of the world economy began to make the skills deficiencies in Britain more glaringly apparent. Though there are several aspects to these deficiencies, the most dramatic failure lies not at degree level but in the numbers of 17-year-olds who were receiving no formal education or training (see Table 7.1). The impact of skill deficiencies on economic performance has been highlighted in an influential research programme of international comparisons initiated by the National Institute of Economic and Social Research (NIESR). The 1980s have seen a number of radical changes in the British training system and in training policy, accompanied by the beginning of educational reform. The course of change is far from coherent: buffeted by policy and events in the economy, each unfolding contradictory aspects of the neo-conservative programme, the training policy manoeuvres have been complex. The government began by retreating from intervention in the training system; later it was forced to raise its input much higher than ever before. It finished the decade by retreating again from direct intervention by returning responsibility for training to local businesses, after having excluded trade unions from their formal part in the training process.

The question to be examined in this chapter is whether the net effect of these changes will be to help arrest the decline of the British economy, and provide a skills base for the accumulation of capital in Britain.[2] We begin in Section 1 by summarising the evidence now amassing that productive performance is strongly correlated with training and education. Section 2 relates the changes brought about through policy and economic events; we concentrate primarily on changes in training, while touching on changes in the school system where the connection is greatest. We develop the idea that the changes lack coherence because they express the contradictory tendencies inherent in the philosophy of the 'free market and the strong state' as applied to training. Section 3 contrasts the British changes with the system in some competing countries. Section 4 concludes with a somewhat pessimistic evaluation of the prospects for the newest system now being erected: the Training and Enterprise Councils.

Table 7.1 Post-compulsory youth education in the 'Group of Seven' countries, 1984.

	Enrolment of 17-year-olds					Ratio of the number of persons taking post-secondary degrees to size of age class[1]
	School education		Apprentice, part-time, etc.	Post-secondary	Total	
	General	Vocational				
Canada	67	0	–	9	76	36
France	25	38	10	2	75	25
Germany	32	18	46	1	97	20
Italy	22[2]	25[2]	23[2]	0[2]	70	12
Japan	63	27	0	0	90	35
United States	81	0	–	6	88	58[2]
United Kingdom	18	12	35[3]	0	65	27

Notes: (1) Both 'batchelors' and lower; (2) 1981; (3) Includes further education, private and public part-time studies and the Youth Training Scheme.
Source: OECD (1987).

7.1 TRAINING AND ECONOMIC PERFORMANCE

The conventional economic approach to evaluating the effectiveness of training, couched in terms of 'human capital' analysis wherein individuals see themselves and are seen as objective repositories of investments in saleable skills, treats the issue in a cost-benefit accounting framework: the benefits being higher wages for individuals, higher productivity for firms. Wages being more visible and measurable than individual productivity, rate-of-return studies have typically allowed wage gains to represent the social benefits from training. Among the problems with such studies (Ashton *et al.*, 1989) are the questionable assumptions underlying the simple theory of marginal productivity, the identification of training as the cause of wage gain and the choice of an appropriate discounting factor.

A more fruitful approach has been the international comparative method – either comparing whole industries and sectors in Britain with those in other countries with known superior productivity records or comparing matched samples of firms having similar equipment but different training systems from different countries. One example of this method is the study of the construction industry by Prais and Steedman (1986), who observed that productivity is much higher in both France and Germany than in Britain and who were able to attribute much of this advantage to their superior training. Not only is training certificated and better integrated into a general education and training system but the numbers trained are much larger: France trains at least twice as many people as Britain, and Germany twice as many as France, even though the construction sectors are about the same size in all countries. Prais and Wagner (1983) compared training standards in five occupations in Britain and Germany and found that the standards in Germany were at least as high as in Britain, yet the proportions in each of the occupations trained in Germany were at least double those in Britain. Steedman and Wagner (1987) attributed much of the inferior productivity of Britain in a matched sample of firms producing furniture and fitted kitchens in Britain and Germany to the lower training standards in Britain which hampered the use of Computer Numerical Controlled machinery and the flexibility of production. A similar study by Daley *et al.,* (1985) also attributed much of the productivity differential between matched British and German manufacturing firms to differences in training, resulting in more frequent breakdowns and generally lower quality products. They cite in addition the relatively poor technological training of British managers which reduces the speed with which new technology is introduced into British firms. The relatively low quality of management training in Britain is also studied by Prais and Wagner (1988). The general inferiority of managerial training in Britain has been recognised for a long time but received further analysis in the joint report by the Manpower Services Commission, the National Economic Development Council and the British Institute of Management (1987), which showed that Britain has neglected the development of managerial skills.

The level of training among the general workforce has also been the focus of a number of studies. Thus, Prais (1981) compared vocational qualifications of the labour force in Britain and Germany in the mid-1970s. The central point of this comparison is that whereas the proportions of the workforces in the two countries with university degrees was very similar, there was a big difference in the proportions with intermediate level qualifications, such as apprenticeships with about 60% of the German workforce having such qualifications but only about 30% in Britain. In a similar comparison between Britain and Japan, Prais (1987) found that Britain was inferior in the general level of educational attainment, and particularly in mathematics. He also noted that Japanese companies operating in Britain found difficulty in recruiting workers with intermediate levels of skill. The deficiency in training in Britain is considered to be particularly acute with the trend towards more technologically advanced products and methods of production. Several studies have emphasised the need for more highly trained and flexible workers as technology changes. Campbell and Warner (1987) found that new production methods required more highly skilled managers and shopfloor workers with more initiative, particularly in companies involved in flexible small-batch production. Northcott and Rogers (1984), in a survey of 1,200 establishments, found that the shortage of microelectronics expertise was the factor most often spontaneously mentioned by their respondents as the factor hampering the introduction of microelectronics into industry.

To sum up, what these and other studies have shown is that there is a significant connection between the productivity performance (hence competitiveness) of industry located in different countries and the training and vocational education systems in force; and the British system has evolved into just about the worst among advanced capitalist countries. This was recognised by the House of Lords Select Committee on Overseas Trade (1985). The significance of this deficiency will no doubt increase as existing engineering industries become more technologically advanced and as the knowledge based industries expand.

7.2 THATCHERISM, INTERNATIONALISATION OF CAPITAL AND TRAINING

7.2.1 Historical background

The origins of the training problem which surfaced so rudely in Margaret Thatcher's era of free-market restructuring lie deep in the British past. Britain entered the industrial era with a model of training provision derived from the Guild system and then alongside it an educational system was constructed that was totally divorced from industry. The result was an institutional structure geared to produce a small highly educated élite and a mass of literate workers, some of whom were trained through the apprenticeship system for the skilled jobs, leaving the majority to enter firms as unskilled or semi-skilled labourers.

The apprenticeship provided a binding contract between parents and employer that the young person would serve the master for a given time period (usually 5–7 years). In return the master would agree to teach the apprentice the secrets of the trade. The cost of entry, of persuading the master to take an apprentice, differed according to skill level and eventual remuneration that could be expected. In the mid-nineteenth century for a sailmaker it was £7, for a cabinet maker who could expect to command much higher wages it was £50. In some instances the apprenticeship was just a channel through which employers secured labour but where few secrets were taught, as with some of the early mill owners. The unions were able to use the apprenticeship system as a means of exerting some control over entry to the trade and to ensure that their monopoly of a particular trade was not undermined. The more technical training required by industry was provided by a small number of institutions established by the larger entrepreneurs in cities such as Birmingham and Manchester.

During the nineteenth century the main preoccupation of the state in the field of education was not with the transmission of technical knowledge, but with the question of the moral and political condition of the lower orders. The state system of education was established on the basis of that previously provided by the major religious organisations; the independently financed working-class schools were closed down (Gardner, 1984). The concern was not to provide the masses with a broadly based technical education but to ensure that they were given some form of instruction appropriate to their rank and, equally important, exposed to the correct moral code. This concern with ensuring that the education delivered was appropriate to the future status and function of young people in the labour market has been a long-standing characteristic of the British education system. In the late 1960s and 1970s, there was an attempt to establish a comprehensive system, but the educational reforms associated with the 'new vocationalism' (Blackman, 1987; Brown, 1988) are rapidly undermining that system and restoring the traditional characteristics.

The ruling élite was always educated outside the state system. The public schools pioneered a curriculum which incorporated a grounding in the classics with modern science. Its function was to prepare young people for careers in politics, the church, law, armed forces and in ruling the Dominions. It was this academic curriculum which came to dominate the state education system, through the leadership of the grammar schools. A strong movement towards a more technical curriculum did emerge in the early twentieth century but was discarded in favour of the classical curriculum of the grammar schools. This heritage has created a strict division at the secondary level between education and training in Britain, one that is not found in other countries such as Germany, where the two are more highly integrated. The division left the task of training each new generation to the employers and unions. By the end of the Second World War the universities were providing those in the professions and top civil servants with a broad-based liberal education. The grammar schools were providing a small administrative élite and the secondary modern schools were created to feed young people into the apprenticeships and the jobs as operatives in the labour-intensive industries. Apart from the apprenticeships, which were still largely time-served, the employers provided the little training that was required for the unskilled and semi-skilled jobs (Ashton, 1988).

Within such a system, the delivery of training was very sensitive to the business cycle. Training was one of the first costs employers cut when they entered a downturn in the business cycle, only to find that as the economy recovered, they were faced with a shortage of skilled labour. These recurrent skill shortages, together with a growing realisation that Britain was falling behind her competitors in the delivery of skills, led to the 1964 Industrial Training Act. This legislation created a national system of Industrial Training Boards (ITBs), which had the responsibility for improving the quantity and quality of training within the firms in their jurisdiction. They had the powers to levy charges and refund those who were deemed to be pulling their weight. In this way the free-rider problem associated with industrial training costs was overcome. Those firms which relied on others and poached trained workers to avoid the costs of training were penalised. In practice the ITBs concerned themselves primarily with the training of operatives and skilled workers. However, because they were imposed on employers there was a continual distrust by firms of their 'bureaucratic interference'. In addition to the ITBs the government also created a series of Skillcentres to provide training for those who wished to change career but lacked the skills to do so. During this period, also, the polytechnics were established from the old colleges of technology and expanded ostensibly to provide vocational education within the higher education system. Although they were intended to have parity of prestige with the universities, this did not occur and in most cases the traditional curriculum of the universities was adopted. For a while at least the only basic difference between the two systems lay in their funding arrangements.

The next major development came in 1973 when the government set up the Manpower Services Commission (MSC). This had the task of bringing together employers, unions and government to create a coherent national approach to the problem of training and manpower supply. The MSC developed a corporatist strategy, producing a consensus on the main issues to be tackled and on the strategy to be adopted (Turbin, 1987). This was a radical departure from previous government strategy which was always to impose policy from Whitehall without much forethought or discussion about how it might be implemented (Marquand, 1989). It was this framework which the Thatcher administration inherited on coming to office.

7.2.2 Private and public sources of change in the training system

The contradictory tensions in the neo-Conservative philosophy of 'the free economy and the strong state' (Gamble, 1988) are nowhere more evident than in the evolution of the government's training policy over the last decade. The 'free economy' principle invokes individuals' incentives to better themselves, through investing in their own 'human capital', sometimes funded and sometimes also delivered by the firms they work for. Without state interference an optimal amount of training would be chosen. Yet education and training are commodities so manifestly overladen with externalities and market imperfections, and in the case of children, so far from fulfilling the requirements for informed choice that no government can leave the matter entirely to the private sector. In the case of education, only the small sector catering for the élite can proceed along free market lines (and these are in practice supported through tax reliefs). As regards training, much more can be left to firms and individuals but without intervention little would be achieved.

The 'strong state' principle involves the government's requirement to improve economic performance by modernising the training system through imposing an enterprise philosophy on the various training institutions, if necessary radically altering them. To do this the government has to weaken the opposition it finds in local education authorities, in trade unions and in the liberal and older conservative establishments of higher education. Further intervention, and a distortion of its basic training objectives, is forced upon the government by the imperfect, even disastrous, functioning of its more general economic policies: the appearance of mass youth unemployment with accompanying political risks compels ameliorative action. The result of these contradictory forces in the 1980s has been a confused picture of both less and more intervention in the training and education field, and elements of devolvement accompanying some unprecedented accumulations of centralised power.   Partial support for the belief that free training markets can provide British capital with an adaptable system comes ironically from the competitive challenge of foreign-owned capital, whose managers tend to be steeped in the institutional background of superior interventionist education and training systems.

The growth of multinationals such as IBM and Nissan brought companies into Britain which highlighted different training practices. IBM devotes considerable resources to training, but does not recognise unions. It has a highly developed internal labour market and can move staff around freely providing retraining where necessary. The Japanese companies recognise only one union but also devote considerable resources to training. Human resource development, as it is called, is central to those companies' product market strategies and not something which is bolted on as an afterthought. Such companies would have challenged existing British stereotypes about training and its role in the firm irrespective of the party in power (Funding Study, 1988).

Another consequence of the extension of global markets has been that the higher levels of productivity and quality associated with the Japanese firms in particular have forced many other companies operating in Britain to reassess their labour management strategies. As it became clear to such companies that their survival in world markets depended on them achieving the same levels of commitment and productivity from their workers that the Japanese had already done, their industrial relations and training practices had to change. Essentially this meant reducing lines of demarcation, reducing staffing levels but making the remaining workers more flexible and multi-skilled. It meant undermining the occupational labour markets which were a product of the old apprenticeship system and making training more firm-specific and creating an internal labour market.

These changes are, however, neither universal nor necessarily a viable model to be applied in all sectors. The essential question is whether the training system in British firms can adapt to the changing requirements of the market. There is overwhelming evidence that it cannot. To start with, there is a long-term history of reported skill shortages in British industry, most apparent in times of cyclical upturn, but remarkably persistent. Beyond that, however, is the evidence of an overall tendency for British industry to special-ise in relatively low-skill lines of production. There are thus two kinds of skill shortage in evidence: the *disequilibrium* kind, where firms queue up to hire skilled workers or try to entice them away from competitors, and the *equi-librium* kind, where industry is short on skills relative to competitors abroad simply because it has settled for low-skill production processes. Even if firms were not reporting skill shortages, this can be because the disequilibria have disappeared along with the industry itself – leaving the rest of industry in a particularly disadvantageous position within the international division of labour.

Over the last decade changes in the economic environment have brought with them changes in the perceived demands placed on the training system. The loss of jobs in manufacturing, especially in the labour-intensive industries where capital has been relocated to lower wage cost countries, has been the most decisive influence. There is far less demand now for the unskilled, semi-skilled worker in manufacturing than there was even a decade ago; one-third of the manual jobs in engineering were lost during the 1981–3 recession alone. The new jobs require knowledge of new technologies and the new conditions of labour involve new forms of flexibility. In addition there has been a rapid expansion outside manufacturing for workers with these skills, in finance, commerce and business services. The new jobs at this level tend to be information-based. Those firms which have survived and expanded are characterised by having a much higher proportion of professional, managerial and technical workers than was the case a decade ago. Finally, within the service sector there has been a rapid growth of part-time employment and jobs which require relatively few skills and to which married women returning to work are recruited. In short, there have been contradictory trends at work, some leading to an upskilling and a growing demand for more highly educated workers, others producing an increase in the demand for unskilled and semi-skilled labour, but not for the heavy manual labour which characterised the old manufacturing industries. Thus, whereas the jobs lost were predominantly manual jobs filled by males, the new unskilled and semi-skilled workers are increasingly service sector jobs filled by married women (Ashton *et al.,* 1989).

Yet these perceived demands on the training system may be very different from the demands that would be necessary if the economy were to be re-oriented to compete in leading high technology and mainline sectors of industry. The perceived demands tend to be related to immediate problems of shortages, and there is evidence that as much as 70% of establishments in Britain simply have no plans for training. Generally, the development of a training strategy is nowhere near the top of the agenda for managerial decision-making (Funding Study, 1988; Training Commission, 1989). Thus, it is possible within a free market approach for the economy to be caught in a low-skills equilibrium.[3] The perceived demands for training from a de-industrialising economy may be adequately met in a self-fulfilling reduction of the skills base. Yet this form of adaptation can hardly be said to reflect the choice and aspirations of employees.

There arises, then, the question as to whether the policy surveys of the Thatcher government are likely to redress these deficiencies. To what extent have its interventions helped to reduce skill shortages of the disequilibrium type by addressing the static and dynamic externalities involved? More important, have they helped to re-orientate industry based in Britain towards a high-skills location in the division of labour?

7.2.3 Training in the 1980s

The actual course of the government's training policy reflects both the tensions between intervention and the free training market, and the contradictions in the free market economy generally.

The initial attitude was revealed after only a few weeks in office. In June 1979, MSC expenditure for the year already begun was cut by £110 million, about 18% of its previous budget.[4] This cut mainly fell on the Special Temporary Employment Programme (STEP) but also affected the Training Opportunities Programme (TOPS) and the number of people completing TOPS courses in this first year fell by about 4,500. These initial reductions in the MSC budget were to be followed by planned further cuts in the following years. The revealed intention of the government appears to have been a progressive reduction in the role played by the MSC.

Further evidence of withdrawal of state involvement came with the decision to abolish 16 of the 23 Industrial Training Boards in 1981. These abolitions were part of a package aimed at cutting public expenditure on education and training but were in line with the policy of cutting bureaucracy and pushing back the responsibility for labour market issues onto employers. The ITBs were to be replaced by voluntary associations with no power to levy. For essentially the same reasons the government reduced the number of Skill-centres and put them on to a self-financing basis. In the future, the provision of training was to be left to market forces. This apparent intention was, however, thwarted by the increase in unemployment in the early 1980s. The increased number of new entrants to the labour market occurred at just the moment when the effects of the first monetarist experiment were being felt in the labour market (Table 7.2). Youth unemployment was already serious when the Conservatives were elected, but the problem soon escalated: by the end of 1981 an estimated one in three of all school-leavers were entering the Youth Opportunities Programmes (YOP) compared with one in six in the previous year. In addition there was a massive collapse in the number of apprentices being trained by private industry, the recession accelerating the long-run de-industrialising trend of decline (Table 7.3). Such devastation of the potential future skills base hardly boded well for a restructured, fitter and more dynamic industry.

This combination of failures lay behind a most significant change in training policy: the introduction by the MSC of its New Training Initiative (NTI). This was an attempt to set into place a national system of vocational training, to make training available to all young people entering the labour market and to those adults who required it. It also involved continuing its efforts to update the apprenticeship system, a process which had been under way for some time. The aim here was to replace the time-served basis with a modular system that was norm referenced.

Central to the NTI was the Youth Training Scheme (YTS). This was a one-year programme of work experience with a minimum component of off-the-job training. It built on previous experience with the Youth Opportunities Programme which had been created in the 1970s, also as a response to the problem of youth unemployment. It differed from previous schemes in that it was delivered primarily through employers on the assumption that they were the best placed to make decisions about what constituted the most appropriate form of training. The YTS was later extended to two years and the quality of the training given was monitored by a new Training Standards Advisory Service. However, while the YTS achieved the political objectives of giving school-leavers an alternative to the dole, it remained largely a low level training scheme, preparing young people for operative level jobs in manufacturing, sales, community and personal care

Table 7.2 Youth labour market and government training programme for young people, 1978–1989.

	1 Civilian labour force, Great Britain: 16–19 '000	*2*[c] Unemployment UK, January numbers 18–19 '000	*3*[c] Unemployment UK rates 18–19 %
1978	2,431	140.0[b]	10.9
1979	2,548	132.7[b]	10.4
1980	2,684	142.1	10.9
1981	2,628	245.6	18.1
1982	2,590	318.2	22.9
1983	2,532	369.8	26.1
1984	2,572	391.1	27.0
1985	2,570	374.0	24.8
1986	2,504	342.1	23.5
1987	2,551	297.9	22.0
1988	2,514[a]	229.6	17.0
1989	2,432[a]	168.9	12.5

	4[d] Entrants to YOP in year commencing	*5* Entrants to YTS in year commencing
1978	162,200	
1979	216,400	
1980	360,000	
1981	553,000	
1982	543,000	
1983	27,000	354,000
1984		389,000
1985		397,700
1986		360,000
1987		327,600
1988		334,400[e]

Notes: (a) Projections; (b) Great Britain; (c) there have been frequent changes in the methods of measuring the unemployed. These are discussed in *Department of Employment Gazette,* October 1986, p. 422 and December 1988, p. 661; (d) YTS succeeded YOP and various other schemes including Training for Skills and Unified Vocational Preparation in 1983. The YOP figures include some people who entered more than one programme in a year; (e) planned entrants 1988–9.
Sources: 1, *Department of Employment Gazette*, May 1987, p. 254; March 1988, p. 118. 2, 3, *Department of Employment Gazette*: various issues Tables 2.7 and 2.15. 4, 5, *MSC* and *TA Annual Reports:* various years.

and clerical work. Provision for adults remained relatively under-developed and was only tackled on a systematic basis when long-term unemployment became a politically sensitive issue. Utilising its experience with the YTS, in 1988 the MSC produced the Employment Training Scheme, a period of training available to all the long-term unemployed following an initial counselling session. Again, this was a low-cost training programme which could at most prepare people for semi-skilled jobs. Relatively poor incentives meant that, in any case, in the first six months there was a poor take-up rate, ranging from 79% in Humberside to only 32% in Surrey.[5]

It would be hard to avoid the conclusion that the key driving force in such interventions is the political problem of unemployment, rather than the structural economic problem of an insufficiently skilled workforce. Noted skill problems, such as the low level of managerial qualifications, have been largely left to a market-led process of adaptation (with gestures such as the 'Enterprise in Higher Education' Scheme), for unemployment among this group is neither large nor a major spur to political action. The government's propensity to withdraw is, moreover, shown in other areas. Under the cloak of the call for greater efficiency and freedom of choice, the government has steadily deprived higher education institutions of public resources.[6] It succeeded in absorbing the increased numbers of students by the simple expedient of expanding the numbers in polytechnics without appropriate resources. The resulting decline in the quality of teaching is both hard to gauge and long to emerge, but nonetheless real. On the other hand, the fact that the 'solution' to youth unemployment was packaged as a training measure (with consequent pressures not least from the union movement

Table 7.3 Apprentices and trainees in manufacturing industries, GB.

	Total appren '000	Total other trainees '000	Total appren. and other trainees[1,2] '000	Males in training as % of all males in manufacturing	Females in training as % of all females in manufacturing
1965	243.3	145.3	388.6	5.8	2.7
1975	155.3	135.2	290.5	4.5	2.5
1976	148.4	116.3	264.7	4.4	2.4
1977	153.1	125.1	278.2	4.5	2.5
1978	156.2	116.3	272.5	4.5	2.4
1979	155.0	111.3	266.3	4.5	2.4
1980	149.5	90.0	239.5	4.4	1.9
1981	147.6	62.9	210.5	4.2	1.5
1982	123.7	56.0	179.7	3.8	1.6
1983	102.4	47.9	150.3	3.3	1.4
1984	82.0	39.7	121.6	2.6	1.3
1985	73.2	39.2	112.4	2.4	1.3
1986	61.8	38.5	100.3	2.2	1.2
1987	58.0	37.4	95.4	2.2	1.1
1988	55.7	37.6	93.3	2.1	1.1

Notes: (1) Many of those receiving training under YTS are excluded if they have no contract of employment. (2) The distinction between 'apprentice' and 'other training' has changed as the conditions of apprenticeship have changed.
Source: Employment Gazette, September 1980 and Table 1.15, various issues.

represented on the MSC to make the training genuine) combined with an increasing public acceptance (reinforced by pressure from within the MSC) that there really was a serious skills disparity between British and continental workers.

On the education front, the MSC instituted the new Technical and Vocational Education Initiative (TVEI), intended to stimulate technical and vocational education among 14–18-year-olds in school and by 1984 there were 20,900 students participating in its courses. In January 1984 the government increased the resources of the MSC to buy work-related non-advanced further education. Not only was the YTS turning into a genuine training programme rather than a palliative for youth unemployment but the MSC was extending its scope into the educational system itself in an attempt to provide for the non-academic school pupil. The TOPS programme to train adults continued to expand and in 1984–5 there were 75,400 completions. A significant aspect of the TOPS programme was that about 30% of its trainees were women, a notable extension of training provision to an increasingly important part of the workforce but one traditionally ill-provided for. Special provision was made for training in skills related to the new information technology with the establishment of 120 Information and Technology Centres (ITECS) by the end of 1984, taking over 4,000 young people under the YTS scheme. By 1988 these had expanded to 175 and offered 10,500 training places.

Significant changes were also made in the training provided by the private sector. Agreement was reached between the Engineering Employers Federation and Confederation of Shipbuilding and Engineering Unions on training standards as laid down by the Engineering Industry Training Board and the Construction Industry Training Board introduced tests for training standards. New training arrangements were established in the electrical contracting sector, the printing industry and in road transport. The City and Guilds, BTEC Council and the Royal Society of Arts began to link their standards, leading to the establishment in 1986 of the National Council for Vocational Qualifications (NCVQ). This council accredits and standardises qualifications awarded by others and is starting to remedy one of the weaknesses of the British training process, namely that even where training was undertaken it did not lead to the formal recognition of the attainment of a clearly defined standard. An early example of the benefits to be gained was a new national training scheme for retailers, recognised by the NCVQ in 1989.

All this activity, together with changes in the educational system, showed some results. An improving trend is shown in the proportions of people in the 16–19 age range recorded as having no qualifications in the General Household Survey. In 1977 this proportion stood at 35% for males and 30% for females. It fell to 33% and 28%, respectively, in 1981 and again to 24% and 22% in 1986. There were also pronounced declines in the proportion of the age range 20–29 recorded as having no qualifications. Although it is difficult to tell exactly at what levels the increased numbers of qualifications were obtained, there is a clear indication that some inroad was made into the ridiculously large proportions of the British workforce having no qualifications at all.

Despite such improvements, and allowing even for the fact that previous governments had made but feeble inroads into the training problems of British industry, the record of the training system after a decade of Conservative government has been poor. When the 'truth was out' in the 1980s and the issue could no longer be politically ignored the *laissez-faire* philosophy in force was singularly unsuitable for effecting requisite changes. Those improvements we have seen have been partly the result of economic circumstances (as with YTS). Any progressive intentions were undermined by the collapse of the apprenticeship system, and the solutions adapted in response to unemployment run counter to the logic of change in the world economy.

As we have seen, there has been a diminishing demand for relatively unskilled workers and a growth in demand (even through the recession) for professional, managerial and technical workers, resulting in persistent disequilibrium skill shortages at this level. Yet the output from the higher education system has not been proportionately increased, neither has there been any increase in the proportions of young people who obtain middle-level educational qualifications, e.g., O-levels. The only solution offered has been to train more young people for low-skilled jobs. The institutions of higher education which were in a position to resolve the problem have had their budgets cut and the universities in particular had strict limits placed on the number they could recruit.

Another contradiction raised by these underlying trends is that the group from which the employers have drawn for their new low-skilled jobs have not been the traditional school-leaver population but married women, yet the training was directed at the school-leaver population. As a resource married women have been largely ignored, yet many of them have the requisite educational background to fill not only the low-level skills jobs but also the higher-level skilled vacancies. It is evident, too, that many of the long-term unemployed, approximately 25% of the 18–25-year-olds, have the requisite educational background (O-levels or above) to enable them to train for the higher-level skill vacancies (Finn and Convery, 1988). Yet what they are offered on the Employment Training Scheme is a one-year package of low-skills training. It is this persistent theme of a low-cost, low-skills solution to the problem of a shortage of highly skilled labour which is the major failure of the government's policy on training. It is a policy forced on the government by its rigid adherence to a belief in the ability of market forces to produce a solution to all economic problems. This has left the state in a position where it will not effectively underwrite the social costs of training or even use its resources to steer the country in the right direction as has been done in other societies.

Finally, the one institution which appears to have done most to bring about changes, the MSC, has now been abolished, replaced by a mere wing of the Department of Employment. One of the last bastions of quasi-corporatism remaining from the 1970s, the MSC survived for nearly a decade because it helped to resolve the various contradictions we have discussed above between the need for a strong state to impose a free market in training and the paradoxical requirements of free market intervention.

The MSC had pioneered a form of consensual policy making, involving the consent, if not always the active co-operation, of both employers and unions. It possessed a degree of independence, but this did not prevent it being used by Government to help resolve its free market political problems. For example, in the case of YTS, the Government's aim was to tackle the problem of mass youth unemployment. In the wake of the 1981 riots it had 'to get the kids off the streets'. The MSC provided the means to do this, but the MSC also had its own agenda for a national system of training, although this was expensive. The result was a compromise with the MSC delivering a training scheme which guaranteed to offer a place to all young people without a major increase in spending. Similarly, the MSC had been pioneering changes in vocational education (and later the NCVQ). What was particularly significant about the MSC was that it offered the means of delivering a coherent national policy on vocational education and training.

The MSC was also able to create at least one change within the educational system – the TVEI. In a teaching profession generally demoralised by cuts and shortages, changes were naturally slow to emerge from within. Reform was also particularly held back by the weight of the élitist British class structure – especially, the dominance of the Public Schools (which form the personal memories of education for cabinet ministers) and the lure of the City. Also, despite the Higginson Committee's recommendation for a wider sixth-form syllabus (which would conform with practice elsewhere), the overly specialised A-level route has been maintained, at the insistence of Margaret Thatcher.

Yet such an institution as the MSC was bound to sit uneasily within a regime which in most other respects is confronting trade unions and diminishing their influence. In addition, the promotion of training among the low-skilled has always been accompanied by the objective of lowering wages – a policy that was bound to conflict with union consensus. Over the years, Margaret Thatcher's administration has slowly undermined the consensual basis of the MSC's mode of operation. The delivery of the Youth Training Scheme strained relationships with some unions and in 1989 the government ended unions' rights to be consulted about specific schemes. In the event, the inability of the unions to wring sufficient concessions on the details of the Employment Training Scheme led to the TUC voting to withdraw co-operation. By this time the MSC had already been transformed into the Training Commission but the refusal of the TUC to co-operate provided the pretext for dismissal of the Commissioners and the incorporation of the Commission into the Department of Employment as the Training Agency. Whatever independence it had possessed has now gone – an outcome entirely consistent with neo-Conservative philosophy. With the MSC's demise the state is now stronger, and the economy seen to be that much freer without this element of union 'interference'.

7.3 TRAINING SYSTEMS IN OTHER COUNTRIES

With a constantly changing international division of labour, in response to a complex pattern of economic crisis, technological changes and the emergence of the Pacific rim, the ability to compete depends on the pace of adjustment to change. In the current era, the ability to capture the high-wage sectors will increasingly depend on competitiveness in the knowledge-based industries which are among the leading sectors. There is a sense, therefore, in which governments with responsibilities for intervening in training and education systems are competing with each other in the process of capital accumulation, reflecting capitalist competition. British-owned (and foreign-owned) firms can choose to locate their investment in the most profitable way – to them, it is relatively unimportant whether the low-wage assembly operations are in Britain or elsewhere as long as there is skilled labour somewhere to draw upon. For a government, to be lumbered with a low-wage region is a different matter, and one of some concern. In this context it is interesting to compare the changes brought about under Margaret Thatcher with the systems, and the improvements, introduced elsewhere. Space permits only a limited range of comparisons.

The British model is distinguished by its focus on low-skills training, providing a major point of contrast with other advanced industrial economies such as Canada, USA, France, Germany and Sweden. When confronted with the need for a more highly trained labour force Canada and France adopted what may be loosely termed a vocational training solution. Canada had traditionally recruited its skilled labour from overseas, frequently Britain, but it became clear in the 1950s and 1960s that this was providing, at best, only a short-term solution. The response was to develop vocational education at the secondary level and to put considerable resources into the expansion of a comprehensive system of higher education (Gaskell (in press)). The result was a substantial increase in the proportion (now estimated to be over 70%) of young people who continued their high-school education until they reached the age of 18. Moreover, once finished with high school, 30–40% stay on into higher education. The result is that Canada is producing a very well educated labour force which industry and commerce then train to meet the requirement of particular firms. However, the open nature of the educational institutions means that there is a constant flow of personnel back and forth between work and education/training. It is not at all uncommon for young people to leave high school or college, take up a job and then return, full-time or part-time, to obtain further educational or training credentials. The strict division which separates education and labour market experience in Britain is unknown there (Krahn and Lowe, 1990).

In France, the vocational solution has taken a different form. Compared with Britain, the French system has always maintained an even more rigid division between education and training. Traditionally, the educational system provided a basic education and those youths not destined for higher education left as soon as possible. A decade ago, the participation rate of 16-year-olds in education was lower than in Britain. Within the labour market the emphasis was on each firm providing forms of training directed exclusively at meeting its own requirements (Maurice *et al.,* 1986). There was little training comparable to the British apprenticeship system which provided, through a combination of work experience and part-time education, a training in occupational-specific as opposed to firm-specific skills. Since then, the most radical response in France to skill problems have been in the middle and lower levels of the education system. For those who opt out of the academic route at 14 they introduced the CAP (Certificat d'Aptitude Professionel) and at a slightly higher level BEP (Brevet d'Etudes Professionel) which keeps young people in full-time education until 18. Unlike the British YTS, access to these courses is not automatic and depends on a prior level of achievement. These courses provide a high level of broad-based vocational training for young people intending to enter a variety of trades, and produce a much larger number of qualified craftworkers than in Britain. In this way, using the educational system the French have upgraded the skill levels of those entering the middle and lower levels of the labour market. However, not content with that, their current reforms are aimed at further improving the qualifications of those entering higher-level jobs. The Technical Baccalaureat, equivalent to a technical A-level, is being supplemented by a Vocational Baccalaureat and the aim is to increase significantly the numbers qualified to technician level and above. Already the achievements are significant, for while Britain produces 26,000 BTEC students per year the French produce 82,000 students per year through the Technical Baccalaureat. In this way the French are well on their way to solving their training problem. The tactics have been to use the public education system to provide 'an all-round technical education combined with mastery of a specific skill' (Steedman, 1988, p. 68). The state has socialised the costs of initial training, imposing a levy of 0.5% of gross wages. In exchange for this employers can recruit from a much more highly qualified pool of labour.

The Germans have adopted a different solution relying on an industrial training base and occupational labour markets to provide the solution. Young people opt for a training in a formally regulated three-year apprenticeship, organised jointly by the employers, unions and state. Participation in education is compulsory for all German youth until they are 18. However, for those on the apprenticeship system this refers to their part-time education which through the German Meister system, also involves intensive supervised training at the work place. The German system has a much longer pedigree than the French: for at least the last two decades it has produced an output of highly qualified workers far in excess of anything achieved in Britain. In the last decade the French and the Canadians have used their educational systems to catch up with the Germans and provide a labour force with the requisite intellectual problem-solving skills required for knowledge-based industries. In Britain, by contrast, the main thrust of policy has been to improve the training of those who choose to enter unskilled and semi-skilled jobs at 16.

Finally, in Sweden there has long been a consensus between the government, employers and unions on the need to pursue a 'high technology' path to economic growth if the country is to maintain full employment and a high standard of living. This has provided the basis from which the labour market policy has been derived. It has meant that as the conditions of international competition have changed, labour market policy has been adjusted to ensure that the economy has remained competitive. The aim has been to ensure the flexibility of the labour market by reducing the costs of mobility by the provision of training and retraining grants, so as to raise the rate of return to vocational education and training.

In practice this has involved substantial shifts in the approach to training policy (Standing, 1988). In the 1950s there was help to ensure geographical mobility of workers in the outer regions, but relatively little attention was paid to training since the industrial structure, based on heavy industries, was fairly stable. The educational system, with its nine years of compulsory education, was sufficient to meet the demand for labour. Since then changes in Sweden's position in world markets and the underlying shifts in the economy, such as the reduction in the demand for unskilled labour and the growing demand for more technically skilled workers, have combined to create a number of changes. Dissatisfaction with the educational system has led to a greater emphasis on vocational education in an attempt to upgrade the skill level of the labour force. Now 90% continue into upper secondary education and since 1983 every local education authority has had to draw up a plan to ensure that 16- and 17-year-olds obtain further (vocational) education. Like Britain, programmes have been introduced for young people, but unlike Britain, one part of the training budget is devoted to 'bottleneck' training, aimed at removing bottlenecks by increasing the upgrading of workers within the firms and by retraining workers displaced for jobs for which there is a perceived skill shortage. This in-firm training is seen as an essential part of the attempt to further enhance the skills base of the economy.

In summary, although considerations of equity determine that most of the training budget is spent on those disadvantaged in the labour market, the unemployed and handicapped, the underlying thrust is now to use public interventions in training to ensure the upgrading of the labour force. Training forms part of an active labour market policy which ensures that 70% of labour market spending goes on counselling, placement, training rehabilitation and job development programmes (Ministry of Labour, 1988). This active labour market policy contrasts dramatically with the British policy. Britain's labour market spending budget (including unemployment benefits) is of comparable size, but only 30% goes to the employment service, training and job development programmes. In Britain, the majority of resources are devoted to supporting the unemployed. The aim of Swedish training policy and the wider labour market policy is to facilitate the necessary economic restructuring by combining the workers' demand for security with the need for flexibility in production. Thus, while some of the components of labour market policy are similar in the two societies, the major difference lies in the Swedish consensus between government, capital and labour, that labour market policy should play a central part in enhancing the competitiveness of Swedish industry.

7.4 CONCLUSION

Technological progress in the UK is being hampered by failure to develop the human resources of the nation ... At stake is the UK's competitive edge in international trade and ultimately therefore the UK's economic future ... The Committee doubts whether there is a more serious challenge facing British industry than the adequate provision of people properly qualified and trained to exploit effectively the new technologies as they emerge. (House of Lords, 1984–5; paras 5.1 and 5.2)

There is now a widespread recognition that industry in Britain has a training 'problem' if it wishes to attract high-paying productive capital investments, and there appears to be any number of specific hitches and problems along the way – the persistence of skill shortages, the regulation of YTS and ET Schemes, the unions' opposition to ET, teacher shortages, the difficulties of recruiting for ET and YTS, and so on. These sorts of problems are inevitable given the contradictory forces pulling in several directions that follow from the neo-Conservative policies and the course of economic events. At least some of the contradictions can be resolved, however, through an essentially political struggle. Lacking an effective opposition either inside or outside the Conservative Party, the government has begun to return the training problem to businesses themselves where, according to the philosophy, it belongs. In the future, training is to be delivered through about 100 local Training and Enterprise Councils which are to be established by private-sector employers; top managers are to comprise at least two-thirds of their membership, the rest to be recruited from co-operating trade unions, local authorities, voluntary organisations and representatives from education. These Councils are to address themselves to the training problems and issues in the local labour market. They are intended to draw up strategies, arrange for the delivery of suitable training programmes by further education colleges and other providers, and tailor YTS and ET schemes to local needs.

There must remain serious doubts whether this system, providing no more resources and devolving a fair amount of control away from the centre, will enable British capital to compete. Even YTS is faltering in areas like the South-east where youth unemployment has fallen sufficiently to make it difficult to recruit at the low pay levels characteristic of the schemes. The TEC schemes are modelled on similar lines to the work of private industry councils introduced in 1983 in the US, a country with an appalling record of productivity growth, and with skills problems of its own. It is true that the councils are somewhat similar in conception to the German local Chambers of Commerce, whose success in managing training is renowned. Whether this solution can work in the less consensual atmosphere in British industries is unclear. The involvement of local employers in training is essential but it is doubtful if voluntary arrangements can be sufficient. In a few cities like Birmingham, with a strong tradition of involvement of businesses in municipal affairs through the Chamber of Commerce, the prospects look brighter,[7] but these traditions do not exist in the vast majority of British towns, and, moreover, private employers have on the whole a notorious unwillingness to provide training in Britain in the absence of a strong push from the state.[8] After a whole decade there is belated talk (but still no action) to extend training and further education to every worker aged under 19.[9] It remains to be seen whether, in the event of this target being achieved, it will substantially open the doors to the acquisition of the higher level of skills which so many British workers are currently barred from.

If the skills problem is not addressed, it may be that the only long-term resolution for UK-based capital is a world-wide equalisation of wage rates for work of equal low-skill content. Only those in the élite high-skill workforces, particularly those able to partake via multinationals in the international rewards for skilled professionals, managers and technicians, will be able to command high and increasing wages. For the rest, a levelling down to those received in the emergent developing nations is not so far-fetched in the long run. In the absence of further change, it seems depressingly likely that the British may yet enter the twenty-first century, in the age of high technology, as still a 'spectacularly ill-educated people'.

NOTES

1. See, e.g., Caves and Krause (1980); Smith (1984); Gamble (1979), none of which address the training issue; these contrast strongly with more recent accounts, e.g., Davies and Caves (1987).
2. In our view proper education and training are legitimate, necessary and immensely

152   *Production Process and Labour Market*

valuable tasks in themselves, justifiable without reference to the economic objectives of any particular kind of society. In this chapter, however, the question is simply: is the new system beneficial for British capital? There are occasions when objectives do not conflict, and this is one such.

3. Finegold and Soskice (1988) define the 'low-skills equilibrium' operating in Britain as a 'self-reinforcing network of societal and state institutions which interact to stifle the demand for improvement in skill levels'.
4. This, and subsequent training data in this section, are extracted from MSC *Annual Reports*; employment and unemployment data are taken from the *Employment Gazette*.
5. *Financial Times*, 16.4.89.
6. *Financial Times*, 13.2.89.
7. *Financial Times*, 14.12.88.
8. In addition, the British Institute of Management and industry training specialists have expressed grave doubts about the viability of devolving training to the private sector, while the Confederation of British Industry called for substantial modifications; *Financial Times*, 15.2.89 and 13.4.89.
9. *Financial Times*, 16.2.89.

REFERENCES

Arnold, M., *Schools and Universities on the Continent*, (Macmillan: London, 1868).

Ashton, D. N., 'Educational institutions, youth and the labour markets', In *Employment in Britain*, (ed. Gallie, D.) (Blackwell: Oxford, 1988).

Ashton, D. N., Green, F. and Hoskins, M. D., *An Overview of the Evaluation of the Net Benefits of Training*, Funding Study Series, Training Commission (in press).

Ashton, D. N. and Lowe, G. S. (eds), *Making Their Way: A Comparative Analysis of the Relationship Between Education, Training and the Labour Market in Canada and Britain*, (Open University Press: Milton Keynes) (in press).

Ashton, D. N., Maguire, M. J. and Spilsbury, M., *Restructuring the Labour Market: The Implications for Youth*, (Macmillan: London, 1989).

Barnett, C., *The Audit of War: the illusion and reality of Britain as a great nation*, (Macmillan: London, 1986).

Blackman, S. J., 'The Labour Market in school: new vocationalism and issues of socially ascribed discrimination', in *Education, Unemployment and Labour Markets*, (eds Brown, P. and Ashton, D. N.) (Falmer: London, 1987).

Bowles, S. and Gintis, H., *Schooling in Capitalist America*, (Routledge & Kegan Paul: London, 1976).

Braverman, H., *Labour and Monopoly Capital*, (Monthly Review Press: New York, 1974).

Brown, P., 'The New Vocationalism: a policy for inequality?' in *Young Careers: The Search for Jobs and the New Vocationalism*, (ed. Coles, R.) (Open University Press: Milton Keynes, 1988).

Campbell, A. and Warner, M., 'New Technology, innovation and training: a survey of British firms', *New Technology, Work and Employment*, 2, 2, 86–99 (1987).

Caves, Richard E. and Krause, Lawrence B. (eds), *Britain's Economic Performance*, (The Brookings Institution: Washington, 1980).

Daley, A., Hitchens, D. M. W. N. and Wagner, K., 'Productivity, machinery and skills in a sample of British and German manufacturing plants: results of a pilot inquiry', *National Institute Economic Review*, 111, 48–61 (1985).

Davies, Stephen and Caves, Richard E., *Britain's Productivity Gap*, (Cambridge University Press: Cambridge, 1987).

Financial Times, 14.12.88.

Financial Times, 13.2.89.

Financial Times, 15.2.89.

Financial Times, 16.2.89.

Financial Times, 13.4.89.

Financial Times, 16.4.89.

Finegold, David and Soskice, David, 'The failure of training in Britain: analysis and prescription', *Oxford Review of Economic Policy*, 4(3), 21–53 (1988).

Finn, D. and Convery, P., *The New Adult Training Programme* (Unemployment Unit: London, 1988).

Funding Study, *The Study of Vocational Education and Training: Some Early Research Findings*, Background Note No. 2 (Sheffield Training Commission, 1988).

Gamble, Andrew, *Britain in Decline*, (Macmillan: London, 1988).

Gamble, Andrew, *The Free Economy and the Strong State* (Macmillan: London, 1988).

Gardner, P., *The Lost Elementary Schools of Victorian England* (Croom Helm: London, 1984).

Gaskell, J., 'The Canadian Educational System' in *op. cit.* (eds Ashton, D. N. and Lowe, G. S.) (in press).

Hobsbawm, E. J., *Industry and Empire* (Penguin: Harmondsworth, 1968).

House of Lords Select Committee on Science and Technology, *Education and Training for New Technologies*, Vol I. Report: House of Lords Session 1984–5, Vol. XVII (1984–5).

House of Lords *Report from the Select Committee on Overseas Trade*, Vol. 1. (HMSO: London, 1985).

Krahn, H. and Lowe, G. S., 'Transition to work: findings from a longitudinal study of high school and university graduates in three Canadian cities', in *op. cit.* (eds Ashton, D. N. and Lowe, G. S.) (in press).

Manpower Services Commission, National Economic Development Council and British Institute of Management, *The Making of Managers: A report on management education, training and development in the USA, W. Germany, France, Japan and the UK* (National Economic Development Office: London, 1987).

Manpower Services Commission: *Annual Report*, various years.

Maurice, M., Sellier, F. and Silvestre, J.-J., *The Social Foundations of Industrial Power* (MIT Press: London, 1986).

Marquand, J., *Sources of Economic Growth* (Harvester Wheatsheaf: Hemel Hempstead, 1989).

Ministry of Labour, *The Labour Market and Labour Market Policy in Sweden: A discussion paper for the 1990s* (Ministry of Labour: Stockholm, 1988).

Northcott, J. and Rogers, P., *Microelectronics in British Industry: The Pattern of Change*, Policy Studies Institute, No 625 (1984).

OECD, *Structural Adjustment and Economic Performance* (OECD: Paris, 1987).

Playfair, L., *Industrial Instruction on the Continent* (Royal School of Mines: London, 1852).

Prais, S. J., 'Vocational qualifications of the labour force in Britain and Germany', *National Institute Economic Review*, 98, 47–59 (1981).

Prais, S. J., 'Education for Productivity: Comparisons of Japanese and English Schooling for Vocational Preparation', *National Institute Economic Review*, 119, 40–56 (1987).

Prais, S. and Wagner, K., 'Some practical aspects of human capital investment: training standards in five occupations in Britain and Germany', *National Institute Economic Review,* **105**, 46–65 (1983).

Prais, S. and Wagner, K., 'Productivity and management: the training of foremen in Britain and Germany', *National Institute Economic Review,* **123**, 34–47 (1988).

Prais, S. and Steedman, H. 'Vocational training in France and Britain: the building trades', *National Institute Economic Review,* **116**, 45–55 (1986).

Smith, Keith, *The British Economic Crisis* (Penguin: Harmondsworth, 1984).

Standing, G., 'Training, flexibility and Swedish full employment', *Oxford Review of Economic Policy,* **4**, 94–107 (1988).

Steedman, H. and Wagner, K., 'A second look at productivity, machinery and skills in Britain and Germany', *National Institute Economic Review,* **122**, 84–95 (1987).

Steedman, H., 'Vocational training in France and Britain: mechanical and electrical craftsmen', *National Institute Economic Review,* **126**, 57–70 (1988).

Training Commission, *Employers' Training Activities (Employers' C)*, Funding Study Series, Training Commission (in press).

Turbin, J., 'State intervention into the labour market for youth: the implementation of the Youth Training Scheme in three local labour markets', Ph.D Thesis, University of Leicester (1987).

8 LABOUR MARKET FLEXIBILITY IN BRITAIN

Jill Rubery

Labour market flexibility is considered to be one of the major social and economic changes of the 1980s. Not only is it a major policy objective of the Thatcher government, but it has also been increasingly identified as a necessary condition for successful adaptation to changing market and technological conditions (Atkinson, 1985; Piore and Sabel, 1984). Moreover, on the basis of evidence of a general growth of non-standard employment in advanced countries it has become in popular perceptions no longer merely a political objective but instead a universal and inevitable characteristic of modern economies (Hakim, 1987b).

The British labour market is thought to be becoming more flexible along several dimensions. There has been a movement away from standard employment forms, and in particular a growth in part-time and self-employment. Trade unions have been weakened through the attack on traditional union strategies of job demarcation and control and through the fragmentation of the regulatory system. New legal constraints on trade union actions at an industrial or labour market level, the progressive dismantlement of the public sector and the continued trend towards firm-specific pay and collective bargaining systems all reduce the ability of unions to establish common standards and regulate the labour market.

These developments have fostered widespread concern with both the need for flexibility and the social and economic costs of flexibility, but there have been relatively few attempts to develop a critical appraisal of the meaning of the term, or the underlying factors which are leading to changes in the methods of labour market operation (see Rubery *et al.*, 1987 and Pollert, 1988 for critical reviews). Without such analysis it is difficult to identify the causes and consequences of such changes. Trends towards 'flexibility' have to be considered within the context of a specific labour market and the economic and social systems of organisation that underpin the operation of that market (Maurice *et al.*, 1986; Rubery, 1988a, Chapter 9, 1988b). Only within this type of analysis is it possible to identify the forms of flexibility and rigidity that

Figure 8.1 Framework for the analysis of labour market flexibility.

Labour market regulation	The industrial system
Legal/individual regulation (i) definition of employee (ii) employee rights (iii) taxation of employee by employment status *Voluntary regulation* (i) mechanisms for generalising standards at industry/national level (ii) union control at plant/industry level – importance of job demarcations (iii) employer and union attitudes (iv) legal constraints on voluntary regulation	*Industry structure* (i) sectoral composition (ii) size composition of firms (iii) vertical and horizontal integration *Employer policy and strategy for competitiveness* (i) variability of product demand (ii) product market and technological conditions (role of labour costs) (iii) managerial ethos (including political context) (iv) impact of labour market conditions on policy

Labour market system	Social reproduction
Labour market flows (i) access to employment for those out of employment (including young, unemployed, etc.) (ii) non-standard employment forms and flows between employment and unemployment (iii) labour supply conditions and non-standard employment (iv) training systems, general and firm-specific skills and flows of skilled labour	*Income maintenance* (i) state and family income support for the young, the unemployed, the old, child-rearers, etc. (ii) regulations on supplementing benefits to non-employed through casual work *Childrearing and the family system* (i) social attitudes to participation (ii) domestic division of labour (iii) state and market provision of services for child-rearing

exist, and the costs and benefits to capital and labour of any changes in the operation of the labour market.

The importance of country-specific characteristics has not been fully recognised because of the persistence of the general and ahistorical neo-classical model of the labour market as the implicit basis for comparison between an actual labour market and an 'ideal' flexible labour market (Rubery, 1987; Deakin, 1988). Not only is the neoclassical labour market model purely abstract, it is also not necessarily an 'efficient' form of labour market organisation, even from the perspective of capital, as recent neoclassical research on asset specificity and information costs has in fact recognised (Green, 1988; Maurice *et al.,* 1986, appendix). Moreover, the concept of flexibility is used to describe both micro- and macro-level flexibility, without identification of the potential contradictions between these levels of 'flexibility'. Thus, a free or flexible market is supposed to allow individual firms to fix pay according to their profitability, to ensure smooth mobility flows between jobs and to ensure downward average real wage flexibility in a recession, even though these different 'requirements' may need different institutional arrangements.

There are four main sets of economic and social institutions which structure an employment system (Rubery, 1988b): the system of labour market regulation, both legal and voluntary; the industrial system; the labour market system; and the system of social reproduction (including the system of income distribution and income maintenance for those not fully participating in the wage labour market). These four sets of institutions determine the demand for labour, the regulations under which labour is employed, the ways in which labour obtains access to employment and to skill and career enhancement, and the types of labour available for low-wage or non-standard employment. In the following sections we use the outline framework described in Fig. 8.1 to discuss the characteristics of the British labour market and their implications for labour market flexibility. We will thereby cover all the various forms of 'flexibility' that have been defined by modern writers, including numerical flexibility (the ability to adjust labour purchased to labour requirements); functional flexibility (the ability to transfer labour between tasks); wage or financial flexibility (the ability to vary wage levels according to the productivity or scarcity value of the employee); and labour market flexibility (the ease with which labour can transfer between organisations, industries, regions, etc.).

8.1 FLEXIBILITY AND THE LABOUR MARKET REGULATION SYSTEM

The system of labour market regulation, both legal and voluntary, shapes the standard employment contract and employment system and determines the incentives and opportunities for employers to develop employment forms outside the normal regulatory framework (Muckenberger, 1988; Deakin, 1986, 1988). Figure 8.1 outlines the range of legal, fiscal and voluntary aspects of a regulatory system which need to be examined to understand the form and degree of flexibility within a specific labour market.

The first two critical factors are the rights which workers acquire within the normal regulatory framework and the eligibility conditions for those rights. In Britain people in employment enjoy relatively few rights as compared to European societies, but in the 1970s there was a marked trend towards the extension of employee rights; these included the basic ones of a right to a contract of employment, to periods of notice before dismissal, to protection against unfair dismissal, to redundancy pay, to maternity leave, to protection against sex and racial discrimination and to rights to participate in union activities. This set of rights, while a major improvement on the almost blank sheet of employment rights that prevailed up to the mid-1960s, is nevertheless extremely limited compared to other societies where there are rights to minimum pay, to minimum holidays, maximum hours or overtime pay, and to be represented by a trade union. Moreover, access to these rights was, as is common in more regulated societies, limited to persons with appropriate employment status, fulfilling minimum working-time and minimum tenure requirements.[1] These trends towards individual employee rights could be expected to encourage the development of non-standard employment forms, including temporary work, self-employment, home-working and part-time work (below 16 hours per week), all of which are likely to fall outside the scope of individual rights.

The trend toward an extension of individual rights has been reversed under Thatcher. In particular, rights to unfair dismissal and maternity leave have been weakened, such minimum wage protection and hours protection as existed previously on a piecemeal basis has either been reduced or abolished[2] and no new rights have been added except for an amendment to the Equal Pay Act to allow claims for equal value, under pressure from the EEC. Eligibility requirements for rights have been strengthened, such as, for example, two years' continuous employment with the same employer is now necessary before unfair dismissal can be claimed and there are currently plans to raise the threshold for employment rights for part-timers from 16 hours to 20 hours. These threshold requirements could in theory be expected to increase the use of non-standard forms of employment. However, the range and level of employment rights are now so limited that it is implausible to presume that most employers design their employment systems in order to evade these rights. Indeed, flexibility here has been achieved more by weakening the rights for all employees than by strengthening distinctions between employment categories.

This type of analysis could help to explain the relatively weak evidence for a growth of temporary working in the UK in the 1980s (Casey, 1988; Dale and Bamford, 1988), despite predictions based on small-scale surveys of a major growth of this employment form (Meager, 1986). Current evidence suggests that it is now roughly at the same level as its previous peak in the late 1970s before the major reduction in temporary working during the crisis of 1979–81; in 1986 less than 6% of those in employment considered that they were in a temporary job. Where levels of legal job protection for all employees are low, there may be little incentive to formalise the category of temporary employee except for industrial relations reasons, as will be discussed below. Home-working has also not shown a major increase in the 1980s after an apparent upsurge in the 1970s; the previous rise may have been sponsored by attempts to evade legal regulation but there is little evidence of systematic attempts to switch from direct employment to home-working in the 1980s and most estimates put the share of home-workers in total employment at only around 1% (Hakim, 1985, 1987b). While there is no overall striking net trend there have been changes in the industrial, occupational and ethnic character of home-working: white-collar home-working has been increasing while manufacturing home-working has been declining, but also probably becoming more concentrated among ethnic minorities in inner-city areas working in particular industries such as clothing (Huws, 1984; Hakim, 1987a; Mitter, 1985).

By contrast there has been substantial growth in both self-employment and in part-time employment in the 1980s. Self-employment increased from 1.9 million to 2.8 million between 1979 and 1987 (Rubery, 1988b) and now accounts for 12% of employment, while part-time work continued its steady upward growth in the 1980s, accounting for 20% of all jobs in 1988. In 1979 3.8 million women worked part-time, but this number had risen to 4.3 million by 1988, and a rising number of men (0.9 million in 1988) are also employed in part-time jobs.

If the system of legal regulation was the most important factor, similar patterns of expansion could be expected in all forms of employment that fell outside the regulatory net. The main explanations for the growth of self-employment and part-time working may be found elsewhere, in changes in the industrial system or in levels of unemployment, but the third aspect of the legal part of the regulatory system listed in Figure 8.1, the tax system, is relevant here. Both forms of employment are subject to particularly favourable tax treatment: part-time working is excluded from national insurance tax by both employer and employee if earnings are below a minimum level[3] and self-employment is the only form of employment where income is not taxed at source, thus increasing scope for evasion and offering legitimate chances to postpone payments. It is indeed the efficiency of the PAYE system in Britain which may provide some clue to the growth of self-employment in the UK at a time when tax avoidance by those in employment is given political support (Pahl, 1988). In contrast, temporary working has been recently brought within the PAYE net and thus its incidence may decline as people are unwilling to be taxed at source when on low earnings. These tax advantages have not changed fundamentally in the 1980s and they thus provide mainly a favourable climate in which part-time and self-employment work could be expected to grow.

The tax and employment protection system in Britain is also important in explaining the availability of a labour supply for these types of non-standard work. On the one hand, the tight rules applied by the social security system on benefit recipients earning extra income reduce the number who seek non-standard employment as a supplement to unemployment. On the other hand, the relatively few benefits that accrue to employees from a standard employment contract increases the supply of labour for non-standard jobs as the costs of being excluded from employee status are relatively small, at least in international comparative terms. In particular, access, for example, to health care is not linked to paying national insurance or having employee status and women who have primary responsibility for childcare can receive credits for state pension entitlement even when not paying national insurance contributions. The main costs of non-standard employment to the individual arise from the exclusion of these types of employees from benefits associated with voluntary regulation such as occupational pension schemes, and it is the opportunity to differentiate employees' access to these types of benefits (Horrell *et al.*, 1988) that may be more important in the development of dualist labour markets in Britain than access to legal protection and state benefits.

Indeed, in Britain most of the discussion of flexibility needs to be focused not on the legal and state forces for regulation but on the system of voluntary regulation, in particular on the increasing lack of legal or other instruments by which voluntary regulation can be extended into the non-unionised sector. The first element in the voluntary regulatory system which must be examined is thus the means that exist for generalising labour standards. Britain, even in the 1970s, had a relatively weak institutional framework for generalising wage increases and other forms of employment protection from the strong to the weak sectors of the economy; not only were there no general minimum wage laws but the system of national-level industry bargaining was being progressively displaced by systems of company and plant bargaining. The main exception to this pattern was the public sector, where strong national bargaining systems continued alongside the development of local-level bargaining and productivity deals. The impact of the Conservative government's policies has been to weaken further the links between unionised sectors and non-union sectors, to encourage fragmentation of the bargaining system, and above all to attack the system of strong national bargaining in the public sector through privatisation of services, sales of nationalised industries, the dismantling of national bargaining systems (for example, abolishing the Burnham committee which negotiated teachers' pay) and by setting rigid cash limits on public expenditure which reduced the unions' opportunities to resist this battery of attacks. Within the private sector the weakening of the Wages Council System (which sets legal minimum wages in a number of industries including retail, catering and clothing), the abolition of the Fair Wages Resolution (which required government contractors to pay fair wages) and restrictions on strike activity which is not a direct dispute between employees and their direct employer have all reduced opportunities to control wage levels at a labour market level or to generalise increases to non-union sectors. Moreover, unions have found employers increasingly reluctant to negotiate, at the industry level, substantive changes in conditions or indeed to maintain existing regulations over such issues as hours of work, which in many industries have traditionally been regulated through national agreements even when pay was effectively negotiated at local level.[4]

These changes have arisen more from the process of decline in national agreements which occurred in the 1960s and 1970s coupled with union weaknesses in the 1980s than as a direct response to Thatcher policies, but the effect has been to fragment further the system of wage regulation in the UK. As a consequence there has been a marked increase in the range of pay settlements (Brown, 1987) and a notable widening in the structure of pay differentials (Rubery, 1986). These increases in pay variation at one level constitute an increase in pay flexibility, if the latter is taken to mean pay varying with the ability to pay of the firm. Flexibility in pay might also imply that earnings should vary with the ability to pay of the economy; that, for example, real wage growth should not exceed the growth in productivity in the economy or should not cause further loss of international competitiveness. The continued growth of average real pay in Britain while the economy remains weak may suggest that the micro-flexibility has not resulted in the type of macro-flexibility that may be necessary for international competitiveness. Mass unemployment has been found not to be an effective means of constraining real wages and Glyn and Rowthorn (1988) have argued that it is, in fact, corporatist systems of pay determination that are most likely to be able to modify real wage growth. Contradictions for neoclassical theory also emerge with the evidence of wider variations in levels of pay for similar work; while under Thatcher a market or flexible pay system fixes pay according to profitability of the enterprise, in textbook economics all enterprises should pay the same going rate for labour of a given quality. Evidence of increasing disparity in pay levels for similar workers could thus be taken as indicating the failure of the market system, and in particular a low degree of labour mobility or flexibility between firms.

Unions may not always seek to extend regulation to the non-union sector or to weak segments of the labour market, particularly if such a policy may reduce security for their members or the core workforce. Indeed, much of the growth of non-standard employment forms may be explained by the joint interests of employers and unions in distinguishing between core and periphery workers, so as not to undermine the morale and the security of the core workforce. Increased use of temporary and fixed-term contracts has been most common in the public sector (Millward and Stevens, 1986). As already argued, such a development cannot be explained by legal regulation *per se*. Much more important is the continued legacy of the public sector as a 'good employer', where jobs are permanent unless otherwise stated. The move towards more insecure jobs has thus involved a distinct division between core and periphery jobs, a strategy also generally preferred by the unions to the alternative of risking redundancies for the core workforce. In general, unions in Britain have adopted a relatively passive approach to the growth of non-standard employment forms such as part-time working. In other European countries unions have actively opposed part-time working on the grounds that this would undermine their system of labour standards. The growth in Britain has met no such opposition, and it could be argued that as a result both of unions' attitudes and the limited degree of legal regulation of employment, flexible employment forms are more fully integrated with the standard labour force and not confined, for example, to the informal economy. However, moves to integrate non-standard employment too far into the regulated economy have been effectively resisted by Thatcher. The unions' relatively successful unionisation of part-time workers in the public sector was thwarted by the privatisation of many services areas where part-time workers were concentrated, so that the advantages of wage as well as numerical flexibility could be realised (Coyle, 1986a, b; Fevre, 1986).

While much of Thatcher's earlier policy was designed to fragment the labour market and to de-regulate the non-union sector, the changes introduced in 1984 and 1988 into employment legislation have increasingly restricted the power of unions within organised plants, for example, by requiring secret ballots before a strike can be called. These changes in legislation have most effect when, as for example in the well-publicised instances of the Wapping dispute and the cross-channel ferry dispute, the employer decides to initiate major changes in work organisation. Most of these examples, as we shall argue below, can be traced to changing conditions in the product market increasing the incentive for restructuring, but the change in the legislative framework under which unions operate was an important facilitating factor, particularly in the way the legislation prevented the development of widespread sympathy action. Most of the changes in work organisation that have been introduced within the unionised sector have been designed either to increase numerical flexibility by changes in working-time legislation or have been designed to increase functional flexibility through reductions in job demarcations. Although there is no legal regulation of working-time in Britain (the fragmentary legislation that previously regulated night work and women's work has been abolished in the 1980s) union regulation of working-time, and in particular over time, systems has been a major element of most industry and plant collective agreements. The move towards more flexible hours contracts is thus a major departure from previous practice and evidence of an increase in managerial control over employment conditions. However, although there are now a large number of well known and publicised examples of changes in working-time arrangements,[5] and many of these clearly indicate an increase in the intensification of the use of labour, there is doubt about how far these developments can be generalised. At the same time there has been a return to high levels of overtime working, with overtime earnings accounting for over 15% of male manual workers' earnings in 1988,[6] slightly more than the percentage when the Conservatives came to power in 1979, and when there was not such a large supply of unemployed labour. These trends suggest that the impact of changes towards, for example, annualised hours, has been, overall, relatively small.

Changes in job demarcations and increased functional flexibility provide a more direct challenge to union power in the UK than in other countries because of the historical organisation of unions along craft lines and the division between manual craft and white-collar technician unions. It is probable, however, that even without Thatcher's employment legislation there would have been a general move towards relaxation of such demarcations as they became clearly technologically obsolete. Recent evidence suggests that such changes in job organisation among craft workers have been fairly widespread, but have usually had the willing co-operation of unions (Daniel, 1987). Where the change in the legislative framework has made a critical difference is in those sectors such as printing, where there was little possibility of a smooth transition towards job flexibility. The change in legislation and in political climate has also encouraged opportunistic moves by right-wing unions such as the EETPU to poach members and establish single-union, no-strike agreements. This aggressive behaviour by the EETPU may in fact have made it more difficult for other unions to find an orderly way to reorganise under the changing job structures, although mergers by unions are facilitating the restructuring by minimising the problem of inter-union competition for members in the new jobs. While not discounting the political significance of the major confrontations with unions, nevertheless it seems reasonable to conclude that most firms have been able to secure some increase in functional flexibility without this involving a major change in union regulation and control and moreover, most evidence would suggest that firms have by and large only sought relatively limited functional flexibility (Atkinson and Meager, 1985, 1986; Rubery *et al.*, 1987; Daniel, 1987), within horizontal occupational groups and not crossing major hierarchical boundaries.

To summarise, the main characteristic of the labour market regulation system in the UK is the absence of formal legal restrictions on flexibility. A recent consultant's report on labour market flexibility in four countries for the OECD remarked: 'The situation in the United Kingdom differs markedly from that in the other three countries [France, Germany, Sweden] insofar as there are virtually no legal or social constraints on flexibility' (Brunhes, 1988, p. 25). Firms in Britain thus have, in principle, the opportunity to introduce numerical, functional or wage flexibility without recourse to the use of special employment forms which in other countries facilitate the evasion of regulation. The explanation of the growth of non-standard employment forms such as part-time and self-employment must thus lie outside the legal employment protection system, in the tax system, the industrial system and the structure of labour supply. Moreover, there is little evidence to suggest that unions have actively resisted the development of flexible employment forms; a recent survey of mainly private manufacturing companies found a relatively high incidence of multiple forms of flexibility within union-recognised plants (ACAS, 1988). Indeed, within the public sector, where most has been done to weaken the unions, it is the continuation of effective forms of labour market regulation that has increased the use of explicitly flexible employment forms. Public-sector employers have not introduced flexible employment conditions for all but instead have created tiers of flexible employment labour through the use of fixed-term contracts and privatisation. This continuation of the voluntary system of regulation is evidence not simply of union power but also of employers' continued need for co-operation from their labour forces. Employers' desire to motivate employees through sharing of productivity gains is also evident in the relatively high rates of wage increases in the more successful plants and sectors. It is this interest in sharing productivity at the micro-level which causes a fragmentary bargaining system to be appropriate for micro- but not macro-level flexibility in wages. These gains within the strong sectors may in fact contribute to the pressures which have been generated to control the incomes of those on social security and other benefits.   The major changes are thus not that firms have discovered that they can manage without unions and co-operation and have rediscovered the flexible, neoclassical labour market, but that gains achieved by some groups of workers through their strategic position in strong industrial sectors are less generalisable through the rest of the economy. Moreover, the power of unions even within the strong sectors is more conditional on employer attitudes, and on the underlying structural conditions in the economy, for the 1980s legal framework for industrial relations has increased the ability of employers to implement radical changes in the employment relationship and labour process whenever changes in markets or technology determine that the existing system of organisation is no longer working to their advantage.

8.2 FLEXIBILITY AND THE INDUSTRIAL SYSTEM

There are two main ways in which the industrial system structures both the demand for and the use of flexible employment; the first is through the structure of industry and system of industrial organisation, including the degree of concentration and vertical integration. Changes in flexible employment that arise through these influences can be regarded as a compositional change. The second factor is employer strategy, which cannot be predicted solely on the basis of industrial and organisational characteristics. This factor thus gives rise to strategic as opposed to compositional flexibility. Much of the debate on flexibility in Britain has focused on strategic changes, notably the adoption of the flexible firm model of a core and periphery sector within the firm as identified by Atkinson (1985). This debate, however, has tended to use changes at the macro-level in the structure of employment as evidence of change at the micro-level in employer strategy, thereby confusing these compositional and strategic effects.

There is, in fact, fairly strong evidence to suggest that changes in the composition of industry are more important for explaining net changes at the aggregate level than changes within existing organisations. For example, the growth of part-time employment is primarily attributable to the continued relative growth of service employment (Rubery and Tarling, 1988), as indeed the share of part-time employment in manufacturing has fallen both absolutely and relatively, thereby casting doubt on how far the core/periphery model has been adopted within manufacturing. Similarly, the growth of self-employment appears to be associated with the expansion of services with little change in the relative share of self-employment in manufacturing. Even the general trend towards a higher share of employment within small firms is found, on careful analysis, to be caused more by the decline of large firms than the autonomous growth of small firms (Storey and Johnson, 1987). The number of small firms, like the number of self-employed, has increased but the average size within the small-firm category has decreased. There is thus little evidence of a major expansion of the small-firm sector, or indeed of the development of the industrial districts and complex forms of subcontracting associated with the model of flexible specialisation and with the pattern of industrial development in Northern Italy (Pyke, 1987). Manufacturing industry has remained comparatively highly vertically and horizontally integrated (Marsden, 1987) and most of the net changes can be explained primarily with reference to the major decline of manufacturing in the 1979–1981 period.

Longer-term trends in industrial integration and concentration may, however, be associated with some of the labour market developments in the 1980s. The high level of concentration in the service sector in Britain may have facilitated the widespread introduction of sophisticated manpower planning based on flexible use of part-time labour. Within manufacturing the process of merger and development of the conglomerate firm which characterised the 1960s and 1970s was also associated with the growth of company over industry-level bargaining (Marginson *et al.,* 1988). The impact of these developments had been felt in the 1980s with the widening of dispersion of wage settlements between firms in the same industry and the breakdown of effective industry-wide training systems. The lack of cohesion and co-operation between employers within sectors in Britain may thus be one cause of the resort to increasingly fragmented pay settlements and firm-specific training systems, developments which allow flexibility for firms to pursue their own policies but which may inhibit the flexibility of the operation of the labour market, and in particular labour market flows between firms.

With regard to the role of employer strategy in increasing flexibility in the labour market, we need not only to identify the extent of policy change but also to distinguish between three different possible causes of changes in employer labour force strategy. These three factors are responses to short-term changes or uncertainty in market conditions, responses to longer-term changes in market or technological conditions and responses to changes in the political or regulatory framework. The importance of the flexible firm model propounded by Atkinson and the flexible specialisation model put forward by Piore and Sabel (1984) is that they purport to be predictors of change brought about by long-term changes in the nature of markets and technologies, and thus a more permanent and inevitable part of the social and economic change in the 1980s than if these strategies were induced by either short-term or by political conditions.

The first point to note is that there is as yet relatively limited evidence to support the proposition that the core/periphery model has been widely adopted within private-sector firms in Britain. Even Atkinson, in his own empirical research, concluded that only a minority of the 70 firms interviewed had fully implemented a core/periphery distinction (Atkinson and Meager, 1985, 1986). There is evidence of fairly widespread movement towards breaking down job demarcations, but within fairly narrowly defined occupational categories; there is also accumulating evidence of new strategies towards working hours (ACAS, 1988), including the introduction of shifts, weekend working and moves towards more flexible payment systems for overtime, but these changes have again been occurring alongside very high levels of overtime working and overtime pay; and although there is increased evidence of the use of non-standard job forms, particularly part-time work and self-employment, these employment forms are concentrated in service sector industries and have not been growing throughout the economy. It is in the public sector that there have been the most evident changes in employer strategy: the internal labour force has been increasingly subdivided into those on permanent and those on temporary contracts (Millward and Stevens, 1986); there has been a large rise in the share of subcontracted work, with subcontractors paying lower wages than the public sector, and there have been major changes in work organisation often associated with more intensive use of labour. These latter changes have come about through the use of competitive tendering, thereby inducing internal employees to agree to work harder to secure the contract against outsiders, through large-scale investment in new technology and new managerial systems prior to privatisation and through the imposition of reductions in manpower relative to demand through the strict cash limits system (Burns *et al.,* 1985; Ferner, 1985; Ferner and Terry, 1985).

Turning now to the explanation of these restricted changes in employer strategy we find only limited support for the hypothesis that the major factor has been response to long-term changes in product market and technological conditions. Britain has been characterised as emphasising the short-term, and not bringing in the type of radical changes, involving a great deal more than labour cost minimisation policies which would be necessary to enhance capacity to produce new and better products (Brunhes, 1988; Rubery *et al.*, 1987). An example of short-term change is provided by the use of temporary labour and the YTS scheme. As we argue below, these developments can be viewed, at least in part, as opportunistic responses to labour market conditions and do not necessarily reflect a permanent change in labour requirements. The major reorganisations of labour relations in the public sector must be attributed to the specific political programme of the government. The level of funding provided for investment in some nationalised industries such as coal was clearly not determined by the type of commercial criteria which are used in the private sector and can only be explained by a policy to undermine union power and control over the labour process prior to nationalisation (Burns *et al.*, 1985). The more dramatic onslaughts on union power in the private sector are also linked to the changes in employment legislation brought in by the Thatcher government, in so far as these prevented the development of effective industry-wide resistance to the sackings of the workers in the Wapping dispute by Murdoch or the ferry workers by Townsend–Thorenson.

However, the concentration of these disputes by industry is related to long-term trends in market and technical conditions, to the computerisation of printing, to the building of the channel tunnel, and in the case of the television technicians' disputes to the de-regulation and expansion of competition in the media (Brown, 1987). For the most part, however, the main obstacles to technical and product market change do not seem to lie in the organisation of labour. Firms' needs for flexibility to respond to market conditions are much greater than the need to deploy labour more flexibly, and while labour reorganisation may be the outcome of the restructuring process it is neither the objective nor the main factor retarding the restructuring of British industry. Indeed, many firms have reported active help and co-operation from their unions in restructuring, and the problem of too little technical change is voiced by unions more frequently than the problem of too much change (Daniel, 1987).

8.3 FLEXIBILITY AND THE OPERATION OF THE LABOUR MARKET

The economic and social significance of flexible employment forms depends on the pattern of labour market flows, in particular the ways in which individuals gain access to employment, acquire and develop skills and obtain access to promotion and career progression.

A central issue is thus whether non-standard employment forms, associated with labour market flexibility, in Britain provide a bridge between unemployment and permanent regular employment, or between school and entry to adult employment, or whether they are either 'dead- ends' or temporary respites from unemployment which are most likely to end with yet another spell of unemployment. These patterns in part depend on the overall level of demand in the labour market but also on the custom and practice and recruitment policies in the specific labour market. Britain has not traditionally had the period of temporary and casual work between school and work that has characterised many European countries (Marsden and Ryan, 1986; Garonna and Ryan, 1986). When youth unemployment increased to unacceptable levels, a transition period of temporary work was introduced first by the Labour government, but considerably extended under the Conservatives, under the guise of a need for work experience or training before entry to permanent employment. The Youth Training Scheme has now been extended to two years and put on a permanent basis. However, the way in which the scheme operates as a form of access to employment varies between regions and between industries (Ashton *et al.*, 1988). In some industries it has become incorporated into the regular training system and has thus become the normal route for entry into primary-type jobs, in practice replacing the old direct entry into apprenticeship system. In other industries it is used primarily to provide subsidised labour for the firm for two years, although a minority may be kept on to fill any permanent vacancies. Interestingly, it is these industries which have been forced in areas of high labour demand to switch back to offering direct employment, thus suggesting that the move towards a transition period of work before permanent direct employment has not been incorporated into the long-term operation of the UK labour market. This absence of a transition period has in fact increased the likely long-term consequences of high youth unemployment: recent research has shown that young adults who failed to gain access to permanent work on leaving school because of the severe recession are now disadvantaged in the labour market relative to current school leavers who are the favoured choice of employers (Ashton *et al.*, 1988). Thus, this group runs the risk of remaining permanently in the unstable part of the labour market.

Temporary work in general in Britain does not tend to act as a bridge into permanent employment. It is the case that the unemployed are more likely to take a temporary job and that some of these manage to make the next step into permanent work, but temporary work is also frequently followed by further spells of unemployment (Casey, 1988). The association with unemployment is evidenced by the higher share of people involuntarily in temporary jobs in high unemployment areas, but temporary work has also been growing in high labour demand areas because of labour shortage and the growing problems caused by firms' 'training strike' in the 1980s.[7]

Other forms of non-standard employment are also not associated with

progression up the employment ladder or with the development and acquisition of skills. Entry into self-employment is often associated with redundancy
or fear of unemployment (Storey and Johnson, 1987). Moreover, it is not
only the birth but also the death rate of new businesses that is high, suggesting
that for many self-employment is not a permanent route out of unemployment. Most entering self-employment have already acquired skills or work
experience, and need indeed to have a skill to sell on the market; few
opportunities exist within self-employment for skill development and enhancement. Women usually enter part-time employment when returning to work
after having children. These jobs are usually 'dead-end' both in the sense that
there are few opportunities for promotion and because they often do not
utilise the existing skills of the workforce (Martin and Roberts, 1984; Dex,
1984). With problems of skill shortage likely to intensify, part-time work may
come to be seen not as a source of flexibility but of rigidity as it fails to
allocate resources efficiently or to develop and expand labour skills.

One of the main ways in which the period of the Thatcher government will
be seen in the future to have contributed to increased rigidity in the labour
market will be through its policy on training (see Ashton, Green and Hoskins,
this volume). A flexible labour market must be one in which it is possible to
expand as well as contract the labour force in response to changes in demand,
but such a requirement necessitates both a policy for the development of skills
prior to the expansion of demand and a policy to ensure skills are transfer-
able. The abolition of any requirement for firms to train (through the dismantlement of the Industrial Training Boards), the encouragement given to firms
to develop firm-specific training and not to adhere necessarily to standards
for general skills, and the restrictions on the development of further and
higher education of all types have not served to secure either of these two
objectives. During the recession of 1979–81 training programmes collapsed
and only the more far-sighted firms foresaw the need to start training before
the upturn in demand was actually upon them. Far from being a flexible
labour market the UK labour market in the late 1980s is proving to be a very
rigid structure, incapable of meeting the increase in demand for labour even
when unemployment levels still stand at historically high levels. Indeed, one
measure of flexibility should be to see if the unemployment rate can fall to a
low level before firms complain that they are operating in an over-employed
labour market with labour scarcities.

8.4 FLEXIBILITY AND THE SYSTEM OF SOCIAL REPRODUCTION

The system of social reproduction, that is the way labour is produced and
reproduced (including here the system of income sharing and income support
for non or part-time labour market participants), structures the supply of
labour, including that for flexible employment. The main source of supply for

flexible employment in Britain is married women and men with family responsibilities seeking second jobs. Students, the unemployed and older workers are more important in other countries than in Britain where the intensive higher education system, the relatively strict regulations on earnings for benefit recipients and universal pension benefits limit the supply compared to other societies, where not only may it be easier for these groups to take on informal work, but earnings from informal work may be built into the system for income maintenance during schooling, unemployment and old age. There is, in fact, very little evidence to support the claims that unemployment in Britain has been accompanied by a large rise in the size of the black economy; most of the unemployed currently lack the capital, the skills and contacts necessary to participate in the informal economy (Thomas, 1988; Pahl, 1988).

However, the availability of married women for part-time work is also country-specific; in, for example, the US or France, a higher percentage of married women with children work full-time (Rubery, 1988a). The explanation of this pattern of labour supply in Britain must lie in the interaction between conditions in the labour market and in the social reproduction system; these include the favourable tax treatment for part-time work, the lack of childcare facilities and the increasing dependence of the family income on two earners (with the wife contributing a lower share of the budget than in countries such as France and the US, but childcare costs are not incurred to the same extent). Once a pattern of labour supply becomes incorporated into normal family income levels this system of participation may become reinforced over time as families seek to secure normal living standards.

The main ways in which the supply of labour for flexible employment have been increased under the Conservatives have all been indirect effects of the increase in unemployment. Young people, as we have already argued, had not traditionally been used for part-time and very temporary employment. However, high unemployment affected young people disproportionately at least at the outset, and they were thus forced into providing labour on new terms. The government has tried to institutionalise this change in their labour supply by establishing the Youth Training Scheme on a permanent basis and restricting young people's rights to unemployment benefit. Thus, families have been required by the changing economic conditions to accept much longer-term responsibility for the 'social reproduction' of their children, although recent scarcities of new recruits have reversed this process to some extent with more school leavers finding permanent jobs. The other main new sources of labour supply for flexible employment have also arisen indirectly out of unemployment; a relatively high share of those becoming self-employed had been unemployed or feared unemployment, those taking early retirement are also more likely to be available for temporary or part-time work than older retired workers, unemployment benefit entitlements have been tightened to reduce the cost thereby expanding the share of labour outside the benefit net with no effective reservation wage, and involuntary employment in temporary jobs is higher in areas of high unemployment. These trends suggest a general increase in supply of labour to non-standard jobs from all groups prone to unemployment. Nevertheless, not all the unemployed are willing to become flexible labour, taking jobs where the wage is geared to labour traditionally considered to have access to income outside the labour market, such as young people and women. The problem for government policy is that the textbooks of free market economics speak of one wage labour market, thus misrepresenting reality, which is a series of segmented markets where pay reflects not the productivity of the worker but their position in the social reproduction system. To try to establish the totally flexible market with one market clearing wage the government has had to resort to strategies such as the top-up payment for six months for the unemployed taking a low-paid job, in part recognition that these jobs are in fact too low-paid for prime age men with family responsibilities.

8.5 CONCLUSIONS

Flexibilisation of the labour market is commonly believed to be one of Thatcher's central objectives which was most essential for British economic recovery, and moreover one of the objectives which has been most successfully achieved. However, the above analysis of the characteristics and trends in the UK labour market has not supported this view in several major respects.

In the first place, the framework we have used to analyse flexibility within a specific labour market has demonstrated that there is no single way of organising a labour market and thus of achieving economic objectives. This fact has indeed been recognised in the OECD which has identified both the US and the Japanese labour markets as alternative efficient models of achieving flexibility, even though they stand at opposite ends of the spectrum, with the former achieving flexibility through 'hire and fire' and the other through lifetime employment commitments (OECD, 1986). This recognition of the possibility of alternative 'efficient' modes marks a major departure from simple neoclassical analysis. The transformation in modes of thinking has only been partial, as the OECD then went on to assume that European labour markets which stand mid-way along this spectrum are inherently less efficient. One of the main implications of the 'societal' approach we have adopted is that labour market restructuring has to be compatible with economic and social institutions. Some of the changes that have been introduced into the British labour market in an effort to achieve 'flexibility' have not proved compatible with such institutions; for example, the attempt to develop a period of flexible employment for young workers has not as yet led to the development of new patterns of recruitment to allow smooth transition into permanent, primary employment from a period of flexible employment. Instead, young adults have fewer options on the labour market than more recent school leavers and there is a potential permanent loss of productive labour to the economy. Thus, the instigation of periods of flexible employment for young people in Britain may have very different costs and benefits from those in other countries where flexible employment already fits the normal transition pattern from school to work and where families are willing to support young adults financially. It must also be recognised that in Britain certain aspects of flexibility, such as the growth of self-employment, are found to be more associated with the impact of recession and the lack of alternative employment than with the rebirth of the entrepreneurial spirit or the emergence of a vibrant small-firm sector as in northern Italy. A further implication of this 'societal' approach is that policies which are justified as economically 'necessary', even if socially undesirable, may lose their economic rationale if the full range of options for the operation of the labour market are taken into account.

Secondly, there are not only different ways of achieving flexibility but also major contradictions between the different elements of a flexibilisation policy. Thus, the British labour market has evolved in the direction of providing increasing opportunities for firms to vary the quantity of labour employed and to determine their own pay and training policies. However, these policies themselves make it more difficult to achieve other aspects of labour market flexibility, namely the control over the rate of growth of real wages and the development of a pool of flexible skilled labour to facilitate flows between firms and ameliorate problems of labour scarcity. In general, Conservative labour market policy has been designed to encourage short-term flexibility and has failed to provide a framework which would foster the type of co-operation both between firms and between capital and labour which is necessary to achieve long-term and significant change in the productivity potential of the British economy. The emerging skills shortage in Britain is finally beginning to focus attention on how recent labour market policies have hampered the development of labour resources, and to divert attention away from the core/periphery-type models of efficient labour managements which have more to do with adjusting to the short than the long term.

These conclusions so far imply that the policy of increasing labour market flexibility has not served the long-term interests of the economy. These interests may be different from those specifically of British capital, even taking a narrow definition of the economy to include productivity, international competitiveness and non-waste of resources, and leaving out any issues of equity, social welfare, power or social justice. The notion that there are different ways of organising societies efficiently in practice implies that there are different ways of accommodating the interests of capital and labour. The Thatcher government has clearly chosen a strategy to advance the interests of capital, whatever the cost in terms of jobs, output or equity, but the question which is unresolved, and potentially unresolvable, is whether in the 1980s such a change in the balance of power in the labour market was in fact required. In short, had the previous system of labour organisation become such a block to economic development (Kilpatrick and Lawson, 1980) that at the least a major 'shock' was needed to force the labour market to adjust to modern economic conditions? Such a shock would need to be both ideological and economic, designed to undermine trade union power (Ghilarducci, 1986) and the institutions of the welfare state by redefining the political agenda. With this type of interpretation, Thatcher's policies cannot necessarily be justified using standard economic analysis, and they appear primarily ideological and often against rational economic management. But their long-term effect, it might be argued, is to restore the appropriate conditions for accumulation in Britain. The main arguments made to support this line of reasoning refer to the restrictive practices of the union movement in Britain which were seen as inhibiting the process of technological and market change. However, while in some industries, for example printing, management may not have been able to make radical changes in job structures and pay bargaining through negotiation, much of the actual empirical evidence suggests not only that unions have co-operated in the process of technological change but that the main obstacles to further development have been inadequate investment and market development strategies on the part of firms.

No substantive body of evidence currently supports the hypothesis that Thatcher's labour market policies were a necessary, even if unpleasant, part of the process of economic restructuring. Indeed, the emerging rigidities in the labour market, the scarcities of skills, the widening dispersion of earnings and growing inequality all suggest instead that these policies have diminished the potential contribution from the labour market to economic growth as well as adding significantly to the extent of economic misery experienced by labour market participants.

NOTES

1. A proviso is that in Britain employment status and employment rights are determined by actual practice, not by the employment contract; thus, a self-employed person who is treated as if an employee over an extended period can in principle obtain employment protection through the courts (Leighton, 1983).
2. Legal minimum wage protection in Britain only applies in those industries covered by the wages council system. Under 21-year-olds have been removed from the scope of the wages councils; the powers of wages councils to set terms and conditions reduced to that of fixing one minimum hourly rate; and the inspectorate which enforces the minima has been reduced in size while the rate of underpayment has grown. There are now plans to abolish the wages councils entirely. Restrictions on hours of work primarily applied to women and children who were not allowed to work nights and required statutory rest periods within factories. These hours restrictions have now been abolished under the guise of enhancing equal opportunities.

3. Schoer (1987) estimated that the difference in the national insurance system was the main reason for a much higher incidence of part-time working in Britain as compared to West Germany.
4. For example, negotiations to reduce the working week in the engineering industry have led the employers' side to try to tie any reduction in the working week to the abolition of industry-wide controls on overtime working arrangements.
5. These disputes include those over rostering on the trains, shift schedules on the channel ferries and the current attempt to introduce six-day working in the mines. In addition to these directly disputed changes, many service industries, for example banks, the retail sector, estate agents, have extended operating hours into evenings and weekends, and other firms have introduced versions of annualised hours contracts. Moreover, a recent report by ACAS (1988) found that one-third of sample of 584 firms, mainly private-sector manufacturing, had introduced shift working over the past 3 years. The same survey found a relatively low incidence of annualised hours, job sharing or flexible working hours.
6. Source: *New Earnings Survey* statistics.
7. The number of apprenticeships fell dramatically in the early 1980s (see Ashton, Green and Hoskins, this volume).

REFERENCES

Advisory, Conciliation and Arbitration Service (ACAS), *Labour Flexibility in Britain: The 1987 Acas Survey,* Occasional Paper No. 41 (1988).

Ashton, D., Maguire, M. and Spilsbury, M., 'The youth market in the United Kingdom and the 1979–82 recession: The effects of cyclical and structural change', *Labour and Society,* **13**, 4, 415–44, Geneva (October, 1988). Geneva.

Atkinson, J., 'Flexibility: planning for an uncertain future', *Manpower Policy and Practice*, Vol. 1, Summer, (Gower: Aldershot 1985).

Atkinson, J. and Meager, N., *Changing Working Patterns*, National Economic Development Council (1985).

Atkinson, J. and Meager, N., 'Is flexibility a flash in the pan?' *Personnel Management*, September (1986).

Brown, W., 'The paradoxical role of pay in eliciting labour productivity', Paper presented to the *Second European Regional Congress on Industrial Relations*, Israel, December (1987).

Brunhes, B., 'Labour market flexibility in Europe: a comparative analysis of four countries', Working paper for the OECD Working Party on Industrial Relations (1988).

Burns, A., Newby, M. and Winterton, J., 'The restructuring of the British Coal industry', *Cambridge Journal of Economics,* 9 (March 1985).

Casey, B., 'The extent and nature of temporary employment in Britain', *Cambridge Journal of Economics*, 12 (1988).

Coyle, A., *Dirty Business* (West Midlands Low Pay Unit: Birmingham, 1986a).

Coyle, A., 'Going Private' in *Feminist Review* (eds) *Waged Work: A Reader* (London: Virago, pp. 222–37, 1986b).

Dale, A. and Bamford, C., 'Temporary Workers; cause for concern and complacency?' *Work, Employment and Society*, June (1988).

Daniel, W. W., *Workplace Industrial Relations and Technical Change* (Frances Pinter and Policy Studies Institute: London, 1987).

Deakin, S., 'Labour law and the developing employment relationship in the UK', *Cambridge Journal of Economics*, Vol. 10, December (1986).

Deakin, S., 'The comparative structure of labour law systems; state systems of regulation and the harmonisation of labour standards in the EEC'. Paper prepared for 10th annual conference of the International Working Party on Labour Market Segmentation, sponsored by the EEC on *The Internationalisation of Markets and Terms and Conditions of Employment*, Oporto, Portugal (1988).

Dex, S., *Women's Work Histories; an Analysis of the Women and Employment Survey*, Department of Employment Research Paper No. 45 (1984).

Ferner, A., 'Political Constraints and Management Strategies: The Case of Working practices in British Rail', *British Journal of Industrial Relations*, Vol. 1, March (1985).

Ferner, A. and Terry, M., 'The crunch had come': a case study of changing industrial relations in the Post Office', *Warwick Papers in Industrial Relations*, No. 1 (Industrial Relations Research Unit: University of Warwick, 1985).

Fevre, R., 'Contract Work in the Recession', in *The Changing Experience of Employment* (eds Purcell, K., Wood, S., Watson, A. and Allen, S.) (Macmillan: Basingstoke, 1986).

Garonna, P. and Ryan, P., 'Youth labour, industrial relations and deregulation in advanced economies', *Economia e Lavoro,* **4**, 3–19 (1986).

Ghilarducci, T., 'When management strikes: PATCO and the British miners', *Industrial Relations Journal,* **2**, 115–28 (1986).

Glyn, A. and Rowthorn, R., 'The Diversity of Unemployment Experience since 1973' *World Institute for Development Economics Research*, WP40, April (1988).

Green, F., 'Neoclassical and Marxian conceptions of production', *Cambridge Journal of Economics,* **12**, 299–312 (1988).

Hakim, C., 'Employers' Use of Outwork', *Department of Employment Research Paper,* No. **44** (1985).

Hakim, C., 'Home-based work in Britain', *Department of Employment Research Paper,* No. **60** (1987a).

Hakim, C., 'Trends in the flexible workforce', *Employment Gazette*, November, 549–60 (1987b).

Horrell, S., Rubery, J. and Burchell, B., 'Unequal jobs or unequal pay', *Social Change and Economic Life Initiative Working Paper*, No. **6**, ESRC (1988).

Huws, U., 'New technology homeworkers', *Employment Gazette,* **92**, 1, 13–17 (January, 1984).

Kilpatrick, A. and Lawson, A., 'On the nature of industrial decline in the UK', *Cambridge Journal of Economics,* **4** (1), 85–102 (1980).

Leighton, P., *Contractural Arrangements in Selected Industries – A Study of Employment Relationships in Industries with Outwork*, Department of Employment Research Paper, No. 39 (1983).

Marginson, P., Edwards, P., Martin, R., Purcell, J. and Sisson, K., *Beyond the Workplace*, (Blackwell: Oxford, 1988).

Marsden, D., 'Small firms and labour markets in the UK', *New Industrial Organisation Programme* (International Institute for Labour Studies: Geneva, 1987).

Marsden, D. and Ryan, P., 'Where do young workers work? Youth employment by industry in various European economies', *British Journal of Industrial Relations,* **24** March (1986).

Martin, J. and Roberts, C., *Women and Employment: a Lifetime Perspective* (HMSO: London, 1984).

Maurice, M., Sellier, F. and Silvestre, J.-J., *The Social Foundations of Industrial*

Power: a comparison of France and Germany (Trans. A. Goldhammer) (MIT Press: Cambridge, Mass., 1986).

Meager, N., 'Temporary work in Britain' *Employment Gazette*, **94**, 1 (1986).

Millward, N. and Stevens, M., *British Workplace Industrial Relations 1980–84* (Gower: Aldershot, 1984).

Mitter, S., 'Industrial restructuring and manufacturing homework: immigrant women in the UK clothing industry', *Capital and Class,* **27** (Autumn 1985).

Muckenberger, U., 'Before the completion of the internal market: laws concerning labour market segmentation in Germany, the UK and France', Paper presented to the *Tenth Conference of the International Working Party on Labour Market Segmentation*, Oporto, Portugal (1988).

OECD, *Flexibility in the Labour Market: The Current Debate* (OECD: Paris, 1986).

Pahl, R. E., 'The Black Economy in the UK', Paper prepared for the European Commission on *The Black Economy in Europe* (1988).

Piore, M. and Sabel, C., *The Second Industrial Divide*, Basic Books: New York, 1984).

Pollert, A., 'Dismantling Flexibility', *Capital and Class*, Spring (1988).

Pyke, F., 'Industrial networks and modes of cooperation in a British context' (North West Industry Research Unit: University of Manchester, 1987).

Rubery, J., 'Trade unions in the 1980s: the case of the United Kingdom', in *Unions in Crisis and Beyond: Perspectives from Six Countries* (ed. Edwards, R.) (Auburn House and Croom Helm: Dover, Mass., 1986).

Rubery, J., 'Flexibility of labour costs in non union firms', in *Flexibility in Labour Markets* (ed. Tarling, R.) (Academic Press: London, 1987).

Rubery, J. (ed.), *Women and Recession* (Routledge & Kegan Paul: London, 1988a).

Rubery, J., 'Precarious forms of work in the UK', paper presented at the *International Institute of Labour Studies' Conference on Precarious Work*, Brussels, September (1988b) in *Precarious Jobs in Labour Market Regulations: The Growth of Atypical Employment in Western Europe* (eds Rogers, G. and Rogers, J.) (International Institute for Labour Studies: Geneva, 1989 forthcoming).

Rubery, J., Tarling, R. and Wilkinson, R., 'Flexibility, marketing and the organisation of production', *Labour and Society,* **12**, 1, 131–51 (January 1987).

Rubery, J. and Tarling, R., 'Women's employment in declining Britain', in *Women and Recession* (ed. Rubery, J.) (Routledge & Kegan Paul: London, 1988).

Schoer, K., 'Part-time employment: Britain and West Germany', *Cambridge Journal of Economics,* **11** (1987).

Storey, D. and Johnson, S., *Job Generation and Labour Market Change* (Macmillan: Basingstoke, 1987).

Thomas, J. J., 'The politics of the black economy', *Work, Employment and Society*, June (1988).

9 THE CHANGING DISTRIBUTION OF INCOME UNDER MRS THATCHER

Thomas Stark

9.1 INTRODUCTION

> The Conservative conception of a social structure not only assumes that marked inequalities are inevitable but also declines to justify them because their inevitability makes justification unnecessary. (Cowling, 1978)

The Conservative philosophy in the Thatcher era is clear-cut. Market forces must be allowed to operate efficiently and effectively. To this end the social fabric of society must be restructured. Thus, we have declining state interference in the economy; reduced direct tax rates in order to increase the rewards of enterprise and initiative; and a state income support system designed to dismantle the 'dependency culture' and serve only those 'genuinely' injured or disadvantaged by economic competition.

The demise of unionised labour and the growth of a 'share-owning' democracy through privatisation policies are part and parcel of this changing social structure. The shift of the relative tax burden from direct to the supposedly less resource distorting ('neutral') indirect taxes is also part of the new pattern. The aim is to increase economic competitiveness at home and abroad with the consequent increase in economic growth. 'If the price of this growth is greater inequality in the distribution of income, then so be it' would not be unfair comment on a Thatcherite approach to inequality. Ultimately it is believed, even predicted, that the fruits of growth will 'trickle down' to all members of society.

Eight years into this social revolution John Rentoul wrote: 'there are now Three Nations ... The Three Nations are the *haves* the *have nots* and the *have lots*' (Rentoul, 1987). In this chapter we aim first to show that Rentoul's statement is broadly correct by demonstrating that inequality has increased greatly. Secondly, we shall endeavour to trace the sources of this increase in inequality and finally we shall address the role of the re-distributive mechanism in the face of increasing inequality.

Gini coefficients

Indices of inter-decile
ratios (1983=100)

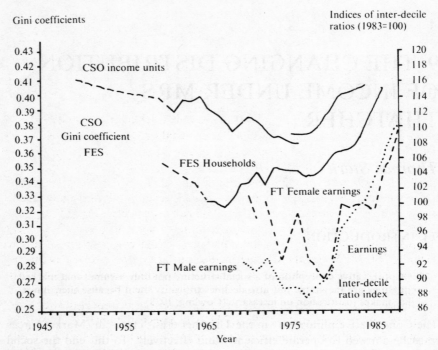

Figure 9.1 Inequality indices.

We start with a sharp statement of fact, namely that since the late 1970s there has been a pronounced and prolonged increase in the inequality of income. This increase is apparent in all major and regular series on income distribution and also under any measure or index of inequality one wishes to use. It is, in fact, one of the few periods since the Second World War when all data sources display an identical pattern. Moreover, the increase in inequality, which in most cases started in 1977, has become the longest period of sustained increase since regular statistics became available in the 1960s.

The above statements are illustrated in Fig. 9.1 using three major sources.[1] The increase in inequality in each source has been particularly sharp since 1980 and from the mid-1980s the levels of inequality recorded are higher than at any time during the previous thirty years.

9.2 THE DATA SOURCES

The three data sources selected were:

1. The CSO distribution by income units.
2. The Family Expenditure Survey (FES) distributions by households.

3. The New Earnings Survey (NES) distributions with respect to full-time adult earners whose pay is not affected by absence.

These are the three most regular and comprehensive UK sources available.

9.2.1 The CSO data

The CSO data is an extension of the Inland Revenue's Survey of Personal Incomes and attempts to allocate a substantial proportion of the National Accounts total for Household Income to income units. Income units are either single adults or married couples. This source has been published periodically since 1949, annually during the 1960s and late 1970s but now on a four-year cycle – the latest for the 1984–5 financial year.

9.2.2 The Family Expenditure Survey (FES)

FES is a continuous annual survey of, currently, 12,000 households. Income data is a by-product and, though often subject to criticism, it is nevertheless a valuable source (Atkinson and Micklewright, 1983). The income recipient is the household – broadly, single adults and families sharing a common address and cooking facilities. The income concept is Gross Weekly Normal Household Income, though the CSO derives annual distributions using various inome concepts – from original, through disposable, to final. The first FES was in 1957.

9.2.3 The New Earnings Survey (NES)

NES is a 1% sample survey (over 150,000 cases) of the wages and salaries in April of all employees above the deduction card limit for National Insurance and Income Tax. It is for main source earnings before tax and other statutory deductions and refers to individuals. Though part-time employees are covered, it is only the distribution for full-time employees whose pay has not been affected by absence that is considered reliable. Finally, the data refers to either hourly or weekly earnings. The NES extends back to 1968.

9.3 THE FACTS

The CSO data display a long, but interrupted, secular decrease in inequality from 1948 to 1978–9. In 1975–6 there was a major change in the compilation of this series, which accounts for the break in the series. We have measured, in this case, inequality using the popular Gini coefficient (see Appendix 9.1). Since 1978–9 the Gini coefficient has risen sharply and for 1984–5 – the latest available figures, which were published in November 1987 – had almost returned to its 1949 level.

The inequality in the distribution of Gross Normal Weekly Income by households from FES is also charted using the Gini coefficient. Since the household is a larger grouping of persons than the income unit, we would expect a lower level of inequality – as is the case. The gap is narrowing, however, perhaps reflecting a closer affinity between the two concepts, which is what we would expect with the long-run fall in the number of persons per household.

The FES displays a fall in inequality from 1959 to 1967. Between 1967 and 1972 inequality increased and then decreased marginally until 1977. Since then inequality has increased and is now at historically unprecedented levels for household data. Some of our later analysis will focus on a comparison of the 1980 and 1986 FES distributions.

The two other charted inequality series are from the NES, one for the Gross Weekly Earnings for full-time males (dotted line) and the other (broken line) for full-time female employees.[2] In these cases we have charted inequality as an index, with 1983 = 100 and inequality measured by the inter-decile ratio (see Appendix 9.1). The year chosen, for technical reasons, was 1983 – a change in definitions which need not concern us. Male earnings inequality decreased from 1970 to 1977 and has risen sharply since then. The pattern for females is more erratic, but basically similar with the turning point being in 1979. Full-time employed men account for over 90% of all employed males and full-time employed females over 55% of female employment. Our

Table 9.1 Distribution of gross normal weekly income by households.

Quantile group (%)	1979	1980	1986	Average Income 1980	1986	% increase in real incomes 1980–86[1]
Top 1	3.9	4.4	5.4	647.7	1261.4	33.0 (55.4)
2–5	9.8	10.1	11.5	371.7	671.6	23.4 (31.7)
6–10	9.8	9.9	10.6	291.5	495.2	16.0 (19.0)
Top 10	23.5	24.4	27.5	359.2	642.4	23.5 (31.4)
11–20	16.5	16.1	16.9	237.0	394.8	13.9 (14.9)
21–30	13.4	13.4	13.5	197.2	315.4	9.3 (13.4)
31–40	11.5	11.4	11.3	167.8	264.0	7.4 (10.3)
41–50	10.0	9.8	9.2	144.3	214.9	1.7 (3.2)
51–60	8.3	8.2	7.4	120.7	172.9	−2.1 (0.1)
61–70	6.6	6.6	5.5	97.1	128.5	−9.6 (−6.4)
71–80	4.7	4.6	4.0	67.7	93.4	−5.7 (−4.5)
81–90	3.3	3.2	2.8	47.1	65.4	−5.2 (−4.9)
91–100	2.2	2.2	1.8	32.4	42.0	−11.5 (−8.2)
Mean Income p.w.	120.5	147.2	233.6	All households		8.4 (12.1)

Note: (1) 1979–1986 real increase in brackets.
Source: Family Expenditure Survey.

indices are thus representative of a substantial proportion of the employed population.

In Table 9.1 we set out a quantile analysis of the FES distribution for the years 1979, 1980 and 1986. This gives us some insight into the changes implied by the rising Gini coefficient. The top 10% of households in this period increased their share of total income by 4 percentage points. The second highest decile group registered a marginal increase, while the third and fourth maintained their shares. The bottom half of the distribution collectively lost 3.6 percentage points. In 1979 households in the top 10% on average received 11 times the Gross Weekly Income of those in the bottom 10%. By 1986 they were receiving 15 times as much.

When we look at the changes in real income – estimated by assuming a common rate of inflation for all income groups – we see that the increases within the top 10% have been substantial and only the top 30% of households have kept above the average increase. The bottom 50% have declined in real terms. In other words, a household in the lower half of the distribution in 1986 was actually worse off than a similarly placed household in 1980.

The 'spoils of economic growth' in real terms in the Thatcher years have largely accrued to the upper echelons of the income distribution and have certainly not 'trickled down' to the bottom half of the distribution.

9.4 SOURCES OF INEQUALITY CHANGES

Distributions by households can, of course, be influenced by changes in the number of persons or income earners per household and by changes in the age structure of the population. Changes in the regional pattern of income distributions could also influence the national distribution.

Mookherjee and Shorrocks (1982) concluded that 'if the "age effect" is subtracted from aggregate inequality, ... the observed upward trend in household inequality either falls to almost zero ... or is reversed (if the Gini coefficient is employed as the measure of inequality).' (p. 901) The 'age effect' referred to incorporated the impact of changes in the age structure of the heads of households and the mean household incomes of each head of household age group. Their analysis referred to the FES statistics on Gross Normal Weekly Income by households for the years 1965 to 1980. What, of course, was not readily apparent at the time was that the years 1978 to 1980 were the start of the sustained and substantial increase in inequality in this series that we can now witness.

9.4.1 The age effect

We repeated Mookherjee and Shorrock's calculations for our period 1980–1986, using the Theil and Gini indices of inequality (see Appendix 9.1). The

Theil index is the most well-known member of the 'Generalised Entropy' indices derived from Information Theory. It has the property that it can be totally decomposed such that we can calculate:

Total inequality = within group inequality +
                   between group inequality

The Gini coefficient cannot be so neatly decomposed such that the difference between total inequality and the pure group effect does not represent just the 'within-age group' component but also includes an 'Interaction effect' (see Mookerjee and Shorrocks, 1982). It is for this reason that we will restrict much of our analysis to the Theil index.

In Table 9.2 we present the results of the age decomposition for the years 1980 and 1986. As can be seen with the Gini coefficient the age inequality effect has diminished marginally, while that in the Theil index has risen slightly. In Table 9.3 we compare the contribution of changes in the age effect to the change in aggregate inequality for successive periods. While in the earlier periods the age factor had dominated the increase in inequality, this is definitely not so in the 1980–6 period. In fact, there was a general increase in inequality for all age groups.[3]

9.4.2 The household size effect

Given that 'age' has had a minor impact on the trend in inequality, we then turned to see if household size may be the explanation. There has been a long-run trend in the FES for the average number of persons per household to fall (from 2.714 in 1980 to 2.554 in 1986). This change, if it represents a reduction in income sharing between single persons and/or families within

Table 9.2 Age decomposition of the inequality in gross normal weekly income of households, 1980 and 1986.

	Theil Index*			Gini Coefficient	
Year	Aggregate inequality	Within-group inequality	Age effect	Aggregate inequality	Age effect
1980	0.2134	0.1542	0.0592	0.3579	0.1877
1986	0.2755	0.2095	0.0660	0.4040	0.1863

*Because we had to infer the 'mean' income per age group, since they were not given in the FES publications, this meant that the Theil coefficient as estimated from the 'de-composition' formula did not precisely equate with that estimated from the aggregate data. In our exercises these differences only affect results at the third or fourth decimal point. We opted to link in with the aggregate distribution Theil value by estimating the within-group inequality directly and thereby leaving the between-group effect as residual. As it happened, this method produced results most favourable to a contributory role by the age factor.

Source: Family Expenditure Survey.

Table 9.3 Contribution of changes within and between age groups components to the trend in total inequality of gross normal weekly income of households.

	Theil Index*			Gini Coefficient	
Period	Aggregate inequality	Within-group inequality	Age effect	Aggregate inequality	Age effect
1965–80*	0.031	0.002	0.028	0.032	0.048
1975–80*	0.013	0.004	0.009	0.011	0.016
1980–86	0.062	0.055	0.007	0.046	−0.002

Note: *Mookherjee's and Shorrocks's figures. See also footnote to Table 9.2.

households, could lead to less concentration of income and hence greater inequality. Following the same method as for age groups, we estimated distributions for five household size groups. The impact of the changing household size pattern is presented in Table 9.4. The results indicate that we can also eliminate this as a major source of the increase in inequality. Inequality has increased across the board in all household size groups.

The combined impact of both age and household size may produce a larger role for these structural factors. However, it is impossible from published data sources to derive the necessary breakdown to estimate this combined impact. Of course, age and household size are not independent and we would anticipate that the combined impact would be somewhat less than the sum of the two individual impacts.

Age and household size are probably the two most important demographic structural factors influencing the distribution of household income. Another structural factor which could play a role would be the number of workers per household This cannot be quantified due to a major change in the definition of a worker in the FES in 1982, rendering pre- and post-1982 comparisons meaningless.

Table 9.4 Household size decomposition in aggregate inequality of gross normal weekly income of households, 1980 and 1986.

	Theil Index*			Gini Coefficient	
Year	Aggregate inequality	Within-group inequality	Size effect	Aggregate inequality	Size effect
1980	0.2134	0.1504	0.0630	0.3579	0.1839
1986	0.2755	0.2098	0.0657	0.4040	0.1879
Change in 1980–86	0.0621	0.0594	0.0027	0.0461	0.0040

Note: *The size groups were for one-, two-, three-, four- and five-or-more-person households. We did know the mean incomes for each group, thus the Theil indices as estimated above correspond exactly with the Theil indices estimated from the aggregate distribution.

Source: Family Expenditure Survey.

9.4.3 Regional income distribution

The FES provides two-yearly data on the distribution of Gross Weekly Income by households for each of the 12 regions of the UK. In the period 1979–80 to 1985–6 inequality increased in all regions. The 'between region' inequality effect also doubled in the same period (see Table 9.5a), giving some credence to the so-called 'North–South divide'. However it is also clear that the contribution of inter-regional inequality still plays a relatively minor role compared to inequality within each region.

The figures in Table 5a are calculated at current prices. A case can be made that regional price differences, if allowed for, may change the inter-regional inequality effect. We devised a regional price index[4] and readjusted the distribution in each region to South-east prices. The results are given in Table 9.5b. In each of the years the 'within-region' inequality factor is marginally increased after the adjustment, but the 'between-group' inequality is noticeably reduced, though it still almost doubles over the period. The overall impact is a very slight reduction in the level and trend of national inequality.

Table 9.5a Decomposition of the inequality in gross normal household weekly income by regions, 1979–80–1985–6.

Theil Index

Year	Total inequality	Within-regions factor	Between-regions factor
1979–80	0.2114	0.2076	0.0038
1985–86	0.2630	0.2549	0.0081
1985–86 – 1979–80	0.0516	0.0473	0.0043

Source: Family Expenditure Survey.

Table 9.5b Decomposition of the inequality in gross normal household weekly income by regions, adjusted to South-east prices.

Theil Index

Year	Total inequality	Within-regions factor	Between-regions factor
1979–80	0.2106	0.2079	0.0027
1985–86	0.2612	0.2561	0.0051
1985–86 – 1979–80	0.0506	0.0482	0.0024

Source: Family Expenditure Survey.

9.5 CHANGES IN THE COMPOSITION OF INCOMES AND THE IMPORTANCE OF WAGE INEQUALITY

Perhaps the most striking feature of the above analysis is that for every age, household size and regional cohort inequality has increased since 1980. The 'within-group' element in the exercises has dominated and the 'between-group' contribution to the increase in inequality is indeed quite minor. This suggests that we must search elsewhere for the sources of the increase in inequality and an obvious direction to follow would be the changing pattern in the types of incomes received by households.

Though declining in relative significance, employment earnings are still the major source of household income. Since 1980 there have been two changing patterns within employment earnings. First is that by 1986 wages and salaries contributed less than 30% to the total income of the poorest 40% of households and only 60% to those in the middle quintile group. In 1980 the equivalent proportions were 45% and 75%, respectively. Secondly there is substantial evidence indicating that among those still receiving wages and salaries, inequality has increased noticeably. These two patterns are, of course, not unrelated.

The contribution of each type of income to total inequality can be quantified by using Concentration Indices[5] (see Table 9.6). In 1986 wages and salaries accounted for 82% of the inequality in the Gross Weekly Income of households. This compared to a 93% contribution in 1980. The contribution of other types of incomes has increased, while the negative impact of state benefits has declined. Though exerting a declining impact, wages and salaries still accounted for approximately 60% of the overall increase in inequality. It is for this reason that we shall focus our attention on changes in the distribution of employment income.

9.5.1 Inequality in employment income

The New Earnings Surveys (NES) show that inequality has increased from 1979 up to the most recently available figures for 1988 (see Table 9.7). The data is restricted to full-time employed adults.

The difference between male and female earnings is a topic of frequent interest. However, this particular difference has not contributed to the general increase in inequality; indeed, quite the reverse (see Table 9.8). The inequality within each sex group has increased. Moreover, throughout the period since 1979, inequality among adult male earners has accounted for over three-quarters of the within-group inequality set out in Table 9.8. For this reason we shall concentrate our analysis on full-time employed adult males.

Adam *et al.* (1988) have concluded: (a) that earnings have risen fastest in the higher-paid occupations, and (b) that the numbers of employees in the top and bottom wage occupations have increased, while those in the middle groups have declined.

Table 9.6 Income inequality by type of income: analysis by concentration indices.

Type of gross normal household weekly income	Concentration index 1980	Concentration index 1986	Proportion of total income 1980	Proportion of total income 1986
Wages and salaries	0.474	0.534	0.712	0.643
Self-employment	0.520	0.600	0.055	0.077
Investment incomes	0.242	0.499	0.030	0.042
Annuities and pensions	0.145	0.270	0.026	0.043
Other	0.291	0.360	0.057	0.065
State benefits	−0.250	−0.214	0.120	0.130

	Contribution to inequality 1980	Contribution to inequality 1986	% contribution to inequality 1980	% contribution to inequality 1986
Wages and salaries	0.338	0.343	92.8	82.2
Self-employment	0.029	0.046	7.9	11.1
Investment incomes	0.007	0.021	2.0	5.0
Annuities and pensions	0.004	0.012	1.0	2.9
Other	0.017	0.023	4.6	5.5
State benefits	−0.030	−0.028	−8.3	−6.7
All income	0.365	0.417		

	% contribution to the change in inequality 1980 base	% contribution to the change in inequality 1986 base	% contribution to the change in inequality Mean* base
Wages and salaries	64.7	55.5	60.0
Self-employment	6.2	8.7	7.5
Investment incomes	12.2	15.9	14.0
Annuities and pensions	4.6	8.7	6.5
Other	6.2	5.8	6.0
State benefits	6.2	5.8	6.0

Note: *Geometric mean
Source: Family Expenditure Survey.

These changes in the occupational structure of employment are reinforced by changes in the industrial structure. Only three of the ten major industrial groups actually increased their employment of employees in the period 1980 to 1986 (see Table 9.9). The main gainers were banking, finance and insurance (512,200), which is a high average-wage industry, with also a very high inter-decile ratio and other services (SIC 9) a low-wage industrial grouping but also with a high inter-decile ratio. As can be seen in Table 9.9 the major employee loss industries were the 'middle' average-wage industries, which also in the main had middle range inter-decile ratios. The notable exception to this pattern was 'other manufacturing' – a low-wage/high dispersion industry, which lost 442,700 employees or approximately 20% of the total employment loss.

Table 9.7 Theil inequality
index for earnings of
employees: full-time adults
(whose pay is not affected by
absence).

Year	All adults
1976*	0.0915
1979*	0.0914
1983*	0.1094
1983†	0.1067
1986†	0.1131
1988†	0.1345

Notes: *For full-time men
over 21 and women over 18.
†For full-time persons on
adult rates of pay.
Source: New Earnings
Survey.

Generally, though, we can conclude that there has been a trend for employment to shift out of middle-wage/dispersion industries and be either replaced in high- or low-wage industries with high levels of dispersion or lost to the distribution of earnings altogether.[6]

The occupational changes outlined by Adams *et al.* can in fact be summarised more generally. The occupations with the faster-rising wages and increasing numbers of employed were in all cases non-manual occupations. In Table 9.10 we perform a decomposition analysis between manual and non-manual male earners. The between-group factor has increased fourfold and accounts for almost 30% of the total increase in overall inequality – a result that supports the conclusions of Adams *et al.*

However, a more meaningful analysis might be to separate out the 'relative mean earnings' and relative occupational numbers effects. This can be done

Table 9.8 Decomposition of the inequality of
earnings by sex.

	Theil Index	
Year	Within-group factor	Between-group factor
1979	0.0705	0.0209
1983*	0.0911	0.0182
1983†	0.0903	0.0164
1988†	0.1182	0.0163
1979–88 change	0.0477	−0.0046

Note: * and †, see Table 9.7.
Source: New Earnings Survey.

Table 9.9 Changes in the industrial composition of employment, 1980–6.

SIC Group	1987 Average full-time adult wages (£)	Increase in employment (1,000) June 1980– June 1986	1987 Inter-decile ratio
1 Energy and water	248.1	−186.6	1.792
8 Banking, finance and insurance	230.7	+512.2	3.887
2 Extraction (not fuels)	216.6	−292.5	2.594
7 Transport and communication	214.9	−142.2	2.632
3 Metal goods, engineering, etc.	207.0	−917.2	2.723
5 Construction	194.1	−239.3	2.656
9 Other services	191.5	+303.3	3.031
4 Other manufacturing	188.7	−442.7	3.255
6 Distribution, hotels, catering	162.2	+ 62.0	3.207
0 Agriculture, forestry, fishing	142.7	− 42.1	2.196
All industries and services	198.9		

Sources: Family Expenditure Survey and *Employment Gazette Historical Supplement*, No. 1, February 1987, 1–4.

by estimating the changes that would have occurred in the Theil index had first, only the relative mean earnings changed and secondly, only the relative numbers of manual and non-manual employees changed. It is an indexing exercise and we took 1979 as our base. The latter estimate gives us the occupational population effect and the former the mean wage effect. The difference between the sum of these two effects and the actual total change in the Theil index we define as the residual effect. The upshot of the exercise was that the residual accounted for approximately 60% of the change, occupational population changes for 30% and relative mean wages 10%.

The residual will include four categories of impact on the distribution. These are as follows:

1. The impact of changes in the industrial structure of employment.
2. The impact of changes in the occupations within the broad bands of the manual and non-manual change.
3. The impact of any other relevant structural or demographic factors, such as the regional element or the small business factor.
4. A market effect, which is not totally independent of any of the above effects, i.e., increasing flexibility in the labour market.

The 'market' effect is basic supply and demand analysis. Wages rise relatively with excess demand and are depressed with excess supply. The weakening role of the trade unions, the encroaching 'fear' of unemployment on those in employment, the absence of 'income policies' and the like, one suspects, have allowed this market effect greater scope than in former periods.

While we cannot isolate the four categories, it would not be unreasonable to conclude that a 'market effect' has undoubtedly played an important role.

Table 9.10 Decomposition of the inequality in earnings of full-time adult male employees in manual/non-manual occupational status.

Year	Total inequality	Within-group factor	Between-group factor
1979	0.0732	0.0691	0.0041
1988	0.1218	0.1039	0.0179
1979–88	0.0486	0.0348	0.0138

Source: New Earnings Survey.

In an era where the philosophy of 'market rule' is paramount, the market has quite clearly played its part in generating a vastly more unequal society.

9.6 CONCLUSIONS ON THE CAUSES OF INCREASING INEQUALITY

Structural and demographic factors such as age, household size and regional patterns have only played a very minor role in the trend of increasing inequality. The main force (60% we estimated) is centred on changes in employment earnings, in spite of the declining role of wages and salaries in total household income. Using data on full-time earnings, which throughout our period accounted for 92% of total wages and salaries, we detected (a) an industrial structural effect; (b) an occupational structural effect; and (c) a 'market' effect, which is probably the dominant factor. Allied to this 'wage effect' will also be the proportionate rise in the numbers of part-time workers, from 19% in 1979 to 23% in 1986, and whose incomes started at 32% of the level of full-time workers in 1979 and grew by 20% less up to 1986.

The remaining factors influencing the increase in inequality were the rise in self-employment and investment income, where inequality is much greater; and the expanding importance of social security benefits throughout the distribution, many of which have fallen behind in average and/or real terms. All of these factors have supplemented the basic increase in wage income inequality, leading to a corresponding increase in total household income inequality.

The dramatic rise in unemployment since 1979, it might be argued, must have played a part in the increase in inequality. The impact of unemployment will manifest itself in three ways. First, as we have already mentioned, by weakening the market position of those most likely to be unemployed. This is part of our 'market effect'. There can also be no doubt that the rise in part-time employment reflects a market reaction to the general rise in unemployment. Secondly, the increasing number of the long-term unemployed, well over 1 million by 1986, has played an important role in the growing dependence on state benefits in the lower half of the distribution. Thirdly, the increasing numbers of short-term unemployed (i.e., unemployed less than one year) – over 2 million in 1986 – means that some multiple of this increasing number will have experienced unemployment during each year. This, in turn, widens the dispersion in annual incomes. This latter effect will not be 'picked up' in the FES Gross 'normal' weekly distributions, though these will possibly overstate the relative significance of the wholly unemployed in the household distribution,[7] by virtue of missing this 'part-year' type of effect.

The upshot is that increasing unemployment has played a part in increasing inequality. To quantify this role, however, would require a major simulation exercise, involving a number of 'what would have been' assumptions.

9.7 THE IMPACT OF REDISTRIBUTION POLICY

The declining contribution of state benefits towards equality in Gross Household Weekly income has already been noted. We can add to this the well-documented estimates that changes in the income tax structure have largely benefited the upper income groups (see *Hansard*, 1988 and Sutherland, 1988).

The CSO derives annual distributions from the FES in order to analyse the impact of taxes and benefits. The conversion of the household distribution from a 'normal' weekly basis to an annual basis results in some marginal changes in the shares of some decile groups. These also show up more strongly when we compare the average real income increases (decreases) per decile groups. This can be seen if we compare the corresponding columns in Tables 9.1 and 9.11. The bottom four deciles fare better on the annual basis

Table 9.11a Distribution of annual household income at each stage of the redistribution process (re-ranked at each stage).

Quantile group (%)	*Quantile shares (%)*							
	By original income		By gross income		By disposable income		By final income	
	1979	1986	1979	1986	1979	1986	1979	1986
Top 10%	26.9	31.9	23.9	27.5	22.9	26.0	22.0 }	42.0
11–20	17.9	18.8	16.2	16.6	15.8	15.6	16.0 }	
21–30	14.7	14.9	13.4	13.3	13.3	13.3 }	24.0	24.0
31–40	12.4	12.0	11.5	11.1	11.4	11.0 }		
41–50	10.4	9.5	9.9	9.0	9.8	9.2 }	18.0	17.0
51–60	8.4	6.9	8.3	7.3	8.4	7.6 }		
61–70	6.1	4.2	6.6	5.6	6.8	6.1 }	12.0	11.0
71–80	2.7	1.5	4.7	4.2	5.3	4.8 }		
81–90	0.5	0.3	3.3	3.1	3.9	3.7	4.3 }	6.3
91–100	0.1	–	2.2	2.1	2.6	2.6	2.8 }	

Table 9.11b Percentage increase (decrease) in average real annual income per decile group of households at each stage in the redistribution process (re-ranked at each stage).

Quantile group	%, 1979–86 By original income	By gross income	By disposable income	By final income
Top 10%	28.7	27.9	26.8 ⎫	19.3
11–20	13.7	13.5	12.8 ⎭	
21–30	10.1	10.8	10.4 ⎫	7.9
31–40	5.8	7.0	7.6 ⎭	
41–50	–1.1	1.8	3.7 ⎫	1.9
51–60	–10.5	–1.9	1.5 ⎭	
61–70	–25.1	–5.6	0.0 ⎫	–1.1
71–80	–37.4	–2.3	1.6 ⎭	
81–90	–44.9	4.5	4.3 ⎫	–4.2
91–100	–72.7	7.5	8.3 ⎭	
Average	8.6	11.0	11.4	7.9

Source: CSO, *Economic Trends* (various).

than on the weekly basis. This is largely due to the inclusion of state transfers of those unemployed for less than 13 weeks and the loss of income for those higher in the distribution who experience temporary unemployment.

In Table 9.11a we present the decile shares for households at each stage in the redistribution process for the years 1979 and 1986.[8] We have re-ranked at each stage. At each stage the greater inequality in 1986 *vis-à-vis* 1979 is quite apparent. Also very apparent is the change in the shape of the distribution as we move from stage to stage. Table 11a shows that the step from original to gross income redistributes in favour of the bottom 60% of households with the bottom 20% being relatively large gainers. This process is reinforced for the bottom half after the imposition of direct taxes. The net impact of indirect taxes (which in fact are mildly regressive) and benefits in kind have only a very marginal impact on decile shares after the disposable income stage.

The changes in average real incomes (Table 9.11b) show up more dramatic impacts. The changing pattern of original income towards greater inequality is glaringly stark. Direct cash benefits rescue all but the fifty-first to eightieth groups in real terms, but only the top 20% exceed the national average real increase. After direct taxes, no one is worse off in real terms, though by Final Income the lowest 40% are.

The major components of the redistribution process are thus state cash benefits and direct taxation (income tax and employee National Insurance contributions). The impact of direct taxes (benefits) will depend on the degree of progressiveness and the average effective tax (benefit) paid (received). These two effects combined with the change in factor income inequality will determine the ultimate change in the inequality of disposable incomes. Follow-

Table 9.12 Percentage contribution to changes in the inequality of disposable income, 1979–86.

	%
Change in the inequality of original income	+154.8
Changes in the progressivity of state benefits	− 7.0
Changes in the average benefit/income ratio	− 28.6
Changes in the progressivity of direct taxes	− 22.5
Changes in the average tax/income ratio	+ 3.3

Source: CSO, *Economic Trends*, December 1988; CSO, *Economic Trends*, January 1981.

ing Kakwani's[9] method for separating out these effects we estimated the percentage contribution of each to the change in the inequality of disposable income (see Table 9.12). The cash benefit system reduced inequality by 35%, compared to 19% for the tax system. A slight decrease in the average tax rate has reduced the effectiveness of the system, though this has been more than offset by an increase in the degree of progressiveness, largely due to increases in personal allowances.

Inflation under a progressive direct tax system with constant tax rates will automatically cause the average effective tax rates to rise. The declining tax rates since 1979 have, when combined with rising levels of personal allowances, offset this inflationary factor. The changes in the tax system are part of the philosophy of reducing the burden of direct taxation and any improvement in the effectiveness of the redistribution mechanism through increasing progressiveness is probably purely coincidental. Similarly, the average effective benefit rate will rise if the proportion of households receiving benefits increases without there being any rise in the rates of benefit. Since many benefit rates have not kept pace with the increase in average earnings, the increasing impact of the benefit system cannot therefore be claimed to be a conscious active response to increasing inequality.

An alternative method of comparing the changing effectiveness of the redistributive system is to examine the percentage change in the Gini coefficients after each stage in 1979 and 1986 (see Table 9.13). The step from original to gross income – the cash benefit factor – reduced inequality by 23.8% in 1986 compared to 22.8% in 1979. Direct taxes contributed a further 8.4% decline in 1986 and 7.4% in 1979, while indirect taxes reversed the change by 10.8% in 1986 compared to 8.6% in 1979. In both years benefits in kind contributed a further 10% reduction in inequality at the final stage. Overall, then, there has been a slight increase in effectiveness at the 'direct' stages of redistribution, though the shift in the tax system toward indirect taxes has clearly reduced the effectiveness of the entire redistribution system.

In our introduction we stated that Thatcherism saw no need to justify the inevitable increase in inequality. The 'new order' would provide growth such

Table 9.13 Gini coefficients for the distribution of income at each stage of the redistribution process.

	1979	1986
Original income	0.451	0.517
Gross income	0.351	0.394
Disposable income	0.324	0.361
Income after cash benefits and all taxes	0.350	0.400
Final income	0.315	0.360

Source: CSO, *Economic Trends*, December 1988.

that all will benefit and a system devised to protect the most 'disadvantaged' in the community. It is not surprising, therefore, that inequality continues to increase even after redistribution. There was, however, by 1986 no sign that there was any system to protect the lowest decile groups, or that the benefits of 'inequality induced and/or accompanied' growth had spread too far down the income scale.

APPENDIX 9.1

Three measures of income inequality are used. First the Gini coefficient, incorporating Sheppard's correction for grouped data, which we calculated following the *Royal Commission on the Distribution of Income and Wealth* (1980) as:

$$G = \frac{N}{N-1} [1 - \{ \Sigma\, n_i(Y^*_i + Y^*_{i-1}) - \Sigma\, (n_i^2 - 1)\, W_i/6 \} / NY] \qquad (1)$$

where: N is the total number of households
n_i is the number of households in the ith income range
Y^*_i is the sum of incomes up to and including the ith range
W_i is the width of the ith range
Y is the total amount of income

The second measure adopted was Theil's (1967) first entropy measure, namely:

$$T = \Sigma\, \frac{y_i}{Y} \log \frac{\bar{y}_i}{\bar{Y}} \qquad (2)$$

where: y_i is the amount of income in the ith range
$\bar{y}_i$ is the average income in the ith range
$\bar{Y}$ is the average income for the whole distribution

We compensated for the 'grouping error' or the 'within-range inequality' for the Theil measure by converting the distributions into percentiles using the

Double-Log proportionate (Pareto) interpolation method. This converted the standard 16 range FES distributions into 100 ranges. It also meant that the Theil measure reduced to:

$$T = \frac{1}{100} \Sigma \, a_i \log a_i \tag{3}$$

where a_i is the income share of the ith percentile. The above simple method (with a convenient percentile distribution as a by-product) gave results which were within the range of those produced by interpolation techniques based on more complex density functions.

The Theil measure readily decomposes into within-group inequality and between-group inequality. Following Mookherjee and Shorrocks (1982) the decomposition is:

$$T = \Sigma \, \frac{y_k}{Y} T_k + \Sigma \, \frac{y_k}{Y} \log \frac{\bar{y}_k}{\bar{Y}} \tag{4}$$

where the k subscript now refers to groups (age, sex, regions, etc.) and T_k is the Theil measure for each group. The first term is the within-group inequality, the second the between-group, which quantifies the impact of the differing group means.

The nature of the Gini coefficient is such that only the 'between-group' element can be meaningfully estimated. Again following Mookherjee and Shorrocks, we estimated:

$$G = \frac{i}{2N^2 \, \bar{Y}} \, \underset{k \, h}{\Sigma \, \Sigma} \, n_k n_h \mid \bar{Y}_k - \bar{Y}_h \mid \tag{5}$$

The third measure used was the inter-decile ratio which is:

Lowest income (earnings) in the top 10% of incomes (earnings)

Highest income (earnings) in the lowest 10% of incomes (earnings)

This measure is easily calculated. It generally shows similar trends as more complex measures. However, it is a 'rough and ready' calculation, since it totally ignores changes in equality both between and outside the two decile points.

NOTES
1. The figures for the series charted are available on request from the author.
2. Both series since 1983 are for full-time persons on adult rates whose pay has not been affected by absence. Prior to 1983 they referred to males over 21 and females over 18 years of age whose pay has not been affected by absence.
3. Inequality indices for the nine age groups in the FES for 1980 and 1986 are

available on request from the author. Indices for each household size group and for the standard regions of the UK are also available on request.

4. Our Regional Price Index was estimated from two sources: first, the Reward Group's 'Cost of Living – Regional Comparisons' data, where we adopted the implicit regional price index in the estimates of consumer expenditure less housing; secondly, the Family Expenditure Survey, where we used the average expenditure per household by five types of housing to construct a regional housing expenditure price index. This latter was achieved by assuming that on average the unit of housing per type of housing was the same in each region, such that average expenditure variations therefore reflected price variations. These were then weighted by the number of households per type of housing and then using the relative weights of housing and other consumer expenditure per region, again from the Family Expenditure Survey, combined with the index from Reward Group data. The final stage was a re-reference with respect to the South-east of England.

5. See Kakwani (1980). Pages 173–81 of this book discuss in detail Concentration Indices, their relationship to the Gini coefficient and how they can be used to estimate the contribution of each type of income to total inequality.

6. Unfortunately, changes in the Standard Industrial Classification (SIC) during our data period make it impossible to compare or quantify precisely an 'industrial effect' between 1979 and 1988.

7. This overstatement will be tempered by virtue that only those unemployed for over 13 weeks have state benefits recorded as 'normal' income. For those unemployed for less than 13 weeks the last recorded employment income is adopted.

8. The CSO, in its estimates of the effects of taxes and benefits, sets out five stages. These are as follows:

(a) Original income   – factor incomes, occupational pensions and annuities and other non-state incomes, e.g., alimony.

(b) Gross income   – original income plus cash benefits from the state.

(c) Disposable income   – gross income less income tax and employee National Insurance contributions.

(d) Post-tax income   – disposable income less indirect taxes.

(e) Final income   – post-tax income plus benefits in kind from the state.

9. See Kakwani (1980), pp. 253–72 for a discussion on the methods of estimation used in this section and for Table 9.12.

REFERENCES

Adams, Mark, Maybury, Ruth, and Smith, William, 'Trends in the distribution of earnings 1973 to 1986', Employment Market Research Unit, *Employment Gazette*, **96**, 2 (1988).

Atkinson, A. B. and Micklewright, J., 'On the reliability of income data in the Family Expenditure Survey, 1970–1977', *Journal of the Royal Statistical Society*, Series A, **1**, 33–61 (1983).

Cowling, M., *Conservative Essays* (Cassells: London, 1978).

Hansard, Written Answers, 27 June 1988, p. 104. Topic; Tax Liabilities.

Kakwani, N. C., *Income Inequality and Poverty. Methods of Estimation and Policy Applications* (Oxford University Press: Oxford, 1980).

Mookherjee, D. and Shorrocks, A., 'A decomposition analysis of the trend in UK income inequality', *Economic Journal*, Vol. 92, 368, 886–902 (1982).

Rentoul, J., *The Rich Get Richer*, (Unwin: London, 1987).
Royal Commission on the Distribution of Income and Wealth, 'Technical Records of the Commission's Methods', Internal mimeograph (1980).
Sutherland, Holly, *The Impact of the 1988 Income Tax Changes*, Taxation Review, Background Paper No. 1, Fabian Society (1988).
Theil, H., *Economics and Information Theory* (North-Holland: Amsterdam, 1967).

PART IV

POLICIES AND AGENCIES FOR MODERNISATION

10 R&D, TECHNICAL CHANGE AND INVESTMENT IN THE UK

Chris Freeman

10.1 INTRODUCTION

It is generally accepted by all schools of economic thought that technical change is vital for the growth of productivity in any economy. Moreover, in the post-war period the role of technological competition in international trade performance has been increasingly acknowledged. Since Posner's seminal paper (Posner, 1961), a large number of empirical studies have confirmed the role of product design and new products in international competition and of process innovation in cost reduction (Soete, 1981). These developments in empirical work have found expression in a substantial revision of international trade theory (Dosi and Soete, 1988) since the Montreal Conference of the International Economics Association. Particularly in the case of the astonishingly successful Japanese export performance in the last thirty years, the role of technology has been amply demonstrated (Freeman, 1987). Conversely, weaknesses in product design, product quality and process innovation have often been advanced to explain the relatively poor British trade performance in the post-war period in such industries as machine tools, passenger cars, ship-building, cutlery, television and many others (Pavitt, 1980).

Consequently, there can be little doubt that those activities which contribute to the efficient introduction and exploitation of new and improved processes and products are extremely important for the competitive performance and long-term growth of any industrial economy. They are especially important for small and medium-sized countries such as Britain, which are highly dependent on international trade and vulnerable to shocks from the international economy. The balance of payments constraint frequently slowed the growth of the British economy in the post-war period.

Nor can the growing importance of services be adduced as a reason for neglecting or belittling the role of technical change in international competition and economic growth. On the contrary, one of the most important features of the rapid process of structural change in the 1980s has been the breakdown of many of the old distinctions between manufacturing and services. At one time it was often said that services were neither capital-intensive nor R&D-intensive (Guy, 1987). This was never strictly true and it is less and less true today. The bulk of investment in computing systems and in software in the 1980s in the UK and other industrial economies has been in the services, rather than manufacturing. Industries such as financial services, distribution and even tourism are becoming much more capital-intensive and already have a heavy investment in computerised equipment. The telecommunication network has always been both highly capital-intensive and R&D-intensive. The revolutionary developments in optical fibres and the convergence of computer and telecommunication technology mean that the telecommunication infrastructure is now at the heart of a whole set of new services, as well as playing a vital role in older service industries (Thomas and Miles, 1989). Moreover, the fact that the maintenance and redesign of software systems is now an essential activity for many service industries is leading to a shift in the *locus* of some design and development activities and the establishment of R&D capacity in areas where none previously existed (Barras, 1986).

Not only is it fallacious to believe that the advent of a 'service economy' will make such economies as Britain and the US less vulnerable to technological competition, it is also a mistake to believe that competitive strength in services is independent of competitive strength in manufacturing. In many areas there is a complex set of customer–supplier interactions in the design and application of the new technologies which mean that there are virtuous circle effects in the simultaneous development of technological strength in both hardware and software activities. Many of the new data banks, software, business service and consultancy activities which have shown such extraordinary growth in the 1980s are essentially *producer* services and benefit generally from a strong domestic market in the *manufacturing* sector. For this reason, among others, the debate on the competitive performance of the US economy in the 1980s has moved strongly towards the recognition that it would be suicidal for the US to opt out of manufacturing and rely on services in the competition with Japan (Cohen and Zysman, 1987; Cuomo Commission Report, 1988; Office of Technology Assessment, 1987). This conclusion is no less valid for the UK, despite the relatively greater decline in the UK manufacturing sector.

Nor do the environmental problems associated with the energy-intensive and materials-intensive phase of growth in the post-war period lessen the need for technological strength. Again, the ability to change direction and to develop energy-saving and material-saving technologies is dependent on technological strength, just as the understanding of such complex problems as the 'greenhouse effect' depends on scientific capability. A new 'green' pattern of sustainable growth and environmental improvement is highly desirable but it is no less dependent on scientific and technical activities in pollution abatement.

This chapter therefore examines the evidence on the performance of the British science–technology system in the UK in the 1970s and 1980s in relation to other OECD economies and considers the main policy changes introduced by the Thatcher government over the past decade and their implications for the future performance of the UK economy. It is first necessary to clarify some of the problems of measurement and definition of scientific and technical activities and their relationship to other indicators of economic performance. This is done in the following section and leads on to consideration of the influence of technology on UK productivity and trade and finally to the discussion of science and technology policy.

10.2 MEASUREMENT OF SCIENTIFIC AND TECHNICAL ACTIVITIES AND UK PERFORMANCE IN R&D

While virtually all economists would agree that technical change is vital for the long-term growth of productivity and for the competitive performance of firms and countries, the *measurement* of technical change and of the activities which contribute to its rate and direction engenders more complex problems. The statistics of Research and Development (R&D) are those which are most commonly used and they will be used also in this chapter. However, for a variety of reasons, the relationship between R&D activities and economic growth is by no means straightforward and unambiguous, *inter alia* for the following reasons.

First, R&D activities are an imperfect measure of the scale and scope of all those inputs which are needed to implement and manage technical innovation efficiently. While the definitions of industrial research and development which are in general use in the OECD areas (OECD, 1981) include the work of specialised R&D laboratories and departments in industrial firms, they do not include much design and engineering work which is necessary to scale up production processes, to improve the efficiency of production, to establish good quality control systems, and to market new and improved products. Nor do they include so-called 'fashion design', which is extremely important in such industries as clothing, footwear, furniture and other consumer goods. Thus, although measures of R&D activity are a good first approximation to the scale of technical effort devoted to the improvement of existing products and processes, and to the invention, design and development of new ones, a high level of R&D activity would not necessarily be accompanied by a proportionately high level of commitment to other technical activities and services, which are just as important for the successful commercialisation of technical innovations arising from R&D activity. These considerations could be important in making international comparisons of R&D activities and

Table 10.1 Intra-European variations in industry-financed and defence R&D.[a]

	Share % (1985)[b]	Proportion of value-added (%) (1985)	US $ 1980 Per capita (1985)	Growth % p.a. 1967–85	Defence as % of GERD[c] (1985)
FRG	35.7	1.99	159.5	5.80	5.1
France	17.9	1.23	88.4	5.63	19.9
UK	17.0	1.32	81.5	1.83	28.7
Italy	9.3	0.71	44.2	5.77	5.8
Switzerland	4.4	n.a.	184.4	1.30	n.a.
Sweden	6.2	2.64	201.6	7.28	10.8
Netherlands	4.5	1.22	84.8	2.29	1.3
Belgium	3.6	1.21	99.1	6.20	( )[d]
Denmark	1.2	0.93	61.9	5.87	( )[d]
Ireland	0.2	0.44	19.0	7.54	( )[d]

[a]R&D expenditures and industrial value-added (at constant 1980 prices) converted to US dollars using 1980 purchasing power parities.
[b]The first four columns refer to industry-financed R&D and the fifth column to defence R&D.
[c]GERD = gross expenditure on R&D.
[d]In Belgium, Denmark and Ireland, defence R&D accounted for less than 1% of GERD.
Source: OECD and see Patel and Pavitt (1989).

national economic performance. Thus, for example, Italy has a much lower level of industrial R&D activity than the other EEC industrial countries of comparable size (Table 10.1) (Patel and Pavitt, 1989), yet Italy's post-war performance in terms of productivity growth and exports of manufactures compares favourably with other EEC countries. While there are many possible explanations for this, an obvious one is that 'non-R&D' types of techical activity have played a very big part in the success of some leading Italian industries and that Italian industrial structure differs from other countries. In machinery and vehicles design, production engineering and technical service have been especially important. In the case of such industries as clothing and footwear, types of fashion design and marketing activities which are not classified as R&D have been important in the commercial success of new and improved Italian products. On the other hand, the highly R&D-intensive aircraft industry is not a major one in the Italian industrial structure.

Secondly, the scale of national R&D activities and other related activities depends both on the structure of industry and on the *level* of economic development and the degree of international *specialisation*. The least-developed countries have little or no R&D but newly industrialising countries can make rapid progress by imports of technical know-how and reverse engineering combined with relatively small-scale R&D. As they become industrialised, they will experience a growing need for more R&D activities, if only to make effective use of imported technology. However, even when they attain high levels of development and per capita income, the scale of R&D and related activities may be lower in countries which are specialised in the production and export of minerals and natural resources (for example, Norway, Australia, Canada, New Zealand) than in countries which have a much more varied industrial structure and strong capital-goods industries, characterised by high R&D intensities. 'Catching-up' countries, such as South Korea, attained very high GNP growth rates with a relatively low level of R&D intensity, although this increased rapidly in the 1970s and South Korea now plans to overtake both USA and Japan in its R&D intensity. On the other hand, the UK and US showed rather low rates of growth by comparison with their high R&D intensity. Comparable measures are not easily available, but the same point is valid for the Soviet Union.

Thirdly, in considering these points it is obviously essential to remember that measures of gross expenditure on R&D (GERD) include both civil and military R&D. It is fairly clear that R&D activities which are *directly* concerned with the introduction and improvement of products and processes for the world civil market are inherently far more likely to have favourable effect on economic performance than military R&D activities which can at best have only an indirect ('spin-off') effect. It seems likely that there has been increasing divergence between the respective requirements of civil and military technology in the 1980s (Walker *et. al.,* 1988; Kaldor and Walker, 1989). Moreover, particularly if there are shortages of skilled engineers and scientists, the deployment of a large proportion of these scarce resources in military R&D may actually have adverse effects on the performance of the rest of the system.

It is not simply a question of resources, but also of effects on firm behaviour. Micro-level studies have found that firms in Britain and the US which see themselves as primarily designing and developing products for defence markets have a style of management behaviour and of marketing which is often not well suited to the differing requirements of civil markets, even when 'spin-off' opportunities exist. All this is not to deny that some 'spin off' has been important for civil industry, particularly in aero-engine development and in the scaling-up of processes for integrated circuit manufacture. But in trying to analyse the relationships between scientific and technological activities and economic performance, it is obviously desirable to consider separately the scale of civil R&D, as in Fig. 10.1.

Fourthly, for all these reasons the statistical correlation between aggregate national measures of R&D activity and rates of economic growth has often been found to be rather a weak one or even, according to some authors, non-existent. However, if the previous three points are taken into account, then there is indeed a definite relationship between technological and economic performance. As Fagerberg points out in the most recent and comprehensive attempt to correlate measures of technology with measures of

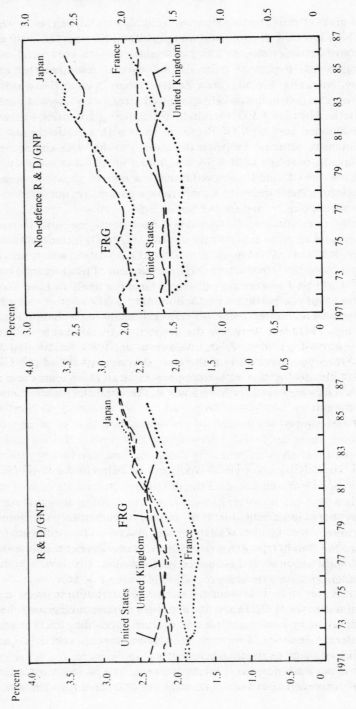

Figure 10.1 R&D/GNP ratios by country and non-defence R&D/GNP by country. (*Source:* National Science Foundation, 1988.)

economic growth, it is necessary to take into account both the technological level and the economic level over a considerable time period, adjusting for cyclical fluctuations and normalising for scale factors (Fagerberg, 1988). It is also necessary to exclude military R&D for the reasons discussed above. Unlike most earlier studies, his analysis includes six NICs (Brazil, Argentina, Hong Kong, Taiwan, South Korea and Mexico) as well as 19 OECD countries. This is obviously an improvement in considering long-term changes in technology and economic performance. He found a closer correlation between an 'output index' (patenting activity) and levels of GDP per capita than with an 'input' index (R&D). This is what could be expected taking into account the comments above. However, his most important results relate to his *dynamic* analysis which shows that long-term economic performance can be statistically 'explained' by a combination of *rates of growth* of technological and investment indicators.

Fifthly, innovative performance depends not simply on the level of *inputs* of R&D and of other technical and marketing activities, but on the *efficiency* with which these resources are managed. Numerous micro-studies, such as the SAPPHO project (Rothwell *et al.,* 1984), have demonstrated that the scale of R&D is no guarantee of successful innovation – although it may often be a *necessary* condition in most branches of industry, it is not a *sufficient* condition. There is usually a rather weak correlation between scale of R&D and the growth of output and profitability at the firm level, but in general the fastest-growing *industries* are the same ones throughout the OECD areas, reflecting the international character of science and technology and of world markets. However, just as firms vary in the efficiency of their innovation management, so do nation-states vary in the efficiency of their *national systems of innovation.*

10.3 THE LEVEL AND TREND OF UK INDUSTRIAL R&D IN THE 1970s AND 1980s

On the basis of this discussion of measurement problems, it is now possible to make some assessment of the level and trend of UK expenditure on R&D during the Thatcher period. The analysis concentrates on industrial R&D, which accounts for about two-thirds of all R&D in most OECD countries.

In terms of *structure* and *specialisation* of the UK economy, it could be expected that the UK would be a highly R&D-intensive economy, comparable to the USA, Japan, the Federal Republic of Germany or Sweden. Indeed, taking into account the far lower level of military R&D in Japan and the Federal Republic of Germany, it could be expected that *aggregate* R&D intensity would be relatively much higher in the UK.

The most R&D-intensive industries were, and to some extent still are, strongly represented in the structure of the UK economy. The UK aircraft industry (the most R&D-intensive of all industries) is the strongest in Western Europe. The electronics industry, although it has experienced relative decline in the area of consumer electronics and components, is still one of the strongest in Europe. The drug industry, although much of it is under multinational ownership, is also strongly represented in the UK. So, too, are other research-intensive sectors of the chemical industry and the oil industry. Finally, although in the 1980s demand has been relatively stagnant, the nuclear industry, both civil and military, is highly R&D-intensive and remains an area which absorbs a high proportion of total UK R&D expenditures.

For all these reasons, it is not at all surprising that in the 1970s and 1980s, the UK was among those industrial countries which had a GERD index between 2 and 3% of GNP (Figure 10.1) (National Science Foundation, 1987), much higher than countries such as Italy, Denmark or Finland, which have an entirely different pattern of specialisation within the world economy. What is disquieting is that over the 1970s and 1980s, the UK's R&D-intensity, relative to competing countries with a similar industrial structure, has been steadily declining. The growth rate of UK industrial R&D activities was the lowest in Europe from 1967 to 1985, except Switzerland (Table 10.1) (the per capita level of Swiss industrial R&D was, however, twice as high as UK in 1985).

Strictly comparable international statistics are not yet available for 1987 or 1988, but there can be little doubt that the *relative* decline of the UK has continued throughout the Thatcher decade of the 1980s. The number of people employed in industrial R&D is probably the best available proxy indicator of the *real* level of resources committed to competitive scientific and technical activities in British industry. There are complex problems involved in estimating the correct 'deflator' for the current expenditures on R&D in the 1970s and 1980s. As Table 10.2 (*British Business*, 3.2.89) shows, there was a fall in total numbers employed from 195,000 in 1981 to 184,000 in 1987, despite a break in the series in 1985 when the AEA was *added* to the sample surveyed. Part of the decline may have been due to the subcontracting of services as expenditures have shown a small increase and the total number of engineers and scientists also showed a small increase (although this was mainly the effect of adding the AEA).

If this relative stagnation in the 1980s had been at a very high level of R&D activity, this would perhaps not have been quite so serious, but the per capita level of *industry-financed* R&D in the UK in 1985 was only about half that of the German Federal Republic, much less than half of the level in Sweden and Switzerland, and lower than the level of Belgium, Netherlands or France (Table 10.1). It is difficult to escape the conclusion that this represents a serious weakening of the long-term competitiveness of the UK economy during the 1980s.

It should be remembered that the *ratios* used in GERD/GNP measures and

Table 10.2 Intramural current and capital R&D expenditure and employment in 1981, 1983, 1985, 1986 and 1987.

	1981	1983	1985r	1986r	1987[1]
Total expenditure £million	3,792	4,163	5,122	5,951	6,337
Expenditure on					
capital items	323	310	515	541	618
current items (total)	3,469	3,853	4,607	5,410	5,719
– salaries and wages	1,703	1,881	2,164	2,535	2,632
– other current items	1,766	1,972	2,443	2,875	3,087
Total employment					
(average for year – thousands)	195	186	173	188	184
– Scientists and engineers	77	77	81	87	87
– Technicians, laboratory assistants and					
draughtsmen	66	60	50	49	49
– Admin., clerical, industrial and other staff	52	49	42	52	48

Notes: ([1]) Includes UKAEA; r: revised.
Source: British Business (1989).

in column 2 of Table 10.1 reflect not only on the numerator but also on the denominator. The UK ratios reflect low levels of productivity rather than high levels of R&D – if UK productivity was closer to the EEC leaders then the UK R&D intensity would appear far lower. For this reason, the per capita measures of R&D used in column 3 of Table 10.1 are in many respects a better guide to the true level of UK industrial R&D.

However, all this might not be so serious if it could be shown *either* that less R&D is actually needed with today's new technologies *or* that military R&D undertaken in Britain has greatly enhanced the competitive position of British industry *or* that British R&D and other technical activities are more productive than similar activities elsewhere. The first two of these propositions are inherently implausible but they are now briefly examined as this actually helps to indicate the true magnitude of the problems which will confront British industry (and any incoming government) in the 1990s and which are already finding their reflection in the acute balance of payments crisis of 1988–9. The third proposition is more complex and is examined in the following section.

As we have seen, civilian non-military R&D intensity has been quite rapidly increasing in the 1980s in most complex industrial economies and particularly in Japan and the Federal Republic of Germany (Figure 10.1). This has been particularly marked in privately financed industrial R&D (Table 10.1) but it has also included publicly financed R&D, which is particularly important everywhere in fundamental scientific research. If privately financed R&D has increased in this way in industries which are the arena of fairly intense world-wide competition, it must surely be mainly because many enterprises have found an increased R&D activity to be important for their competitive survival and long-term growth. The implementation of many new technologies is in fact impossbile without some considerable commitments to R&D. This is obvious in the case of successive generations of integrated circuits, digitised telephone exchanges, FMS, CAD, CNC and other computerised equipment and systems, but it also applies in the whole burgeoning areas of biotechnology and in materials technology. These are all *generic* technologies with a host of actual and potential applications which pervade the entire economic system. It is this change of techno-economic paradigm (Freeman and Soete, 1987) which has triggered the need for many new departures in R&D activities in the 1970s and 1980s and for an increased intensity of research, design and development in many established areas.

British industry cannot opt out of this world-wide technological revolution and the restructuring which it entails. Some British firms, such as ICI, have responded to this challenge and have remained serious contenders in the new types of world technological competition (Patel and Pavitt, 1987b). Many others have either lacked the resources, the incentives or the pressures to strengthen their long-term investment in R&D and other scientific and technical activities. The government's role in creating a climate which generates such incentives and pressures and helps to make the resources available is considered in the final section of this chapter. But here it must be stressed that incentives and pressures which push management towards *short-term* profit maximisation may actually be inimical to the type of long-term investment needed for the new technologies.

The notion that the heavy orientation of British R&D towards military objectives might strengthen its technological capacity in civil markets is even more implausible. In fact, successive British governments ever since the Wilson administration in the 1960s have shown growing awareness that the military bias in British R&D has been more of a hindrance than a help. The government's own scientific advisers, both in the Department of Industry and in the Cabinet Office, have repeatedly warned of some of the adverse consequences of this over-dependence, especially in electronics. In his previous career at IBM, the present scientific adviser to the Prime Minister was in a unique position to observe some of these adverse consequences. In 1985 the Chairman of IBM (UK) pointed out that:

> UK Sources are becoming a serious concern. Our primary concern relates chiefly to the technological needs we foresee we will need in the coming years in ever greater quantities. This includes magnetic and optical storage, printing technologies, display devices and communications. While the UK does have a presence in some of these technologies, much of it is bound up in aerospace, communications and defence, with little or no native capacity in the commercial sector. (Bird, 1985)

But although good advice and good intentions have not been lacking in the 1970s and 1980s, no government has actually shown the political determination to grasp this nettle and make a decisive break with the past. This government must, however, be credited with a few tentative steps in the direction which will be essential if the long-term competitiveness of the British electronics industry is ever to be restored (Walker *et al.,* 1988). The GEC–Siemens bid for Plessey opened up some of the key issues and highlighted the extent to which many of the leading UK firms have been dependent on military contracts and military R&D for a long time (Morgan *et al.,* 1989). GEC's defence sales were just over £2 billion in 1988 – about a third of group turnover and over half of electronics turnover, while Plessey's were 40% of total output. The R&D effort has been even more heavily oriented towards military markets, so that the opportunity cost in terms of skilled engineers, scientists and software people (often in short supply over long periods) must have been enormous.

Thus, in the industry which is at the heart of the technological revolution – microelectronics – the two key British firms have not been primarily oriented towards the major civil markets for a long time and it is hardly surprising that there has been a serious loss of competitiveness outside the limited defence sector.

Finally, we turn now to consider the possibility that Britain's limited R&D resources, although declining in relation to world competition in the 1980s, have been more efficiently used, i.e., that 'R&D productivity' has in some sense improved more than that of other countries.

10.4 THE OUTPUTS OF THE R&D SYSTEM

Since the first surveys of R&D expenditures and personnel in the 1950s, a great deal of progress has been made in the development and application of a wide variety of other quantitative indicators of national scientific and technological activities, including output indicators. Despite the inherent problems associated with various types of measurement in this field, it is now increasingly possible to make broad-based international comparisons with some confidence (Patel and Pavitt, 1987a).

Two qualifications to this general statement must be made. First, the specific limitations of each type of measurement must always be taken into account (this applies of course to all types of national statistics, including those that are most widely used, such as GNP or employment statistics). Secondly, the degree of *international* comparability varies with different types of measurement. In the case of science and technology indicators, such as patents, publications and citations, the increasingly international character of science and technology and the computerisation of the main data sources has permitted a major expansion of the internationally comparable data in the last two decades. This analysis concentrates on the use of patent statistics as measures of inventive activity and on the use of bibliometric data and citation analysis as a measure of scientific activity.

Table 10.3 US patents applications by national origin of inventors as percentage of total applications.

Country	1970–6	1980–6
USA	65.6	55.7
UK	4.1	3.4
Japan	8.4	19.1
FRG	8.2	9.2
France	3.2	3.3

Source: National Science Foundation (1987).

The problems in the use of patent statistics have been extensively discussed for a long time and these discussions are well summarised by Pavitt (1985). The major problems of differences in national patent systems can be resolved for many purposes by using patents in a single foreign country as the basis for international comparisons. In the most recent period, trends in patenting in the US have been widely used. This method has the advantage that almost all firms will wish to protect their most significant patentable inventions in the largest industrial country, although of course the scale of patenting activity will also be influenced by marketing strategies and by inter-firm and inter-industry variations in the propensity to patent. Nevertheless, the evidence is still very strong that patents do provide an indicator which reflects major changes in the effectiveness of inventive activities in most industries world-wide. In the future, it will be increasingly possible to use EEC patent statistics to complement comparisons based on US statistics, but the community patent has not been in use long enough to use the statistics with confidence here.

The number of patent applications in the US was about the same in the 1980s as in the 1970s, but the national origin of inventors changed as shown in Table 10.3 (National Science Foundation, 1987). The dramatic increase in the Japanese share of patents taken out in the US from 8 to 19% is at least prima-facie evidence that Japanese R&D and other inventive activities resulted in an output of inventions proportionately greater than that of other leading industrial countries. Over the same period, the share of patents originating from British inventors in the US declined to 3% and the share of West German inventors increased from 8 to 9%, while the French share remained fairly steady at about 3%.

It is sometimes suggested that these comparisons reflect *not* the trend of inventive output of various countries but the commercial tactics of the leading firms. The declining share of US and British inventors is sometimes explained by a preference for secrecy or a more precise calculation of the relative costs and benefits of taking out patents. Such explanations may be partly valid for the *general* world-wide tendency of patenting, particularly in defence-related areas or in process technology. They may also explain the slow growth in

Table 10.4 Ten classes with highest national dominance, 1975–84 (only classes with more than 100 total patents are included).

	No. of patents	% of class	Activity* index
Japan			
354: Photography	2,167	52.5	4.4
334: Tuners	51	45.9	3.9
368: Time measurement	831	44.4	3.7
133: Coin handling	68	39.1	3.3
369: Dynamic information storage	555	37.5	3.2
360: Dynamic magnetic information	1,244	37.3	3.1
355: Photocopying	1,204	35.6	3.0
430: Radiation imagery	2,273	34.7	2.9
346: Recorders	802	33.8	2.9
123: Internal combustion engines	2,706	31.5	2.7
United States			
232: Deposit and collection receptacles	158	94.6	1.6
7: Compound tools	144	91.4	1.5
166: Wells	2,707	89.9	1.5
224: Package carriers	946	87.9	1.4
124: Guns and projectors	421	87.4	1.4
281: Books, strips and leaves	120	85.4	1.4
272: Amusement and exercise	1,058	84.6	1.4
410: Freight accommodations	350	84.5	1.4
150: Cloth, leather	208	84.2	1.4
190: Baggage	132	84.1	1.4
United Kingdom			
303: Fluid pressure brakes, etc.	148	11.7	3.0
131: Tobacco	116	9.8	2.5
188: Brakes	191	9.3	2.4
299: Mining or *in situ* degradation	112	9.3	2.4
424: Drugs, bio-affecting and body treating compositions	1,554	8.7	2.3
546: Organic compounds	199	7.2	1.9
378: X-Ray or gamma ray systems	117	7.2	1.9
405: Hydraulic and earth engineering	183	6.8	1.7
106: Compositions, coating or plastic	199	6.5	1.7
277: Joint packing	115	5.3	1.6

Notes: *The 'activity index' is a measure of relative national concentration in each class and is measured as a percentage of national patents in each class over the percentage of patents in all classes.
Source: Freeman (1987).

total patent numbers. But if they are offered as explanations of variations in *national* patenting behaviour then, although this may be flattering to national vanity, they presuppose that the Japanese and Germans are uniquely misguided in taking out a large number of patents in the US while the British are more cunning in their strategic behaviour. Such explanations seem

Table 10.5 Ten classes with largest increase in national patents, 1975–84.

Classification	No. of patents			% of class		
	1975–9	*1980–4*	*increase*	*1975–9*	*1980–4*	*increase*
Japanese						
123: Internal combustion engines	985	1,721	736	26.0	35.9	9.9
424: Drug, bio-affecting	636	1,183	547	7.7	12.3	4.6
428: Stock material or miscellaneous articles	583	1,113	530	13.1	20.0	6.9
364: Electronic computers and DP systems	359	843	484	10.9	18.3	7.4
430: Radiation imagery	895	1,378	483	29.9	38.9	9.0
358: Pictorial communication	486	946	460	22.2	31.4	9.2
355: Photocopying	410	793	383	26.3	43.6	17.3
346: Recorders	211	591	380	22.6	41.1	18.5
354: Photography	909	1,258	349	46.8	57.6	10.8
219: Electric heating	299	642	343	12.5	21.5	9.0
American						
364: Electronic computers and DP systems	2,302	3,028	726	69.9	65.6	–4.3
128: Surgery, miscellaneous	2,752	3,170	418	75.6	72.6	–3.0
126: Stoves and furnaces	1,299	1,707	408	84.3	79.8	–4.5
62: Refrigeration	1,118	1,465	347	73.3	69.1	–4.3
435: Chem: molecular biology and microbiology	810	1,153	343	52.3	54.6	2.3
428: Stock material or miscellaneous articles	2,907	3,209	302	65.2	57.7	–7.5
502: Catalytic solid sorbent	1,088	1,363	275	63.7	68.4	4.7
362: Illumination	662	885	223	72.8	72.5	–0.3
358: Pictorial communication	1,214	1,433	219	55.6	47.7	–7.9
424: Drug, bio-affecting	4,234	4,448	214	51.0	46.3	–4.8
British						
474: Drugs, bio-affecting	683	866	183	8.2	9.0	0.8
340: Communication, electrical	119	162	43	3.6	4.5	0.9
430: Radiation imagery	68	101	33	2.3	2.8	0.5
277: Joint packing	44	71	27	5.7	6.6	0.9
60: Power plants	143	169	26	5.1	7.0	1.9
324: Electronic measuring and testing	86	111	25	4.1	6.0	1.9
166: Wells	18	43	25	1.3	2.7	1.4
350: Optics, systems and elements	142	166	24	5.0	5.2	1.1

Classification	No. of patents			% of class		
	1975–9	*1980–4*	*increase*	*1975–9*	*1980–4*	*increase*
364: Electronic computer and DP systems	114	136	22	3.5	3.0	–0.5
239: Fluid sprinkers, etc.	61	83	22	3.9	5.6	1.7

Source: Freeman (1987).

improbable in the extreme. What is certainly true, however, is that the Japanese patenting behaviour is indeed linked to the successful penetration of the US market by Japanese firms on an increasing scale.

Unless it is assumed that British firms operating in world markets have no desire to export to the US market even in areas of technical strength, then the declining British share must be viewed as a measure *both* of declining relative competitive inventive activity and an associated decline in relative competitiveness in commodity trade, and conversely in the case of Japan.

Even more significant than the change in total share of patents taken out in the US is the Japanese position in specific technologies and product groups. Table 10.4 shows the patent classes with the highest 'national dominance' of Japan, the US and the UK, and Table 10.5 the classes showing the largest increases. What is impressive about these different forms of representation is the Japanese strength in patent classes related to information technology and engines. The 'activity index' in the right-hand column of Table 10.4 is a measure of the Japanese concentration in these classes and is calculated as the percentage of patents in each class over the percentage of patents in all classes. A similar analysis of the 'activity index' of British patents shows brakes, drugs and tobacco as the classes with highest national dominance. In absolute terms US firms continue to take out more patents in electronic computers than Japanese firms, but the UK has fallen far behind both.

Thus, except for a few areas such as chemicals and drugs where UK firms have done relatively well, the evidence from patent statistics does not suggest that the UK has performed relatively better than other countries in terms of the inventive output from the R&D system. Rather the reverse: they confirm the relative decline of UK technological competitiveness, particularly in relation to Japan, but also in relation to the Federal Republic of Germany.

Patents are a reasonably good proxy indicator of some areas of inventive output but they reflect mainly the activities on the 'D' side of R&D. What about research? Although it accounts for a relatively small proportion of total R&D, fundamental research is increasingly important for the effective working of the entire science–technology system. This was indeed recognised explicitly by the Prime Minister herself in her address to the Royal Society on 25 September 1988. But the Government's actions have belied its words (Table 10.6). The general constraints on the Universities in the 1980s and the restrictions on Research Council expenditure have resulted in a weakening of Britain's relative performance in this area, too, which has been well

Table 10.6 UK government R&D expenditure – breakdown by department[a] (1983–84 £million[b]).

	1981–2	1983–4	1985–6[c]	1987–8[c]
Civil departments				
Agriculture	119	119	118	113
Energy	40	34	35	34
UKAEA	226	204	173	151
Environment	43	32	39	39
Health	31	28	24	23
Trade & industry	317	313	356	253
Transport	31	28	24	23
Other	147	149	161	151
Total civil departments	954	907	930	787
Research councils				
Agricultural	46	44	45	40
Economic and social	17	18	17	16
Medical	112	113	111	109
Natural environment	58	60	59	57
Science and engineering	236	245	262	255
Total, research councils	469	480	495	477
Universities, etc.	539	551	531	520
Total, civil	1,962	1,938	1,956	1,784
Ministry of Defence	1,943	1,984	2,181	2,181
Total	3,905	3,923	4,137	3,966

[a]figures taken from *Annual Review of Science Statistics*.
[b]converted to 1983–4 prices using GDP deflator.
[c]estimates only.
Source: Martin (1987).

documented by Irvine and Martin (Irvine *et al.*, 1985, 1987; Martin, 1987). The forward estimates up to 1991 show no significant increase in real terms in civil R&D over 1985 to 1986 levels (Cabinet Office, 1988).

While this will affect the performance of the British economy mainly in the long term, the links between fundamental research and industrial technology have become much closer in recent years. Biotechnology, new materials technology and microelectronics are all characterised by strong inter-dependencies between basic science and technology. For this reason Japanese, German and US industry *and* the Japanese, German and US governments, have greatly increased their fundamental research activities during the 1980s. The relative decline in support for British scientific research has thus come at a time when its economic effects will be more serious than at any previous period. Historically, fundamental research has been one of the strongest elements in the British R&D system and it remains relatively strong by most of the available indicators of scientific performance. But it is particularly unfortunate that even in areas of great British relative strength in international terms, the scale of support should decline. However, Irvine and Martin (Irvine *et al.*, 1985, 1987) have shown that, measured by numbers of papers and citations, output was still strong in the 1980s.

10.5 INNOVATION, DIFFUSION OF INNOVATIONS AND PRODUCTIVITY

As we have seen, the evidence from 'output' measures does not suggest that British R&D has been more productive than that of other leading industrial countries in the 1980s, with the exception of fundamental research. But for the outputs of R&D to be converted into improved *economic* performance, much more is needed than R&D itself. The evidence of such vastly expensive projects as Concorde, Nimrod and the Fast Breeder Reactor, as well as the military bias and the trend of patent statistics, suggests that in all probability the British R&D system has been *less* efficient than the Japanese or the German. But even if this was not the case and the British R&D system had been more efficient and productive, this would still not be enough in itself to ensure that the British economy derived the benefit from this R&D by translating the results into higher productivity, new and better products or improved international trade performance.

The outputs of the R&D system which have been discussed above in Section 10.4 affect economic performance only *indirectly* rather than directly. Even when a prototype of a new product reaches high technical performance standards during the development stage and many patents are taken out, this is, of course, no guarantee that it will be a commercial success. The results of R&D and other scientific and technical activities for economic objectives are brought to fruition only through *innovation* and *diffusion* of innovations.

We owe to Schumpeter the distinction between invention, innovation and diffusion of innovations which has since been generally adopted in most research on technical change and economic growth. Inventions are identifiable contributions to technology, many of which may be patented. But, whether patented or not, they become economically significant only when embodied in *innovations*. Innovation is the first introduction of new products, processes and systems into the economy, i.e., the commercialisation of the outputs of R&D and other inventive activities. But whereas we have *direct* measures of the *inputs* into R&D and of 'intermediate' outputs, such as patents and scientific papers, we do not have measures of *innovation*, except in a few industries for specific periods. There are no general internationally comparable measures of innovation and diffusion of innovations. Yet, ultimately it is only the successful *diffusion* of innovations which leads to perceptible and widespread effects on the growth of productivity or trade competitiveness and on aggregate economic performance.

The diffusion of innovations is of course not a simple process of replication and copying. Although there is an element of replication, diffusion is almost always accompanied by improvements and modifications to a new product or process. Sometimes these 'improvements' may be so important that they are just as significant as the original innovation. Consequently, the product or process which is being sold at the later stages of a diffusion process may bear little resemblance to the very first models. We have only to think of computers, robots or passenger cars to recognise the truth of this proposition.

It follows that scientific and technical competence, creativity and managerial skills are important at all stages of diffusion including 'learning by doing' and 'learning by using' as well as original scientific discovery and innovation. Indeed, it is often the case that the greatest productivity gains and quality improvements may be achieved with later generations of products as a result of follow-up R&D and feedback from users.

Hence, the effectiveness of the 'outputs' of R&D and other technical services depends on the wide availability of skills and strong user feedback throughout the system. Education and training are therefore of crucial importance for the successful attainment of the potential productivity gains from any new technology. It can *never* be enough to have a few brilliant scientists in élite laboratories. That may be a recipe for a few Nobel prizes, but it can never generate widespread productivity gains or a high level of competitiveness in industry generally.

Moreover, successful diffusion of almost all new products and processes depends on new *investment* embodying the results of R&D in new capital equipment as well as 'intangible investment' in education, training, information services and other scientific and technical activities.

Although we do not have any general overall measures of innovation diffusion, there have been an increasing number of case studies of particular products and processes. There has also been one major international comparative study of diffusion in the leading industrial countries. This was carried out by a number of European economic research institutes, including IFO in Germany, IUI in Sweden and NIESR in Britain. The study was recently updated by one of the leading investigators (Ray, 1984), thus providing a unique longitudinal perspective on diffusion of some key processes in eight different countries from the 1960s to the 1980s. In terms of the UK performance, the most significant finding was that although the UK was often the *first* among the eight countries surveyed to *introduce* an innovation, it was often the *last* to *diffuse* it through the potential adopter population. This and other studies have shown that Swedish, German and Japanese firms, on the other hand, although not usually the innovators, were usually the quickest to diffuse innovations through entire industries. They also achieved more efficient exploitation of the new processes during diffusion.

Such studies have obvious implications for the low levels of productivity in much of British industry. Among the products which have had relatively slow rates of diffusion compared with other leading industrial countries are such

Table 10.7 Performance in manufacturing trade.

	Export/import ratios		
	1965	*1975*	*1985*
OECD (total)	1.29	1.36	1.12
United States	1.55	1.38	0.60
United Kingdom	1.78	1.29	0.90
France	1.40	1.31	1.12
Sweden	0.90	1.09	1.25
Italy	1.92	1.72	1.47
FRG	1.71	1.89	1.69
Japan	4.22	4.58	4.25

Source: Kaldor and Walker (1988).

key technologies as computer controlled machine tools and robotics. While there has been some improvement in relative UK productivity performance in the mid-1980s, this was clearly related in part to higher rates of capacity utilisation compared with the depressed level of 1981 and in part (as in the case of Spain) to 'catching-up' effects as the leading industrial countries had drawn so far ahead of Britain in absolute levels of productivity (see also Chapters 5 & 6, this volume). To achieve Japanese, US and German levels of productivity in the 1990s would be impossible in most sectors without much higher levels of investment in training and plant and equipment. By the end of the 1980s, UK manufacturing investment had barely recovered its 1979 level, although there was a more substantial increase in services investment.

The low levels of investment in training and new capital equipment throughout the 1980s, as well as the inadequate levels of expenditure on R&D, must inevitably have adverse consequences for international technological competition in foreign trade. Some of these implications have already been discussed, particularly in Chapter 2. In concluding this section, we focus especially on the case of *electronics* as one illustration of the general problem and the specific importance of technological competition.

Table 10.7 (Kaldor and Walker, 1988) illustrates the generally poor performance of the US and UK in manufacturing trade from 1965 to 1985, by comparison with countries such as Sweden, Italy and the Federal Republic of Germany, as well as Japan. The general position and the further recent deterioration of the UK position is well known. What is not so well recognised is that the performance has been particularly poor in some of those areas which are the most important for future growth in the 1990s – especially electronics and machinery. Table 10.8 shows the overwhelming success of Japan in electronics compared with all other countries, but it also shows that the relative deterioration of the US and UK trade position in this crucial sector was even greater than for trade in general. Yet the electronics

Table 10.8 Performance in electronics trade.

	Export/import ratios		
	1965	*1975*	*1985*
OECD (total)	1.26	1.22	1.02
United States	1.08	1.42	0.54
United Kingdom	1.60	1.04	0.60
France	1.11	0.95	0.71
Sweden	0.98	1.43	1.10
Italy	0.93	1.11	0.73
FRG	1.47	1.45	0.95
Japan	11.32	5.88	13.90

Source: Kaldor and Walker (1988).

industry has accounted for over 30% of all UK industrial R&D throughout the 1980s and has been the focus of several major government policy initiatives, which are discussed in the final section of this chapter.

10.6 TECHNOLOGY POLICY AND ECONOMIC POLICY: CONCLUSIONS

Although there are numerous inconsistencies in its position, the basic stance of the Thatcher government in relation to technology policy, as in all other aspects of economic policy, has been to minimise the role of the government and the public sector. Even though, at least since Arrow's (1962) seminal paper, there is ample warrant within the framework of neoclassical theory of market failure to justify public funding of generic research, basic science and technology, as well as of education, training, information services and dissemination activities, the government has generally shown a miserly attitude towards most of these activities throughout the 1980s with the consequences which have been described and are illustrated in Table 10.6.

The major exceptions to this have been in the field of information technology and biotechnology where some of the initiatives which started in the 1970s, under a previous government, were continued in the 1980s and a number of new programmes were started in support of industrial innovation (Table 10.9) (*Financial Times*, 20.3.84).

The most important of the new initiatives was undoubtedly the 'Alvey Programme' (1983–8). This was initiated in response to what was perceived as a competitive threat from Japanese programmes of support for so-called 'Fifth Generation' computing. The Alvey Committee proposed a major programme of research in the area of information technology to strengthen the technological capability of British industry for future generations of

Table 10.9 UK government support for innovation.

Scheme	Period	Funds available (£million)
Misp-1 (micro-electronics innovation)	1978–5	55
Misp-2	1985–90	120
Map (microprocessor application scheme)	1978– *	85
Computer-aided design:		
Cadmet (manufacture and test)	1982–5	9
Cadtes (test equipment)	1982– *	24
Cadcam (design and manufacture)	1981–6	16
Flexible manufacturing	1982–6	35
Robotics	1981– *	10
Fibre optics	1982–6	40
Joint opto-electronics	1982–7	15
Software products	1982– *	15
Biotechnology	1982–5	16

Note: *Denotes that scheme lasts until funds are exhausted.
Source: Financial Times, 20.3.84.

software, components (VLSI), computers and 'expert systems' (Alvey Report, 1983). While not accepting the full scale and scope of the Committee's recommendations and insisting that most of the money should come either from industry or from the reallocation of funds already committed to the SERC, the DTI and the MOD, the government did, nevertheless, support a £350 million programme of 'pre-competitive' research for six years and has since continued some support on a smaller scale through the Information Engineering Directorate.

This programme, however, was remarkable not so much for its scale as for some novel features, largely based on Japanese experience. First of all, there was an implicit (and perhaps unintended) recognition that government has a role in setting strategic priorities for national innovation policy. Secondly, the commitment to a programme of several hundred projects spread over a large number of firms, universities and polytechnics differed sharply from the single giant project approach. Thirdly, the principle of collaboration between firms and between firms and universities was relatively novel in the British context. Finally, a fairly independent and energetic Directorate and an excellent Director contributed to a relatively successful programme with important lessons for the future.

Independent evaluation of the Alvey programme both by technical consultants and by university evaluation teams confirmed that the technical objectives of the programme were in the main achieved (Science Policy Research Unit (SPRU) and Programme of Policy Research in Engineering, Science and Technology, 1988; Hobday, 1989). However, the description of the programme as 'successful' must be qualified. As we have seen, technical success is by no means the same as commercial success. Whether the programme leads to any long-term improvements in the competitive performance of the electronics and software industries remains to be seen. But there are strong reasons for doubting whether the commercial exploitation will match up to the technical achievements.

The former Director of the programme, Brian Oakley, pointed to the main problems in translating the technical achievements into commercially success-ful products and systems: the structure of the British electronics industry and the pressures on firms to put short-term profitability above long-term strategic investment in new equipment and systems.

The relative decline of the British electronics industry has been apparent not only in relation to Japan, but also in relation to other European countries such as the Federal Republic of Germany and France. The joint bid by GEC and Siemens for Plessey illustrated the relative weakness of the two leading British firms by comparison with the German giant in almost all areas except defence electronics (Figs 10.2, 10.3) (Morgan *et al.*, 1989). In 1987 the UK had a deficit of £2.5 billion in foreign trade in civil electronics but a surplus of £0.7 billion in defence-related electronics.

In the 1950s and even in the early 1960s, the UK electronics industry was still leading in Europe in many areas of electronics and was the strongest country in terms of foreign patenting in the USA in computers and communications. But as Fig. 10.3 shows, the UK had fallen well behind

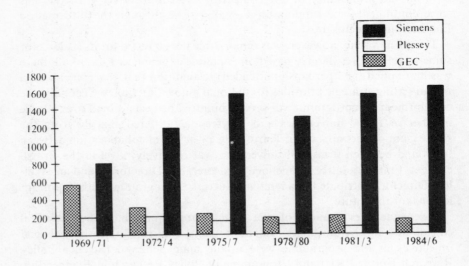

Figure 10.2 Patent numbers by firm, 1969–86. (*Source:* Morgan *et al.*, 1989.)

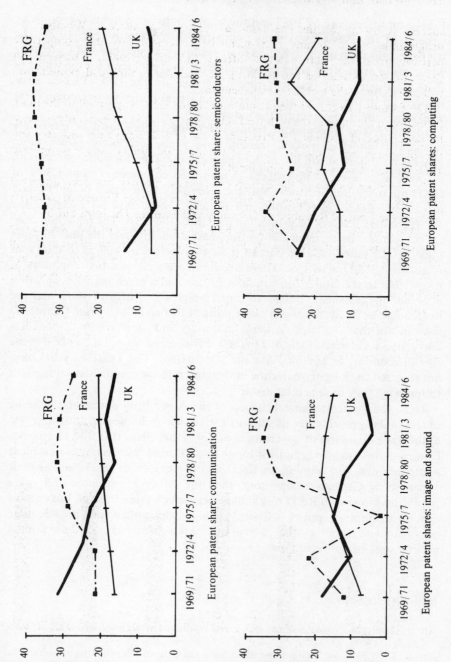

Figure 10.3 Proportion of patenting by large European electronics firms, 1969–86, according to country of company headquarters. (*Source:* Morgan *et al.*, 1989.)

France and Germany by 1985 and the total number of patents taken out by either GEC or Plessey was puny compared with Siemens (Fig. 10.2). The over-specialisation of the UK electronics industry on defence and its relative weakness in most other areas are serious structural problems for the whole of British industry, but the government's stance on the GEC/Plessey issue showed up in the lack of any coherent industrial policy to overcome these weaknesses and to restructure the industry.

To be effective in economic terms, technology policy must be intimately related to industrial policy, training policy and economic policy more generally. Almost all studies of Japanese economic performance stress both the very high levels of investment in plant and equipment (around 30% of GNP for quite long periods) and the extremely high levels of public and private investment in education and training. These have far exceeded the corresponding levels of investment in the UK or the USA. The highly success-ful competitive performance of the Japanese economy over the past 20 years must be attributed in large part to these two factors as well as to the rapid increase in R&D activities. There are far more well-qualified engineers in proportion to the labour force than in Britain and a much higher proportion in senior management. But more importantly, the dearth of skills and the inadequate levels of training in many parts of British industry (see Chapter 7) have meant that the improvements in *quality* and *productivity* of products and processes characteristic of Japanese diffusion have not taken place in the British economy to anything like the same extent. The Thatcher years have not reversed the long-term decline in Britain's relative competitive strength in technology; they have accelerated it.

Thus, the limited technical success of the Alvey Programme and of some other similar programmes of support for generic technologies illustrates one of the basic dilemmas of government policy in the 1980s. If British electronics firms had been as strong in their long-term strategic investment in new plant and equipment, on training, in R&D and in world-wide marketing as their Japanese or German competitors, then the Alvey Programme and other public investments in R&D would have been much more fruitful. But to have generic technology policy without an industrial policy and an adequate education and training policy is to prejudice the success of even those limited programmes of public support.

REFERENCES

Alvey Report, *A Programme for Advanced Information Technology* (DTI, HMSO: London, 1983).
Arrow, K., 'Economic Welfare and the Allocation of Resources for Invention', in *The Rate and Direction of Innovation Activity* (ed. Nelson, R.) (NBER and Princeton: USA, 1962).

Barras, R., 'Towards a Theory of Innovation in Services', *Research Policy*, 15, 4, 161–73 (1986).

Bird, J., 'IBM Suppliers get First Public Warning', *Sunday Times*, 19.5.85.

Blackaby, F., *De-Industrialisation*, NIESR Policy Papers no. 2 (Heinemann: London, 1978).

British Business, 3.2.89, pp. 24–25.

Cabinet Office, *R & D 1988: Annual Review of Government Funded Research and Development*, Table 1.2 (HMSO: London, 1988).

Cohen, S. and Zysman, J., *Manufacturing Matters: The Myth of the Post-Industrial Economy* (Basic Books: New York, 1988).

Cuomo Commission Report (Simon & Schuster: New York, 1988).

Dosi, G. and Soete, L. L. G., 'Technical Change and International Trade', *Technical Change and Economic Theory*, Chapter 19 (eds Dosi, G., Freeman, C., Nelson, R., Silverberg, G. and Soete, L. L. G.) (Pinter: London, 1988).

Fagerberg, J., 'Why Growth Rates Differ', *Technical Change and Economic Theory*, Chapter 20 (eds Dosi, G., Freeman, C., Nelson, R., Silverberg, G. and Soete, L. L. G.) (Pinter: London; Columbia University Press, 1988).

Financial Times, 20.3.84.

Freeman, C., *Technology Policy and Economic Performance: Lessons from Japan* (Pinter: London, 1987).

Freeman, C. and Soete, L., *Technical Change and Full Employment*, Chapter 4 (Blackwell: Oxford, 1987).

Guy, K., 'The UK Tertiary Service Sector', *Technical Change and Full Employment*, Chapter 9 (eds Freeman, C. and Soete, L.) (Blackwell: Oxford, 1987).

Hobday, M., 'Strategies for the UK Semiconductor Industry: Lessons from the Alvey Programme' (SPRU: University of Sussex (mimeo), 1989).

Irvine, J. *et al.*, 'Charting the Decline in British Science', *Nature*, 316, 6029, 587–90 (1985).

Irvine, J. *et al.*, 'The Continuing Decline of British Science', *Nature*, 330, 318, 123–6 (1985).

Kaldor, M. and Walker, W., 'Military Technology and the Loss of Industrial Dynamism', *La Recherche*, October, pp. 1270–77 (1988).

Martin, B. R., 'The Structure and Funding of UK Research: A Statistical Overview', *Electronics and Power*, January, pp. 31–6 (1987).

Morgan, K., Harbor, B., Hobday, M., Tunzelmann, N. von and Walker, W., *The GEC-Siemens Bid for Plessey: The Wider European Issues*, CICT Working Paper no. 2 (SPRU: University of Sussex, 1989).

National Science Foundation, *Science and Technology Data Book*, figure 35 (Washington DC: USA 1988).

National Science Foundation, *Science and Engineering Indicators* (Washington DC: USA 1987).

OECD, *The Measurement of Scientific and Technical Activities: Proposed Standard Practice for Surveys of Research and Development* (Frascati Manual), Paris (4th Revision) (1981).

Office of Technology Assessment, *Technology and the American Economic Transition* (Congress of the United States: Washington, 1987).

Patel, P. and Pavitt, K., 'Is Western Europe Losing the Technological Race?', *Research Policy*, 16, 2, 59–85 (1987a).

Patel, P. and Pavitt, K., 'The Elements of British Technological Competitiveness', *National Institute Economic Review* (November 1987b).

Patel, P. and Pavitt, K., *Measuring Europe's Technological Performance: Results and Prospects* (CEPS Paper no. 36: Brussels, 1989).

Pavitt, K., (ed.) *Technical Innovation and British Economic Performance* (Macmillan: London, 1980).

Pavitt, K., 'Patent Statistics as Indicators of Innovative Activities: Possibilities and Problems', *Scientometrics,* **7**, 1–2, 77–99 (1985).

Posner, M. V., 'International Trade and Technical Change', *Oxford Economic Papers,* **13**, 3, 323–41 (1961).

Ray, G. F., *The Diffusion of Mature Technologies* (Cambridge University Press: Cambridge, 1984).

Ray, G. F., 'Full Circle: The Diffusion of Technology', *Research Policy* (in press).

Rothwell, R., 'SAPPHO Updated – Project SAPPHO Phase 2', *Research Policy,* **13**, 3, 258–91 (1984).

Soete, L. L. G., 'A General Test of Technological Gap Trade Theory', *Weltwirtschaftliches Archiv,* **117**, 4, 638–66 (1981).

Science Policy Research Unit (SPRU) and Programme of Policy Research in Engineering, Science and Technology (PREST), *Evaluation of the Alvey Programme* (HMSO: London, 1988).

Thomas, G. and Miles, I., 'Telecommunication Services' in *Technology Strategy and the Firm* (ed. Dodgson, M.) (Longman: London, 1989).

Walker, W., *et al.*, 'From Components to Integrated Systems: Technological Diversity and Integration between the Military and Civilian Sectors' in *The Relations between Defence and Civil Technologies* (eds Gummett, P. and Reppy, J.) (Kluwer: Dordrecht, Boston, London, 1988).

11 DENATIONALISATION

Ben Fine

11.1 INTRODUCTION

In late 1988, there was wide coverage of the birth of Britain's latest export. The country that had given the world Keynesianism had lost the intellectual race to popularise monetarism to the US in the person of Milton Friedman, but it had regained the initiative in the export of economic policy with its newest discovery, privatisation. While this might do little to improve the balance of trade, it promised much more in the balance of invisibles through City consultancies. For a package of advice had been put together and was to be 'marketed' by the British Overseas Development Agency (ODA) to other countries overseas.

Admittedly, this was being done in conjunction with the US, with pressure to be added by supranational agencies such as the IMF and the World Bank. But it was ample testimony to the leadership that the UK has taken in privatisation, even though the latter was already a global phenomenon with nearly a hundred countries adopting such policies, as well as there being the affinities with *perestroika* in the Soviet Union and the use of the profit motive elsewhere in the socialist world.

At the immediate ideological level, the justification in the West for privatisation is said to be based upon the need to roll back the economic frontiers of the state. State intervention in general, economic or otherwise, is increasingly being constructed ideologically as a violation of individual freedom. One effect of this breach with the ideology of Keynesian welfarism has been to sweep into prominence the proponents of *laissez-faire*, a select group of monetarist and neo-Austrian advisers to the government, who have been nurtured at the right-wing think-tanks such as the Centre for Policy Studies (CPS), the Institute for Economic Affairs (IEA) and the Adam Smith Institute.

As will be seen, it would be a mistake to reduce the virulence of the UK privatisation programme to the mere influence and activities of a few individuals who, by their own confession, were intellectually considered 'cranks' not so long ago (and still are by the majority of the academic economists in the UK).[1] On the other hand, nor was the privatisation programme an inevitable outcome of Thatcherite policies. For, while some individuals have been unduly influential, this would leave still open the need to explain both the timing and the extent of their effectiveness in the formulation and implementation of policy. The denationalisation programme began quite late in the day. It was seriously put forward only after the 1983 election[2] and seems to have been adopted rapidly to sustain what was judged to be the favourable political momentum created by council house sales (which had themselves up to the beginning of 1989 matched in value the revenue raised by denationalisation). For Letwin (1988a, p. 66), 'Before 1983 ... nobody had a coherent policy, nobody knew how to overcome the tremendous inertia and obstacles inside the bureaucracy ... there was a universal dither'.

One way of overcoming the inertia was to 'go forth and privatise' with sufficiently flexible *ad hoc* legislation to overcome any future objections and difficulties (Walker 1988, p. 14) and, as Letwin suggests:

> So, my first advice is to take the plunge. My second advice is, don't listen too much to too many experienced professionals. Choose advisers who will take the plunge with you and get on with it. You will find, as I say, that it's not perfect, but it does work. (Letwin, 1988a, p. 61)

And, since 1983, the British Government certainly has taken the plunge. It had by 1988 sold off almost £20 billion worth of assets in eleven billion shares, including eleven listed companies with a total capitalisation of over £58 billion.[3] This is two-fifths of the public corporation sector inherited by Mrs Thatcher.

Most prominent have been the sale of British Airways, British Gas and British Telecom, but for each of these the potential role played by competition as traditionally understood is negligible, with the first being transformed from a public into a private monopoly and the third competing with a single subordinate rival in Mercury. It is generally recognised that the only competition available to the privatised water industry is through the stock market, for the regionally separate water authorities do not have overlapping markets. The imperative to introduce competition into the generation and distribution of electricity is heavily circumscribed by the size in England and Wales of the two incumbent companies. Their existing plans to expand capacity and the large-scale investment requirements for any newcomer able to make an impact, even presuming the absence of collusion, make effective competitive entry extremely unlikely. The significance of this privatisation can be judged by its worth, matching alone the value of the whole of the previous privatisation programme. On the horizon looms what has been described as the ultimate privatisation, that of British Coal, presumably a target as much motivated by a political as an economic logic with its associated assault on the miners.

Within Marxism, there has been very little specific analysis of the nationalised industries. They have an ideological association with socialism and planning, but one that is tainted by their incorporation within the capitalist system. A more general view from the left, such as from trade unions, is that privatisation is a policy that furthers the interests of capital and its accumulation by handing over the productive assets or activities of the state to the private sector.

This is, however, an understanding that is both too superficial and too general. It has its counterpart, again never substantively documented, in the earlier notion that nationalisations were equally a strategy to benefit private capital through the provision of a widely conceived infrastructure, or to supply essential inputs at cheap prices in what were otherwise unprofitable sectors. This is the approach to be found in Gough (1979), for example, in his consideration of state expenditure in general. He essentially employs a distributional framework as between capital and labour, with different activities being assigned to the public or private sector according to the rhythm of class conflict, efficiency and the needs of capital.

In this way, whether it be privatisation or public ownership, each is viewed as a strategy to benefit private capital. This may be ethically appealing to the socialist outlook or analytically appealing to the exponents of conspiracy theory, but it is futile analytically in explaining the course or cause of historical change.

Accordingly, in Section 2, some attention is devoted to theoretical considerations. It is argued that privatisation is the result of a combination of economic factors, some operating over a long period, others conjunctural. These, together with the political imperatives of the Tory Government, have led to privatisation as the culmination of a process restoring previously eroded capitalistic conditions to the industries that were taken into public ownership after the war.

In Section 3, the problems of assessing the impact of privatisation are discussed. It is suggested that comparison of indices of economic performance, such as (total factor) productivity change are an inadequate basis on which to judge the impact of privatisation as a strategy for accumulation. Rather, some account has to be taken of the specific conditions in which accumulation is now taking place, such as rapid introduction of new technology and high levels of unemployment. And the significance of the peculiar position of the British economy has to be assessed in terms of its relative decline.

Section 4 illustrates some of the earlier arguments by reference to privatisation of electricity supply, and emphasis is placed on the continuity of policy that will involve in many instances. Finally, in Section 5 it is concluded that privatisation does advantage capital accumulation in the UK in some respects. But more important is the extent to which it will consolidate existing structural causes of economic decline.

11.2 THEORETICAL CONSIDERATIONS

Any analysis of denationalisation needs to embody a number of features. First, there must be an underlying economic theory containing, in particular, a view of industrial change and development. Secondly, there must be an understanding of the relationship between the economy and society more generally, incorporating the role of politics and the state. Otherwise, there is no possibility of addressing the significance of state ownership. Thirdly, there must be a broader historical and empirical judgement of the specific conditions in which the state's economic policies are being formulated and implemented.

The approach adopted here is, on the first point, in line with Marx's theory of capital accumulation. This associates accumulations with increasingly capital-intensive methods of production and concentration of ownership and control. The process as a whole is uneven, both spatially and sectorally, and includes other contradictory features such as de-skilling for some, as jobs are simplified by machinery, while re-skilling for others, as previously separate tasks are combined. This reflects the tension between the fragmentation and separation of production processes into separate units, as in component manufacture, and their consolidation as in the classic motor car assembly line.

The individual capitals that persist must succeed in a competitive process. This is fought predominantly through productivity increase. But this in turn depends upon a number of factors such as access to technology, finance and markets and in which conflicts with labour over wages and conditions of work are paramount. For each of these in the current period of capitalism, the economic interventions of the state at a general level, as well as at a detailed level, assume enormous importance. Thus, on the second point of the relationship between economy and society, the policies and role of the state must be assessed.

Finally, a historical assessment within these briefly outlined and abstract perspectives has a number of components.[4] The major nationalisations that took place in the UK after the Second World War were the consequences of an erosion, partly during the war itself but over a longer period, of effective capitalist command of the industries concerned. This is more deep-seated than a (temporary) lack of profitability which affects many capitals in a downswing. Rather, it reflected a combination of developments in technical, industrial, marketing, financial, political and ideological relations. These different aspects, taken together, undermined the possibility of the capitals concerned being restructured under private ownership without considerable intensification of class conflict.

The subsequent history of these industries has been one of restoration of directly capitalistic forms of organisations and command, most noticeably in the increasing imposition of commercial criteria, but ranging across all of the other aspects as well. In the 1960s and 1970s this meant that state ownership could be used temporarily to restructure the private sector as in lame-duck policy. It has certainly made denationalisation a policy option in the 1980s as the outcome of the increasingly capitalistic command over each of the industries. Here a contrast, at least into the early 1990s, is found with the NHS. For while privatisation has more than nibbled around its edges, the principle of free provision has kept the private sector at arm's or, more exactly, queue's length, not only through the practices of non-payment but in the more general absence of the direct predominance of commercial criteria throughout the organisation of health provision.

These features of the nationalised industries have coincided with specific aspects of the UK economy more generally. Within the advanced capitalist economies, it is best described as the three-low economy.[5] It is low-wage, low-investment and low-productivity. This is explained by a lack of coherent long-term industrial planning to bring about domestic reorganisation of the economy.[6] This reflects (a) the international and predominantly short-term perspective of the City, whereby it neither provides long-term investment to industry nor undertakes a supervisory role in industrial development; (b) the dominance of the British economy by multinational corporations which restructure on a world scale, relying upon and reproducing the three-low economy, particularly by using Britain as a low-technology assembler; and (c) the limited long-term influence of the British labour movement on industrial strategy (the post-war nationalisations standing out as an exception which subsequently became the victims of macroeconomic policy for wages, prices and budgetary control rather than a base for planning and co-ordinating the economy). Further, this has led, not to a lack of state industrial policy – this has in fact been extensive – but to fragmented responses to a variety of globally oriented interests, as organised within multinational corporations.

Such interests are liable to welcome privatisation. New technology has tended to break down divisions between sectors of the economy, most clearly demonstrated in terms of information technology where the distinctions between telecommunications and data processing and office equipment are disappearing. Accordingly, the traditional divisions between public and private sectors had to be broken down, with the statutory monopolies of the former constraining diversification both in and out of their own spheres of operation. High levels of unemployment of both labour and capital have also made attractive to the private sector what were formerly perceived to be unprofitable areas, although this is more important in the contracting out of public services than for denationalisation.[7]

There have also been the specific motives of the Thatcher government. Politically, this has been part and parcel of a strategy to undermine the organisational basis of the Labour movement, for which the nationalised industries are perceived to be institutional strongholds. As Pirie, President of the Adam Smith Institute, puts it in a fictional portrayal of Mrs Thatcher's motives[8]:

> 'Who else tends to vote against us?'
> 'Prime Minister, we do find that people who work for the state-owned firms in the public sector tend to vote against the Conservative Party.'
> 'Right, I want less of them.' So, there are now two-thirds of a million fewer of those. (Walker, 1988, p. 3–5)

Together with legislation to abolish the metropolitan authorities and to reform education (opting out and core curriculum) and local government finance (poll tax), the attempt is being made through privatisation to undermine not the politics as such but the labour politics of government expenditure.

The assault on the labour market has been more overt, particularly in the 'reform' of industrial relations to restore 'balance' between the two sides of industry, but also in the high levels of unemployment brought about through the deflationary policies of the early Thatcher years. This has all had its ideological counterpart in the attack on socialism. Under the guise of promoting a people's capitalism[9] this has taken the form of seeking wider share-ownership in the denationalised corporations and home-ownership in place of public housing.[10] This strategy has also had its successes at the level of political ideology with the retreat of the Labour Party leadership (Redwood in the introduction to Letwin):

> Privatisation and success are increasingly identified with one another. A particular testimony to the extent of this success is the change in the British Labour Party's attitude towards privatisation ... Between 1983 and 1987, as the scale and pace of the privatisation programme increased, the Labour Party gradually abandoned this sort of rhetoric (increasingly in favour of public owner-ship) ... talked of 'social ownership'.[11] (Letwin, 1986b, p. 13)

Consideration must also be given to whether denationalisation is itself a policy for weakening the Labour movement. This issue has to be treated with some caution. For, at other times, it has often been suggested that the power of the state as employer can also be used to engage in wage and other conflicts more successfully than the isolated private employer, despite the latter's relative freedom from political constraints. Privatisation might also, at least temporarily, enhance the bargaining position of the workforce, and not just managers, in order to smooth the transition.[12] It follows that the role of public ownership in the balance of class forces cannot be simply read off as positive or negative. Nonetheless, a change in ownership does open the way for managers to push through changes, including those affecting wages and conditions of work. But the outcome is not pre-determined by virtue of denationalisation in itself.

Denationalisation has also been seen as a means of raising government finance in order to pay for electorally popular tax cuts, the selling-off of the family silver, as Harold Macmillan put it. Once again, this argument has to be treated with some caution for, in the context of a perfectly operating capital market, the capital sums gained would be exactly off-set by the discounted present value of the lost income. With an imperfect market for finance, there is every reason to believe that privatisation will even worsen the government's and the economy's position. For there are the costs of handling the deals themselves, which are far from negligible, and there is the net loss of government assets involved in sales at prices below value. This has generally been the case with the trading price rapidly rising above issue price, to the gain of those buying shares.[13] There is also the potential crowding-out or delaying effects on other stock issues as a result of large issues for privatisation on the stock market.

It is against factors such as these that the privatisation programme has to be explained and its likely effects assessed. Orthodox accounts have often considered some of these influences, but usually only in isolation from one another and in the context of a limited economic theory. Over the past five years, however, a new orthodoxy has gripped the study of the nationalised industries and the stance adopted towards them.[14] It considers that ownership as such does not matter. For academics, much more emphasis has been placed upon the regulatory and competitive environment and the nature of managerial motivation.[15] This has had its counterpart in the political arena, where the Labour Party's traditional commitment to public ownership has been weakening towards the objectives of control (through regulation) rather than ownership as such.

There are certain strengths to this new approach, which places more emphasis on mechanisms of control than the earlier emphasis on optimality criteria for objectives, such as long-run marginal cost pricing. It rejects the notion that ownership as between the public and the private sector is the only or even the primary factor in determining performance. As a corollary, it necessarily sets aside the crude neo-Austrian view that the market is the best option in an imperfect world.[16]

There are, however, arguably greater weaknesses than strengths. These are the limited scope of the factors other than ownership that are considered through a tendency to focus on static optimality rather than developmental gains (which is where the neo-Austrians have an advantage), and a lack of historical perspective within which to set the current phase of privatisation – with reliance instead upon rather informal, abstract principles at one extreme and empirical narrative at the other. The weakness of the orthodoxy lies in its theoretical reliance upon instances of market failure derived as a deviation from perfect competition or from technical conditions associated with natural monopoly or externalities. This leaves it more than unusually uncomfortable in dealing with the issue of the active agency of ownership in bringing about industrial development. And the same discomfort applies to the assessment of the specific historical and political circumstances in which privatisation is occurring.

While the neo-Austrians offer an alternative, the one most favoured by the government, it rarely progresses analytically beyond the level of dogma. While emphasising the dynamic gains to be achieved through free-market incentives to entrepreneurs and all who engage in economic activity, they do little more than assert that such gains are superior to those that could arise from state intervention and that the nebulous dynamic benefits outweigh the static losses associated with monopoly, externalities and market failure. An empirical study to assess the performance of entrepreneurs in the British context is notable only by its absence. Ultimately, faith is held in the financial markets as sufficient to ensure adequate competitiveness where, as in water, product competition is impossible. Excess profits, or deficiencies in service, so the story goes, would lead to a predatory takeover to realise and eliminate the gains and losses associated with monopoly and/or inefficiency.[17]

From this discussion of the causes, effects and motives associated with privatisation, the following conclusion can be drawn. The underlying problems of the British economy derive from its lack of a coherent agency for long-term direction of industry. This has led to increasing reliance upon lower levels of wages to compensate competitively for low levels of investment and productivity. In the current period of radical restructuring of economic and social life in the wake of new technology and high levels of unemployment, privatisation does open avenues for concentration, diversification and expansion of capital in the drive to accumulate. But, in the British context, the privatisation programme tends to consolidate existing weaknesses, including the rejection of coherent industrial policy, and fails to break with the 'three-low' characteristics of the past.

11.3   ASSESSING THE IMPACT?

Judging the impact of privatisations against this analytical background is fraught with difficulties. First, there is as yet little evidence on which to make an assessment, partly because privatisation is so recent and partly because it is hard to separate out the privatisation effect from other influences at work. For example, measures of productivity growth might show an improvement because of the availability of new technology. Customer service might be improved only in an initial attempt to please and to secure contracts. High unemployment might be associated with downward pressures on wages and working conditions and lead to the concentration of output on the more productive capacity at low levels of aggregate demand. These render productivity/performance assessment complex and difficult, and the comparative performance of newly privatised companies has to be set against the general productivity 'improvement' in the UK of all industries from the early 1980s onwards, which is discussed in Chapters 5 and 6.

To a large extent, even on the basis of an agreed theory of cause and effect, these difficulties of assessment can only be overcome with the passage of time and it has been suggested that a full business cycle is the appropriate period.[18] In the case of public services rather than corporations, as in building repair and maintenance work, it is known that the private sector tends to withdraw from provision during periods of expansion to seek out more profitable work in the private sector. But in periods of slack demand, the private sector insists that it be allowed to compete with the public sector Direct Labour Organisations. More generally, whether contracting out of public services has been a success or not remains highly controversial – for, as well as costs, the changing level of service and conditions of work have to be continually monitored. The problems of assessing the denationalised industries are even more intractable because of the long gestation period of the fixed capital involved, as in power station construction and planning. There are also the related 'infrastructural' requirements, such as R&D, innovation and training of a skilled workforce.

The second difficulty of assessment is brought out by the studies of the comparative performance of public and private enterprise in the past. For the circumstances in which the enterprises compete directly with each other are relatively rare.[19] In general, in these circumstances, there is a slight favour to be found in the performance of the private over the public sector. This is usually, however, the result of judging by the criteria which are associated with the measurement of private-sector performance – with profit-related indices to the fore. Crudely put, the ideology for the nationalised industries has often been that profits mean exploitation of monopoly power, losses mean inefficiency. This puts the public sector at a disadvantage, partly because it has objectives, such as security and right of supply, other than those associated with private profitability, and partly because it does not tend to operate in so free an environment with, for example, more severe restrictions through state policy on access to finance, diversification and price and wage increases.

These broader considerations need to be extended even further to encompass the strategic role played by the development of new technology and in providing a skilled workforce. What is significant in the following conclusion from an early study of post-privatisation British Telecom is how these and other broader considerations have been left aside, although privatisation still does not emerge as superior:

> Put another way, different standards of service, waiting times for connections, national topography or social obligations were not taken into consideration in computing these results. More work on refining both output and input measures is obviously desirable. However, we are inclinded to think that allowances for omissions would not greatly affect the ranking of telecommunications organisa-

tions. The total factor productivity indices do markedly improve British Telecom's performance in international perspective compared with the simplistic number of lines per employee measure, but they do not show British Telecom performing better than its state-owned monopolistic counterparts in continental Europe. (Foreman-Peck and Manning, 1988)

It is not, perhaps, surprising that given equal availability of factor inputs, two different phone companies, private and public, perform at much the same level. But the significance of what is the second largest purchaser of electronic products after government cannot be reduced to measurements of total factor productivity, however broadly defined and accurately measured. And much the same is true of aerospace, the major absorber of R&D expenditure, and of electricity, etc. Each of these has an internal dynamic of development as well as an impact on the economy more generally.

These observations point to the conclusion that, in order to capture the presumed effects of competition and managerial responsiveness to incentives, an assessment of comparative performance depends upon a full and proper sectoral industrial study rather than confinement to measures of costing, pricing, productivity and profitability. However, the discussion here has not been entirely negative, since it has highlighted some of the factors that need to be considered in assessing the significance of denationalisation. In this there is, however, a danger of overlooking the woods for the trees. For the marginal differences in performance as between the public and private sector, industry by industry, are of less significance in the case of the British economy than the absolute performance of each. It seems extremely unlikely that any variance of performance between the public and the private sector is the source of the UK's economic decline.

To put it differently, suppose that the public-sector performance was lifted up to the level of the private sector. Are we to believe there would be a further effect lifting the whole economy's performance even higher through some systemic effect? Consequently, the role of the privatisation programme should be judged on the extent to which it transforms the conditions for restructuring the economy, as suggested previously in the case of the strategic role of telecommunications.

Significantly, this is precisely the ideological basis on which the Tory government justifies privatisation. It is posed as part and parcel of a strategy to reintroduce market forces. Thus, the government has consistently argued that civil servants are not the appropriate individuals to pick industrial winners (the presumption being that such winners are there to be picked rather than actively to be created).[20] Even if this neo-Austrian outlook could be accepted, and the economy is best left to the animal spirits of entrepreneurs and the market, this would leave unexplained the poor performance of the British economy over the past century.

For, as previously argued, a major weakness of the British economy has been the absence of an agency formulating long-term and coherent industrial policy, although industrial intervention has been extensive. This weakness will be consolidated by the privatisation programme. For, by a perverse logic, the *laissez-faire* policy of the Government requires it to create new institutions, as in the Regulatory Offices, or to expand the activities of those that already exist, most notably in the Monopolies and Mergers Committee. Consequently, a major part of the making of industrial policy will be devolved upon these bodies but with their influence being restricted in both scope and power. In other words, civil servants will still be picking winners, but they will not be calling the name of the game and the options open to them will be limited.

11.4 THE PRIVATISATION OF ELECTRICITY

The discussion of the previous sections can be illustrated by reference to the privatisation of electricity, although a comprehensive coverage of the issues is not possible here.[21] Very few, other than neo-Austrians, have been prepared to support the privatisation of electricity or, at least, the form it has taken – and this is true even of neo-Austrians where the featherbedding of nuclear power is concerned.

First, from an orthodox economic stance, there will be static dead-weight losses. The cost of undertaking the sale may be as much as £500 million or about half the price of a new power station and this leaves aside the vast amount of staff and parliamentary time engaged in formulating and pushing through the reorganisation. Again, it is paradoxical that the civil servants are presumed able to establish the appropriate industrial structure and regulatory regime for post-privatisation but unable to dictate policy on a continuing basis.

For England and Wales, there are to be two generating companies with the power stations divided between them, although the larger is to have all the nuclear power stations. In so far as they compete with each other by negotiating binding contracts, this may well conflict with the previous adoption of the merit order whereby the most efficient stations are used first. It has been estimated that the loss of the merit order could impose an annual cost of £1 billion,[22] although this is contingent on the contractual arrangements made, the extent to which there is a spot market for electricity and the way in which it is run.

Secondly, little account is taken by policymakers of the macroeconomic effects of privatisation, i.e., its wider economic repercussions. The wish to import coal, currently cheapened by temporary world excess capacity, will have profound effects. Since the miners' strike of 1984-5, it has been consistently argued by those opposing colliery closures that the pits are economic once account is taken of the full costs of closure. This includes redundancy payments and dole payments, loss of national insurance, direct and indirect taxes and the multiplier effects of reduced wages in a depressed economy.[23] There are also balance of payments implications of some importance, as adverse exchange rate movements are necessary to make up the deterioration in the balance of trade. At no time have these arguments, supplemented by detailed calculations, been answered. This points to the political motive of running down the coal industry in order to weaken the NUM as a focus for labour movement activism and militancy. But it has its costs in terms of higher levels of unemployment and deterioration in the balance of trade.

Thirdly, an explicit continuity of policy, and one unlikely to foster accumulation, has been forged in the strengthened commitment to nuclear power. Legislation provides for it to expand as an obligation upon the industry, so that at least 20% of supply is nuclear. This is despite the knowledge that nuclear power is now at last admitted to be more costly than coal-fired power stations so that no private company would build nuclear power stations without subsidy. This has given rise to the notion of a nuclear tax with a dispute about who should bear it. This is less relevant than the glaring fact of economic inefficiency whether the cost is ultimately borne proximately by price, tax or wage levels.

Fourthly, moving to more dynamic factors, damaging continuity of policy is also exhibited in the field of R&D. In general, government R&D in the past has been disproportionately allocated to sectors around defence such as aerospace with limited spin-off for civil application. Within energy, there has been a predominance of expenditure on nuclear power, with resources devoted by Government to nuclear power and coal in 1988–9 standing at £209 million and £1.4 million, respectively. In comparison to other countries, expenditure on R&D per tonne of coal burnt is 5p for the UK, as opposed to 31p for the USA, 34p for West Germany and 105p for Japan![24]

Despite this, there are some indications of changing priorities, with the decision to phase out the experimental fast breeder reactor at Dounreay over the next few years. Consider also the United Kingdom Atomic Energy Authority (UKAEA), the largest R&D organisation in Western Europe. Under financial pressure it is seeking in 1989 to diversify commercially by contracting privately for non-nuclear activities. This may appear desirable in the sense of cutting wasteful nuclear research. But it is more a step forward by default, representing a cost-cutting exercise rather than a forward-thinking strategy. Once again this reveals the lack of a coherent strategy for the development of new technology across the economy as a whole.

Fifthly, it has long been argued that the industry suffers from institutional bias, not only towards nuclear power, but also towards 'gigantism', with the imperatives of supply taking precedence over the needs of consumers. This confirms the capture of policy by interest groups in supply in the absence of long-term planning. In particular, there is backwardness both in developing combined heat and power and in pushing through measures of energy conservation, both of which are liable to yield higher rates of return than generating more electricity.[25] However, the plans to privatise add no incentive to overcome these deficiencies. And no sooner had the privatisation Bill been published than the Government announced a cut in the budget of the Energy Efficiency Office from £24.5 million to £15 million.

Finally, consider the construction of new power stations. This is known to be unsatisfactory in Britain with poor performance in both completion times and cost targets. Privatisation is thought to be able to deal with this at a stroke through much tougher contracts and penalty clauses. This, however, is to overlook the causal factors concerned. Some of these are general to large-scale construction, whether power stations, building sites or motorways. They concern the nature of the construction industry with its structure of fragmented firms offering casualised employment through subcontracting to the major contractors involved.[26] In addition, the major suppliers of power station equipment are part of an international cartel which has agreed not to compete in each other's domestic markets. They operate in concert and consortia to raise prices in tendering for export orders. Despite the Single Market in 1992, the prospects are either for this cartel to continue or, more likely, for it to be reorganised through merger and acquisition, with GEC, the most important UK company, open to being taken over. Consequently, privatisation's dependence on competitive tendering for cheaper power station construction is ill-founded. Once again, the opportunity is lost to intervene in this sector despite its importance as part of the electricity/electronics complex that the companies involved tend to straddle, usually along with their substantial defence interests.

In short, privatisation of electricity is liable to lead to a consolidation of underlying weaknesses in the restructuring of the British economy, R&D, conservation and energy efficiency will continue to be at comparatively low levels. The sacrifice of the merit order in pursuit of competition will give rise to dead-weight losses. Building power stations to cost and on time will not be enhanced and restructuring around the sectors of electrical and electronic goods will be determined by the global interests of multinationals which have traditionally treated the UK as a location for low-wage, low-technology assembly. The preference for increasingly expensive nuclear power is to be enshrined in the commitment to supply, and the wish to emasculate the NUM and the British coal industry through import of coal at temporarily depressed world prices will lead to higher fuel and generating costs and macroeconomic inefficiency. The pre-emptive increase in electricity prices in two stages prior to privatisation was justified by the claim that it was necessary in order to fund a future investment programme of £40 billion.[27] Free marketeers should, however, argue that funds would be raised on private capital markets if the investment were justified. Moreover, this projection of investment requirements is itself the major decision to be made in electricity supply. Perversely, it is being made by a Government as a matter of pricing policy in preparation for privatisation.

11.5 CONCLUDING REMARKS

There are a number of themes to this chapter. The first is that privatisation as such does not represent such a break with the past as might be supposed by the switch from public to private ownership. At the level of industrial policy-making, it exhibits continuities with what has gone before and brings to fruition the re-commercialisation of the public enterprises over the past 40 years.

Secondly, while ownership as such does matter, and the difference between public and private ownership is and has been a significant factor in industrial development and the conflicts over it, its impact can only be properly assessed in a broader context combining both economic and political factors.

Thirdly, the implications for accumulation of capital in the UK are complex and should not be seen in such stark terms of remorseless economic decline. Privatisation is part of a strategy that eschews coherent long-term intervention to restructure British industry on a domestic basis. As such it reinforces the three-low economy within the industries themselves, across the economy as a whole and, more generally, in the level and direction of social and infrastructural provision.

This is not, however, to deny the potential for phases of expansion, some of it at the forefront of technology and productivity with skilled and well-paid jobs. But it will have as its counterpart increasing dependence on low-paying assembly-type jobs and a continuation of economic weakness within the advanced capitalist countries.

NOTES

1. See Walters (1981, p. 5).
2. See Brittan (1986).
3. For a listing of the privatisations that have occurred, see Price-Waterhouse (1987). This booklet has a preface from Howard Hyman, previously seconded to the Treasury to advise on privatisation, now Director of Privatisation Services at Price-Waterhouse.
4. For a fuller account, see Fine and O'Donnell (1985).
5. For greater detail, see Fine and Harris (1985).
6. This is documented by comparison to other countries in Hesselman (1983), for example.
7. See Ascher (1987), for example.
8. Other social groups as potential voters to be increased (+) or reduced (–) include home-owners (+), shareholders (+), the self-employed (+), trade unionists (–), council house tenants (–) and civil servants (–!).
9. For a critique of people's capitalism, see Fine (1988).
10. On council house sales, see Forrest and Murie (1988).
11. That this was before rather than a response to shifts in public opinion is also testified by the right:

> I tend to think it [privatisation] was an accident ... we didn't get public opinion to support it until after it was done. (Walker, 1988, p. 15)

12. For a discussion of some of these issues, see Thomas (1984).
13. See Mayer and Meadowcroft (1985) and, a little more surprisingly, from the World Bank (Mansoor 1987). The UK's poor performance in getting the issue price has been rationalised thus:

> There is a mansion somewhere in South America where retired Nazi generals argue with British financiers, and the Nazi generals show that in hindsight they, in fact, won World War II seven times over. And the British financiers show that with hindsight they could have gotten a very much better price for Telecom, British Gas or whatever. (Walker, 1988, p. 20)

14. An early presentation of the new orthodoxy is to be found in Kay and Silberston (1984). The standard text is Vickers and Yarrow (1988). For a critique, see Fine (1989a).
15. So much so that industrial economics has been successively reduced to competition and regulation policy rather than strategy for industry in terms of how much investment, what industrial structure, etc.
16. A most influential representative of the neo-Austrian school is Littlechild, at least for his role in advising government. See Fine and Harris (1987) for references to his work and for a critique of his views.
17. As in Littlechild's (1986) claims on behalf of the Government for the privatisation of water.
18. Although not, presumably, over a long wave; see Byatt (1985).
19. See Vickers and Yarrow (1988), Pryke (1982), Millward (1982) and Molyneux and Thompson (1987).
20. The Government does, however, appear to take its responsibility seriously in picking stockbrokers and advisers to arrange the issues, this being described as a competition akin to a beauty contest, so closely are the candidates scrutinised; Letwin (1986b, p. 136) Judging by the under-pricing, as compared, say, to France, it does not appear to have been too successful!
21. For an excellent critique on the Government's plans from an orthodox standpoint, see Energy Select Committee (1987/88a). For an elaboration of the points made here, see Fine (1989b).
22. See evidence presented to the Energy Select Committee (1987/88a).
23. Such evidence was first presented by Glyn (1984) and has subsequently been considered at independent colliery reviews, public inquiries such as Sizewell and parliamentary committees.
24. Energy Select Committee (1987/88b).
25. See Hillman (1984) and Chesshire (1986).
26. See Ball (1988).
27. All in all, *Private Eye* got it right when it pictured Cecil Parkinson in late 1988 claiming that he was putting up electricity prices by 15%, as indeed he was to make the sell-off attractive, to prove prices would be lower under privatisation!

REFERENCES

Ascher, K., *The Politics of Privatisation: Contracting Out Public Services.* (Macmillan: London, 1987).
Ball, M., *Rebuilding Construction: Economic Change in the British Construction Industry*, (Routledge: London, 1988).
Brittan, S., 'Privatisation: a comment on Kay and Thompson', *Economic Journal*, **96**, March, 33–8 (1986).

Byatt, I., 'Market and non-market alternatives in the supply of public services: British experience with privatisation', in *Political Economy and Government Growth* (eds Forte and Peacock) (Blackwell: Oxford, 1985).

Chesshire, J., 'An energy efficient future: a strategy for the UK', *Energy Policy*, **14**, 5, 395–412 (1986).

Energy Select Committee, *The Structure, Regulation and Economic Consequences of Electricity Supply in the Private Sector*, Third Report, HC 307 (HMSO: London, 1987/88a).

Energy Select Committee, *The Department of Energy's Spending Plans, 1988–89*, Fourth Report, HC 513 (HMSO: London, 1987/88b).

Fine, B., 'Is there such a thing as "People's Capitalism"?', *World Marxist Review*, **31**, 2, 129–36 (1988).

Fine, B., 'Scaling the commanding heights of public sector economics', *Cambridge Journal of Economics* (1989a) (in press).

Fine, B., 'Privatisation of the Electricity Supply Industry: broadening the debate', *Energy Policy* (1989b) (in press).

Fine, B. and Harris, L., *The Peculiarities of the British Economy* (Lawrence & Wishart: London, 1985).

Fine, B. and Harris, L., 'Ideology and markets: economic theory and the "New Right"', in *Socialist Register* (eds Miliband, R. *et al.*) (Merlin Press: London, 1987).

Fine, B. and O'Donnell, K., 'The Nationalised Industries', in *The Peculiarities of the British Economy* (1985) (eds Fine, B. and Harris, L.) (Lawrence & Wishart: London, 1985).

Foreman-Peck, J. and Manning, D., 'How well is British Telecom Performing? An international comparison of Telecommunications Total Factor Productivity', *Fiscal Studies*, **9**, 3, 54–67 (1988).

Forrest, R. and Murie, A., *Selling the Welfare State: the privatisation of public housing* (Routledge: London, 1988).

Glyn, A., *The Economic Case against Pit Closures* (NUM: Sheffield, 1984).

Gough, I., *The Political Economy of the Welfare State* (Macmillan: London, 1979).

Hesselman, L., 'Trends in European industrial intervention', *Cambridge Journal of Economics*, **7**, 2, 197–208 (1983).

Hillman, M., *Conservation's Contribution to UK Self Sufficiency*, Energy Paper no. 13, (Heinemann: London, 1984).

Kay, J. and Silberston, A. 'The New Industrial Policy – Privatisation and Competition', *Midland Bank Quarterly Review*, Spring, pp. 8–16 (1984).

Kay, J., Mayer, C. and Thompson, D. (eds) *Privatisation and Regulation: The UK Experience* (Clarendon Press: Oxford, 1987).

Letwin, O., 'International experience in the politics of privatisation', in *Privatisation: Tactics and Techniques* (ed. Walker, M.) (Fraser Institute: Vancouver, 1988a).

Letwin, O., *Privatising the World: a Study of International Privatisation in Theory and Practice* (Cassell Educational: London, 1988b).

Littlechild, S., *Economic Regulation of Privatised Water Authorities* HMSO: Department of Environment, reproduced in part with some further reflections in *Oxford Review of Economic Policy*, **4**, 2, 40–67 (1986).

Mansoor, A., 'The Budgetary impact on Privatisation', *IMF Working Paper*, no. WP/87/68, (IMF: Washington DC, 1987).

Mayer, C. and Meadowcroft, S., 'Selling public assets: techniques and financial implications', *Fiscal Studies*, **6**, 4, 42–56 (1985) reproduced in Kay *et al.* (1987).

Millward, R., 'The comparative performance of public and private enterprise', in *The Mixed Economy* (ed. Roll, E.) (Macmillan: London, 1982).

Molyneux, R. and Thompson, D., 'Nationalised industry performance: still third-rate?', *Fiscal Studies,* **8**, 1, 48–82 (1987).

Price-Waterhouse, *Privatisation: the Facts* (Price-Waterhouse: London, 1987).

Pryke, R., 'The comparative performance of public and private enterprise', *Fiscal Studies,* **3**, 2, 68–81 (1982).

Thomas, D., 'The Union response to denationalisation', in ibid. (1984); reproduced in Kay *et al.* (eds) (1987).

Vickers, J. and Yarrow, G., *Privatisation: an Economic Analysis*, (MIT: Cambridge, 1988).

Walker, M. (ed.), *Privatisation: Tactics and Techniques* (Fraser Institute: Vancouver, 1988).

Walters, A., *The Economic Adviser's Role: Scope and Limitations* (Centre for Policy Studies: London, 1981).

12 THE FINANCIAL SYSTEM AND CAPITAL ACCUMULATION IN THE 1980s

Jan Toporowski

During the 1980s the financial system in the UK and, to a lesser extent, abroad, has been a public laboratory testing out monetarist and neo-conservative policies on money, credit, banking, securities and free markets generally. The most revolutionary of these policies, financial de-regulation, is said to be a major factor behind the economic revival of the mid-1980s. Leaving aside the authorities' ideological commitment to free markets, the fundamental rationale for these policies has been the creation of financial conditions that would be more favourable to capital accumulation.

The actual performance of the economy in the second half of the 1980s does suggest that de-regulation of financial markets has given rise to a certain acceleration in economic activity. Moreover, new capital markets have established themselves, old ones have been reformed, and this has coincided, albeit with something of a lag, with an investment boom in the economy.

Such evidence may be interpreted as proof of the existence of more enterprising financial markets directing 'savings' more efficiently to higher-yielding projects. This conclusion is based on a set of interdependent assumptions about government policy and the relationship between the financial system and the rest of the economy. In practice, many other factors affecting investment have also changed. The economic revival of the second half of the 1980s may owe more to a rise in consumption than investment efficiency.

In order to draw more specific conclusions, it is necessary to look at the nature of financial accumulation and its relation to capital accumulation generally. This question lies at the heart of the current controversy over the role that savings play in capital accumulation, and whether indeed the availability of savings is an actual restraint on accumulation. It will be argued that in a capitalist economy, savings do not in fact constrain investment. This has important implications for the theoretical debate over whether financial service activity is indeed a 'productive' activity. On a more practical level, it suggests that financial capital outflows have not in themselves adversely affected domestic investment.

In this chapter we shall examine first of all the role of financial services and their relative growth in employment and total economic activity in the UK. Secondly, we shall look at the measures of financial de-regulation that have been implemented, their theoretical justification, and the actual role of the financial sector in the UK economy. Finally, it will be argued that reform in the financial system has not increased the share of profits in income in the economy, despite a recovery after the recession of the early 1980s. Continuing inflation in the financial markets without corresponding increases in profits is likely to precipitate a recession in which financial instability and more widespread price inflation become preconditions for restoring capital accumulation.

12.1 BOOM AND REFORM IN THE FINANCIAL SYSTEM

By the standards of employment and their share in economic activity, financial services have, until recently, been one of the success stories of reform under the monetarist regime of the conservative government since 1979. As Table 12.1 shows, employment in banking and finance in Great Britain rose by 16% between June 1979 and June 1986 to 524,000 in the latter year. Employment in insurance, which has remained somewhat on the periphery of the financial services reform programme (see below), has risen by only 6.5% – the same rate of increase as service employment generally. Consultancy, Accounting, Leasing, Property Dealing and Management Services, which are associated with corporate finance in the economy, have shown the greatest increase in employment – 45% between 1979 and 1986. This brought employment in financial services in the broadest sense to 2.175 million, an increase of 32% since 1979.

Table 12.1 Employment in banking, finance and insurance in Great Britain 1979–86.

1,000s in June	1979	1982	1984	1986
Banking and bill discounting	n.a.	362	384	397
Other financial institutions	n.a.	105	116	127
Total banking and finance	451*	467	499	524
Insurance	216	220	221	230
Consultancy and leasing services, property dealing (SIC 83–85)	981	1,084	1,221	1,421
Total financial services (SIC 8)	1,648*	1,771	1,941	2,175
Total services employment	13,279	13,117	13,503	14,161
Total employment	22,500	20,916	20,741	21,105

Note: *Adjusted for discontinuity of data.
Source: Department of Employment and own calculations.

By contrast, total employment in services in the economy has risen by a mere 6.6%. There is an even greater contrast with total employment in the economy, which fell by 6.2% over this period, from 22.5 million in June 1979 to 21.1 million in June 1986.

The robustness of the boom in financial services is seen in particular if we compare the years 1979 and 1982, the latter being in the trough of the 1980s business cycle. Total employment in this downturn fell by 7% and employment in services shrank by 1.2%. Meanwhile, financial services did more than just weather the recession. They thrived, albeit at a more modest pace than they were to achieve later. Between 1979 and 1982, employment in financial services rose by 7.5%.

Taken in this context, the most alarmist estimates of job losses following the stock market crash of 1987 of up to 50,000 jobs ('Economists Cast Doubt on City Job Loss Forecast', (*Financial Times*, 25.1.88) represent a moderate set-back, offsetting only partially the increase in employment of the mid-1980s. In the context of the 2.3 million jobs lost outside services in the primary and manufacturing sectors, such a shrinkage of employment in the City is trivial.

A more serious study by the Institute of Manpower Studies (Institute of Manpower Studies, 1988) showed that in the seven months following the crash, employment in securities trading fell by 1,500, out of just over 25,000 employed in this activity in and around the City of London. A similar net loss of jobs in that activity was expected up to 1990, but overall employment in financial services in this part of London was expected to rise by around 13.5% (37,000 jobs) between 1987 and 1992. The increase was expected to occur mostly in banking, accountancy and management consultancy. Between 1984 and 1987, the increase in financial services employment in this area had been 51,000, so a halving in the rate of employment increase is expected at the end of the 1980s.

The increase in employment reflects in part the positive income elasticity of demand for such services (Economists Advisory Group, 1984), but much of this increased activity has been due to the structural reforms that have been implemented in the financial sector over the decade. These structural reforms fall broadly under two related headings: de-regulation and the emergence of new markets.

By the de-regulation of financial markets is meant the removal of controls exercised over prices in financial markets (interest, commission and exchange rates) and over financial flows in the economy (capital exports and credit) by the 'authorities', primarily the government and its agent in the City, the Bank of England. The controls ranged from fixed commission rates in Stock Exchange dealing to special deposits as a check on the liquidity of domestic banks, and hence their credit creation. They included regulations concerning holdings by UK residents of capital in foreign currencies, as a support for the government's attempts to manipulate sterling exchange rates, and restrictions on the range of business that could be undertaken by banks and building societies (Congdon, 1982).

This system of interlocking controls over financial markets was intended to make effective the government's monetary policy and provide a stable financial environment in which business and, to a lesser extent, household, decisions could be made. In fact, with the periodic sterling crises of the 1970s and the tying of the previous Labour government to targets for money supply expansion by its agreement with the International Monetary Fund in 1976, it was already apparent when the Conservative government entered office in 1979 that either monetary policy targets were inconsistent, or the instruments available to the authorities were ineffective.

This was confirmed in the Wilson Report that was published in 1980, which enunciated many of the principles of financial market organisation that became conventional wisdom and were now put into practice. Most important among them was scepticism about the efficacy of financial regulation and a belief in the benefits of allowing market forces and greater competition to operate in financial markets (Committee to Review the Functioning of Financial Institutions, 1980).

The newly elected Conservative government proceeded to de-regulate and restructure financial markets. The process had already been started with the passing of the 1979 Banking Act in the twilight of the previous Labour government. This established a two-tier system of designated banks and licensed deposit takers. It also formalised the relationship between the Bank of England, as the guardian of the banking system, and the institutions whose probity and integrity it was supposed to supervise. By specifying the criteria which had to be satisfied before a firm could operate legally in the UK as a bank, the Act took the first step towards opening up the banking cartel to greater competition.

These measures were followed by new monetary control arrangements that largely dismantled the complex of banking regulations and gave more institutions equal status in the banking system. A new, much wider, monetary sector, now including foreign banks, replaced the smaller banking sector with privileged access to Bank of England support, through having their acceptances eligible for discount by it. Reserve ratios were replaced by a non-operational cash requirement of 0.5% of eligible liabilities for institutions with liabilities in excess of £10 million. Such institutions were also to remain liable to make special deposits, but these were placed in abeyance and the Bank indicated that it would now make more use of open market operations as a control over banks' liquidity. The Minimum Lending Rate was formally suspended (*Bank of England Quarterly Bulletin*, September 1981a; Hall, 1983, chapter 9).

Most dramatic of all was the announcement in July 1979, within weeks of the election of the Conservative government, that exchange controls on the movement of capital into and out of the economy were to be abolished three months later. The result was an outflow of capital abroad in the third and fourth quarters of 1979 amounting to some £0.5 billion in excess of previous outflows. In 1980 and 1981, the capital outflow (UK private-sector overseas investment) totalled £15.467 billion, some £7.5 billion greater than the most recent capital outflows under the previous foreign exchange regime (Hall, 1983, p. 80). We shall return to the significance of these outflows below.

Despite considerable doubt as to the effectiveness of the government's monetary policy in this new system of controls through markets, as opposed to the previous more direct controls, the government has stuck to the new system, perhaps because so far it has managed to avoid the kind of crisis that brought down the previous experiment in *laissez-faire* monetarism, the Competition and Credit Control policy in the early 1970s. At the beginning there were doubts as to the extent of the de-regulation, for example over short-term interest rates, which the government has in effect treated as an instrument of monetary policy (Llewellyn and Tew, 1988). This was done without quite formalising the situation by suspending Minimum Lending Rate (although this was resurrected for one day in January 1985 in a vain attempt to stem a run on sterling).

The combination of banking de-regulation with a monetary policy that gave priority to control over the growth of the monetary aggregate M3 under the Medium Term Financial Strategy meant that to be effective monetary policy had to be considerably more deflationary than it would have needed to be in a more controlled banking system. The result of the de-regulation was to inaugurate a decade of very high interest rates (see Table 4 below) which did little to prevent a persistent over-shooting of targets for monetary expansion.

The two-tier banking system itself fell into some disrepute after the Johnson Matthey Bankers collapse in 1985, in particular since that institution had been in the allegedly more trustworthy bank tier of the system. The 1979 Banking Act was therefore amended by a new Banking Act in 1987. This tightened up controls over bank lending to individual borrowers and made all banks subject to the same degree of supervision.

Competition was further intensified when the Trustee Savings Banks were amalgamated and floated off as a highly capitalised joint stock bank in 1986.

De-regulation extended also to the other major domestic banking sector, the building societies. Under government encouragement, the Building Societies' Association interest rate cartel was allowed to break down in 1984 – its removal had earlier been recommended by the Wilson Report. With the removal of informal controls over clearing bank business, the banks began to enter the home purchase loans market, principally at the higher price end of the market. The pressure of this competition for the best end of the lucrative housing market of the mid-1980s caused the building societies to demand access to a wider range of banking business, and they were supported in this by many critics of the existing clearing banks.

In 1986, the government passed the Building Societies Act, which went some way towards meeting those demands, although it insisted that domestic mortgages should remain the main business of the societies. A Building Societies' Commission was set up to supervise the finances and probity of the societies. More importantly, the societies were given a procedure whereby they could cease being mutual funds and become limited liability companies. From 1987 the societies started to offer a wider range of banking services.

The outcome of all this enhanced competition in the banking sector and from overseas banks and building societies was pressure on the clearing banks to open their clearing arrangements to other institutions. The advent of electronic means of transmitting funds in the 1970s had already forced the clearing banks to consider more open, efficient and flexible methods of clearing. The Child Report in 1984 (Members of the Bankers' Clearing House, 1984) paved the way for the admission of these new competitors into the clearing system.

In the capital markets, the upheaval was much greater. The Wilson Report had criticised the narrow and cartelised nature of the Stock Exchange, and the apparently inadequate range of corporate financial services available to all but large companies. Despite minority dissent, it stopped short of endorsing direct state participation in capital accumulation outside the nationalised industries. The 'radical conservative' consensus that emerged was that if there was a problem with the narrowness of financial markets then this was a problem that was best resolved by releasing the forces of competition in markets. The result was a complex programme of developing new financial markets and expanding and integrating existing ones.

The foundations of the new system were the existing Stock Exchange and the Eurobond market. In 1980, the Stock Exchange started an Unlisted Securities Market, in which smaller and less well established companies could issue shares. In 1982, the London International Financial Futures Exchange (LIFFE) was set up. This gave traders an opportunity to hedge against changes in interest rates, exchange rates and financial stock prices. This was, it should be noted, over two years before the Plaza Accord in September 1985, at a time when official *désintéressement* in financial markets was regarded as a natural corollary of the monetarist doctrines espoused by the governments of the major capitalist countries. The resulting volatility of prices in financial markets virtually created the business of the financial futures exchange.

There still remained the question of the reform of the Stock Exchange. The Exchange had been referred to the Restrictive Practices Court by the previous Labour government on the grounds that its fixed rates of commission and restrictions on membership were an undue restraint on competition in that market for financial services. In May 1983, an agreement to withdraw this referral was reached between the Department of Trade and Industry and the Stock Exchange. In return for this withdrawal, the Exchange was to make its membership easier to obtain, and to have commission rates fixed by negotiation in the market (Reid, 1988, chapter 2).

It was apparent that if this agreement were to be implemented, the traditional distinction between jobbers and brokers would also have to be abolished. This was because brokers would need to have an opportunity to compensate themselves for the expected lower commissions by being able to 'take positions' in stock and profit from capital gains. Acting as a principal in this way was hitherto restricted to jobbers, since brokers were only allowed to act as agents.

The Stock Exchange eventually went over to a new system combining 'market makers', or brokers who 'stood ready' to buy and sell stock, and brokers who acted as pure agents, in October 1986. Commission rates for dealing were also made subject to negotiation at that time. With the open encouragement of the Bank of England, banks and other financial firms were encouraged to enter the securities markets by buying up existing firms, or becoming recognised as new firms under the easier new membership regime. In practice, this ended up increasing trading capacity more than fivefold (Hewlett and Toporowski, 1985, chapter 4).

In its technology, securities trading now shifted from the floor of the Stock Exchange dealing hall to electronic screens and telephone communication. This reform was associated with a restructuring of the gilts, or government bond market. The Bank of England set up its own gilts dealing room and, also in 1986, started to deal with a wider range of institutions on a more competitive basis. In 1987, auctions of government stock began (Reid, 1988, pp. 63–6). However, with the public sector in surplus at the end of the 1980s, official funding policy was dedicated to paying back the National Debt. This starvation of the gilts market was supposed to 'crowd in' a company debenture market. In the event, it merely precipitated the withdrawal of gilts dealing firms from a market that, if anything, had become even more over-endowed with trading firms than the company stock market (Hewlett and Toporowski, 1985).

In 1987, in a further attempt to reach those companies which were not being served by existing arrangements, the Stock Exchange started up what was called the Third Market to trade in stock issued by companies too small or insufficiently established to obtain registration with the Unlisted Securities Market.

This burgeoning activity, and in particular the encouragement that was now being given to wider share ownership and personal pension schemes among the financially unsophisticated, raised questions of the prevention of fraud, or 'investor protection' as it now became fashionable to call it. Such frauds had usually precipitated the puncturing of financial bubbles, and the authorities generally took the view, in particular as the stock market reached spectacular heights in the summer before the crash of 1987, that if fraud could be prevented, then so could the bubble.

The government commissioned the Gower Report (Gower, 1984), which recommended that the firms undertaking various types of investment business should be associated into self-regulating organisations licensed by the government, each having their own formal and informal rules of conduct. Five of these were eventually set up under the overall supervision of the Securities and Investments Board in a system that was given the stamp of legality by the Financial Services Act of 1986. A notable exception were banks which have remained under direct Bank of England supervision.

12.2 FINANCIAL REFORM AND ECONOMIC EFFICIENCY

The significance of these changes remains a matter of some controversy. The evident intention of the Wilson committee and the government had been to make the operations of financial, and in particular capital, markets more efficient. The conventional wisdom of economists in the 1980s has been that regulation is supposed to distort price signals indicating where capital should be redistributed in order to obtain a better social return on it, while regulated markets are held to tie up capital in industries where investment opportunities are unprofitable (Mayes and Hunn, 1987, chapter 3).

This function of a free social capital market had been anticipated in nineteenth-century political economy:

> capital withdraws from a sphere with a low rate of profit and invades others which yield a higher profit. Through this incessant outflow and influx, or, briefly, through its distribution among the various spheres, which depends on how the rate of profit falls here and rises there, it creates such a ratio of supply to demand that the average rate of profit in the various spheres of production becomes the same, and values are, therefore, converted into prices of production. Capital succeeds in this equalization, to a greater or lesser degree, depending on the extent of capitalist development in the given nation, i.e., on the extent to which the conditions in the country are adapted to the capitalist mode of production. (Marx, 1959, pp. 195–6)

In this view, the capital market is the market in which the capitals, tied up in various industries and undertakings, compete with each other, maximising their returns relative to each other. The process does indeed have a progressive function, tending towards the elimination of activities and undertakings that have lower than average rates of return and expanding those activities which have higher than average rates of return. With an assumed declining marginal efficiency of investment, the latter activities have capital transferred to them until the return on investment therein is reduced to the average in the economy.

In practice, however, even the most financially sophisticated economies have not achieved such a thoroughly transparent system of social capital allocation. In the UK, which has a relatively active stock market, most fixed capital investment actually takes place out of retained profits (including depreciation). A negligible amount is financed from the issue of stock

(Committee to Review the Functioning of Financial Institutions, 1980, pp. 131–4; Fine and Harris, 1985, chapter 4). The usual method of expanding the firm's productive capital has been traditionally to reinvest existing profits, with stock market issues being undertaken on completion of the productive capital expansion as a means of switching to cheaper finance.

A more subtle point concerning the financing of investment is how this is related to the size of the firm undertaking it. Kalecki's Principle of Increasing Risk argues that the larger the firm (i.e., the amount of accumulated retained profits owned by the firm), the easier it is for that firm to obtain additional quantities of finance for its expansion and investment (Kalecki, 1954).

This principle interposes into the process of obtaining an equilibrium rate of return in all economic activities the institutional factor of the respective sizes of the firms in which social capital is organised. Small firms are deprived of funds for investment in a free market financial system in which future returns are uncertain. In the financial reform programme of the 1980s, smaller firms were recognised as having particular difficulties in financing capital expansion (Committee to Review the Functioning of Financial Institutions, 1980, p. 157 and appendix 2).

From this point of view, there is no doubt that the changes and reforms that were undertaken have expanded considerably the access of smaller firms to finance. The setting up of the Unlisted Securities Market and the Third Market has enabled smaller less established firms to issue securities and raise more liquid capital. The government's Loan Guarantee Scheme, whereby the government has guaranteed banks' lending to small companies up to a high proportion of the value of such loans, has eased the purse-strings of finance: Business Expansion Schemes, introduced in 1984 and giving tax benefits to investors in small growing companies, have encouraged and complemented another type of financing introduced from the US, namely venture capital. (The home-grown version of this, the Industrial and Commercial Finance Corporation, now Investors in Industry, or 3i, was established in 1946.) Starting in the early 1980s, venture capital has boomed through the decade. In 1987, £953 million was invested in British projects – an increase of 77% on 1986 (*Financial Times*, 28.4.88).

However, to an extent these innovations merely lowered the credibility threshold of financiers offering the money. There has been a high failure rate among the businesses supported by venture capital, sometimes as high as 80% or 90% of the number of projects in a venture capital 'portfolio'.

More importantly from the point of view of innovative fixed capital restructuring in the economy, the strain of this failure rate on the credulity of venture capitalists eventually resulted in a tendency for finance for new ventures to concentrate more on proven technologies and methods of expanding the market value of capital. Until the mid-1980s, scientific innovations in electronics and biotechnology were favoured by venture capital funds. Afterwards, however, the uncertainty and high risks associated with such schemes provoked a return to safer projects in retail trades, clothing, construction and property development, and management buy-outs that were not linked to larger investment programmes (*Financial Times*, 14.3.88; *Supplement on Venture Capital*, 30.11.88).

At least two other interpretations have been attached to the changes that took place in the 1980s in the financial system. There was an ideological purpose in making citizens more aware of how the system of accumulating and allocating finance capital was supposed to benefit them, in particular through owning shares. In the flotation of shares in companies that were being transferred to the private sector, allocations were deliberately skewed to create premiums over the issue price during initial trading, thereby creating a direct financial incentive to buying those shares.

Tax reliefs have also been granted to workers and managers obtaining shares in their enterprise, either through purchase options or Personal Equity Plans, in which money was saved for investment in such shares. By the beginning of 1988 nine million adults, or 20.5% of the adult population in Britain, were estimated to own shares directly, albeit half of those share-owners only held shares in one company (HM Treasury, April 1988).

Following the stock market crash of 1987, the share-marketing efforts of the government and stockbrokers diminished: 'Share shops' in Debenhams and other retail outlets were shut down. Official pronouncements, which had previously scarcely veiled the speculative gains to be made from share owner-ship, now switched to emphasising the 'long-term' commitments involved in owning shares.

The other importance that was attached to the restructuring activity in financial markets was as a substitute for economic decline elsewhere. In the first half of the 1980s, the growing employment, investment in offices and technological advances in trading and funds transmission and rising salaries in the financial sector all contrasted sharply with the decline of manufacturing industry that gave rise to the then current debate on 'de-industrialisation'. The official view of the government was that the services sector, including financial services, could replace industries which were 'no longer viable'. This conviction was put quite succinctly by the Governor of the Bank of England, Robin Leigh-Pemberton:

> given the substantial sums that have been invested in financial services in this period [i.e., in the early 1980s – J.T.] the inference is irresistible that the prospec-tive rate of return in much of this sector is seen as at least as high or higher than that elsewhere. This being so, and given the decline in our manufacturing capability, the fact that our oil and gas reserves will not last indefinitely, and thus the need to develop new areas of wealth generation, we cannot as a nation afford to neglect financial services. It is true that investment in financial service activity tends to create less jobs than, say, a comparable investment in manufacturing; but our primary concern must be to ensure that new areas of wealth-generating activity develop to take the place of those that are actually or prospectively in decline. (*Bank of England Quarterly Bulletin*, March 1984)

Table 12.2 Private transfers overseas 1978–88.

£million Year	UK investment overseas		Overseas investment in the UK		Balance of capital flows	
	Direct	Portfolio	Direct	Portfolio	Direct	Portfolio
1978	3,520	1,073	1,962	−139	−1,558	1,212
1979	5,889	887	3,030	1,549	−2,859	662
1980	4,886	3,230	4,335	1,499	−531	−1,731
1981	6,005	4,300	2,932	323	−3,073	−3,977
1982	4,091	7,563	3,027	225	−1,064	−7,338
1983	5,417	7,193	3,386	1,888	−2,031	−5,305
1984	6,003	9,866	−181	1,419	−6,184	−8,447
1985	8,653	19,440	4,213	7,121	−4,440	−12,319
1986	11,525	25,243	4,176	8,447	−7,349	−16,796
1987	15,372	6,463	5,953	10,805	−9,419	4,342
1988*	6,918	6,600	2,969	981	−3,949	−5,619

Note: *First six months.
Source: CSO, *Economic Trends.*

It is of course true that, as commercial operations, financial firms make profits or losses. But from the point of view of its function in capital accumulation, the financial system does not itself create wealth. It is actually responsible for creating a money equivalent of it, or realising wealth, gathering it together, and reallocating the surpluses or deficits generated in the productive (surplus-creating) economy. In this respect, the profits of financial firms are derived from surpluses created elsewhere (Marx, 1956, chapters 1 and 2; Ruffini, 1983, pp. 108–11).

By implication, the financial sector cannot substitute itself for declining productive activity in the economy. What it can do is to transfer capital to production elsewhere, abroad for example, and derive profits from the surpluses generated there.

Such transfers of capital were greatly facilitated by the abolition of exchange controls in 1979. This gave rise to the huge net outflows of private capital that we have already mentioned. These outflows and the inflow of funds into capital markets in the UK, or portfolio investment, are shown in Table 12.2.[1]

British direct investment overseas has been greater than overseas direct investment in Britain throughout the 1980s, and it has been rising much more rapidly than the much-publicised investment of overseas companies in the UK. There has also been a net outflow of portfolio funds, mainly due to the rising proportion of overseas assets held in the portfolios of investment funds managed in London. Their share rose from around 5% at the start of the 1980s to around 20% on the eve of the 1987 crash (*Bank of England Quarterly Bulletin*, December 1986).

The crash precipitated a sudden reversal of this trend in portfolio investment, as funds sought greater security in the markets that they knew in London: in the final quarter of 1987, a total of £9.1 billion was realised and returned to the UK by British financial institutions. By comparison, in 1986 those institutions had purchased £14.4 billion in overseas securities.[2] However, as the figures in Table 12.2 show, the trend towards net portfolio investment overseas returned in 1988.

The rising net outflow of direct investment aroused some criticism, especially in the early years of the decade. Capital investment overseas was said to be at least partially responsible for reducing capital investment in the UK. The point was put by the TUC:

> The common characteristic of both overseas investment and mergers is that in general they will result in less not more industrial capacity in the UK, and fewer not more jobs. (Trades Union Congress, 1986)

This argument has in common with the view enunciated by the Governor of the Bank of England above a belief that the flow of funds in an economy is a 'wealth-creating' activity. The TUC view is perhaps less extreme in that it does go on to state that it is the putting of funds into British industry that is productive, rather than merely turning them over. But it still seems to regard a flow of funds as a *prior* condition for social capital expansion.

The argument about funds deficiency through leakage overseas is lent superficial plausibility by the fact that the 1980s really have seen a collapse in fixed capital investment in the UK (Table 12.3). Investment in general in all sectors of the economy fell by 12% between 1979 and 1981, since when it has risen,

Table 12.3 Real gross investment in the UK 1979–88.

£million 1985 prices

Year	Non-dwelling building and works	Vehicles ships and aircraft	Plant and machinery	Total	of which manufacturing investment
1979	16,171	7,514	19,736	43,421	10,136
1980	15,334	6,296	19,660	41,290	8,761
1981	14,859	4,895	18,269	38,023	6,579
1982	16,377	5,028	18,478	39,883	6,360
1983	16,651	5,177	19,401	41,229	6,422
1984	18,135	6,107	21,262	45,504	7,810
1985	18,178	6,433	23,744	48,355	8,735
1986	18,365	5,627	24,013	48,005	8,477
1987	19,092	6,099	25,599	50,790	9,090
1988*	9,959	3,074	13,803	26,836	5,008

Note: First six months, preliminary data.
Source: CSO, *Economic Trends.*

albeit at a rate somewhat faster than the general economic growth rate. However, investment in manufacturing industry fell by 37% between 1979 and 1982, and only reached its 1979 level again in 1988.

There are nevertheless problems in drawing firm conclusions from this data. In particular, it is not possible to assume that the productivity of this investment has been constant over what amounts to a trade cycle. The analysis of those conclusions that may be drawn from these statistics lies beyond the scope of this chapter. What we can argue is that the availability of funds was not a determining factor in the investment behaviour of British firms. To argue that it is would be to revert, by implication, to the Treasury View of the 1930s, according to which only finite sums are available for investment. These place a limit on how much investment may be undertaken, whether absolutely or through some comparison of the rate of interest and the return on investment.

Such comparisons may be a factor in investment decisions as a subjective consideration in those decisions. But the relevance of monetary policy here is through its effects on expenditure decisions, and not on some notional supply of savings. In an economy with a credit system working through commercial firms, the general availability of funds, as opposed to its specific rationing by bank managers to, say, small businesses in accordance with the Principle of Increasing Risk (see above), does not constrain business investment.

For example, should investment exceed the current level of savings after taking into account capital outflows then the problem of financing the excess is one of creating liquidity against existing or future assets. There is no reason why properly functioning banking or securities systems should not generate this extra liquidity (cf. Sawyer, 1985, pp. 91–101; Asimakopulos, 1983; Reynolds, 1988, chapter 12).

Should savings exceed investment, then they will simply inflate financial markets in the way in which, as we shall argue in the final section of this chapter, financial markets have been inflated during the 1980s.

12.3 THE FINANCIAL MARKETS AND PROFITS

We shall now move on to the significance of the changes in the financial system for the process of generating profits and capital accumulation. Broadly speaking, and according to conventional economic theory (e.g., Carter and Partington, 1984), circumstances in the financial markets through most of the 1980s have not favoured profits or capital accumulation outside the financial sector. Interest rates, whether real or nominal, have stayed at high levels throughout most of this period in accordance with the monetarist doctrine that this acts as a restraint on inflation (see Table 12.4). Exchange rates have been volatile and, at the start of the decade and recently, have reduced the profitability of the exporting trades. At the same time, however,

Table 12.4 Financial markets 1978–88.

Year	Three month inter-bank interest rate	Sterling exchange rate index (1975 = 100)	FT 30-share index (average of working days 1 July 1935 = 100)
1978	12.44–12.63	81.5	479.4
1979	16.81–17.06	87.3	475.5
1980	14.75–14.88	96.1	464.5
1981	15.56–15.75	95.3	518.5
1982	10.44–10.63	90.7	574.7
1983	9.34– 9.41	83.2	692.6
1984	10.00–10.13	78.6	854.9
1985	11.81–11.94	78.3	1,004.6
1986	11.00–11.13	72.8	1,287.1
1987	8.75– 9.00	72.7	1,600.0
1988*	9.20– 9.44	76.4	1,433.2

Note: *First eight months.
Sources: Bank of England Quarterly Bulletin, Financial Times.

securities prices have experienced a record boom which seems to have been punctured only temporarily by the stock market crash of October 1987.

The effects of these price changes, and the changes that have taken place in the financial system and the way in which it operates, may be argued to influence directly the notional profits or capital accumulation that would occur if all business decisions were entirely rational and realised. Yet, as those who make such decisions know, they are not always made in a spirit of enlightened rationality. The expectations that are such an important factor in investment decision-making have a social context and can be the result of social pressures. These are frequently combined with that element of faith that is an essential feature of entrepreneurial activity, and is apparent in projects from the Stockton to Darlington Railway to the Channel Tunnel of today.

The business intentions and calculations of businessmen are therefore a poor guide to the profits that they will actually make. Those profits will depend on how expenditure in the economy enables notional or planned investments to be realised. This realised, or actual, profit is then the key to capital accumulation as being the variable that signals to the capital markets where further investment should take place, and where realised profits should be reinvested.

What has happened to profits over this period, and can they substantiate the hypothesis that the reform of the financial markets and other supply side measures have made Britain a more profitable and efficient economy? The official data that is shown in Table 12.5 suggests that, with only a minor

Table 12.5 Official estimates of profits in the UK 1978–88.

£million Year	Profits* (1)	GDP at factor cost income estimate (2)	Share of profits in National Income (1)/(2) × 100
1978	24,453	147,966	16.5
1979	31,225	171,696	18.2
1980	31,100	199,377	15.6
1981	33,074	217,716	15.2
1982	37,540	238,025	15.8
1983	43,998	260,925	16.8
1984	51,153	278,742	18.4
1985	58,548	305,262	19.2
1986	55,994	323,976	17.3
1987	68,991	354,400	19.5
1988†	38,002	190,105	20.0

Notes: *Gross profits of industrial and commercial companies
including stock appreciation.
† First six months.
Sources: CSO, *Economic Trends* and own calculations.

set-back in 1980 and a more significant one in 1986 (the result of the slump in
oil prices that occurred in that year), profits have hardly ceased to rise over
the decade. The share of profits in total income in the economy has also been
rising steadily after the recession of the early 1980s. This would appear to
substantiate a view that supply side measures have been effective in shifting
the distribution firmly in favour of profits and capital accumulation.

However, it is not difficult to cast doubt on the reliability of these statistics.
The profit estimates are subject to lags and distortions in reporting which are
likely to have been enhanced in a decade of radical change in corporate
taxation and accounting practice. The series is also inconsistent, with profits
from the major privatised corporations artificially inflating the figures in the
second half of the decade, as those corporations were added to the industrial
and commercial companies sector. Finally, the figures also include overseas
profits made by UK-based multinational companies.[3]

A more consistent series without these disadvantages has been obtained
using a methodology developed from the profits equation that Kalecki derives
from the national income accounts identity between income and expenditure.
Briefly, this identity can be rearranged to give an equation in which actual
(realised) profits after tax are equal to investment, plus the government's
budget deficit, plus the foreign trade surplus, plus capitalists' consumption,
minus workers' savings. Using the sectoral balance statistics of the CSO, a
consistent statistical series for profits in the UK economy has been estimated
(Kalecki, 1971, chapter 7; Toporowski, 1989). These figures are shown in
Table 12.6 below.

Table 12.6 Profits in the UK economy 1978–88 (consistent).

£million Year	Estimated profits	Share of profits in National Income
1978	25,001	16.9
1979	27,991	16.3
1980	25,459	12.8
1981	25,242	11.6
1982	25,604	10.8
1983	33,945	13.0
1984	39,167	14.1
1985	41,773	13.7
1986	43,519	13.4
1987	51,475	14.5
1988*	22,869	12.0

Note: *First six months.
Source: Toporowski, 1989.

The table suggests that, although profits have been rising over the decade, the share of profits in national income was still, in the first half of 1988, below the share obtained by profits at the end of the 1970s. This is even after a recovery from a fall of about a third in that share between 1979 and 1982. This does not support the view that financial and capital market reforms have made the process of capital accumulation more effective or profitable. At the very least, it suggests that any improvement due to these reforms has been more than outweighed by the failure of other supply side measures by the government.

One conclusion that may be drawn from our argument above, that realised profits depend on the amount and patterns of expenditure in the economy (an argument that is also implicit in the Kalecki profits equation), is that microeconomic, supply side measures are irrelevant in determining profits in the economy. In fact, this is not strictly speaking the case if we accept the Kalecki profits analysis. Greater microeconomic efficiency would have an effect on the balance of foreign trade that enters into the profits equation. However, by this standard the supply side measures of the 1980s have been worse than ineffective, as the balance of payments accounts have recorded a surplus in the early 1980s reversed into a huge deficit of approximately £15 billion in 1988.

The results of this analysis are also consistent with the 'blocking hypothesis' about the relationship between finance and industry in the UK that has been put forward by Fine and Harris (Fine and Harris, 1985, chapter 4). In brief, these authors emphasise the role of bank credit in the financing of investment, with the role of the capital markets being mainly to facilitate the restructuring of existing corporate capital. Fine and Harris argue that the very availability of this credit discourages long-term investment because banks assign their highest credit rating to liquid collateral.

This view is a useful antidote to the eventually rather sterile debate that split the Wilson Committee about whether or not the City provides enough finance for industrial investment. It can be added that a system of bank lending that favours liquid collateral also discourages long-term investment from retained profits, since companies then prefer to keep their reserves liquid in order to maximise the lines of credit (overdraft limits) that are available to them. From this point of view, the programme of financial market reforms has hardly improved matters, with enhanced competition between banks mainly concentrated on lending against theoretically realizable assets such as property.

12.4 THE FINANCIAL MARKETS AND CAPITAL ACCUMULATION IN THE 1990s

It is in the context of the relatively stagnating share of profits of British industry that the boom in financial markets, the takeover and speculative activity associated with it and the panic at the end of 1987 need to be seen. Broadly, prices in securities markets are determined by two factors: the inflow of funds into them (cf. Kaufman, 1986, chapter 13) and the level of profits in the rest of the economy. As we have argued above, the profits of the financial system are derived from the profits of the productive economy. Inflation in financial markets therefore requires some corresponding increase in profits from that 'real' economy, in order that profit claims in financial markets can be realised without putting a stop to capital accumulation (cf. Minsky, 1978, 1986).

There is no doubt that financial markets have been greatly inflated during the 1980s, as the industrial share index shown in Table 12.4 testifies. Realised claims in the form of dividends and interest payments have also been correspondingly inflated: dividends, interest and other transfer payments quadrupled from £6.17 billion in 1978 to 23.85 billion in 1987 (CSO data). During this same period, the profits of the companies officially classified in the industrial and commercial sector rose from £24,453 billion in 1978 to £68.99 billion in 1987 (see Table 12.5), or by a factor of less than three. But even that, as we have argued, considerably over-estimates the actual growth of profits in the economy. High levels of net overseas investment (see Table 12.2) can therefore be seen as functionally necessary to maintain the flow of dividends, interest and other transfer payments into the UK's financial markets at levels commensurate with the inflation in financial asset markets.

In large part this inflation of the financial markets has been due to the reform and restructuring of those markets to which we referred in the first

Table 12.7 Investment fund inflows 1979-88.

£m			
Year	Unit Trusts	Life Assurance and Pension Funds	Total
1979	90	9,966	10,056
1980	88	11,568	11,656
1981	186	12,624	12,810
1982	148	13,375	13,523
1983	601	14,453	15,054
1984	608	16,520	17,128
1985	950	16,823	17,773
1986	2,275	19,202	21,477
1987	3,713	20,258	23,971
1988*	-275	5,501	5,226

Note: *First quarter.
Source: Bank of England Quarterly Bulletin.

section of this chapter. However, little of this restructuring would have been possible without the accompanying rise in the inflow of investment funds into the markets. An important factor has been the Social Security and Pensions Act of 1975 and, to a lesser extent, the 1986 Social Security Act. The first formalised a system of funded pension schemes, while the second made private pension schemes more widely available.

The effect of both measures, and the government's encouragement to households to invest directly or through fund intermediaries in securities markets, has been huge financial surpluses or cash inflows into pension, insurance and investment funds. These inflows (which also include investment income) are shown in Table 12.7. The figures show rising net inflows as the scope of funded pension schemes was gradually extended, but also as the boom in financial markets attracted savings into securities investment vehicles such as unit trusts and life assurance funds. By 1987 the total cash inflow, including investment income, but after payments to policy-holders, pensioners and investors, had reached nearly £24 billion.

While the discretionary savings vehicles of unit trusts saw their inflows reversed after the stock market crash of 1987, life assurance and pension funds, contributions to which are contractual, had their inflows undiminished by the crash and went on to fund the recovery of the stock market in 1988 and 1989.

A Bank of England study published in 1986 revealed that something like a quarter of the cash inflow of life assurance and pension funds was placed on the Stock Exchange in company equity shares, and a further quarter approximately (but considerably more during the recession of the early 1980s) in overseas assets. However, the surpluses of these funds that have been invested in UK securities have been augmented by the growing internationalisation of foreign investment funds. Since the mid-1970s US pension funds have been allowed to invest abroad, and in the latter half of the 1980s the Japanese government has encouraged the investment of its country's financial surpluses abroad, primarily in the US, but also in London.

This vast cash flow into securities markets is likely to continue until at least the end of the century. Indeed, it is not until well into the next century, some three decades from now, that the inflow is likely to fall, and even then it is likely to remain substantial (Committee to Review the Functioning of Financial Institutions, 1980).

The stock market crash of 1987 has already indicated what happens when continuing accumulation in the financial sector is combined with stagnating profitability in the productive economy. If the claims of the financial sector on the profits of the real economy are rising, while those profits are falling, then it is necessary either to increase profits in order to realise those claims and sustain the pace of capital accumulation, or those claims must be devalued or made worthless. The first alternative would require a relative contraction of consumption (equivalent in our Kaleckian analysis to a reduction in the relative income of workers). By reducing the overseas sector deficit and the public sector surplus (the latter through reduced indirect tax revenues and increased social security payments to those formerly employed in the consumption goods industries) such reduced consumption would, according to our equation, result in higher profits. After a temporary recession, the process of capital accumulation would proceed with minimal disturbance in financial markets.

The second alternative would require a re-balancing between profits and financial sector claims. This need not necessarily happen through a financial crash. One way is for claims on the productive sectors of overseas economies to be increased, with greater capital outflows, and an enhanced risk of repeated sterling crises in the foreign exchange markets.

A less destabilising way is for this accommodation between the financial and industrial sectors to take place through a period of differentiated rates of increase in nominal values in the two sectors, for example, by a bout of price inflation in the real economy, devaluing debt and other nominal claims. What makes such an inflationary outcome unlikely is the government's very public commitment to restraining inflation as an overriding priority in its economic policy. One irony in this is that the present government seems to feel no such qualms about inflationary processes in financial markets. A second irony is that it is precisely those financial markets that are most likely to hold the government to its commitment.

12.5 CONCLUSION

The financial system has experienced major changes in the 1980s with reforms aimed at a freer operation of market forces in that system. However, the effect of these reforms on the efficiency of capital accumulation in the economy is likely to have been marginal, and to have been outweighed by other changes holding down the share of profits in the economy in the latter half of the 1980s. Nevertheless, the decade has witnessed a boom in securities markets, and the financial sector is continuing to inflate its claims on the profits generated in the productive economy. Those claims may be met and capital accumulation sustained by a redistribution of income between wages and profits. The alternative is either a period of considerable instability in financial markets or a bout of inflation to balance those claims against profits in the economy. History does not manifest itself in exclusive categories: 'muddling through' in some combination of the three alternatives seems most likely in the 1990s.

NOTES

1. These figures, like the other financial statistics given elsewhere in this chapter, need to be treated with some caution. They are rarely an accurate measure of the variables that they are supposed to represent: the restructuring of financial markets that we are discussing here has itself given rise to changes in category definitions, while financial innovation has altered the scope of those categories.
2. *Financial Times*, 22.4.88.
3. A recent article in *Economic Trends* admitted that company profits have been 'consistently over-stated' and that in 1987 they are likely to have risen by 21% rather than the 23% reported. CSO, 1989.

REFERENCES

Asimakopulos, A., 'Kalecki and Keynes on finance, investment and saving', *Cambridge Journal of Economics,* 7 (1983).
Bank of England Quarterly Bulletin, 'Monetary Control – Provisions' (September 1981a).
Bank of England Quarterly Bulletin, 'The Effects of Exchange Control Abolition on Capital Flows' (September 1981b).
Bank of England Quarterly Bulletin, Speech by the Governor of the Bank of England to a Joint Meeting of the Glasgow Discussion Group in Finance and Investment and the Edinburgh–Stirling Finance and Investment Seminar (6 March 1984).
Bank of England Quarterly Bulletin, 'Life Assurance Companies and Private Pension Fund Investment 1962–1984' (December 1986).
Carter, H. and Partington, I., *Applied Economics in Banking and Finance* (Oxford University Press: Oxford, 1984).
Central Statistical Office, 'An investigation into balancing the U.K. national and financial accounts', *Economic Trends* No. 424 (HMSO: London, 1989).
Committee to Review the Functioning of Financial Institutions, *Report* and *Appendices* (The Wilson Report) (Cmnd 7937) (HMSO: London, 1980).
Congdon, T. *Monetary Control in Britain* (Macmillan: London, 1982).
Economists Advisory Group *City 2000: The Future of London as a Financial Centre* (Lafferty Publications: London, 1984).

Financial Times, 25.1.88
Financial Times, 14.3.88
Financial Times, 22.4.88
Financial Times, 28.4.88
Financial Times: Supplement on Venture Capital, 30.11.88
Fine, B. and Harris, L., *The Peculiarities of the British Economy* (Lawrence & Wishart: London, 1985).
Gower, L. C. B., *Review of Investor Protection, Report Part 1* (Cmnd 9125) (HMSO: London, 1984).
Hall, M., *Monetary Policy since 1971: Conduct and Performance* (Macmillan: London, 1983).
Hewlett, N. and Toporowski, J., *All Change in the City: A Report on Recent Changes and Future Prospects in London's Financial Markets* (Economist Publications: London, 1985).
HM Treasury, 'Share Ownership in Britain', *Economic Progress Report* No. 189 (London, March – April 1987).
HM Treasury, 'Share Ownership in Britain' *Economic Progress Report* No. 195 (London, April 1988).
Institute of Manpower Studies, *Create or Abdicate: The City's Human Resource Choice for the 1990s* (Witherby: London, 1988).
Kalecki, M., *Theory of Economic Dynamics* (Allen & Unwin: London, 1954).
Kalecki, M., *Selected Essays on the Dynamics of the Capitalist Economy 1933 – 1970* (Cambridge University Press: Cambridge, 1970).
Kaufman, H., *Interest Rates, The Markets and the New Financial World* (I. B. Taurus: London, 1986).
Llewellyn, D. and Tew, B., 'The Sterling Money Market and the Determination of Interest Rates', *National Westminster Bank Quarterly Review* (May 1988).
Marx, K., *Capital: A Critique of Political Economy Vol. II* (Progress Publishers: Moscow, 1956).
Marx, K., *Capital: A Critique of Political Economy Vol. III* (Progress Publishers: Moscow, 1959).
Mayes, D. G. and Hunn, N., 'The Macro-Economic Effects of Financial Deregulation', *Economic Working Paper* (National Economic Development Office: London, 1987).
Members of the Bankers Clearing House, *Payments Clearing Systems: Review of Organization, Membership and Control* (Banking Information Service: London, 1984).
Minsky, H. P., 'The Financial Instability Hypothesis: A Restatement', *Thames Papers in Political Economy* (Thames Polytechnic: London, 1978).
Minsky, H. P., *Stabilising an Unstable Economy* (Yale University Press: New Haven, 1986).
Reid, M., *All-Change in the City: The Revolution in Britain's Financial Sector* (Macmillan: London, 1988).
Reynolds, P. J., *Political Economy: A Synthesis of Kaleckian and Post-Keynesian Economics* (Harvester Wheatsheaf: Hemel Hempstead, 1988).
Ruffini, P.-B., *Les Banques Multinationales* (Presses Universitaires de France: Paris, 1983).
Sawyer, M., *The Economics of Michal Kalecki* (Macmillan: London, 1985).
Sayers, R. S. (ed.), *Banking in Western Europe* (Oxford University Press: Oxford, 1962).
Toporowski, J., 'The Reform of Financial Markets and Profits in the U.K. Economy: A Kaleckian View' (Mimeo, South Bank Polytechnic, 1989).
Trades Union Congress, *TUC Report on the City* (TUC: London, 1986).

13 MULTINATIONALS AND THE BRITISH ECONOMY

Paul Auerbach

Britain has the distinction, dubious or not, of having become a world class multinational power – as the home of multinationals which invest abroad it is second only to the US, and as a host nation it falls behind only the US and Canada in terms of the stock of foreign investment. In 1988, Britain was the world leader in foreign acquisitions, with an absolute level (£26 billion) four times as high as that of its nearest rivals. It also possessed the highest ratio in the world (34%) of foreign acquisitions to gross domestic fixed capital formation, other large countries having ratios such as 6% (France), 1.3% (the US and Japan) and 1.1% (West Germany) (*Financial Times*, 13.3.89). The impact of inward investment in the UK may be seen in the fact that one in seven workers in manufacturing is employed by a foreign-owned firm.

In the presentation offered here, the multinational is not seen as an isolated phenomenon – a view often taken by the academic industry devoted to the analysis of multinationals[1] – but as part of a host of factors that are making the UK and other countries ever more 'open' and exposed in both industrial and financial matters. The key questions to be confronted are the following: how has this ever-increasing openness shaped the development of British capitalism since 1979, and to what extent has this progressive internationalisation been promoted by the policies of financial liberalisation operating within the UK economy and elsewhere?

13.1 TWO CONTRASTING VIEWS OF MULTINATIONAL DEVELOPMENT

In order to deal with these issues we must first consider the alternative conceptualisations that have been put forth for the multinational phenomenon. The multinational enterprise has been thought to pose particular difficulties for economic orthodoxy. Why indeed should such a phenomenon exist at all? In a world with a free flow of goods and capital and complete information, specialisation on the part of enterprises and countries would take place. There is little room in such a world for the sprawling, trans-national entity. In the familiar terms which are used to justify the existence of the firm itself (Coase, 1937), the multinational only comes forth because of the presence of market imperfections – to preserve an inherent technological, managerial or marketing advantage that might be dissipated through, for instance, licensing. A strong prediction emerging from this 'internalisation' paradigm as exposited by (mainly) British economists is that multinational investment should be concentrated in high technology sectors. Ironically, the strongest counter-example is Britian itself, the second greatest multinational investor, with its concentration on such low technology sectors as tobacco, alcohol and food products.

There is, however, an important element of validity in the internalisation story. In the early part of 1989, for instance, Amstrad, the highly successful UK electronics company, saw its profits fall back sharply (*Financial Times*, 15.2.89). The company's strategy traditionally had been to run a vertically dis-integrated operation – a mere 1,600 employees for £350 million in turnover – by maintaining fierce competition among its Far Eastern sub-contractors. Serious problems with these 'arm's length' arrangements have emerged in the price, availability and quality of semiconductors, and Amstrad is now integrating backward to purchase an equity stake and to form a 'relationship' with at least one US semiconductor supplier; similar moves are also taking place to get more direct control over international distribution of Amstrad's products. We have here an example of the internalisation imperative bearing upon the international firm, as it is forced by failures in the use of the market mechanism to move from existing as a mere international trader to being a true multinational with equity stakes abroad. Furthermore, a great deal of multinational investment through the century and, most specifically, all of the recent market-led multinational investment by Japan in the US and Western Europe has been motivated by a desire to overcome the 'imperfections' posed by the real or potential restrictions on Japanese exports to these areas. In the absence of these restrictions, the present wave of Japanese investment in advanced countries would not have taken place.

But of far greater significance than any of Amstrad's current difficulties is its very existence: dis-integrated international trading companies functioning on the basis of 'arm's length' agreements in countries across the globe for the production of highly sophisticated products are now becoming common-place. A prominent example of this phenomenon may be found in the machine tool industry (see Rendeiro, 1988). The ratio of foreign direct investment to current output for this sector, approximately 4.5 to 5% in the leading OECD countries, is very low relative to other industries (O'Brien, 1987). Even though there have been moves towards limited forms of foreign direct investment, such developments seem to be linked either to the need to surmount protectionism or to complement exports with direct marketing outlets abroad, as several Japanese machine tool firms have done (*Financial Times*, 26.1.89): an, albeit limited, form of direct investment. In other cases, multinational investment and agreements with domestic firms are provoked by governmental restrictions, as in the case of forays by the US giant AT&T into Western Europe, but these acts must be seen in the context of the growing international competitiveness of the telecommunications industry, with the breakup of national monopolies provoking both the desire to expand abroad in the case of AT&T and the willingness of countries to sanction outside investment to maintain international technological standards in the current, more aggressive environment (*Financial Times*, 8, 9.2.89).

The orthodox approach is irrelevant to the historical development of the multinational. At any given moment, a firm may face a choice between exporting and indulging in foreign direct investment. It is relatively trivial to suggest that the greater the market imperfections, the more likely that the firm will internalise the production decision and indulge in a vertically integrated, foreign direct investment solution. When, in the extreme case, no local markets in the relevant services needed by the firm exist, the firm indulges in almost total vertical integration.

The fundamental problem with the internalisation approach is that it skirts over a central historical fact: the great explosion of multinational activity which took place after the Second World War was coincident with an explosion of trade and the lessening of market imperfections of all kinds – the stabilisation of the international monetary system, the introduction of the GATT and a host of other measures. Those very conditions which have been conducive to an expansion of trade have also promoted the growth of multi-national activity. The essential and implicit assumption embodied in the orthodox approach is that the firm, at any point in historical time is making its calculations along the outer frontier of trade-offs between alternative methods of maximising wealth: no possibilities have escaped our Benthamite rational calculator, even in an international context.[2] If the Benthamite firm is led in the direction of multinational activity because it is not confronted with suitably rich market alternatives, this 'market failure' results either from government interference or one of the specific forms of this failure (e.g. the 'public good' aspects surrounding the dissipation of knowledge), legitimated in orthodox economic theory.

Such an approach leaves no room for the kinds of systematic growth and development that have always characterised the world of international investment and trade, most especially in the post-war years. Continuous trans-formations in the skills and ambitions of managers to think in ever broader, more world-wide terms about possibilities for the manufacture and sale of the firm's products, the expanding facilities for transportation, communication and monitoring of these possibilities and the 'demonstration effect' of rivals in the international arena are of far more significance to long run developments than any static decision on whether to 'use the market' or to invest directly in international facilities.

The orthodox tendency to view managerial activity in 'optimising' terms rather than in an historical, relativist perspective is coupled with a belief in the ubiquitous presence of rich markets in all goods and services whenever there is no governmental interference or any specific form of market failure. But rich markets may be absent for other reasons. In many goods and services, markets may be thin simply because of the relatively low level of economic development of the participants in the economic region under consideration. The conventional approach to multinational investment has been taken to have a modicum of plausibility because it appeared to give a satisfactory explanation of a phenomenon at a particular historical disjuncture: many post-war multinationals, especially those from the US, seemed to function at exceptionally high levels of vertical integration, bringing with them their own home-based resources even for marketing and finance. This was taken as the response of those firms able to 'internalise' – the multinational was a triumph of vertical integration.

Of course, it was no such thing. It was a response to the fact that in the immediate post-war world, even in Western Europe, there were few domestic infrastructures – industrial, financial or in marketing which American multi-nationals felt could fulfil their needs. But vertical integration is not the magic 'key' to the multinational, as so many contemporary writers believe.

There is, certainly, an important sense in which the multinational has continued to develop as a 'planned' entity. Sophisticated multinationals such as Ford and IBM have been progressing from the running of collections of 'truncated replicas' in Western Europe to carefully planned, specialised and co-ordinated roles for their various subsidiaries as part of European and world-wide strategies. This is a fact of central significance for the UK, as the country finds itself the host of specialised facilities which are mere cogs in the grand strategies of giant firms.[3] These circumstances may yield possible advantages in leverage for domestic labour groups, when a stoppage at Ford in the UK in 1988 could close down internationally integrated production. (The stoppage itself was engendered by Ford's attempt to introduce work rules analogous to those of Nissan, its multinational rival in Britain.) This fragmentation of production at a national level may well be a cause for disillusionment about British pretensions to world class status in certain sectors, as it finds itself not with whole industries, but mere specialised 'bits' of, for instance, the car and computer industries. The growth of international integration, however, has been tempered by the fashion emerging from Japanese firms for tight 'just-in-time'-type inventory controls and quality monitoring of suppliers, which constrains the extent of geographical dispersion in many industries and demonstrates that growing sophistication within firms will not necessarily register as increases in cross-border production.

But a far more significant fact countervailing against the growth of cross-border vertical integration is the fact that growing sophistication has not been a phenomenon exclusive to the multinationals, but has affected *all* firms and institutions, and therefore the 'markets' which are created by the activities of these firms and institutions. These rich economic infrastructures have progressively become more widely dispersed and are no longer the almost exclusive domain of the US, as they appeared to be in the immediate post-war period. By the early 1970s, manufacturing and resource-based multinationals setting up in Western Europe had been followed by a 'second wave' of supporting companies such as component suppliers, financial institutions, including such lesser manifestations as the growth of international factoring (bill collecting and paperwork), which are of special interest to smaller firms (*Financial Times*, 24.1.89) and advertising agencies. 'Do-it-yourself' activities become less of a necessity for multinational enterprises attempting to function at a world class level, as they may use financial, marketing and other infrastructures across the world when it seems advantageous to do so.

Thus, as can be seen in Britain and even more dramatically in economies such as South Korea, the multinational has been the key device for the diffusion of managerial technique (and 'efficient' labour relations, a price often extracted by multinationals as a condition of entry), thereby accelerating the level of competition in the world economy. Indeed, the success with which Japanese multinationals have inculcated their own standards of quality control and on-time delivery to domestic suppliers may be one of the most significant side effects of their investment in Britain.

The opposite line of causation also holds: not only does multinational activity promote competition, but an increasingly competitive environment has helped to engender multinational activity. Inter-war cartels, by cutting up the world into economic spheres of interest, inhibited not only international trade in the industries affected, but international investment as well. In the post-war world, earlier phases of multinational activity, especially from the US, were often characterised by a 'product life cycle' model: once products had been fully exploited in the US, they were fobbed off to the rest of the world. The present, more competitive environment encourages international investment, as it pressurises firms' managements to think about simultaneous world-wide distribution and sales of new goods, either as uniform 'world products' or, more likely, as modified for the specific needs of national markets before any 'competitive advantages' are snapped up by rivals. Further pressures in this direction result from the 'supply side': the need to amortise as broadly and as quickly as possible the (ever increasing) fixed costs of marketing new products in many industries, and the need for giant firms once secure in the computer, telecommunications and car industries to merge both within and across national boundaries, and/or to make international cross-border links (e.g. joint ventures) to preserve or extend their technological, marketing or other capabilities in this atmosphere of greater international competitiveness.

Policies and Agencies for Modernisation

There are thus two alternative approaches to multinational development – an orthodox one which emphasises the role of the multinational in surmounting market failure, and an evolutionist one in which the expansion of business horizons dictates that the developing richness and 'perfection' of markets is a process complementing multinational expansion rather than countervailing against it.

The evolutionist approach perceives multinational evolution in ways which significantly contradict orthodoxy: first, the multinational is viewed in the context of complementary developments, and not as an isolated phenomenon. Those very factors which are conducive to the developing richness of markets will also promote multinational expansion; secondly, as market imperfections lessen, as with the moves towards European integration in 1992, the orthodox approach logically must presume a tendency towards a lessening of multinational activity, at least from firms based within the Community. Indeed, an existent conundrum in the orthodox multinational literature is the fact that the Treaty of Rome of 1957 was followed by a significant expansion in intra-Community trade *and* investment. Contrarily, from the evolutionist perspective, it is predicted that international economic activity of all kinds – trade, including intra-industry trade, a result which stands in contradiction to orthodox theory (Greenway, 1988), joint ventures and agreements and multinational investment are likely to increase with growing integration, the investment in many cases merely intended as an 'opening' for exports in markets habituated to using local suppliers. British Steel is the relatively rare case of foreign investment being so motivated from the British side (see *Financial Times*, 27.1.89). In other cases, international investment is promoted by those very kinds of financial and legal uniformity which also facilitate international trade. And contrary to the orthodox perception of the multinational as evidence of 'the growing significance of hierarchical advantages' (Dunning, 1983), the evolutionist perspective predicts the presence of an ever-increasing number of smaller, dis-integrated multinational firms alongside continuing developments in the sophistication of the operations of mature multinational firms.

13.2 BRITISH OUTWARD MULTINATIONAL INVESTMENT

Britain has functioned as a major international investor since the latter part of the nineteenth century. It is commonplace to emphasise that the forms of portfolio investment which were used in this period may be distinguished from foreign direct investment, in which direct managerial influence may be evidenced. While such a distinction is relevant to the managerial analyst, since direct investment implies a level of managerial commitment to foreign activities, it is of less significance from the point of view of its effects on the home nation's fiscal affairs, since in both cases there is a present outflow of funds as a result of the investment coupled with a prospect of future returns which may or may not be repatriated. Many analysts believe that Britain's commitment to overseas activities in the period before World War I denuded the country's industrial and infrastructural developments: such an interpretation of past events informs contemporary discussions on both British portfolio and direct investment (see Rowthorn and Wells, 1987).

The present debates concerning the role of de-industrialisation and Britain's foreign direct investment in the present period are solely concerned with its possibly negative balance of payments effects: unlike the earlier period, there is little chance that British multinationals will be dissipating its precious technological secrets to the rest of the world, for in the current period its multinationals are, as noted, of a definitively 'low tech' variety, with the exception of specific sectors such as chemicals and pharmaceuticals. A difficulty with having multinationals concentrated in, for instance, consumer products and in services is that compared to industries such as electronics and machinery they perform their services locally and do not feed back with substantial technological or export advantages for the home country: from a domestic British perspective, they might as well be portfolio investments. Even so, on one estimate one-quarter of British export flows would not have been possible without an investment presence overseas (Stopford and Turner, 1985, chapter 7). In the case of ICI, its director of research and technology forecasts that the firm in the future will invest more heavily in research outside Britain 'not because the UK is an unsuitable place to do research, but because we need to be working with scientists in countries like the US and Japan if we are to be part of their society' (*Financial Times*, 31.1.89); it is to be doubted whether the apparent past success of outward direct investment by ICI (Britain's largest exporter in 1987) in stimulating domestic economic activity can be taken as typical of other firms and industries in the UK.

On the whole, the record of British direct investment in the twentieth century closely tracks the general performance record of British business in this period: it has been mindless and slothful. Both in the inter-war and the post-war period until the early 1960s, foreign direct investment was dominated by the Commonwealth, the same region in which secured, uncompetitive markets were present for exports of British goods; only in 1971 did investment flows to Western Europe move ahead of those to Commonwealth countries. Then, on the verge of EEC entry, a surge of involvement in Western Europe raised the share of outward investment flows to almost 50%. But, by the early 1980s, this share had fallen below 10% again (while 50% went to the US).

The cultural, legal and linguistic obstacles to investment on the Continent came to be treated as insurmountable. Obstacles for British business to investing in Western Europe were sometimes a reflection of conditions in Britain: since such a large part of British overseas direct investment has taken the form of takeovers, legal and institutional barriers on the Continent to this form of industrial expansion prove more inhibiting for the British than, for instance, for the Japanese. Current moves in the direction of financial and capital market liberalisation on the Continent and the prospects for 1992 have promoted merger activity, and indeed British acquisition expenditure in the EEC was at an all-time high in 1988.

But even with prospective liberalisation in the EC, little serious movement can be seen in the direction of exploiting British advantages in marketing, finance and other areas over their Continental rivals: British firms have perferred to invest in the US, a country whose currency has for many years been notoriously volatile and whose sophistication in the very areas where British companies are strong dictates that substantial unexploited rents are unlikely to be revealed. Thus, for the UK from 1986 to 1988, the ratio of the value of outward to inward acquisitions has been three to one, with 80% of the outward acquisitions directed to the US (*Bank of England Quarterly Bulletin*, 1989). The record £32.5 billion spent in the UK in 1988 was equivalent to 4.5% of its GDP and 4.7% of its total stock market capitalisation (*Business Week*, 13.2.89).

While some British investors in the US such as Hanson Trust have been manifestly successful, the continued, even increased popularity of British investment in the US has to be seen in the context of the fact that, as a whole, foreign investments in the US gained average rates of return ranging between 6 and 13% from 1975 to 1981, but only ranging between 1.5 and 6% from 1982 to 1987 (*Fortune*, 13.2.89).[4] It may be conjectured on the basis of this (limited) evidence that the return on British acquisition is poor: such an outcome would be well in line with the 'disappointing' performance of British acquisitions domestically (see Meeks, 1977). If this be the case, then the search for the motivations of British firms in foreign direct investment may have to go outside the boundaries of the rational choice methodology of the internalisation paradigm and explore other, less salubrious explanations such as the managerial (Mueller, 1969) and exchange rate (Aliber, 1970) motivations for these trans-national acquisitions.

Have policy decisions taken since 1979 made a decisive difference on the flow of outward investment? It is usually suggested that while the lifting of exchange controls for portfolio investment in 1979 opened the floodgates for an outflow of funds (see Toporowski, Table 12.2, this volume), foreign direct investment had never been constrained by existing regulations and in the period subsequent to the lifting of exchange controls did not exceed levels already reached in the early 1970s. But note that the rise in the deficit in foreign direct investment since the mid 1980s has been more substantial than it was formerly, a fact which may be partially attributable to leakage from portfolio funds freed from exchange controls after 1979. (When Sir Gordon White of Hanson Trust originally came to the US on his acquisitions quest, he was restricted to the $3,000 he had been allowed to take out of Britain under currency controls.)

Britain has run rising deficits on both the direct and portfolio capital accounts of the balance of payments throughout this period. The claim has been made (Stopford and Turner, 1985, chapter 7) that when net income inflows and royalties from the stock of past direct investments (including the assumption that one-quarter of British exports are linked to direct investments) are added to the deficit on the capital account, the overall balance of payments effect of outward foreign direct investment is positive through 1983, and when updated, through 1987.[5] Furthermore, given the unimaginative mentality of British capitalists described above, it could be argued that the investment funds of such firms would not have been used more productively or indeed had a more favourable effect on the balance of payments if these firms (otherwise unconstrained) were forced to use these funds 'at home' through some (governmental) administrative measure.

Such arguments are far from decisive. The flow of income from past investments should be thought of as irrelevant to current decisions, and it is not surprising that the inflows from such a substantial accumulation of investments overwhelm current outflows. Even if one believes that domestic capitalists and nationalised industries were incapable of earning higher *commercial* returns on investment than were earned abroad, there is still a question to answer: could the net deficits on the capital account, inflated by oil revenues, have been used more beneficially for investments in the *social* productivity of the domestic economy – in education and in social and physical infrastructure? If so, the apparently higher returns to investment abroad can be seen as merely self-fulfilling prophecy, in which the deprived domestic social environment inevitably sees its 'productivity' deteriorate *vis-à-vis* its foreign competitors.

13.3 INWARD MULTINATIONAL INVESTMENT

Britain has for a long time been 'lucky' as a host of multinational investment. Among Ford's multinational investments before World War I, only the one in Britain was a full fledged commitment, one that managed to transform the state of the domestic industry through its effect on its rivals and permit Britain to function as a world class car producer. In the post-war world, Britain has received a disproportionate amount of first US (an absolute majority of US investments until 1956), and then Japanese investment. These disproportions are especially notable in the context of an economy growing far more slowly than its Continental rivals and, no less importantly, having a currency which throughout much of the period has appeared to possess significant 'downside risk'. The favourable US attitude changed somewhat with signing of the Treaty of Rome and the move to full convertibility on the Continent but, following Britain's entry into the EEC, it once again became a gateway to Western Europe for the US, with Britain still possessing almost one-third of the stock of US investment as of the early 1980s. The reliance by Britain on the US as a source of direct investment continued until recently to be substantial, with US firms investing £1.4, £2.3 and £1.3 billion in the years 1984 to 1986, while the totals from the world as a whole in this period were –£0.25, £4.1 and £4.1 billion, respectively (Department of Trade and Industry, 1986, Table 4.1). Note, however, that in the period 1986 to 1988, the value of disposals in the UK by US companies exceeded acquisitions; over half the acquisition expenditure in the UK in this period came from developed countries outside the EC and North America, such as Switzerland and Australia (*Bank of England Quarterly Bulletin*, 1989).

The Japanese preference for Britain is particularly striking: in the 18 months up to September 1988, Britain attracted nearly four times as much Japanese investment as West Germany, Italy and France combined (*Business Week*, 20.2.89). The stock of Japanese foreign direct investment is still small (less than 10% of the book value of all direct investments in the UK), but this fact is of less significance than certain qualitative aspects of this investment – its use of 'greenfield' sites rather than acquisition as a means of investment, its role in sectors such as electronics and cars, where the domestic presence is weak, and the fact that the investment brings along with it Japanese managerial and labour practices, as well as manufacturing procedures.

The dominant reason for Britain's popularity is almost too simple to be believed: the English language. Japanese firms also cite the presence of a skilled work force and low wage bills as subsidiary reasons (*Financial Times*, 23.1.89). UK labour costs (gross hourly wages, benefits and social costs) in the car industry are, along with those in Spain, the lowest in Western Europe by a significant margin, and British car workers labour (including overtime) the greatest number of hours per year (*Financial Times*, 24.2.89; it is unclear whether these rankings are indicative of the situation in industry as a whole: see *Business Week*, 13.3.89). For many US firms, especially in the early post-war years and for those firms venturing into Western Europe for the first time, the linguistic links as well as the cultural and legal parallels made business easy to do in the UK. The strength makes itself felt as well for Japanese and other firms: it is said that Japanese multinational executives in France conduct business with their French underlings in English.

The weight of inward investment in the UK economy is undeniable (as we have noted earlier, one in seven workers in manufacturing is employed by a foreign company), as is the overall beneficial nature of this investment for British capitalism. Some questions can perhaps be raised about the resources expended by this and other nations' governments to attract this investment: it was alleged that Hoffman–La Roche received £350,000 of public money for every permanent job created at a vitamin factory in Scotland (Young *et al.*, 1988), and the roles that can and should be played by host governments to regulate this investment. Yet the industrial activity in the UK surrounding cars (with 55% of the production foreign owned), North Sea oil and Scottish electronics (which employs more people in albeit relatively low technology enterprises than any two of the three traditional industries, coal, shipbuilding and steel) would barely exist on the basis of domestic resources. Even such 'domestic' stalwarts as GEC have their origins in foreign investment.

Foreign entrants have also been crucial to the stimulation of the use of contemporary methods of management. The supermarket would eventually have come to Britain in any case, but there is little doubt that multinational entry (Canada's Fine Fare and Safeway from the US) speeded the development through the 'emulation effect'. Unlike the car industry, the major participants in British (food and other) retailing remain domestically owned, the stimulative effect of the entrants helping to make the sector an exceptionally strong one by West European standards.

There is some truth in the notion that multinationals have often used Britain for assemblage operations, with many of the jobs created part-time and peripheral, and with research facilities consigned to the home country or to other centres. Such a happenstance is unsurprising, given the infrastructural weaknesses clearly evident in British manufacturing industry as a whole. An exception 'proves the rule': the strength of British manufacturers in pharmaceuticals is complemented by a substantial multinational presence pursuing research projects in this country; of the 30 largest pharmaceutical companies in the world in 1982, 23 have research and development facilities in the US, 16 in the UK, 11 in France, 7 in West Germany and 7 in Italy. Yet in the car industry, foreign multinationals have moved research away from the UK, and this is typical of many industries (Cantwell, 1988).

13.4 1992

Britain has to be seen as a stopping point for many firms in a growing internationalisation of capital which, in the industrial sphere, has several major tendencies. First, there is the continuing growth in the sophistication of the major existent vertically integrated firms, which both desire and feel the necessity to allocate their multinational investment in an 'optimal' manner. This development implies that host countries will find themselves in competition with a broader range of countries than heretofore: even relatively sophisticated production and assemblage operations can be shifted to Southeast Asia if conditions in Western Europe are inappropriate. (The lowering of the labour content of many of these operations and the shifts to 'just-in-time' manufacturing procedures has, however, reduced the incentive for firms to shift away from their large markets in Western Europe.)

An equally significant development, one which has been obscured by the 'multinational as the overcoming of market imperfections' literature, is the growth of vertically disintegrated multinational trade which takes advantage of growing market richness for the purchase of necessary inputs, including the growing sophistication of international financial operations. Many of these developments have taken place in the financial services sector, an area which has made a major and growing contribution to the domestic balance of payments. Here the extremely liberal regulatory atmosphere since 1979 may have made a contribution to the promotion of the domestic 'industry' in financial services. For Britain, non-manufacturing industry is dominant in foreign direct investment, accounting for two-thirds of outward activity and three-fifths of inflows.

Cross-border mergers register as multinational investment, whatever their initial cause. It is difficult to generalise about some of the motives which are now central (e.g., the desire of firms outside the EC to 'leap over' barriers which will emerge in 1992; the myopia of British firms, which directs their investment to the US), but two factors are distinctive. First is the general liberalisation of domestic capital markets which is taking place in many countries, even Japan, and which facilitates multinational investment, either in the form of merger or 'greenfield' investment. (This includes multinational 'investment' by Japanese investment houses.)

Secondly, there is the growing merger activity within the EC in preparation for the projected liberalisation of trade in 1992. This is a highly predictable development: increases in actual or expected competitiveness (witness the industrial reorganisations in Britain in response to post-war competition) commonly result in the desire to integrate to realise supposed economies of scale, in this case at a world class level. For the EC, this phenomenon poses genuine policy conundrums: 'If the EC leans towards trying to preserve competition inside Europe, it may well be to the advantage of US or Japanese multinationals' (*Business Week*, 6.2.89), this at a time when European Community 'champions' are eager to use acquisition as part of their strategy for matching the size and scope of their international rivals. Furthermore, US and Japanese multinationals are in many cases the likely beneficiaries 'if Europe's hodgepodge of product specifications were standardised' (*Business Week*, 12.12.88). The increasing number of joint ventures and other kinds of links with both EC and non EC partners will not register as multinational production, but emerge from the same desire to respond to an increasingly competitive environment.

The need for massive conglomeration inside the EC to realise scale economies can easily be exaggerated. But in electronics, for instance, it is widely believed that West European firms are too small to compete on a world-wide basis for the development of new technologies in telecommunications, and this belief has been a major motivation (and excuse) for the games of merger musical chairs in 1988 and 1989 between Siemens, GEC and Plessey (as well as non-EC firms such as AT&T). Deficiencies in semiconductor production in Western Europe (only Philips ranks in the top ten world-wide, with 28% of the production of the leader, NEC of Japan) are thought to threaten the future viability of the whole electronics industry; joint research projects, sometimes sponsored at the governmental or EC level (e.g. the JESSI project), are thus attempts to respond to the competitive environment, which is perceived in world-wide rather than West European terms.

In other cases, mergers eliminate capacity which has only existed up to the present by grace of an uncompetitive environment, as in the case of the West European power engineering industry (*Financial Times,* 20.1.89). Whether for good or ill, the shopkeepers and middle-sized retail outlets which still hold 80% of retail sales in the southern part of Western Europe are bound to be either driven out of business or swallowed up in merger by the hypermarkets of France and West Germany. British retail firms would also be well placed for expansion on the Continent if they could be bothered.

13.5 CONCLUSIONS

Britain has done remarkably well in recent years for a nation whose industrial base has deteriorated seriously in a 'negative' way (see Rowthorn and Wells, 1987). For various fortuitous reasons, multinationals have come to Britain and implanted world class manufacturing and other facilities in a society where, with few exceptions, 'large' organisations (i.e. those having more than 5,000 employees) have not proved internationally competitive. This widely quoted '5,000 rule' may emerge from difficulties deep in national singularities at the level of management technique and of labour relations, but may be more directly attributed to the problems of a nation which is now vastly under-skilled and under-educated compared with its presumptive competitors. It may be ruefully suggested that given these structural realities and the attitudes that engender them, it is much to the advantage of British capital to find itself part of as 'open' an economy as possible. If this be the case, then a possible argument in favour of the freeing of exchange controls in 1979, even in spite of its otherwise negative consequences, may be that it promoted British capital by enhancing the perceived 'solidity' of the British currency in the eyes of potential multinational investors.

On the whole, however, no specific governmental policy since 1979 has been decisive in promoting this indubitably beneficial inward multinational investment (Young *et al.,* chapter 6); the incentives offered by various governments competing against each other are generally held to be self-cancelling. The main way in which British governmental action since 1979 has enticed multinational entry has been to transform the reputation of the British labour force from one which is particulary 'difficult' to one relatively pliable with regard to wages and especially working practices through the creation of mass unemployment. Ford, however, still thinks it will be easier to introduce a 24-hour, three-shift system in Belgium than in the UK (*Financial Times,* 30.1.89).

The government's freeing of exchange controls in 1979, however, has promoted outward foreign direct and portfolio investment, most directly the latter, which has siphoned off the wealth gains of North Sea oil into overseas investments in a superficially productive way. The possibilities for domestic social renewal now seem lost forever. The prospective decline in North Sea revenues and the growing moves internationally towards capital flow liberalisation indicate that Britain will have to continue to rely on its 'lucky' positioning in the world of international capital flows rather than taking any decisive steps to redirect resources based in this country.

Some readers, fearing the loss of domestic control over the national economy, may question the 'indubitable beneficial effects' of foreign ownership of domestic resources. But does it in fact matter whether or not the companies for which the British population works are 'native' or not? Domestic British firms, as we have seen, have a high propensity to invest and reinvest their earnings abroad, and the experience with sanctions in Southern Africa demonstrates that a government's influence even on their 'own' multinationals may be of a very limited kind, either because of the government's lack of leverage or of the ability of the domestically based multinational to bear influence on that government which is supposedly regulating it. Contrarily, foreign firms like IBM (Britain's third largest exporter) often feel constrained to proceed with some rule (e.g. making the level of production in a country proportionate to its sales there) which limits any perceived damage of the multinational's presence in the host country. With multinational giants such as IBM, Toyota and their West European equivalents thinking more than ever before in global terms, we may be emerging into an era in which all the old slogans about capitalism as an international system are more fully realised than ever before. In such a situation, the European Community may emerge as the minimum unit in which it is possible to speak about the regulation and control of multinationals, and indeed of all of international economic activity.

NOTES

1. It is perhaps a bit churlish to complain of this 'industry' here, given the extensive use made here of these sources. Representative of the works used are Young *et al.*, 1988; Shepherd *et al.*, 1985 and Stopford and Turner, 1985. Dunning, 1988 contains an elaboration and a bibliography of the 'internalisation paradigm' to be discussed below.

2. This assumption is particularly inappropriate at present in many cross-border contexts. In the West European domestic appliances industry 'the quality of information is disparate. In the course of the research, we found many examples of senior managers who did not know in detail what investments (and their cost consequences) had been made by foreign competitors ... This problem of unequal information and strategic intelligence does not seem to apply within countries; it is a product of internationality' (Stopford and Baden-Fuller, 1988, p. 82).

3. Note, however, that 'it is by no means clear that the trend is one way. Persistent differences in national income levels and taste, combined with changing economics of supply as more flexible manufacturing systems are introduced, can halt and even reverse the trend' (Stopford and Boden-Fuller, 1988, p. 15).
4. The graph from which these figures are drawn seems to ignore any effects from exchange rate movements and has no accompanying explanation or detailing of sources.
5. A task not made easier by the lack of precision in the text on how the data were calculated.

REFERENCES

Aliber, R., 'A Theory of Foreign Direct Investment', in *The International Corporation* (ed. Kindleberger, C.) (MIT: Cambridge, Mass., 1970).
Baden-Fuller, C. and J. Stopford, 'Why Global Manufacturing?' *Multinational Business,* **1**, Spring, 15–25 (1988).
Bank of England Quarterly Bulletin, 'Takeover Activity in the 1980s', **29**, 1, 78–85 (1989).
Business Week, 12.12.88.
Business Week, 6.2.89.
Business Week, 13.2.89.
Business Week, 20.2.89.
Business Week, 13.3.89.
Cantwell, J., 'The Reorganization of European Industries After Integration: Selected Evidence on the Role of Multinational Enterprises', in *Multinationals and the European Community* (eds Dunning, J. and Robson, P.) (Blackwell: Oxford, 1988).
Coase, R., 'The Nature of the Firm', *Economica* New Series **IV**, 386–405 (1937).
Department of Trade and Industry *Business Monitor,* MA4 (1986).
Dunning, J., 'Changes in the Level and Structure of International Production: the Last One Hundred Years' in *The Growth of International Business* (ed. Casson, M.) (George Allen: London, 1983).
Dunning, J., *Explaining International Production* (Unwin Hyman: London, 1988).
Financial Times, 20.1.89.
Financial Times, 23.1.89.
Financial Times, 24.1.89.
Financial Times, 26.1.89.
Financial Times, 27.1.89.
Financial Times, 30.1.89.
Financial Times, 31.1.89.
Financial Times, 8.2.89.
Financial Times, 9.2.89.
Financial Times, 15.2.89.
Financial Times, 24.2.89.
Financial Times, 13.3.89.
Fortune, 13.2.89.
Greenway, D., 'Intra-Industry Trade, Intra-Firm Trade and European Integration: Evidence, Gains and Policy Aspects', in *Multinationals and the European Community* (eds Dunning, J. and Robson, P.) (Blackwell: Oxford, 1988).
United Kingdom Balance of Payments (HMSO: London, 1988).
Meeks, G., *Disappointing Marriage: A Study of the Gains From Merger* (Cambridge University Press: Cambridge, 1977).

Mueller, D., 'A Theory of Conglomerate Mergers', *Quarterly Journal of Economics*, Vol. 83 (November 1969).

O'Brien, P., 'Machine Tools: Growing Internationalisation in a Small Firm Industry', *Multinational Business*, 2, Summer, 23–34 (1987).

Rendeiro, J., 'Technical Change and Vertical Disintegration in Global Competition: Lessons from Machine Tools', in *Strategies in Global Competition* (eds Hood, N. and Vahlne, J.) (Croom Helm: London, 1988).

Rowthorn, R. and Wells, J., *De-Industrialization and Foreign Trade* (Cambridge University Press: Cambridge 1987).

Shepherd, D., Silberston, A. and Strange, R., *British Manufacturing Investment Overseas* (Methuen: London, 1985).

Stopford, J. and Baden-Fuller, C., 'Regional-Level Competition in a Mature Industry: the Case of European Domestic Appliances', in *Multinationals and the European Community* (eds Dunning, J. and Robson, P.) (Blackwell: Oxford, 1988).

Stopford, J. and Turner, L., *Britain and the Multinationals* (Wiley: Chichester, 1985).

Young, S., Hood, N. and Hamill, J., *Foreign Multinationals and the British Economy* (Croom Helm: London, 1988).

PART V

THATCHERISM IN HISTORICAL PERSPECTIVE

14 THE THATCHER REVOLUTION

Bob Rowthorn

During the decade since Margaret Thatcher became Prime Minister, her rule has been marked by a determination and ruthlessness without equal in modern Britain. She has pursued a relentless crusade against socialism and all its manifestations, vigorously promoting her harsh philosophy of individualism and self-help, while dismantling the collectivist legacy inherited from earlier governments. Much of the country's nationalised industries and public housing stock have already been sold off to the private sector, and further disposals are in the pipeline. Throughout the economy there has been a single-minded pursuit of de-regulation and promotion of market forces. In the sphere of industrial policy, the already somewhat limited role of the state in strategically shaping long-term economic development has been largely abandoned. Instead, this task has been assigned almost entirely to the automatic mechanisms of competition and the market. Taken as a whole, these measures amount to a virtual revolution. Many well-established institutions and procedures have been either swept away or transformed almost beyond recognition. Others are about to suffer the same fate. The revolution is not over yet.

In its early years, the Thatcher government presided over the worst industrial recession in British history. During the period 1979–81, this recession decimated Britain's manufacturing base, laid waste whole regions of the country and threw millions out of work. Her harsh social policies have condemned millions to a life of poverty and insecurity. Yet for most of the past decade her government has enjoyed considerable support and held a commanding lead in the public opinion polls over a confused and divided opposition. A major factor behind this popularity has been the impressive recovery experienced by the British economy over the past few years. Output has grown almost continuously since 1982 and there has been a spectacular increase in productivity. The scars of the preceding recession still remain, many parts of the country are still virtually derelict and the number of people

I should like to thank Wendy Carlin, Andrew Glyn, Geoff Harcourt and Paul Seabright for their comments on an earlier draft of this chapter.

unemployed or in poverty is still enormous. But these people are in the minority. For a majority of the population economic recovery has brought security and rising incomes. It has also created in many quarters a feeling of optimism, indeed euphoria, about Britain's future. This euphoria has been punctured recently by fears about Britain's mushrooming trade deficit and rising interest rates, and government popularity may now be on the wane. Even so, it still retains a great deal of support.

The duration and obvious dynamism of the British recovery has been widely hailed, both at home and abroad, as an economic miracle. The Thatcher revolution, it is said, has reversed Britain's long-term decline and set the country on a Japanese-style growth path. Indeed, one of Thatcher's main advisors, Alan Walters, has written a book entitled *Britain's Economic Renaissance* (1986).[1] This claim is, in my view, grossly exaggerated and in the following pages I shall explain why. I shall concentrate mainly on the manufacturing sector, for it is this sector which has performed so badly in the past, and upon which the future prosperity of the country above all depends. It is also the sector where the impact of Thatcherism is allegedly so miraculous. To say this is not to denigrate the role of services. Services are clearly of great importance and they play a major role in the modern British economy, but they cannot conceivably compensate for serious weaknesses in the manufacturing sector. Without a strong manufacturing sector the country will face chronic balance of payments difficulties, its long-run growth will be severely constrained and unemployment will remain unacceptably high for the indefinite future.[2] Moreover, the performance of the service sector in Britain has always been quite strong, and few people seriously claim that there has been a miraculous improvement in this sector under the Thatcher regime.

14.1 GENERAL OBSERVATIONS

Before considering in detail what has happened under the Thatcher regime, I should make two points clear. The first concerns my attitude towards this regime. As a socialist, I am naturally hostile towards the Thatcherites and much of what they stand for – their blatant promotion of privilege and greed, their indifference to the needs of the weak and dispossessed. At the same time, however, I must recognise that many of the changes they have made were genuinely needed – not, perhaps, in the specific form actually implemented by the Thatcherites, but certainly in some form. Many of the old collectivist institutions and habits were profoundly conservative and increasingly out of touch with modern realities. Some kind of shake-up was needed. Nationalised industries like coal and steel, for example, were extremely inefficient and grossly unprofitable. Something eventually had to be done about them. The Thatcherite solution was to close down many plants and coal-mines and sack or prematurely retire over half the workforce. This caused enormous suffering, since the communities affected were often geographically isolated and virtually no attempt was made to provide alternative work. However, the Thatcherites did at least face up to the problem. It would be comforting to believe that a Labour government would have done things differently, eliminating loss-making capacity and overmanning, of course, but also ensuring the simultaneous provision of new jobs for those displaced. However, given the hostility of many trade unions to restructuring, and the poor record of the 1974–9 Labour government in this area, the most likely outcome would have been paralysis, with the problem of overmanning and unprofitability festering on indefinitely.

Trade union reform provides another example of where change was required. For years critics had been pointing to the undemocratic nature of Britain's trade union movement, and there was a groundswell of dissatisfaction amongst union members with the situation. Yet calls for reform were ignored, especially by the Left-wing establishment in the unions, who thought that more democracy would reduce their influence. This belief was shared by the Thatcher government, who imposed new rules and procedures on the unions in the hope that this would break the power of the Left. In the event, the Left survived and is still quite powerful. But the lesson is obvious. With the Labour movement unable to put its own house in order, the Thatcherites could take the initiative and impose reforms on the unions. Not only was the nature of these reforms less than ideal, but the whole process helped to discredit the unions and was an important propaganda victory for the government.

My second point concerns the objectives of the Thatcher revolution.[3] This revolution is often perceived in narrowly economic terms, as a crusade for efficiency and for the revitalisation of an ailing British economy. These are certainly important goals, but they are not the most fundamental aspect of Thatcherism. The Thatcher revolution is above all a *counter*-revolution, whose primary aim has always been to turn the clock back and reverse the tide of collectivism, which at one time seemed to be engulfing the country. The victory of Thatcherism inside the Tory Party during the 1970s and the defeat of the consensus-oriented old guard was partly due to an internal shift in the balance of power – the rising strength of what might be loosely called *petit bourgeois* forces within this Party and the declining influence of the traditional upper classes. It also reflected widespread alarm throughout the Tory Party about the long-term political implications of increasing trade union power combined with growing state intervention in the economy. Many believed that, pushed to its logical conclusion, this combination would lead to the eventual destruction of capitalism in Britain and the effective socialisation of the economy. Reversing this trend became their overriding goal, to be given priority over all other objectives.

The Thatcher government pursued its basic goal on a number of levels. Its first aim was to weaken and demobilise the forces of organised labour. This was achieved in stages through a string of ever more stringent legal restrictions on the activities of trade unions, and a series of confrontations culminating in the mid-1980s in the brutal repression of protesting miners and printworkers. Since then, the trade union movement has been fairly quiescent. The government's longer-run aim is to consolidate these victories and prevent the re-emergence of the vanquished enemy. This is to be achieved through an ambitious programme of social engineering, designed both to discredit socialist ideas and create a web of personal interests hostile to socialism. Collective institutions of every kind – nationalised industries, public housing, public transport, the welfare state – have all been mercilessly attacked for inefficiency, poor quality, lack of choice and bureaucracy. In every case the remedy for these alleged defects has been the same – privatisation. Much of the public sector has been sold off to private individuals, often at well below its true value. Public services like transport, health and education have been deliberately starved of funds so as to encourage the growth of private alternatives. British experience is not, of course, entirely unique in this area. Privatisation of public assets and activities has occurred to some degree in most Western countries over the past decade. But nowhere has it been pursued with anything like the single-mindedness witnessed in Britain during these years. This single-mindedness is a direct result of the fact that privatisation is no mere economic policy for the Thatcher government, but is the cornerstone of a political strategy whose aim is to make socialism impossible, indeed unthinkable, in modern Britain.

In some cases, of course, Thatcherite criticisms of the public sector have been quite justified, and privatisation an appropriate remedy. The sale of council house to their occupants is, perhaps, an example.[4] For the most part, however, criticisms have been either grossly exaggerated or, where correct, there has been no evidence that privatisation would bring a significant improvement. This is most obvious in the case of nationalised industries, where the general rule has been that only *profitable* enterprises are privatised. Unprofitable enterprises are normally kept in the public sector while they are restructured and made financially viable. Only later, when they have been made efficient and profitable, are they sold off to the private sector. This procedure makes nonsense of the claim that privatisation is designed to increase efficiency. Its aim is fundamentally political – to discredit the idea of public ownership and create such a highly privatised and fragmented economy that socialism, as traditionally conceived at least, becomes virtually unthinkable. The same motivation can be seen in Thatcherite policy towards the Welfare State. Wherever possible, collective provision is being phased out and replaced by private provision – private pensions, private or semi-private schools, private health and so on. As always, the justification is efficiency or freedom of choice, but the fundamental reason is political. It is to undermine collective consciousness and create a vast reservoir of atomised individuals, whose interests and perceptions make them hostile or simply indifferent to socialist aims and policies. Such an approach is not only extremely inegalitarian. It is often also very inefficient. Nowhere is this more clear than in the case of transport, where public facilities of all kinds – buses, metros, railways – are deliberately starved of funds with the aim of forcing people to use motor cars and other forms of private transport. This has enormous costs in terms of congestion, noise and pollution. But in ideological terms it serves once again to promote individualism and discredit the notion of collective provision.

The strategy just outlined has so far been very successful. Many collectivist solutions, which ten years ago seemed both practical and desirable, now seem hopelessly archaic. This is not, of course, universally the case. For example, there has been strong opposition to government plans to privatise the National Health Service and it has been forced to back down, for the time being at least. This particular form of collective provision remains extremely popular. Potentially, there is also considerable support for renewed investment in public transport, especially in metropolitan areas where services are run down and road congestion is acute. But these are the exception. Overall, the Thatcherites have been remarkably successful in discrediting collectivist ideas and solutions, and in fostering the spread of individualism in society. This is now widely recognised even on the Left, where there is quite a debate about the relevance of socialist ideas in this new and more individualist context. It is generally agreed that many of the old policies are now either irrelevant or politically impractical; that new ways must be found for achieving such traditional socialist goals as equality and social justice. Of course, these developments are not unique to Britain. Collectivism has been on the retreat almost everywhere, East and West, and there is clearly a trend towards individualism in all modern societies. And almost everywhere the Left is having difficulty in coming to grips with this new reality. What is unique about Britain is the extremism and ruthlessness of the Right in exploiting and magnifying these tendencies, and the difficulties experienced by the Left in mounting an effective opposition.

14.2 THE ECONOMIC MIRACLE

There is no simple way of summarising economic performance under the Thatcher regime. The picture depends on which indicator is chosen and which time period is considered. The most favourable picture emerges if we look at labour productivity. Here performance has been dramatic. After a brief fall at the very beginning of the Thatcher era, output per worker has grown strongly for the past eight years. Over this period, labour productivity in British manufacturing has grown almost as fast as in Japan. Over the Thatcher decade as a whole, 1979–89, output per worker in this sector has risen by approximately 50%. It is difficult to compare absolute levels but available estimates indicate that, despite recent growth, labour productivity in British manufacturing remains well below the levels achieved abroad in countries like

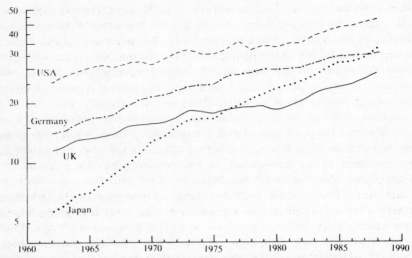

Figure 14.1 Labour productivity in manufacturing industry. Real value added per worker measured at purchasing power parity, measured in thousands of 1985 international dollars as defined by the UN International Comparison Project.

Germany, Japan and the USA (see Fig. 14.1).[5] The recent growth in output per worker has not been sufficient to make up for the country's previously poor performance in this area.

The spectacular increase in labour productivity under Thatcher is often ascribed to the tough anti-trade union laws enacted by her government, and to her readiness to confront and defeat militant unions. This is true in a few nationalised industries like coal, shipbuilding or British Leyland cars, where there have been massive layoffs despite fierce union opposition. But this is not the main explanation. In a recent paper, David Metcalfe of the London School of Economics has shown that labour productivity has increased dramatically throughout manufacturing industry in both unionised and non-unionised plants.[6] Productivity is slightly lower in unionised plants than their non-unionised counterparts, but the gap has remained roughly constant throughout the Thatcher regime. What, then, accounts for the so-called miracle? One important factor is fear. During the terrible recession of the early 1980s, around a quarter of the manufacturing workforce lost their jobs and numerous plants were closed down. Many of these plants were very large and even previously secure companies were faced with bankruptcy. Nobody's job was safe and it became a matter of life and death for managers and workers to co-operate to raise productivity and save their company. The alternative was often the complete closure of the plant concerned. The recession provided a massive shock forcing new working methods on workers and managers alike. This happened in both unionised and non-unionised plants.

There is something ironic in this story. It is widely agreed that the recession of the early 1980s was greatly exacerbated by government mistakes, in particular by the pursuit of an unduly deflationary monetary policy.[7] This is accepted even by many of the people who were responsible for the policy at the time. Yet it was the recession which provided the shock which shook up the manufacturing sector and forced the adoption of new working methods. If government policy had been better designed and functioned as expected, the recession would have been much less severe, the shake-up would have been less dramatic and productivity growth would have been much slower. In short, there would have been no productivity miracle. It is ironic that the one apparent miracle of the Thatcher regime should be the result of a mistake!

There is some doubt about how permanent the effects of the shock will be, whether productivity growth will slow down as memories of the recession gradually wear off. There is also a question of how far it will be feasible to raise productivity in the future without additional investment. Productivity growth over the decade has been achieved partly through labour-saving investment and partly through reorganisation and more intensive use of existing equipment. There are obvious limits to the latter methods, and to sustain rapid productivity growth in the future will require large-scale investment. In 1988 there was something of a boom in manufacturing investment, but by early 1989 this boom was already tailing off and over the medium-term it seems likely that productivity growth will be inhibited by inadequate investment.

Finally, there are dynamic economies of scale, or so-called 'Verdoorn effects', to consider. There is evidence that output and labour productivity are inter-related, in the sense that fast growth in output may stimulate productivity growth.[8] This was obviously not the case during the early 1980s, when it was the shock effect of the recession which increased productivity by forcing the adoption of new working practices. During the more recent period of economic recovery, on the other hand, dynamic economies of scale may have played some role, and the rapid growth in output has probably helped to raise productivity. However, the recovery is now coming to an end. As it does so, the dynamic benefits of fast output growth will evaporate and the resulting stimulus to productivity will be lost. Taking all these factors into account – fading memories of the recession, reduced investment, and slower output growth – it is unlikely that labour productivity in British manufacturing will grow at anything like the rate witnessed over the past decade. This does not mean that productivity will completely stagnate. Merely, that Britain's performance in this area will no longer appear so miraculous.

14.3 PRODUCTION

On this note, let us now examine other negative aspects of the Thatcher 'miracle'. This will help us to understand both its limitations and weaknesses.

Consider first what has happened to manufacturing output. In the initial years of the Thatcher regime, production in this sector fell sharply and then staged the prolonged recovery which is only now coming to an end. However, these recent gains are just sufficient to offset previous losses, with the result that total manufacturing output is now much the same as it was when Thatcher first came to power in 1979. Taking the Thatcher period as a whole, the impressive increase in productivity described previously has been almost entirely of the labour-shedding variety, in which employment is reduced but output remains the same as before. This is in striking contrast to what has happened in countries like Japan and the USA, where advances in labour productivity have been accompanied by very large increases in total output. For example, between 1979 and 1987, manufacturing output and employment in Japan rose by 62% and 7%, respectively (See Table 14.1). The corresponding figures for the UK were 0% and –27%.

Table 14.1 Manufacturing industry 1979–87.

	% change in:				
	Output per worker	*Employment*	*Output*	*Real (1) earnings*	*Product (2) wage*
USA	29.8	–6.3	21.6	–3.9	17.3
Japan	52.2	6.7	62.4	13.4	51.9
FRG	16.5	–7.5	7.6	10.4	9.9
UK	37.8	–27.5	0.0	25.8	28.8

Notes: (1) Hourly earnings deflated by consumer price index.
(2) Hourly earnings deflated by implicit price index of manufacturing value-added (final year estimated).
Source: OECD.

It is a strange miracle indeed which can make millions of industrial workers unemployed and lay waste whole regions of the country, yet finish up producing virtually no more output at the end of the process than it did at the beginning. Yet this is just what has happened in Britain. It is true that a lot of new employment has been created in the service sector under Thatcher, but these are mainly part-time jobs for married women previously outside the labour force. Very little full-time employment has been created to replace the millions of full-time jobs destroyed by productivity growth in the industrial sector, which explains why unemployment is still so high. To describe what has happened under the Thatcher regime as a 'miracle' is a complete misnomer: 'social disaster' would be more accurate.

The huge increase in industrial productivity during the Thatcher period has been accompanied by a very large increase in real wages for most workers fortunate enough to keep their jobs. Real hourly earnings in manufacturing, for example, rose by 26% during the period 1979–87 and by another 4% in 1988. No other Western country has experienced wage increases on anything like this scale in recent years. Moreover, in the UK, higher wages in the manufacturing sector have been financed almost entirely by shedding labour, and hence at the expense of those workers displaced and deprived of their livelihood during the shake-up.[9] What has happened under Thatcher is an example of the divisive social consequences of higher productivity when it is not matched by a corresponding rise in output. If output is stationary, productivity growth merely serves to redistribute income. Nothing extra is produced, but fewer people share in the fruits of production. Those who keep their jobs get more income, while those who lose their jobs get less.

In moral terms such a redistribution may be repugnant. In political terms, however, it can be extremely popular. For those who lose their jobs, rapid productivity growth appears as a curse. For those in employment it appears as a miracle and a blessing, which brings them ever-rising incomes. And so long as it lasts, they are likely to support whomever they think is responsible for this 'miracle'. This is one reason why, despite its failure to increase manufacturing output significantly over the past decade, the Thatcher government remained so popular and enjoyed so much working-class support. It is not simply that the costs of the recession in 1979–81 were off-loaded onto a minority of the population. The benefits of rising productivity have also been confined to those fortunate enough to have a job.

One argument sometimes heard is that the events of the past decade have been merely a preparation. The full dimensions of the alleged miracle, we are told, will only become clear in the future, when rapid output growth will ensure work and prosperity for the whole population.[10] It will then be recognised that the upheaval and misery of the early Thatcher years were a necessary evil required to increase the long-term growth rate of the British economy. There is, unfortunately, little evidence to support this view. Most professional forecasters now believe that balance of payments problems, inflation and capacity constraints will combine to bring the present boom to a virtual end. For example, the National Institute of Economic and Social Research predicts that the economy will limp along for the next few years with manufacturing output and GDP rising at around $2\frac{1}{2}\%$ p.a. and productivity growth much reduced.[11] Employment will stagnate and unemployment will rise to around $2\frac{1}{2}$ million or 10% of the labour force by 1992. What happens after that is anybody's guess. These predictions suggest that talk of a miracle is, to say the least, premature. There has certainly been a spectacular improvement in labour productivity under the Thatcher government, especially in the manufacturing industry. But this has not been translated into a rapid and *sustainable* rate of output growth. Indeed, if the National Institute forecasts up to 1992 are correct, they imply that manufacturing output will have grown at an average rate of just 1.0% per annum over the entire period 1979–92. It seems inconceivable that output performance in this sector would have been so bad under a different regime, with a Labour or non-Thatcherite Tory government in power.

As for other sectors of the economy, they would probably have performed just about as well, or even better, under another government. The Thatcher government can take no credit for the exploitation of North Sea oil, which was largely organised by the preceding Labour government. Nor can it take much credit for the development of financial services, where exports have grown rapidly in the past decade. Even if there had been a Labour government in power during the 1980s, the City of London would still have experienced a considerable boom, just as it did under a Labour government during the 1970s. The reality is that, provided they are not actively hostile to the City, it makes only a marginal difference which government is in power. My conclusion, therefore, is that despite a spectacular increase in labour productivity, the Thatcher government has damaged the manufacturing sector and done little to help most of the rest of the economy. Over the coming years, as problems multiply, the truth of this assertion will become evident.

14.4 SOME HISTORICAL COMPARISONS

To put the Thatcher era into perspective, it is interesting to compare this period with some previous episodes in British history. Figure 14.2 (a–d) plots the behaviour of some key economic variables during three major cycles in the manufacturing sector. Each of these cycles is of nine years' duration and they cover the periods 1920–9, 1929–38 and 1979–88. In each case the cycle begins with a deep slump, which is then followed by a prolonged economic recovery. In all three cycles there is a noticeable increase in labour productivity. This increase is greatest during the 1980s, which have experienced a more rapid and more sustained rise in output per worker than occurred in either of the inter-war cycles. Thus, as far as productivity is concerned, the performance of manufacturing under the Thatcher regime is impressive even by historical standards.

The picture is quite different if we look at other economic variables, such as employment or output. In both inter-war cycles, manufacturing employment at first experienced a sharp fall, but then began to recover and rose strongly for the next seven or eight years (Fig. 14.2b). During the Thatcher period, however, there has been no recovery at all in manufacturing employment. On the contrary, employment in this sector has continued falling right up to the present and is now 30% below its initial level in 1979. This contrast in employment experience is reflected in the behaviour of output. The recovery in manufacturing output during the later years of the Thatcher era is often described as spectacular. In fact, when compared to what happened in the inter-war cycles, this recovery is really rather modest. It is both shorter in duration and less rapid than either of its inter-war counterparts. Even during the two years of exceptional 'supergrowth' in 1987–8 manufacturing output

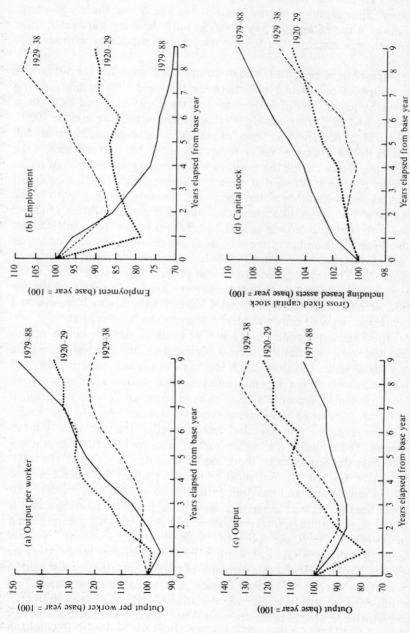

Figure 14.2 UK manufacturing industry: three cycles compared. (*Sources*: (a)–(c), CSO, *Economic Trends Annual Supplement* (Leisner, 1985); (d), *UK National Accounts, 1988* (Feinstein, 1972). *Note*: (d), figures for the inter-war period include construction; 1988 figure is an estimate.

rose no faster than it did throughout most of the 1920s and 1930s (Fig. 14.2c). After only two years of alleged supergrowth, there developed quite a severe shortage of capacity, the economy began to 'overheat' and there was a huge deterioration in the balance of payments. In both the inter-war cycles, quite rapid growth was sustained for five or six years continuously without such difficulties.

The contrast can be best illustrated by comparing cumulative output growth over the course of complete cycles. Between 1979 and 1988, manufacturing output rose by just 5%. During the inter-war cycles, 1920-9 and 1929-38, it rose by 22% and 29%, respectively. Perhaps most interesting are the 1920s, which are widely perceived as years of stagnation and persistent structural problems in British industry. Yet, in terms of output, the performance of the manufacturing sector during the twenties was considerably better than under the Thatcher regime. It is true that there were serious problems in such staple industries as textiles and steel, but there was also impressive growth in the so-called new industries like chemicals and consumer durables. Indeed, throughout the entire inter-war period, apart from brief slumps in 1920 and 1929, there was rapid and almost continuous expansion in the new industries and it was this expansion which contributed so much to Britain's later post-war prosperity. The rapid growth of output in the new industries during the inter-war period was achieved with relatively little investment. With the exception of chemicals, these industries were mostly labour-intensive and their expansion required only a modest investment in fixed capital.[12]

Under the Thatcher regime, there has been some investment in new manu-facturing activities, especially electrical engineering, but this has been on a relatively small scale, certainly much less than in the inter-war period. The inter-war years were an era of genuine and massive structural transformation in the manufacturing sector. Painful losses in some areas were outweighed many times over by huge gains elsewhere. This has not been the case under the Thatcher regime, nor for that matter under the previous Labour Government. There has been a fair amount of investment in the manufactur-ing sector over the past decade, more indeed than during either of the inter-war cycles (see Fig. 14.2d). But most of this investment has been designed primarily to save labour and has done little to raise productive capacity. This is evident from the fact that capacity utilisation in the manufacturing sector is now very high, even though total production is only marginally greater than it was in 1979. While some potential growth industries have recently experienced a spurt in capacity-creating investment, this does not compensate for previous neglect, and the total amount of additional capacity installed in these industries over the Thatcher decade as a whole is quite small. This decade has witnessed nothing like the dynamic transformation in industrial structure which occurred between the wars. The special feature of manufactur-ing industry under Thatcher, as compared to the inter-war period or indeed the 1950s and 1960s, is not the growth of new activities but the decline of old ones. In the past, structural change in the manufacturing sector came about mainly through expansion into new areas, and the decline of the old was of secondary importance. Under Thatcher, the order has almost been reversed.

15.4 CRUCIAL WEAKNESSES

Two problems of central importance have become evident in the late 1980s: a shortage of productive capacity in the manufacturing sector and a mushrooming balance of payments deficit. New investment in manufacturing in recent years has been just sufficient to compensate for the widespread scrapping of capital stock caused by the 1979–81 slump. As a result, total productive capacity is now much the same as it was when Thatcher first came into office. Obviously, there have been changes in composition – there is less steel-making capacity, for example, and more capacity in chemicals and electrical engineering – but overall the total amount has not changed much. The paucity of capacity-creating investment in manufacturing is the result of several factors. The first concerns profitability. The pre-tax rate of return in manufacturing has recovered fairly strongly and has now returned to its 1973 level. However, it is still below the level observed in countries like Germany or Japan (Fig. 14.3). Moreover, to induce a given rate of productive investment nowadays requires a higher pre-tax profit rate than was the case in 1973. Real interest rates on competing financial assets are higher than they were then. The government has also abolished subsidies and tax incentives for investment. Finally, there is less optimism about long-term growth rates in the world economy than was the case in the early 1970s. This in itself has a depressing influence on British investment independently of the rate of profit currently achieved. When these various factors are taken into account the recovery in profits is no longer quite so impressive, and it is not surprising that there has been so little capacity-creating investment in manufacturing industry.

The modest scale of the profits recovery points to a major weakness in the Thatcher miracle. It is true that productivity has risen spectacularly in manufacturing industry. But so, too, have wages. During the depths of the recession in 1979–81 workers felt extremely vulnerable and were compelled by the fear of redundancy to co-operate in raising productivity without receiving additional wages. During the subsequent economic recovery they have continued to co-operate but they no longer feel so vulnerable, and firms have been obliged to pay very large wage increases in return for this co-operation. The Thatcher revolution has thus been incomplete. It has failed to subordinate labour sufficiently to generate rapid productivity growth without at the same time granting massive wage increases. This helps to explain why profits in British manufacturing are still below what is achieved abroad, and why they have not been sufficient to generate investment on anything like the

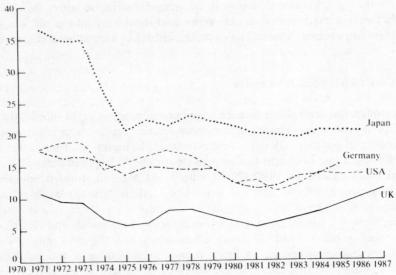

Figure 14.3 Rate of profit in manufacturing industry, gross pre-tax rate of return. (*Source:* OECD.)

required scale.

Another factor behind the paucity of capacity-creating investment has been the absence of any coherent long-term government programme for the manufacturing sector. Economic policy has been strongly free-market in orientation and the government has firmly rejected a strategic approach to industrial investment of the kind so successful in countries like Japan and South Korea. Many of the incentives and mechanisms for stimulating investment in the manufacturing sector as a whole, or in particular sub-sectors, have been dismantled. It is not, therefore, surprising that so little new capacity has been installed.

Government policy towards investment partly reflects a genuine belief in the efficacy of undiluted market forces. It is also a matter of political priorities. As mentioned above, the Thatcher revolution is above all a *counter-*revolution, whose overriding goal has always been to defeat and discredit socialism in Britain. Such a goal takes precedence over subordinate objectives like promoting investment and long-term growth. This has major implications for economic policy. Economic policies are rarely politically neutral and many have significant ideological consequences. Some policies, for example, are associated in the public mind with socialism, or may lead people to think in socialist terms. No matter what their economic benefits, such policies are potentially dangerous and are a threat to the basic political objectives of Thatcherism. Whenever possible they must, therefore, be avoided. This helps to explain the hostility of the present government towards any form of comprehensive strategy for stimulating and guiding industrial investment. In Britain, unlike many other countries, strategies of this variety are traditionally associated with the Left, and to discredit them has been an important ideological weapon of the government. The Thatcherite approach has been to deride interventionism as bureaucratic and counterproductive, and to promulgate the virtues of the free market. In ideological terms, this approach has been highly successful and has put the Left on the defensive, especially during the past couple of years, during which the economic boom

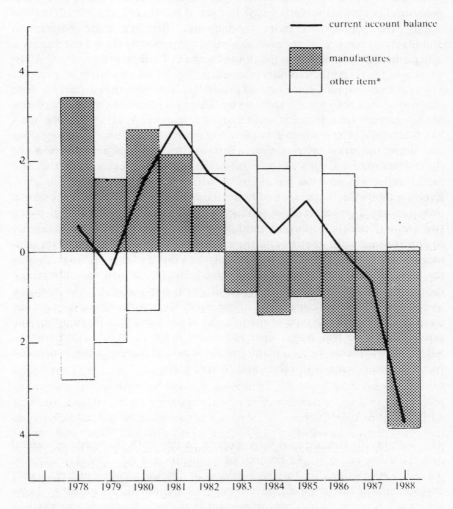

Figure 14.4 UK balance of payments (% GDP at factor cost).
(*Source:* CSO)
*Food, materials, oil and other fuels, invisibles and transfers.

has led to a euphoric but mistaken confidence in free market solutions. In economic terms, however, it has been extremely harmful. The failure to develop a coherent long-term strategy for industrial investment is a major factor behind the present shortage of productive capacity in the manufacturing sector. It has also contributed to Britain's looming balance of payments crisis.

The balance of payments deficit is now around 4% of GDP at factor cost and according to some forecasters is still rising (Fig. 14.4). This deficit is sometimes blamed on the excessive growth of consumer credit and over-generous tax cuts in the Spring 1988 budget. While there is some truth in these claims, the problem is more fundamental. Britain's trade balance in manufactures has been deteriorating almost continuously since Thatcher took office and is now in deficit to the tune of some £14 billion per annum.[13] A few years ago, the then much smaller manufacturing deficit was offset by a surplus on other items, in particular oil and invisibles. However, the surplus on these other items has been greatly reduced by falling oil prices and a poor performance in services such as tourism, air and sea transport. Apart from a few items like financial services, which are still doing quite well, there has been a serious and almost universal deterioration in Britain's international position. Some of these developments, such as lower oil prices, are due to external factors and are no reflection on what has occurred within the country under Thatcher. Even so, their effects are real and bode ill for the future. Other developments, however, are a direct result of failings in the Thatcher revolution, of which two are particularly important and have already been described: its inability to control real wage growth and the absence of a coherent strategy for promoting and guiding industrial investment. As a result of these failings, despite the spectacular increase in labour productivity, British manufacturing industry is still not adequately competitive; in particular it lacks both the ability and productive capacity required either to export on a sufficient scale or to compete with the type of manufactured products now flooding in. The rapid growth in real wages also has other negative implications for the balance of payments, being a major influence behind the explosion in demand for imported consumer durables and foreign travel.

14.6 CONCLUSIONS

The inability to contain real wage growth in line with the needs of capital accumulation and a sound balance of payments is a basic weakness of the Thatcher revolution. So, too, is its refusal to develop a coherent strategy for investment and the long-term development of manufacturing industry. These issues will become increasingly important in the next few years and a failure to resolve them could spell the end of the Thatcher regime. Just what might replace this regime is an open question.

NOTES

1. Walters (1986).
2. This role of manufacturing and its relation to services is extensively discussed in Rowthorn and Wells (1987) and in Wells, this volume.
3. For a good discussion of the politics of the Thatcher regime see Gamble (1988).
4. Although justifiable in general terms, the sale of council housing under the Tories has been pursued with complete disregard for the needs of the poor and the homeless. It was orginally promised that the funds raised from the sale of existing dwellings would be used to finance the construction of new public housing for such people. If actually implemented, this would have been an intelligent and human policy. But the promise has never been kept. Instead, the money has either been frozen or diverted to other uses, and councils have been deliberately starved of funds to prevent them from building new housing. The result has been a drastic reduction in the stock of public housing and a dramatic increase in homelessness. The latter is symbolised by the ragged army of outcasts now living in cardboard boxes and the like in the centres of Britain's major cities.
5. The figures illustrated in this diagram are derived by combining two kinds of data: (1) time series indices for labour productivity within individual countries for the period 1962–88; (2) internationally comparable estimates of absolute productivity levels in the year 1985. The former are taken from the usual OECD publications, while the latter are from an unpublished paper by D. J. Roy. Roy's estimates for 1985 are themselves an update of earlier estimates for 1980 published in *Economic Trends* (see Roy, 1987).
6. Metcalf (1988). See also Nolan, this volume.
7. This point is made by Maynard (1988).
8. There is now a voluminous literature on 'Verdoorn's Law'. For a fairly recent sample see the special issues of the *Journal of Post-Keynesian Economics* devoted to this topic (Spring, 1983).
9. On this point see Glyn, this volume.
10. This argument is an underlying theme in Maynard (1988).
11. National Institute (1988).
12. For a discussion of modernisation and structural change in British manufacturing industry during the inter-war period see Von Tunzelmann (1982). An article of related interest is Gregg and Worswick (1988).
13. The UK balance of payments is analysed at length in an article by Wells, this volume.

REFERENCES

Feinstein, C. H., *National Income, Expenditure and Output of the United Kingdom 1855–1965* (Cambridge University Press: Cambridge, 1972).

Gamble, A., *The Free Economy And The Strong State: The Politics of Thatcherism* (Macmillan: Basingstoke, 1988).

Gregg, P. A. and Worswick, G. D. N., 'Recession and Recovery in Britain: the 1930s and the 1980s', *National Institute Economic Review*, (London, November 1988).

Maynard, G., *The Economy under Mrs Thatcher* Blackwell: Oxford, 1988).

Metcalf, D., *Water Notes Dry Up*, Centre for Labour Economics Working Paper (London School of Economics: London, 1988).

National Institute for Economic and Social Research, *National Institute Economic Review*, (London, November 1988).

Rowthorn, R. E. and Wells, J. R., *De-industrialisation and Foreign Trade* (Cambridge University Press: Cambridge, 1987).

Roy, D. J., 'International Comparisons of Real Value-Added, Productivity and Energy Intensity', *Economic Trends* (CSO: London, June 1987).

Von Tunzelmann, G. N., 'Structural Change, Leading Sectors in British Manufacturing 1907–1968' in *Economics in the Long View, Essays in Honour of W. W. Rostow* (eds Kindleberger, C. P. and di Tella, G.) Part II (Macmillan: London, 1982).

Walters, A. A., *Britain's Economic Renaissance* (Oxford University Press: Oxford, 1986).

15 IS THATCHERISM THE CURE FOR THE BRITISH DISEASE?

Meghnad Desai

Most discussions of Thatcherism have to face the basic problem as to whether it is a contingent, short-run phenomenon or a fundamental, permanent shift in the political system of the UK. A separate question is whether, on balance, it has been a success in terms of the objectives Margaret Thatcher set, or a failure. Finally, there is the question whether from the point of view of the economy, successful or not on its own terms, the Thatcher programme has been of net benefit.

One incontrovertible sense in which the Thatcher era has been unique is in terms of electoral success. Three consecutive victories under the same leader have not occurred in the twentieth century in UK politics; no Prime Minister has served ten years in this century and not since Lord Liverpool in the early nineteenth century. But the uniqueness of this achievement is very easily rationalised *ex post* as inevitable. There is a tendency to cast the 1974–9 Labour government in very dark terms and assert that in some sense Thatcherism was the *only* response which could solve the problems of the UK economy. In *ex ante* terms, it must be remembered that by mid-1978 the Callaghan–Healey regime was thought to be a relative success; inflation was coming down rapidly from its height of 25% to single digit levels, while unemployment, though high in terms of economic history up to 1978, was only 1.3 million. The Labour Party led in the opinion polls up to Autumn 1978 and conventional wisdom told us that the City loved Callaghan and that Labour could have won the election if one had been called in Autumn 1978.

But that being said, let bygones be bygones. The fact is that by March 1979 the 'Winter of Discontent' had happened. The Tories fought the election on the 'Labour Isn't Working' slogan, with pictures of unemployment queues. Margaret Thatcher also held out the seductive promise of 'free' collective bargaining and no incomes policies. Inflation, which had come down to 8% by the last quarter of 1978, was once again rising and being seen as the major economic problem in light of the breakdown of incomes policies. In addition to that, the episode of the UK going cap-in-hand to the IMF in 1976 was also subtly used by the opposition to establish their alternative programme as likely to tackle these problems – inflation, unemployment, balance of payments.

In fighting the election, the Conservatives projected a less ideological image than has come to be the case subsequently. Thus, the free market thrust of Thatcher was only an echo of the 'Selsdon man' of 1970. But to that now-embarrassing episode, a firm control of money supply was added. A point was made that, unlike the after-effects of incomes policies, money supply control would bring inflation down without increasing unemployment. In addition, the Conservatives championed free collective bargaining so loved by the militant left. Thus, in 1979 Thatcherism (not yet invented as a term) projected itself as tough but not radical. It is only subsequently that the full extent of the departure from previous governments became clear. In the first period, liberalisation of foreign exchange markets and removal of the 'corset' on commercial banks were the only market-oriented policies which marked some change. Control of the money supply, cuts in public expenditure, sale of assets of publicly owned corporations – all these had already occurred under the previous Labour government. The difference was that while that government was forced into it against its wishes, the Thatcher government saw these as principal weapons in its economic policy. Only as time passed, and especially after 1983, did the longer-run policies such as privatisation, reform of local authority financing, shifting the tax burden onto the poor, etc., take shape. Thatcherism is not, then, the same in 1989 as in 1979. There have been adjustments, adoption of the policies of the opposition (the 'green' phase of Thatcherism), even some U-turns, but the public image projected has been that of a single consistent and coherent programme.

In this chapter I intend to adopt the view that, despite the many contingent shifts, Thatcherism is a coherent and consistent package. Putting it in a long-run historical perspective, it is a *modernising strategy* to tackle the structural problems of British capitalism. In this it is not unique, but only one among the several strategies that have been proposed and in some cases even implemented by one or another post-war government. In particular we shall consider the Labour governments of 1964–70 and 1974–9 and the Conservative government of 1970–4. There have also been other strategies proposed, especially by the Left: the Alternative Economic Strategy, for example, which has not been implemented but could be seen as responding to the structural problems of British capitalism.

15.1 STRUCTURAL PROBLEMS OF BRITISH CAPITALISM

There is a widespread and long-ranging debate among historians, economic historians and general political writers about the British 'disease'. Surprising as it may seem, the literature is thick in the period before the First World War when there is a contemporary self-consciousness that things could be better, although it is by no means a majority view. There has been a revival in the interest in this question since the 1960s, as a frequency analysis of the rather comprehensive bibliography in Pollard (1989) confirms. Thus, the concern with the decline is itself endogenous. There is, of course, no unanimous agreement among economic historians about the timing, the extent or even the existence of the decline. But there is an overwhelming majority which agrees that there *was* a decline, and that it can be placed *before* the First World War in the 1870s, the 1890s or the decade before the War. No one places the 'crisis' in the inter-war period, traumatic as it was. Indeed, the inter-war period is viewed as a period of economic restructuring rather than one of decline. The literature on this topic is extensive and full of controversy. Some, like Perry Anderson (1964), push the crisis much further back to the seventeenth century; Thompson (1965) also disagrees. Anderson (1987) has revisited the debate. Pollard (1989) is sceptical. The authors to note in the Pollard bibliography are Corelli Barnett, Phelphs Brown, D. McCloskey and Eric Hobsbawm.

The endogeneity of the timing of the debate is not a trivial matter. If we find a foreshadowing of our current concern in the 1880s and 1890s, it is somewhat because we are looking for it. The contemporary Victorian was not troubled: he was enjoying a high level of income and enjoying the sensation of being a member of a (relatively, as of then) high consumption society (John Fowles re-constructs this feeling nicely in his book *The French Lieutenant's Woman* (Fowles, 1970)). There was unhappiness in Royal Commissions, in delegations visiting Germany and in some political debates. But the economy had responses to these early premonitions of crisis which staved off any ill feeling. The awareness of the disease only came on acutely after the Second World War, especially in the late 1950s and early 1960s. Historians may debate whether the decline was *actually* there in the data for the pre-1914 period. The important point is that the UK citizen of the 1960s and 1970s was convinced that something was wrong and that it went back much further than the previous twenty years. Intellectuals, rightly or not, felt this presumption. Once the argument that the disease went back a hundred years was popularly accepted, it was hard to dislodge this belief from the public's mind.

The beginning of the 'crisis' of British capitalism is located in the last quarter of the nineteenth century, some time after the turning point in the early 1870s which marked the beginning of the long depression. Having been the first industrialising country, Britain had enjoyed a monopoly position in international trade despite the multiplicity of small firms in each industry. Having been the leader in industrial growth through early cotton textiles, iron and coal and railways, Britain began to fall behind with the newer industrial processes which occurred in the 1860s and later. Already, by the time of the Great Exhibition, American technology was moving ahead of the British in some respects. With the new steel-making processes and later electricity and chemicals in the Third Industrial Revolution, it was clear to contemporaries that something was wrong. The Royal Commission on the Depression in Trade, parliamentary debates and contemporary literature all show that while the *levels* of income, or the share in world trade, etc., were high, in terms of rates of *growth* the USA and Germany were racing ahead.

The symptoms that were diagnosed can be grouped, somewhat schematically, under four headings. There is in the nature of any such simple classification the obvious additional danger that these four would be seen as mutually exclusive and collectively exhaustive. They are not. There is much overlap and interaction between them, and what is included under one of the headings could easily be under another. Nor can exhaustiveness be claimed: after all, we have not yet arrived at a consensus among historians and there are still many who dispute that there has been any crisis whatever. With these caveats, the four headings under which all the symptoms of the 1873–1963 period could be grouped are as follows:

1. Industrial relations.
2. Industrial structure.
3. Economic structure.
4. Class structure.

In what follows we shall take each one of these in turn. Needless to say, given the space limitations, the treatment of each can only be brief. What is more, these are symptoms. Their causes are also under dispute. Early maturity, the problem of being pioneering, the commitment made to police the world in the empire and out of it, the archaic constitution and the very stability of the polity that had seen no major crisis since 1688 – we could go on listing the causes cited in the literature. (The constitutional/political factors are debated in the Anderson–Thompson exchange; most of the economic causes are discussed by Pollard (1989)).

15.2 INDUSTRIAL RELATIONS

British industrial relations evolved during the phase in which the early lead had given Britain an advantage in international markets. In the established industries which led the First and Second Industrial Revolutions, a craft and guild logic prevailed. Britain had trade unions which organised each craft (boilermakers, for example) across industries rather than as industrial unions. More pre-capitalist elements of deference and truculence survive simultaneously, as in the feudal master–serf relations, than in the more egalitarian ideologies in many newly settled countries such as the USA or Australia, or in countries where feudalism was smashed in violent upheavals or wars, such as France, Germany or Italy. Thus, industrial bargaining takes place under the presumption that workers care only about job security and pay, and especially overtime. Efficiency, productivity and quality of the final product are all seen to be the bosses' concern. Wage bargains concentrate not on raising the basic wage but on extending hours worked, especially the overtime component. The British working week continues to be abnormally long in the OECD countries.

Parallel to the us–them attitude is the reluctance to take control over the production process. Thus, in 1945 when after the war it was in its most powerful position to date, with Labour in power and Ernest Bevin its most powerful personality, it was made clear by the TUC that it was not interested in having workers' representatives on the boards of nationalised industries. Nor has the TUC been partial to workers' control. Only in the UK could there be a militant trade union, the NUM, fighting for the right of a miner's son to his father's job. Mining is a hard, dangerous and unhealthy job. To preserve rather than eliminate such hard work is one testimony to the conservatism of the militant miners. Nor was there any concrete proposal during the bitter miners' strike of 1984–5 for a workers' buy-out of management. There was no desire for workers' ownership or control. It was militant to stay as employees, with no control and no responsibility except to fight for higher wages and hereditary jobs.

These particular facts about trade unionisation should not deter us from seeing that the British trade union movement was a very powerful social force. From the craft unions of the old industrial revolution, the 'new' unions came into being in the 1890s. These covered areas such as dock labour. Historians who see labour unions as a severe problem for the British economy point to the Taff Vale decision in 1904 as establishing the immunity of trade unions from their responsibility as 'legal' persons, as firms are. Thus, unions could not be sued for the losses incurred due to strikes by the losing firm; and thus, trade unions had a special status in corporate law.

Another sign of the strength of the TUC was the crucial part it played in the creation of the Parliamentary Labour Committee, which later became the Labour Party – this tied the TUC to the Labour Party irretrievably. The relationship has not always been a happy one, and in the period since 1964 it became more of a problem for both sides.

Trade unions were admitted as a major force in British society in the official tripartite committees set up during the First World War. With full employment guaranteed, the power of the trade unions grew until, in a famous episode in 1919, Lloyd George confessed to a small group of powerful trade union leaders that they could take over the country if they wished. They demurred and once again revealed that they did not wish to be in power, but only to extract their share of the surplus.

The labour–capital relationship in Britain is characterised by compromise rather than conflict, and the state has played an active role in defusing any situation that could have led to conflict. Keith Middlemas, in a work which was said to be influential in the early years of Thatcherism, argues that it was this consensus/compromise climate that was debilitating and postponed the structural changes that were required to make British capitalism dynamic (Middlemas, 1980).

The result of a powerful but premature trade union movement was, if anything, a paradox. A high-wage, high-skill country in the nineteenth century, Britain ended up as a low-wage, low-productivity one by the second half of the twentieth century. The trade union movement was *powerful* in resisting any attack on it, but *ineffective* in reforming itself even when it acknowledged that such reform was necessary. The history of the attempts to reform it from outside, if not above, constitutes the entire period of 1966–85.

15.3 INDUSTRIAL STRUCTURE

Early maturity is said to have also led to a structure of industry in which small single-owner firms predominated. These entrepreneurs were self-made persons who despised professional management and prized practical knowledge above book learning. When R&D-intensive products came with the Third Industrial Revolution, a different management style was required. The transformation that railways, steel, electricity and chemicals wrought in US business has been well described by Alfred Chandler in his classic *The Visible Hand* (Chandler, 1977). A contempt for education was transmuted into a neglect of industrial training and also influenced the suppliers of education. Universities saw that it was not worth their while to educate industrial technicians, engineers, managers (Weiner, 1981).

Self-made entrepreneurs did not breach the class barrier between workers and employers. They aspired to join the 'gentlemen' and cease to be 'players'. Their sons went to public schools and tried to join the club of the élite. To this day, managers are recruited from this élite and taught to maintain their distance from workers.

Unlike later arrivals, in Britain banks played little part in helping to put together large vertically integrated firms or horizontally integrated cartels. Although country banks had played a part in financing the early industrial revolutions, by the 1880s the concentration in the banking industry created the large London-based clearing banks. They and the merchant banks did not play an active part in industrial financing. The British firms depended on the equity market or private sources for financing.

Another puzzling feature of British business has been that it is more successful abroad than at home. British multinationals perform better abroad than at home. By a similar token, foreign companies, the American ones for nearly fifty years as well as the Japanese more recently, perform better than their domestic rivals when they operate in the UK.

It has to be said that many of these contentions are debatable. Some historians doubt the universality of these attributes and point to exceptions to all of these. There has also been a significant body of mainly US-based economic historians of the new cliometric school who have argued that, far from being a failure, the Victorian businessman was optimising, given the constraints that he faced. Of course, the issue is that these constraints may have been *exogenous* to the individual businessman but they were *endogenous* to the economy; so the Victorian debate does not prove much except that in the circumstances these businessmen were not stupid.

15.4 ECONOMIC STRUCTURE

This constraint refers to the mix of economic activities. The contention is that the financial sector – the city – is relatively much more important than the manufacturing sector. This fact has the consequence that orthodox (deflationary) economic policies are favoured above expansionary policies. The Treasury view is supposed to be an instance of this, with the return to the $4.86 pound in 1925 the most glaring example. An additional implication is that London and the South-east are favoured at the expense of the north of England and Scotland.

The domination of the City can be dated from the 1880s. It was during the last quarter of the nineteenth century that a concentration and centralisation movement took place in retail banking. Unlike manufacturing, banks were able to evolve from single-owner small country banks into a few large banks, with London as headquarters, and with a nation-wide branch network. Banks also managed to be innovative and internationally competitive. As Britain was losing its lead in manufacturing, it was emerging as the financial centre of the world.

The argument, then, becomes that financial capital is opposed to industrial capital and, being more powerful, imposes its policy. Industrial capital is expected to favour an expanding domestic market, secured if possible by tariffs or some other form of protection and subsidies for export growth, if possible in the form of devaluation. There is obviously a conflict here between different parts of industrial capital, as those firms which are export-oriented may not favour tariffs in fear of retaliation, while those who like an expanding domestic market may fear inflation via devaluation. This segmentation within industrial capital is not found in financial capital, which presents a united front.

15.5 CLASS STRUCTURE

The language of class occurs more frequently in British discussions than in many other modern economies. This language refers often to the cultural codification of certain consumer activities. Soccer versus cricket, tabloids versus serious newspapers, saloon bars and public bar – these are outward manifestations of a working class/middle class divide. Such a notion of class is only loosely defined and often more an invention of marketing experts than of Marxist sociology.

There is, however, a serious argument that there are class rigidities in British society and that mobility is limited. Access to the best civil service jobs or managerial jobs is gained through Eton/Horseguards/Oxbridge connections rather than through ability or on-the-job experience. It is peculiar to Britain that education is devalued and its provision at the primary and secondary levels is so bad as to constitute a barrier to mobility. Up to 60% of school-leaving children at 16 exit without qualifications, and this number is an improvement over the previous grammar school/secondary modern system. Education caters to the élite who are so defined by their ability to reason with the written word and verbally, rather than by their practical or industrial skills. The record on vocational or industrial training is bad for a modern industrial economy. The provision of free primary education was resisted in Britain long after the USA, Germany and Japan had adopted it. The reform of education is fought along class lines although disguised in a rhetoric about quality and choice.

On the other hand, managers are educated to regard themselves as a race apart from workers, even from skilled personnel such as engineers. In any case, they are in a management position not as a result of professional training but by virtue of ownership, family or school ties. They bring a financial rather than industrial approach to management, but this is what is prized. Even a Labour government preferred a 'City' banker, Charles Villiers, to an engineer, Monty Finiston, when it came to choosing the head of British Steel, despite Finiston's long work experience.

15.6 COPING WITH CONSTRAINTS

These four constraints overlap and interact. There has been a frequent tendency to single one of them out as fundamental and ignore or even deny the others, but they have to be seen as an integrated whole. It is also clear that once such an integrated set of constraints exists, a rational response on the part of individuals would be to make the best of them. No individual person or sector can remove this set. While some other countries have had the 'benefit' of a defeat in war to destroy their old structures – Japan and Germany come to mind – or of revolutions which have led to new constitutions – France, for example – Britain is unique in having had an uninterrupted and unchallenged (internally or externally) political system since 1688 if not before.

While it seemed to previous generations that this long continuity along with a moderate and non-conflictual pace of reform was the principal and proud achievement of British politics, with the post-1945 world doubts began to be raised as to whether this solution was not the problem. The unpreparedness for the Second World War and the many class-ridden features of the society that total mobilisation had exposed put modernisation on the political agenda. To begin with, there was a consensus on the sort of reforms needed. Expert bodies such as Political and Economic Planning (PEP) had listed the reforms necessary. It fell to the 1945 Labour government to implement this consensus package, although parliamentary debates sought to give it an adversarial edge (Addison, 1975).

The harsh economic climate of the late 1940s changed as the 1950s arrived. Having started the economic reconstruction early, British exports and economic growth picked up. At this juncture the continental European economies, especially Germany, and Japan were still recovering. European currencies did not become fully convertible till 1960 and sterling enjoyed, along with the dollar, a key currency status. The economic growth rate in this 1945–60 period exceeded anything that the economy had experienced in any previous period of similar length, and Macmillan could with justification say in 1959: 'You never had it so good'. One may, at least with hindsight, argue that the Conservatives, in creating a mass consumer society and in rapidly liberalising the economy, postponed the painful process of modernisation begun under Labour. The Labour government had inaugurated the bonfire of controls but with the Conservative victory in 1951 this bonfire became a conflagration. Keynesian demand management, an expanding world economy and falling raw material prices (after the Korean War boom) all helped to sustain the illusion that the good times had arrived permanently.

It was in the early 1960s, indeed, soon after the Macmillan election victory, that the concern about Britain's growth performance became acute. This concern was part of an international debate which made international 'league table' comparisons. John Kennedy made the poor growth performance of the USA a part of his election campaign. In Britain, many pointed out the relevance of the French example with its economic plan and its method of training civil servants through their *grandes écoles*. It was in response to this that NEDO was started, the Plowden Report was issued and the London Business School came into being. The Robbins Report on higher education was a part of this renaissance with its total commitment to an open-ended expansion of university education.

15.7 MODERNISATION STRATEGIES 1964–79

It would be fair to say that Harold Wilson was the first consciously modernising political leader. Although 'the white heat of the technological revolution' has survived only as a cliché, Wilson projected a meritocratic, technology oriented programme for modernisation. Comprehensive schooling, the expansion of the polytechnic sector, the efforts at facilitating mergers and large industrial units via the Industrial Reorganisation Corporation, the establishment of the Department of Economic Affairs to counter the Treasury, the inception of a Ministry for Technology, the enunciation of a National Plan – all these were modernising moves. The Wilson strategy could be seen as concentrating on the industrial structure and the class structure. While there was much rhetoric about defying the Treasury and the City, it was a weakness of the Wilson government that it failed to tackle that constraint. In effect, the Wilson government failed to overcome one of the major conse-quences of the set of structural constraints – the tendency of the British economy to run into a balance of payments deficit.

The tendency towards trade deficit is a post-1945 manifestation of struc-tural constraints. Through much of the nineteenth century, the British economy generated a trade surplus which was then exported on capital account. This capital export strengthened the City. There was also an imperial context and in the case of India, the Indian surplus was manipulated via monetary policy to help London's gold reserves (see de Cecco (1974) for the pre-1914 context and Balachandran (1989) for the inter-war period). During the inter-war period the trade surplus began to be a problem as markets for British products shrank in the wake of industrial development in the periphery, but the compulsion to export capital was strong. It was here that, until 1931 and the abandonment of the Gold Standard, the City extracted a heavy price from the economy by insisting on a restoration of pre-1914 parity. After 1945 India was soon lost, but the imperial commitment was not fully shed till the 1960s. The Sterling Area, with the cosy practice of colonial sterling balances being kept in London, was an advantage to the City but it delayed devaluation to the detriment of the economy. It was in attempting to forestall devaluation that the Wilson government lost its battle with the City.

An interrelated consequence of this set of constraints is the tendency to wage and price inflation in full employment phases. Being a low-wage/low productivity economy, any increase in wages soon translates itself into an increase in unit labour costs and hence prices. International competitiveness suffered and this linked domestic inflation to the trade deficit. The Wilson government switched soon after its re-election in 1966 to identify industrial relations as the key constraint and accept the economic structure (the City) as unalterable. Through the Donovan Commission on trade union reform, the White Paper *In Place of Strife* and incomes policies, it sought to reform the archaic trade union structures, but eventually failed. The modern-isation experiment of the Labour government of 1964–70 ended in much recrimination and a feeling that in pursuing its modernising strategy, Wilson had abandoned/betrayed/compromised the socialist programme of the Labour Party.

The Heath–Barber government of 1970–4 arrived with a commitment to tackle trade union reform as its principal platform. It sought to tackle the industrial structure constraint by relying on an attack on monopoly and restrictive practices. Its principal achievement in this respect was the reform of the banking cartel with Competition and Credit Control. Its other tactic was one which had been tried unsuccessfully before by Macmillan as well as Wilson – entry into the European Community. In this it was successful, and of all the economic reforms of the post-1945 period this is one that has proved irreversible so far.

But the Heath–Barber government fell foul of the interaction of the industrial relations/economic structure constraints. It did not defy the City; indeed, its competition legislation expanded the financial sector. Its growth strategy ran into the problems of inflation and the balance of payments. When its income policies were breached by the trade unions, especially the dock workers, the electricians and the miners, the Heath modernisation programme ended in disarray. Starting from a liberal rhetoric of free markets, the Health government moved to a corporatist solution but in this policy it could not elicit the co-operation of the trade unions, which were antagonised by the reforming legislation.

The Wilson–Callaghan governments of 1974–9 had slender majorities. Facing the severe shock of a quadrupling of oil prices, and coming in the wake of an embattled history of two governments' failure to reform industrial relations, it chose not to be a modernising government at all. Modernisation involved a conflictual approach; after all, some toes had to be stepped on. Instead the approach was to bet on consensus. This strategy seemed to have worked in the (now seemingly) golden period of the 1950s. A Social Contract with the trade unions and no overt defiance of the City were tried. While Tony Benn may have had a strategy to tackle the industrial structure, he was soon replaced. A consensual way of tackling inflation and avoiding a severe deflation was tried; there was an attempt to engineer a mild devaluation in early 1976 to relieve the balance of trade problem. It ended, however, in disaster. By mid-1976 the run on the pound required going cap-in-hand to the IMF. If by 1978 this problem was under control and the pound was drifting up, the consensual approach to inflation broke down in the 'Winter of Discontent'. By the beginning of 1979, a non-modernising government had also collapsed in ignominy. It had almost succeeded, but fell at the last crucial hurdle of industrial relations/inflation.

15.8 THATCHERISM ARRIVES

It is against this background that Thatcherism has to be viewed. While in opposition, the Conservatives analysed their failure to carry on in 1974. It was obvious to them that industrial relations remained *the* principal constraint. But it was also clear that, despite the rhetoric of the 'Selsdon man', the Heath government had not been market-oriented. Revival of the libertarian theories in the late 1970s helped here. Monetarism, which emerged as the Right's version of anti-Keynesian macroeconomic policy, combining at once fiscal conservatism and economic centralisation of power in the hands of the monetary authorities, was harnessed to mount a critique of the 1970–4 government.

However, more important than any of these intellectual developments was the conviction that consensus politics was a problem. Reform and restructuring of the economy could not be carried out without a conflictual approach. It is in embracing conflict and in sharpening rather than glossing over differences that Thatcherism sank deepest into the national psyche. Keith Middlemas, the Conservative historian, explained the British sclerosis precisely in terms of the tendency of the government to intervene in capital–labour conflict with a view to reconciliation. This fudge compromise or consensus was the reason why problems had not been resolved.

In terms of the tradition of British politics dating back to the 1870s, if not before, this is a revolutionary departure. Although conflicts did occur, most notably in the 1920s and 1930s, it was unusual for a British government to be openly partisan in the class war. What is more, Thatcherism sought to appeal to the skilled working class that its interest was in this conflictual strategy. Hence, no incomes policy and free collective bargaining. Hence, the reform of trade unions to weaken the power of the union leadership.

Thatcherism had no explicit strategy for industrial structure except market discipline, but unlike the Heath government, it did not panic in face of recession and did not make a U-turn. Indeed, its policies engineered the deepest recession the British economy has faced since records have been kept. Thatcherism stood firm in the face of a doubling of unemployment, a totem statistic of the post-1945 British economy. This happened within two years of its coming to power. Not turning around, and refusing to reflate, established the credibility of the government and ensured its tough reputation against all subsequent vacillations and inconsistencies.

Thatcherism does not admit that the economic structure is at all a problem. It holds no special brief for industrial capital or indeed for any other fraction of capital. Its cure for industrial structure was recession with consequent bankruptcies and the slimming effect of the market. It does not treat class structure as a problem, except in as much as it wishes to destroy the notion of a solid working class. Its propagandists highlight evidences of upward mobility – share ownership, ownership of council houses, the paraphernalia of yuppiedom, etc. It has not attacked the upper-class cultural habits, though it has antagonised the old-style Tory faction in Parliament. Since class privilege is defined along the private/public provision axis in education, housing and health, and since its assault on the class structure has been inegalitarian, the constraints of an anti-industrial culture, the gentrification of the industrial entrepreneur, the feudal pretensions of royalty and the aristocracy have all been left untouched. But its assault on the Civil Service, the BBC, the Church of England, the universities and the legal profession shows that the educated middle-class professional is seen as an enemy rather than an ally. The old concensus politics with Royal Commissions and quangos is deeply suspect, and the professional middle class is seen as the army of that consensus.

The paradox which faces old-style politics is that this conflictual approach has also proved popular. *Populist* policies have been only occasionally followed – the Falklands War being a prime example – but even that was popular only after the victory. Thatcher's gamble succeeded in the Falklands War and converted a risky ploy into a popular and a populist strategy. However, that apart, it is the unrelenting image of a permanent revolution, constant assault on one preconception after another, one pillar of the establishment after another, dividing and ruling the middle class and the working class, that has kept it re-elected if not emotionally popular.

By dividing the working class, Thatcherism has created an underclass of the unemployed and all the other sections that depend on transfer payments from the state. It has given the 'upper' working class the impression that it has arrived out of the ghetto where Labour politicians and trade unions would like to keep it. Its attack on local authority finance is part and parcel of this strategy, since the local authority sector, though centrally funded to a large extent, had become an autonomous part of the welfare state. In 'rolling back the state', Thatcherism centralised the British state more than it had ever been.

Yet even after ten years of this relentless attack, it is not clear that Thatcherism has succeeded where others have failed. It has done better in terms of re-elections, but there are already signs that its attack on the set of constraints is just as partial, and hence as flawed, as that of previous attempts at modernisation. It has been exposed during 1988–9 for its inability to tackle the balance of trade problem. Inflation has come back despite the best efforts on its part. Its promise of a new dawn to the property-owning sections is compromised by the high interest rates. These high rates are not accidental; they are the symptom of the failure of the economy to generate enough surplus to have a reasonable growth of GDP without running into trade deficit or inflation. Having eschewed incomes policies and devaluation, it is left with only one weapon – interest rates. Having no explicit industrial strategy, it finds that the supply-side miracle has run its course. It finds the class structure unreformed as it faces the problems of football hooliganism with incomprehension and can only propose repression as a cure.

But there are also doctrinal inconsistencies in Thatcherism. These have been exposed in the context of European integration in 1992. It likes de-regulation but not harmonisation. Its preferred variant of capitalism is the nineteenth-century single entrepreneur, not the multinational corporatism of the German variety. Thus, it resists the Social Europe of Delors. But it is also curiously old-fashioned in its notion of sovereignty. Hence, it resists a single currency, money being of totemic significance for Thatcherism; it will thereby find itself in conflict with the City and with those large and powerful sections of British capitalism which stand to benefit from 1992 and a single-currency Europe. It may yet be capitalism which defeats Thatcher.

REFERENCES

Addison, Paul, *The Road to 1945: British Politics and the Second World War* (Jonathan Cape: London, 1975).
Anderson, Perry, 'Origins of the present crisis', *New Left Review,* **23** (1964).
Anderson, Perry, 'The figures of descent', *New Left Review,* **161** (1987).
Balachandran, G., 'Indian monetary policy and the international liquidity crisis 1919–1939', Ph.D. thesis, University of London (1989).
Cecco, M. de, *Money and Empire: The International Gold Standard 1890–1914* (Blackwell: Oxford, 1974).
Chandler, A. D., *The Visible Hand: The Managerial Revolution in American Business* (Belknap Press: Cambridge, Mass., 1977).
Fowles, J., *The French Lieutenant's Woman* (Panther: St Albans, 1970).
Middlemas, Keith, *Politics in Industrial Society* (André Deutsch: London, 1980).
Pollard, S., *Britain's Prime and Britain's Decline: The British Economy 1890–1914* (Edward Arnold: London, 1989).
Thompson, E. P., 'The peculiarities of the English', in *The Socialist Register* (eds Miliband, R. and Saville, J.) (Merlin Press: London, 1965).
Weiner, M., *English Culture and the Decline of the Industrial Spirit 1850–1980* (Cambridge University Press: Cambridge, 1981).

INDEX